WHITELAW REID

Whitelaw Reid

WHITELAW REID

JOURNALIST, POLITICIAN, DIPLOMAT

BINGHAM
DUNCAN

THE UNIVERSITY OF GEORGIA PRESS

ATHENS

Library of Congress Catalog Card Number: 73–90844
International Standard Book Number: 0–8203–0353–4

The University of Georgia Press, Athens 30602

Printed in the United States of America

Contents

Preface

WHITELAW REID (1837–1912) was a journalist and a politician. He was also a business man and, in the latter part of his life, a diplomat. Less important men have been the subjects of recent studies, but the only complete biography of Reid that has been published is a well-written work done fifty years ago by a close friend and strong admirer. It is time for a new account of the life of a man who owned and edited one of the great newspapers of his time, was an important political figure for more than a quarter of a century, and who represented his country abroad in major diplomatic posts.

A lack of all the information needed to answer all the questions that arise about the actions, motivations, and relationships of another person who lived in another century makes for inevitable errors in judgment and leaves some questions unanswered. Within these limitations my effort here is to present as accurate an account as possible of Reid's public life, with some discussion of other interests that absorbed his thoughts and his energies.

I have not tried to support or destroy any preconceived theory of Reid's significance nor to make him seem to be a force for progress or a negative influence on developments in his period. The Reid in the following pages is the Reid of his letters and of his newspaper, with some material from other sources to fill gaps in the account.

Research for this book was supported, in part, by a grant from Emory University.

I am indebted to the publisher of *Agricultural History* for permission to use material from an article of mine that first appeared in that journal.

WHITELAW REID

I

Years of Uncertainty: 1837–60

In 1853, in the cool predawn of an October day in southern Ohio, a slender fifteen-year-old boy who called himself J. W. Reid sat in a plainly furnished dormitory room at Miami University writing a weekly letter to his older brother. Both the act of writing and the hour were more prophetic than the boy realized. He had not then formed any ideas of a career, but as Whitelaw Reid he was to spend innumerable mornings, as well as days and evenings, writing tens of thousands of letters and millions of words of copy as reporter, editor, essayist, historian, diplomat, and politician-statesman.[1]

In October of 1853 young Reid was in the first month of his three years at Miami University in Oxford, Ohio. The college was a neat and orderly place to live. The main building, a three-story brick structure plus a wing, had been built thirty years earlier. Three slightly newer additions to the campus, two dormitories, and a small science laboratory comprised the remainder of the physical plant. A fence enclosed four or five acres around the buildings to keep out stray farm animals, and a path led toward the village of Oxford. Here Reid frequently walked in the morning before chapel. On Sundays he sometimes visited the nearby home of an uncle, a minister, whose apple trees were of as much attraction as were his friendship and counsel. Sunday visits to a minister's home were familiar experiences for a boy brought up in a sternly religious household. His father, Robert Charlton Reid, was a veritable pillar of the Reformed Presbyterian Church, and his mother, Marion Whitelaw Ronalds Reid, was no less devout. Xenia's dozen-odd churches, including two for Negro residents, could accommodate the entire population of the town at one sitting. The family was accustomed to spend many hours in church on Sunday, and the son evidently found it no hardship since he continued the practice voluntarily while away from home at the university.[2]

Reid's childhood had been a sober one. His only brother was nine years older, his only sister seven years younger, and there seem to have been few playmates. As a child he lived in the soundly built house in

1

which he was born, one put up by his father. Located on a low knoll in a forested area that in Reid's youth was being cleared for planting, it was a two-story frame structure with a one-story wing containing sitting and dining rooms and a kitchen. The floors were of oak, the doors, stairs, and interior of black walnut. The first-floor rooms had large marble fireplaces, and the windows throughout the house had eight-by-ten-inch glass panes. The home was near Xenia, seat of Greene County, a corn, wheat, and wool-producing section of steadily increasing wealth and growing population.

When Reid was eight years old the Lake-River railroad, pushing northward from Cincinnati, reached Xenia. When he was eleven the second district fair to be held in Ohio attracted to the town agricultural exhibits of all kinds, including blooded livestock from as far away as eastern Pennsylvania. Xenia's three thousand inhabitants were largely of Kentucky and Virginia origin, with a few from the middle states; less than 10 percent were foreign born. Even fewer were Negroes, although they were increasing more rapidly than the general population and by 1860 would become a source of concern to some of the town fathers. Only some 4 to 5 percent of the adults could not read, and the people were proud of the Xenia Academy. In short, Reid spent his childhood and youth in a town that resembled scores of others in the upper Ohio River region.[3]

The Xenia Academy was presided over by Reid's uncle, Hugh MacMillan, D.D., who was the principal and who taught classical studies. Although the youth was an irregular pupil at the academy, he received much instruction from MacMillan. The teacher provided his young kinsman with the basic skills in Latin, with some knowledge of classical literature, and with some groundwork in mathematics. Further supplementing the meager fare of a grammar school irregularly attended, the boy read a great deal, sometimes sitting by one of the large windows in his room, sometimes lying on his bed. Literary fare in Greene County was thin, and literarily inclined youths read anything that came to hand—the Bible always, Shakespeare frequently, a metropolitan newspaper sometimes, and in Reid's case, Plutarch's *Lives*. The combination of some formal schooling, some tutoring, and some self-instruction enabled him at fifteen to enter Miami University with the status of a second-year student.[4]

The university was to the youth's liking. He not only could read at will, but he was expected to do so. In 1853 Miami was headed by a Presbyterian minister, as it had been since its founding. Neither Dr. William C. Anderson nor Dr. John W. Hall, the presidents during Reid's college years, seems to have made much impression on the youthful scholar. Hall preached Sunday afternoon sermons in the chapel, but since Reid was frequently at his uncle's eating apples and getting news from Xenia, he was not exposed to the president's sermons.

The school where the boy established his first social relations outside the immediate neighborhood of his birth did not make a very great impression on the young man on his arrival. Located forty miles northwest of Cincinnati, Oxford boasted the Oxford Female College as well as Miami University. The town had half-a-dozen churches, including modest Negro Methodist and Baptist edifices. Two decades earlier Miami had been the largest institution of higher learning west of Pennsylvania; in Reid's time it had lost its position of preeminence, but it still ranked next to Oberlin and Ohio Wesleyan among Ohio institutions.[5]

The cost of attending this institution was modest even by the standards of the mid–nineteenth century. Tuition was ten dollars per session, twenty dollars per year. Reid lived frugally; his expenses amounted to no more than fourteen dollars per month. His father's total outlay probably did not exceed a hundred and fifty dollars for the school year of ten months.[6]

The six-member faculty of Miami was adequate but not outstanding. John W. Hall came in 1854 from a pastorate in Huntsville, Alabama, to be president. Since the faculty and virtually all the students, approximately 250 in Reid's term, were unassailably sound Christians, Hall left them to their own devices, delivering sermons at appropriate times but not requiring attendance if legitimate reasons for being absent were presented. For his part, young Reid accepted religion as a vital part of life, but his principal interests lay outside the church. He never became concerned with or involved in the sectarian strife that beset mid–nineteenth century middle-western Protestantism. Religion did not interfere with his studies or with his extracurricular activities, which occupied his time fully, and his diaries do not refer to the subject. President Hall also left free from interference the six professors who

3

made up the faculty of the university, and the professors in turn did not interfere with the students. These were largely left to educate themselves.

Reid worked hard at first, harder than most of his fellow students. Even so, he took few notes and handed in few written assignments. Only one purely academic item may have had an exceptional effect on his career and on his thinking. During his years there, Miami briefly experimented with an elective system, permitting French or German to be substituted for Greek. This innovation was too radical for the time and place, and the option was withdrawn in 1858, but in the meantime Reid learned a good deal of French and became an advocate of the study of modern languages. Other minor experiments were tried in Hall's administration, which, while ephemeral, at least indicate that the curriculum was not entirely without imagination.[7]

In addition to the solid fare of the Latin readers and mathematics texts, Reid was taught that there were three political parties in England: the aristocratic Tories, the liberal Whigs, and the radical Manchester Free Trade Men; that the wild peach was rank poison but the wild cherry was not; that studies inculcating mental discipline were more practical than any others, because they induced skill in all things; that the Democrats in Ohio were largely engaged in attempts to destroy the whole system of vested rights; that southern hospitality was a sham, since the southerner was hospitable only because of near death from ennui and because of his overweening desire to boast of his possessions. The young student merely noted these pearls, usually without comment.[8]

His studies did not keep Reid from participating in the doings of the literary and social clubs of the university or from carrying on other activities including some writing for local newspapers. In all of these areas, however, the beginnings at Miami were far too modest to constitute a hint of his later stature as a clubman, literary figure, or reporter-editor. He joined the Delta Kappa Epsilon fraternity without enthusiasm. DKE had come to Miami in 1852 and the university had three older Greek letter fraternities at the time. A fifth was added in 1855. Usually, inclination, a reasonably acceptable sociability, and a modest sum were the principal requirements for membership. Of much more importance were the literary societies. Reid joined one of the older ones, Erodelphian, whose motto—"scienta eloquentia et amicitiae"—meant interest in (political) science, a liking for (impassioned) eloquence

4

and a desire for friends with similar tastes. South and North, both well represented at Miami, engaged in intellectual battles of such intensity that occasionally feeling was expressed physically as well as verbally.

The literary halls were more attractive than the classrooms physically and far more emotionally appealing. They were also better equipped to serve the intellectual needs of the students. Indeed, sometimes the halls served the university. The Erodelphian Society loaned some 1,551 books to the Miami library in the 1853–54 session. Within a few months the library could account for only 1,287 of them. Thus we find Reid, in October of 1855, in behalf of his society admonishing the Miami trustees and suggesting that more care be taken in the use of the society's books.[9]

The college literary societies of the mid–nineteenth century also bred politicians, and more of Reid's classmates achieved success in the political world than in intellectual or in economic pursuits. In the last decades of the century several of his schoolmates served in Congress (during one term no fewer than four of Reid's Miami college mates were members) and in other branches of the national government. Many were legislators, judges, or members of state executive departments in Ohio, Indiana, Illinois, Iowa, Michigan, Missouri, and Kentucky. Not all these men were close to Reid at college, but all walked on the same small campus and lived in the same two dormitories in the three years of Reid's sojourn. That a score of his schoolmates achieved at least a measure of success and prominence in public life is one indication of the kind of student he found at Miami in the mid-fifties.[10]

There is no suggestion that J. W. Reid thought of the newspaper as a career while he was in college. Yet it is an index to his abilities that he wrote better, more often, and more easily than most of his friends. Perhaps this was a result of much reading, perhaps an inborn knack coupled with a surplus of time. Before his seventeenth birthday he had made contributions to the *Xenia News*, the *Oxford Citizen*, and the *Hamilton Intelligencer*. Most of this writing consisted of items of local interest or was the sort of thing that might be expected of a reasonably well read college youth of the time. Dull matter such as comments on European historical events predominated. These were occasionally enlivened by such pieces as his "Resolutions on the Funeral of Logic." Twice in his college years he contributed to papers beyond the bounds of his native heath. The sixteen-year-old Xenia youth sent a piece to the *New York Tribune* in the spring of 1854. True, it was only a report on the

5

Miami commencement, but the mighty *Tribune* printed it. Only once did a newspaper effort hint of a characteristic that later would help to make him an outstanding journalist. When the reverberations of the debate on Stephen Douglas's bill to organize the Kansas Territory and open that vast area to slavery reached Miami, Reid determined to get into the fight. Utilizing his main talent he wrote three articles on freedom for a Kansas newspaper. This effort also constituted his closest approach to politics and is the most conspicuous effort he made in that direction in his college days.[11]

Reid's record at Miami University was an excellent one. He was highly competitive and strove for perfection. He was, academically, the outstanding member of his class and graduated as its brightest scholar. He had learned much while at the university—chiefly how to live among others of his own age, and that his intellectual capabilities were of a high order. He could indulge his favorite pastime of reading and could think of it as a useful and necessary part of life; such an attitude had not been possible when, as a lad, he had been the only bookworm in town. The chief failure in his college years was that he did not find an answer to his need for a role in life. He knew that he did not want to farm, but he doubtless knew this before leaving Xenia for Oxford. He was averse to participation in mercantile pursuits, and he did not want to become a minister—this too he knew without a college education. He could have moved without effort into any of these areas of activity. Indeed, it took some effort to avoid the three, as they were his family's main, if not only, pursuits and interests. Beyond this negative knowledge young Reid was at sea. After graduating he took a place as principal of a small grade school in South Charleston a few miles from Xenia, probably to avoid making a decision or taking a step that might lead to permanent involvement.[12]

The principal's duties at South Charleston did not begin until fall, and Reid returned to his father's house from the university. He spent some time as a clerk, as he had done intermittently for several years, in his brother Gavin's dry goods store. In this summer he followed the presidential campaign closely, clipping many columns of news stories and commentaries about the candidates and issues. The Republican candidate, the romantic and adventurous young man of action with his "Free Land, Free Men, Frémont" slogan, caught the imagination of the young intellectual who was already disposed to oppose the Democrats and ripe for a new and fresh political movement. Reid, still two years under voting age, considered himself a follower of Thomas Hart Benton's protégé.[13]

In South Charleston he found that his duties included teaching French, Latin, and mathematics as well as supervising the teachers. The school term was short, six months, and he spent the long summer vacation in Xenia, much as he had spent the previous one. Having nothing better to do, he returned to South Charleston in September 1857, but he found school work still unsatisfying and gave up the dull and arduous task at the end of the spring term in 1858. He had searched, in the meantime, for other jobs. Suitable employment for talented and dissatisfied intellectuals uninterested in agricultural, mercantile, or teaching pursuits, were rare in Greene County, and Reid was not yet mature or adventurous enough to break away from the security of his father's roof. He whiled away the summer of 1858 largely as he had earlier ones, the horizons expanding slowly in keeping with his own growth.

Reid was now in his twenty-first year. His tastes had changed little but had broadened somewhat. His reading included at least something of D'Aubigne, Racine, Voltaire, Rousseau, Longfellow, De Quincey, De Toqueville, Scott, Keats, Carlyle, and Charles Sumner. In contrast, his newspaper fare was limited, including only the two Xenia papers and the weekly *Tribune*. These, however, seemed to satisfy him. Attendance at church, walks or rides into Xenia and nearby Cedarville, tutoring a friend in French, and occasional errands or services for Gavin were his principal activities.

Three times during this summer Reid left his home paths. Early in June he went to Paris, Illinois, as an agent for a mail-order fruit tree nursery. The trip was long and dirty, the countryside flat and without interest, and other travelers dull, and the role of fruit-tree peddler was uninspiring. He sold no trees and probably resolved to avoid the life of a traveling salesman in the future.[14]

Three weeks after the Paris trip Reid again shook the Cedarville-Xenia dust from his heels. The countryside was still dull, the travelers nondescript, and the weather hotter than before, but this time Reid's role was inspiring and his errand a joyful one. Miami University friends had invited him to speak during the commencement exercises. Characteristically, he had scoffed on first receiving the invitation. "Spent the forenoon trying to see what old truisms I ought to throw together, to make a speech for Oxford," he said toward the end of May. Again characteristically, he spent many hours working on the speech—most of three consecutive days. He then memorized it. Two days before he was to leave, Reid packed his hand trunk in anticipation and set his alarm clock so as to be up early on the day of departure.

At Miami for four days, Reid mingled with his intellectual and cultural peers for the first time in two years. He saw and talked to some of the professors, but spent most of his time "visiting and gassing" with other returned alumni and with students he had known, agreeing ardently with some and quarreling with others. The social and intellectual air was so rich that the carefully worked out speech became an incidental thing, and Reid's confidence was so buoyed up that he departed from the memorized text and extemporized.[15]

So stimulated was he by the four days at Oxford that he barely stopped on his return to Xenia but hurried on to Charleston to renew his associations there and avoid the enervating dullness of Xenia. Different from Oxford and less rewarding, Charleston was also different from Xenia—at least the people were not the same, and the trip was worthwhile. He dined with some friends and had tea with others, walked in the woods with girls, was urged on every hand to return to the school, and was easily persuaded to stop over for another day. He stayed three. He found the girls diverting and the attractions of one held Reid's attention until two hours past midnight. But he was not interested in discussing another year of teaching and so he returned to his father's house and spent the next day with DeQuincey, Keats, and Carlyle.

The Oxford and Charleston journeys had stirred the young man out of his lethargy, and in the week following his return to Xenia he was more alive to potential opportunity. A chance conversation in a Xenia store led to lengthy discussions of a responsible role in newspaper work. The talk ranged from the idea of Reid's employment as editor of the *Xenia News* to the more ambitious consideration of an investment large enough to control both Xenia papers with the object of combining them under Reid's management. The enterprise was too ambitious an undertaking for the inexperienced intellectual. His brother Gavin, however, nine years older and a well-established merchant, lent his aid. The Reids bought the *News*, J. Whitelaw became its editor, and Gavin, with his business friend R. P. Gray, managed the financial side of the enterprise.[16]

The *Xenia News* was no great prize. It was four years old and had been in as many hands when the Reids took it over. But it was the fledgling journalist's first venture, and while he was not entirely in charge of the whole enterprise, his responsibilities were measurably greater than at South Charleston. He moved into the editor's chair with more interest and less need for adjustment than might have been the case in almost any other activity he could have undertaken. He had practiced his talents for writing when making contributions of essays, editorial matter, and occasional news reports to the Oxford, Hamilton, and other papers two and three years earlier. He had supplied local items to the *Xenia News* while he was clerking in Gavin's store when the paper was in the hands of Preston B. Plumb.

With the position of editor went the obligation to take a stand in politics. This, too, was easy and necessitated no new adjustment. In 1858 the citizenry of Xenia, particularly the Reids and their associates, were already imbued with Republicanism. The impressions he had received at Miami University had influenced him along with scores of other young intellectuals who could not accept the slavery-oriented party of James Buchanan and Jefferson Davis. They had nowhere else to turn, and so they followed Frémont in 1856.[17] The Democrats were still strong in Ohio, but the tide was running swiftly against that party in the state; the *Xenia News*, with Reid's name at the masthead, rode the wave whose crest later carried Lincoln to the White House. Indeed, Reid—with scores of other editors of small country papers—in an important sense constituted the wave. The editor, his town, the county, and Ohio went Republican in 1859. Reid's own political creed was remarkable chiefly in that he formulated it in the first days of his editorship and employed the same phrases and held to the same principles throughout his career. He adopted the words used by the *Cincinnati Commercial*, "independent, not neutral," stated that he intended to support the Republican Party because of the superior virtues of its principles, and declared that he was neither party slave nor blind follower of partisan leaders. On local issues the youthful editor wrote of slavery, Negroes, local politicians, and state leaders. For national topics he followed the same themes. He had not met any of the leading candidates for the

Republican nomination but had a clear preference for Lincoln. Reid believed with a prescience beyond his years that the soundness of Lincoln's principles, the brevity of his political record, and the popular nature of his appeal made him a probable winner. He better than Seward, Chase, or Cameron could carry the doubtful voters of Pennsylvania, New Jersey, Indiana, and Illinois, Reid thought.[18] He supported the Republican ticket strongly in the early stages of the campaign and met the nominee when Lincoln stopped briefly in Xenia on a speaking tour.

Even with this personal touch the campaign did not fill Reid's need for something he did not describe and probably did not understand. Nor did directing the destiny of the *Xenia News*, which made little more progress under his direction than it had under previous proprietors, and he gave up the paper. Perhaps because of the responsibility, or as a result of his inability to take frequent days off, or because of the routine and boredom of life in Xenia, the editor had lost weight and appetite. His family became alarmed, and R. C. Reid and Gavin sent J. Whitelaw on a trip.

With a friend he left Xenia in the summer of 1860 and traveled into sparsely settled northern Minnesota, going as far as the headwaters of the Mississippi and St. Louis rivers, traveling by train, river boat, stagecoach, and horseback. The journey covered nearly three thousand miles, much of it through extremely rugged country. It was the first of many trips Reid would take "for his health." It was the first journey into a region entirely different from the environment he had known from birth and to an area that did not appeal to one with Reid's interests. The experience did broaden his outlook, however, and he had the foresight to arrange to send a series of letters to the *Cincinnati Gazette*. The reports both provided some funds and constituted an entrée into newspaper circles more to Reid's taste than those of Xenia.[19]

2

War Reporter

REID stayed at home to the end of 1860. He sought jobs as a lockmaker's agent, as a distributor for a new writing fluid, and as a salesman of apple trees. His only steady work came in the first two months of 1861, when he taught spelling, reading, penmanship, mental arithmetic, written arithmetic, geography, English grammar, and physiology to fourteen boys and thirteen girls in the Cedarville Township school. His salary was based on the number of pupils he taught and their average daily attendance; it came to $36.66 a month.[1] He did not like the work and he wanted to get away from Xenia and Cedarville. Hence, when an opportunity arose in March to go to Columbus and report the annual session of the Ohio legislature for the *Cincinnati Times*, he was glad for the chance to leave his native grounds. Although the *Xenia News* venture had not been satisfying, newspaper writing was still the only thing he had tried that he was willing to try again. He was to write a letter each day, and he thought of himself as the legislative correspondent of the *Times*.[2]

The pay was poor, and expenses in the capital center greater than in Oxford or Charleston. But his touch with the pen was sure, and once more he walked and talked with his intellectual peers who, this time, were in many cases his superiors as men of the world and in most cases his elders. Giving him just time to find a room and boarding table, to learn his way about the streets of Columbus and the halls of the state house, fortune fairly beamed on the twenty-three-year-old reporter.

The Howellses, father and son, long established printers and journalists, had served as correspondents for several papers in Columbus for some time. William Dean Howells gave up two of them, the *Cleveland Herald* and the *Cincinnati Gazette*, and the elder Howells, William Cooper, wrote the legislative reports for these for a while. When he too decided to give up the correspondence he recommended his Greene County neighbor Reid to the *Gazette* editors. Reid, of course, was already known to the *Gazette* through the letters he had sent while on his junket through upper Minnesota, so the connection was easily

11

arranged. It was customary for reporters to sign their letters, but not with their own names. Reid used the word "Agate" to identify his reports to the *Gazette*.[3]

Meanwhile, the *Cleveland Herald* editors had also approached young Reid, and within less than a month he found himself well established as the legislative reporter for the *Herald* and the *Gazette* as well as for the *Cincinnati Times*. The task of writing three letters nearly every day about the same happenings, ones that were sufficiently different in tone to satisfy Reid's own ethical standards as well as those of his three editors, was more drudgery than challenge. Yet the drudgery was discipline and he became a newspaper man in the exacting sense of the term. The work was far more demanding than the *Xenia News* task, but the total income of thirty-eight dollars a week was a princely sum for a fledgling correspondent. He required only a small part of this for necessities, and so for the first time in his life he had a surplus with which to indulge his appetites. His principal appetite was soon revealed to be for growth investments. He conserved most of his income by living on a spartan scale while he associated with many who did not.[4]

In Columbus he knew, besides the Howellses, the editor of the state Republican organ, the *Ohio State Journal*, Henry D. Cooke. He also came to know the red-haired, red-bearded John Quincy Adams Ward, then beginning his career as a sculptor. Most of the young men with whom he ate at boarding houses were, like Reid, Republicans. Some of them had southern influence in their backgrounds, and at this time Reid seemed southern, at least in appearance, to many observers. Above medium height, with a dark mustache and imperial, his hair worn long in the southern fashion, he was personable and attractive. More important, his background equipped him well to understand many groups. His New England mother, the sternly religious father, the southwestern Ohio population more influenced by the upper South than by the East, his distaste for slavery and the presence of Negro churches in Xenia, made him aware of the diverse elements that were dividing the nation as well as his own state.[5]

Reid had been at his tasks less than a month when the secessionist brushfire in the lower South was fanned into a conflagration by the fighting at Sumter. Flags, drums, and marching men appeared in the streets of Columbus. For the legislative correspondents the chief news was in the house, for it was there that the Democratic strength lay—the senate had passed a war bill quickly. Even in the house, however, party lines rapidly disappeared under the pressures and demands for defense of the flag and the union.[6] The session lasted a month after Sumter, by which time Reid had made such an impression on the *Gazette* owners that they offered their young correspondent the desk of city editor, which then meant the local reporting. He accepted and moved from Ohio's political capital to her commercial and cultural center in May.[7]

Local news in Cincinnati in the spring of 1861 was of far less moment than war news. In May the nearest skirmishing was some 250 miles east of the new city editor's desk. From the beginning of hostilities, federal strategists understood that the Baltimore and Ohio Railroad, stretching westward from Washington to the Ohio River at Parkersburg, Virginia, was highly vulnerable. As one of the most important spans in the iron bridge connecting the East with the Midwest, the road had to be controlled. To keep it free from interference United States troops were collected in the vicinity of a junction at Grafton, Virginia. Their mission was not only to guard the rail line but also to clear confederate forces from northwestern Virginia. Ohio troops were included in the forces at Grafton, and the *Gazette* converted its city editor into a voluntary aide-de-camp with the rank of captain and attached to forces under the command of Ohio's George B. McClellan. Reid arrived at Grafton early in June and found it securely in the hands of federal forces.

For a month after the reporter's arrival there was no military action, so the letters he sent to his paper were of life in camp. He told of the high morale of the troops who sang, complained about the undeserved reputation the Virginians had as fighting men, spirited away each other's equipment more as fun than for profit, and in general had "an uprorious [*sic*] time" in their camps. He also told of the disgracefully poor quality of the uniforms the men had been furnished and of the boredom of camp life despite all efforts to relieve the monotony. In his dispatches to the *Gazette* he continued to use "Agate" as his pen name.

Reid was in an excellent situation for reporting news of any action that might take place in his area. He explained his position to Gavin late in June as he was setting out for Philippi, Virginia, expecting an important and bloody battle. He would be with Gen. Thomas A. Morris and his staff, Reid told his brother, but had orders to keep with the advance elements of the army. He could go with the staff or with any of the generals as circumstances dictated, including McClellan, who was in overall command of the forces in the area Reid was assigned to cover.[8]

When action came Agate was ready to report it. Confederates under Gen. Robert Seldon Garnett had fortified a position at Rich Mountain, Virginia, a few miles from Grafton, and McClellan moved to dislodge them late in June. On the twenty-seventh, Reid left Grafton, traveling with the federal headquarters, on his first military campaign. He thought the way would be exceedingly dangerous but that he would be in Richmond within a few weeks. For ten days he saw much marching, heard firing occasionally, and talked to skirmishers who had brushed with rebel scouting parties. As the main federal body neared Rich Mountain, heavy reconnaissance units succeeded in getting behind Garnett and captured more than five hundred of his troops. The confederate force split up and early on July 12 began to retreat in five separate fragments. Reid, still in the federal headquarters, accompanied the troops that followed some three confederate regiments with accompanying cavalry, artillery, and wagons, all under Garnett's personal command. The drama was played slowly. Heavy rains, muddied roads, and filled streams hampered both pursued and pursuer. Federal advanced elements managed to maintain contact with rebel rear guards and had hopes of overtaking the main body. At Carrick's Ford, Virginia, which was swollen by the rains, the eager pursuers were blocked by a confederate regiment detached to delay the federals. Here on July 13, a Saturday, Reid saw his first battle, watched men die violently, and experienced the helpless disappointment of seeing victory elude a superior force. For, although Garnett was killed, the confederate units escaped.[9]

After Carrick's Ford the futility of further pursuit ended temporarily the pressures on union officers. But the crisis for the union reporters was yet ahead. News had been made, and at Rowlesburg, thirty miles away, there was a telegraph office. Without horses of his own, Reid was forced to rely on the army. He learned that General Garnett's body was to be sent to Washington and that it would go by way of Rowlesburg. It was no great trick for Reid and another reporter to secure permission to go with the wagon as escorts, but to hurry the departure was more difficult. Not until noon on Sunday did the group set out.

The route was over rough terrain; remains of roadblocks impeded progress; stragglers from both forces proved nerve-wracking. Reid, anxious to reach the telegraph key in time for his story to appear in the

14

Monday papers, urged speed and even drove the recalcitrant mules himself when a wagoner's nerve failed as the road narrowed to skirt a bluff above the Cheat River. The effort was sufficient to overcome the resistance of roads, weather, and mulishness, but could not cope with overeager union pickets who fired on the forlorn little party in the dark, less than an hour from Rowlesburg. Reid and the others were forced to hide from their own soldiers until daylight and missed the Monday papers.[10]

Reid's reports on the campaign in the Rich Mountain area included full accounts of the battles with proper credit for all the regiments that participated. He blamed McClellan for failure to capture or destroy the enemy, and he commented sarcastically on the difference between McClellan's performance and the predictions made for him by friendly newspapers. He gave little consideration to the influence of weather and terrain (although he described these in his battle report), none to the work of Garnett's doggedly determined troops, and he ignored the inexperience of the federal soliders. Nor did the reporter point out that the brief campaign was highly successful in that it established union domination of the rail line and of the western approaches to the Shenandoah Valley.[11]

From Rowlesburg Reid went to Ohio for a month. He spent most of the time in Cincinnati or on *Gazette* assignments, including one to report politics in Columbus. He also found some hours for personal visiting and was with his family in Xenia for a time, where he got some much needed rest.

After his short sojourn in Ohio he went to William S. Rosecrans' headquarters at Clarksburg, Virginia, to report news of that Ohioan's activities, resuming the status of aide-de-camp. During the remainder of the year he moved about frequently, following the army headquarters and returning at times to Cincinnati. In these weeks Reid's pen was not used only in comments on battles. A penetrating observer and a severe critic, he wrote of what he saw everywhere. The exorbitant cost of supplies, wasteful and inefficient practices in headquarters offices, inadequately trained and irresponsible officers—not worthy of the men they commanded, he thought—all were bared in Reid's reports. Eventually one of his criticisms, in this case concerning defective ammunition and inadequate medical care, caused him to be denied further access to the area where he was then stationed, Camp Nevin, and he returned to Cincinnati in February 1862.[12]

In the months he was with Rosecrans' headquarters, Reid's battle experience had been further developed at Carnifex's Ferry. At the end of the first week in September Rosecrans moved from the vicinity of Clarksburg toward confederate forces collected near Summersville, Virginia, and Reid traveled with the headquarters wagons. He did not think highly of the movement and wrote that a small force of disciplined troops could have routed Rosecrans' forces at any time. But no such opposition appeared, and the federal troops reached Carnifex's Ferry on September 9 in sufficiently good order to win an unquestioned victory. Reid worked much harder for his story than he had previously. He missed the beginning of the battle, arriving at the scene after dark on the ninth and getting little rest. He was up at dawn, the tenth, trying to see something of the actual fighting, interviewing those who had, and making notes, spending most of the day on horseback sustained by excitement, coffee, and hard biscuit. Thoroughly exhausted, he and another reporter repaired to a fence corner and rolled up in blankets. They did not know until morning that their bed was a pile of stable manure.[13]

Reid wrote two stories on the Carnifex's Ferry engagements. The first, dated September 11, was a full account of the action including troops involved, highlights, and an evaluation of the importance of Rosecrans' victory, which the reporter perhaps overestimated. After thinking things over for two weeks and talking further to participants, he revised his views and wrote a critique. As had been his opinion at Carrick's Ford, he thought the confederates' escape due to federal incompetence. In addition he thought that if sound tactics had been used, the Carnifex's Ferry fights could have been won with little bloodshed. These reports showed some improvement in their appraisal of the broader aspects of war. Reid was an accurate reporter, and he had begun to apply his talents for criticism to analyzing the work of military commanders. Throughout 1861 his work had a limited audience, however, for the events he described were overshadowed by developments in Washington and Richmond.[14]

Reid's eviction from Camp Nevin excluded him only from that area, and when action developed at Fort Donelson, Tenn., about as far west and south of Cincinnati as Grafton was to the east, Reid was dispatched to the scene. Again he was in the headquarters of an active military force. It was much larger than any he had previously seen and its achievements in capturing Fort Henry and Fort Donelson were greater by far than the accomplishments of federal units at Grafton and Clarksburg. As this force, commanded by Brig. Gen. Ulysses S. Grant, moved slowly up the Tennessee River, Reid became acquainted with the officers, visited division headquarters and the regimental and company bivouac areas, and interviewed freely.

After Donelson the confederates abandoned Nashville and seemed to be falling back on a Memphis-Chattanooga line. When Reid arrived at the Henry-Donelson area, Grant was engaged in consolidating control of the lower Tennessee-Cumberland landings and was preparing to move up the Tennessee toward the area of confederate movement. Agate's reports of patrols, leisure activities, and of discipline and organization were more sophisticated than his efforts of the preceding year. As action did not seem imminent he was more relaxed and could enjoy the organized life of large headquarters establishments, far more comfortable ones than he had previously seen in the field. As he rode over the lowlands south of Fort Henry he was part guest and part participant in the movement of Ohio, Indiana, and other western units, in the state of his father's birth.

When Albert Sidney Johnston's confederates struck the bivouacked union army at daybreak on Sunday, April 6, 1862, Reid was as much surprised as Grant was. Upon hearing firing up the river, Reid sought the most certain means of transportation and the best available source of information, Gen. Lew Wallace's headquarters steamboat tied up at Crump's Landing. His instinct was sound. Within two hours Grant arrived aboard his own boat, the *Tigress*, to confer with Wallace, and when the *Tigress* moved on up the river Reid was aboard.[15] For two days the battle raged in confusion and disorder while reporters walked, rode, listened, and looked, attempting to evaluate disjointed, conflicting, and contradictory reports. The six weeks Reid had spent on the ground and among the units now enabled him to move surely about the battle areas and to comprehend the action. The skirmishes at Carrick's Ford and at Carnifex's Ferry had not prepared the young reporter for the carnage of Pittsburg Landing, Tennessee, but there was no doubt in his mind that history was being made and that this was a chance to write it. An interview with a wounded soldier, a straggler, a refugee, or a messenger, whether officer or private, meant almost as much to Reid as it did to the general officers. For the reporter knew much about the locations and makeup of the regiments, their commanders, and in many cases could appraise morale and fighting qualities with accuracy. After two days of intense and bloody fighting, the confederates were forced to break off the action and withdraw to the south. By the following afternoon the weary and bedraggled Reid was on a steamboat that was moving wounded men to Fort Henry and to Cairo. En route he arranged his jumbled and crumpled notes and joined in his mind the terrain and the military units he had visited in the weeks before the battle with the scenes and sounds of April 6–7. The experiences had been harrowing, and the river trip with wounded men was not calculated to sooth frazzled nerves. Reid arrived in Cairo an awed and frightened reporter. His account of the battle, written in Cairo and on the train to Cincinnati, proved he was also inspired. His nineteen-thousand-word story became the classic newspaper account of the Battle of Shiloh.[16]

The story might well have stood out in competition with other war news, but fortunately for its author it stood alone. The only near events that might have competed for attention and space, the capture of New Orleans and the fighting when McClellan moved on Richmond, were yet weeks away. Reid's gloomy story of an army attacked in bivouac, of Grant caught napping, of heroic courage and broad confusion, and of narrowly averted disaster appeared in the *Gazette* on Monday, April 14, filling thirteen columns. The reporter criticized the lack of preparation for an attack, although there had been some skirmishing in the days preceding the confederate assault. He described the topography of the area, the ravines, the thick woods, and the maze of roads and crossroads in the area where union troops had camped in random fashion as they arrived. The rebel attack at dawn on Sunday, he reported, caused near chaos in the federal camps. It was not until late in the afternoon that a defense line was finally established around the landing, where two union gunboats could bring their firepower to bear on the enemy. At dusk northern reinforcements arrived, and when the fighting resumed on Monday the augmented forces gradually gained the initiative. Hard fighting by troops who did not let the near disaster of the previous day destroy their spirits, under officers who showed ability despite a lack of planning, forced the confederates into a general retreat by mid-afternoon.

Agate's account of the battle was widely reprinted, not only in Ohio but in papers in St. Louis and Chicago and in Horace Greeley's *Tribune*. In less than a week's time the twenty-five-year-old reporter achieved a reputation and a standing for which many newsmen strive for a lifetime. Anger of the union generals at his critical appraisal of military leadership only strengthened his position, for the press and the public agreed with Reid.[17] Agate was now a nationally known journalist, respected by the public and by editors not only in the West but also in New York and Washington, and when the press was excluded from areas under Henry Wager Halleck's command in May 1862, Agate was ready for promotion, a salary increase, or both. The *Gazette* sent him to Washington, for that was the news center of the nation and Agate was the *Gazette*'s outstanding correspondent.

In the three years he was in the capital Reid had opportunities not available elsewhere in the country for talented and ambitious intellectuals. In May 1862 Washington was attaining a position of political dominance in American life it had not previously held, and it was a center of intellectual ferment such as would not be seen there again until Theodore Roosevelt's administration. There was also corruption on a vast scale and tempting opportunities for advancement in many fields for the not overscrupulous. As were the others of his craft, Reid was in an excellent position to take advantage of the widespread need for friendly newsmen who were willing to wear rose-colored glasses or to turn their eyes aside on occasion. But if he was still uncertain about his permanent career, he was in no doubt at all as to his ultimate objectives. He wanted a place in the world, money, and a name for himself. The name was not the least important, and one of its essential attributes had to be personal integrity. This conviction was bred in him under his father's roof. It was strengthened by the fact that he had the soul of a critic, and if he is to have inner security a critic must be above suspicion.

Early in the Washington period Reid made the first important financial decision of his life. The Shiloh story brought an offer from the *St. Louis Democrat*, whose managers offered him the position of leading editor at a salary of thirteen hundred dollars a year. Reid considered this carefully. St. Louis seemed to offer a better future than Cincinnati and the *Democrat* was the equal of the *Gazette*. He asked his father for advice. The conservative R. C. Reid was doubtful of the wisdom of making a change, but thought his son should make his own decision.[18] When the *Gazette* learned of the offer, its response was more positive.

Richard Smith, the proprietor, unable or unwilling to increase his star reporter's salary, hit upon an unanswerable argument—he offered to sell high-dividend stock in an amount sufficient to give Reid a twelfth interest in the *Gazette*. Reid accepted but he was unable to take up the handsome opportunity at once; Smith consented to hold the stock until his partner-to-be could make the necessary financial arrangements. Before the end of 1864 Reid had available some $4,000, about a third the amount he needed. Anxious to complete the purchase, he sought Henry Cooke, whom he had known since their Columbus days and whom he occasionally saw in Washington. Through his friend, Reid was able to borrow from Jay Cooke the necessary funds, which he secured with the stock certificates he then obtained from Smith.

That he could first get the money and then produce the collateral, a privilege frequently accorded men of established financial position but seldom available to newspaper reporters, was a measure of Reid's growing reputation among men of substance in Washington. The brief meeting with Jay Cooke and the ease with which a sum greater than his life's earnings up to that time was made available to him left an indelible impression.[19] In turn, he made an impression on the Cookes, and the great financier sought his aid, as he sought that of many others, in publicizing the "seven-thirty" loan early in 1865. Reid did not join Cooke's staff of writers but he did mention the bonds in his letters and dispatches and encouraged others to do likewise.

Perhaps because he did not become identified with the Cookes, the banker asked the reporter to undertake a confidential mission to investigate irregularities in the sale of the bonds in Pittsburgh. Hard-working, earnest, and fully aware of the gravity of the mission, which he performed to Cooke's satisfaction and without offending a guilty banker, Reid was nevertheless cognizant of the humor of the situation. As he put it in a letter to John Nicolay, "You ought to see me, with all the solid men of Pittsburgh. . . . They evidently think me the boiled down concentration and quintessence of Jay Cooke and Co.; but it's confoundedly troublesome to keep on a look of solemn wisdom befitting the occasion."[20]

Meantime, Reid was Agate and Agate's primary responsibility was to the *Gazette*. He had become a skilled analyst of military affairs but he now wrote principally from information supplied by others, for his days as a field reporter were almost over. As in Cincinnati his chief work in

Washington was in the *Gazette* office. From these rooms he occasionally traveled to cover an especially important military action or to make a personal check on controversial matters. In October 1862 he went to Kentucky to learn for the *Gazette* how much foundation there was for the serious criticism of Ohio's Don Carlos Buell that appeared in the press and elsewhere. A year later he took up the cudgels for fellow newsmen by attempting to secure the release of two former Cincinnatians who had fallen into the hands of the confederates. The men, both *New York Tribune* reporters, were in Libby Prison, and Reid urged retaliation against confederates in union custody.[21] In 1864, some months after this unsuccessful effort, Reid became enraged when a reporter was publicly humiliated and sent in disgrace out of areas under Gen. George Gordon Meade's command. He wrote, but did not print, a wickedly critical comment in which he said Meade might have the physical courage of bulls and bulldogs "but he is as leprous with moral cowardice as the brute that kicks a helpless cripple on the street." Reid himself did not lack the moral courage to print this, but newsmen agreed among themselves to ignore the general. The silent treatment accorded him was worse than condemnation, for the hero of Gettysburg virtually disappeared from the papers for several months.[22]

In 1863 Reid covered the only major military action he saw during his Washington years. The *Gazette* editors watched Lee's progress into Pennsylvania in June, and when it appeared to them that a battle was imminent ordered their chief eastern correspondent to join Joseph (Fighting Joe) Hooker's army. Agate received the wire on June 28, a Sunday. Less eager than when a fledgling, he put off his departure until Monday, then allowed an interruption in the Washington-Baltimore rail service to delay him for another twenty-four hours, and almost missed the Battle of Gettysburg. He did not arrive at the federal headquarters, where Meade had replaced Hooker, until the late afternoon of July 1. There he pored over maps, asked questions, made preliminary notes, and got some sleep. He was, therefore, somewhat prepared to understand what he saw during two days (July 2–3) of intensive travel by horseback and by foot over areas held by Meade's veterans against Lee's desperately attacking confederates. He left the battlefield early on July 4, unable to telegraph his story over the army wires, and rode thirty wet and muddy miles to the nearest railroad. There he managed to catch a hospital train for Baltimore where he sent in his story. Despite the obstacles, Agate's account of the battle was outstanding for its clarity and for its feeling of drama. The story was also remarkable, under the circumstances, for its accurate portrayal of the course of the fighting, although it was not the equal of the Shiloh report.[23]

Reid's other important military writings were produced in his role as commentator and critic rather than as reporter. Two dispatches were of especial interest, although the second was not printed. During the furious and bloody Wilderness Campaign in the spring of 1864, Grant, no enemy of the press but well aware of Lee's ability to analyze newspaper reports, kept his movements hidden from reporters and editors and even from Washington officials for several days. Criticism mounted and rumors of disaster floated about the capital. Explanations were demanded, and Agate took up the challenge. He wrote a long and careful analysis, based on information generally available and drawing on his intuition and his knowledge of Grant. The general strategy was described as being sound and effective, and the ultimate objectives, Reid said, would bring the end of the war measurably closer. At the same time Agate excoriated the already unpopular Secretary of War Edwin M. Stanton for his handling of military news and censorship. Reid's analysis proved to be as accurate as Grant's strategy was sound.[24]

Two months later Agate again proved his skill in an analysis of Jubal Early's raid with some fifteen to eighteen thousand confederates in the direction of Washington. Fearful correspondents reported that rebel forces of forty, sixty, perhaps eighty thousand, threatened the capital. Reid, with no more opportunity or information than the rest, decided with considerable accuracy that Early had no more than twenty-five thousand men, and that possibly a third of these approached Washington to screen the main operation of collecting supplies and booty. By the time the report was ready the danger had disappeared, and the unprinted story remains only as evidence of Agate's analytical skill.[25]

Reid's value to the *Gazette* during the war years was not only for his reporting of military affairs but also in his letters of comments, analysis, criticism, and prognostication about politics and politicians. Most of these letters originated in the *Gazette* rooms in Washington, but sometimes he left the city to cover special events elsewhere such as the Democratic convention in Ohio in 1863 and the Republican and Democratic conventions of 1864 in Baltimore and Chicago. For this work the Columbus experience of 1861 proved useful.

In Washington, the great size of the national stage and the kaleidoscopic character of the action made the selection and interpretation of matter for comment far more difficult than had been the case in Ohio's capital. In this situation, Reid's Ohio-Republican background was a valuable asset. In striking contrast to treatment it accorded some opposition papers, including suspension and the arrest of editors, the party in power was more than kind to its friends. Along with a small and elite group of writers, Reid had a privileged position from which to watch and record the great dramas of the war. He enjoyed a national reputation as a newsman and a growing reputation for personal integrity. As one reward he was made librarian of the House of Representatives throughout the war years. From time to time, when congressional leaders felt it expedient, they appointed friendly news correspondents to clerkships of committees. In December 1863 some of Reid's fellow journalists, representatives of the *New York Evening Post*, of the *Sacramento Union*, and of the *Boston Journal*, were appointed to House clerkships while *Chicago Tribune* and *Cincinnati Commercial* correspondents held Senate sinecures. In the third session of the thirty-seventh Congress, Reid was clerk of the House Committee on Military Affairs.[26]

Relationships established through the librarianship and the clerkship helped expand his widening circle of friends. The dominating and attractive secretary of the treasury, Salmon P. Chase, knew his young fellow Ohioan well and liked him, and Reid responded by giving strong support to Chase's presidential ambitions. Thaddeus Stevens knew him by reputation, and Reid was once astonished when he was confronted by a smiling Stevens and given a compliment. "I'd as soon have expected compliments from a vinegar barrel—or father Wickliffe," he later told William Henry Smith.[27] Sen. John Sherman complimented him extravagantly on his skill in describing events and persons for his readers, and he was well acquainted with Congressman General James A. Garfield and a host of lesser Ohio politicians. Most of the newsmen in Washington knew each other, although at least one seems sadly to have misjudged Reid, writing later that Agate sometimes had to share his fellow journalist's room for lack of funds to pay his rent. Reid may have lacked ready cash from time to time, but a likely explanation is that he probably had banked too large a portion of his salary and did not want to withdraw funds earmarked for investment.[28]

Agate was not as close to the executive branch of the government as to the legislative. In the cabinet only Chase was his friend. He admired but did not know Secretary of State William H. Seward personally. He disliked Secretary of War Stanton and he had a strong distaste for Postmaster General Montgomery Blair. His White House entrée was the least of his privileges in Washington. Lincoln's secretaries, John Nicolay and John Hay he knew as fellow bachelors who were from, but not of, the West. They were personal friends but could not become allies, for Reid was not a Lincoln admirer. As editor of the *Xenia News* he had felt that Lincoln was the nominee most likely to succeed in 1860 and accordingly had supported him. But he had quickly become disenchanted. He preferred Chase very strongly and in 1864 was honest in his opinion that the president did not have the qualities needed for coping with the dangers of war and the problems of peace. He could explain all this openly to the *Gazette* readers because Richard Smith also thought poorly of the president. So plain-spoken was Reid in his dispatches that John Hay once made an effort to reduce Reid's effectiveness as a critic and to have him discharged as a Washington correspondent for a press association, but the president's secretary was unsuccessful. Reid was always a realist and did not let his preferences and prejudices blind him to the facts. In January 1864, he told Greeley that he had little hope of making headway against "the Lincoln delusion." Even so, he made an effort, joining strongly in the movement to deprive the president of renomination in the summer of 1864. Even the Emancipation Proclamation, Agate told his readers, owed much of its success to Seward's suggestion as to timing and some to "the concluding and golden sentence" of the January 1 proclamation, which he said came from Chase's pen.[29]

As the convention met, Reid analyzed Lincoln's strength, finding it in the people's faith in his common sense and honesty, in the wide appeal of his homespun character, the stubborn support he gave his friends even when they were unpopular, and the standing he gained from Grant's successes. The very lukewarmness, or even the opposition, of Republican leaders gave fresh zest to the liking of the people, Reid thought, and he said, "I believe him today to be the most popular man we have ever had in the history of this nation." But Reid classed himself with the leaders rather than with the people. He joined in the active postnomination moves of Benjamin F. Wade, Henry W. Davis, James

W. Grimes, and John A. Andrew, working with many newspapers including the *Gazette* and with the passive acquiescence but not the active support of scores of others, including Charles Sumner, in an unsuccessful last-ditch move to have Lincoln withdraw and leave the way open for a candidate more acceptable to the radical Republican leadership. By mid-September he was resigned but unconverted, as he told his friend Anna Dickinson, and would vote for Lincoln very much as he swallowed pills. Later he thought the surrender of Atlanta responsible for Lincoln's election.[30]

Reid's reporting, political as well as military, and his analysis and criticism, reached an ever-widening circle during the war years. His principal outlet, of course, was the *Cincinnati Gazette* where Richard Smith agreed with his Washington correspondent on most subjects. The Agate letters appeared frequently in the *Gazette*, usually on subjects of their author's choosing but at times on a topic about which Smith sent a query. Reid also sent dispatches with some frequency to the *New York Times*, the *Pittsburgh Gazette*, the *Cleveland Leader*, the *Detroit Tribune*, the *Chicago Tribune*, and the *St. Louis Democrat*. By 1863 the young Ohioan had so well established himself as an accurate and colorful writer that the newly formed Western Associated Press made him one of its first eastern correspondents, thus widening further the influence of his pen.

Richard Smith felt that this success had gone to his reporter's head. His suspicions were crystallized when Reid sent a special article to the *New York Tribune* without informing the *Gazette*. Material for the article, purporting to be on the real bases for the removal of Rosecrans, certainly came to Reid through congressional connections, probably from members of the House Committee on Military Affairs, for the data used were taken from official correspondence and were not known to be available. The story attracted wide interest in the army and elsewhere, and Smith printed it in the *Gazette*. He guessed that Agate, in sending the article to Greeley, was seeking a quarrel with the *Gazette* while maneuvering for a job with the *Tribune*. Smith did not know his own man. There was very little likelihood of Reid's leaving him without very substantial remuneration elsewhere as long as the *Gazette* stock agreement remained unconsummated.[31]

The war years were crucial ones for Reid. He had gone to Cincinnati in 1861 as a youth, well read and with some talent as a writer, but provincial, unsure of himself, and uncertain in his ambitions. Four years later he was an established journalist, his talents proven, his abilities recognized, and his goals visualized, albeit imperfectly. It had been his fortune not only to witness two of the great battles of the war at Pittsburg Landing and at Gettysburg but also to report and interpret them to his countrymen. He had played a smaller but still significant role when he helped to quiet northern anxieties by his analysis of Grant's Wilderness Campaign. In another field, through his short but not unproductive association with Jay Cooke's bond programs, he had had an opportunity to see from within a pioneering financial operation of far-reaching influence in federal policies. Here Reid's contributions were small, but his personal knowledge of public finance was greatly broadened.[32] His financial status was also strengthened; in mid-1863 he was trading profitably in stocks through Samuel Hallet Co. and Jay Cooke and Co. in four-figure sums. Perhaps his greatest gain came through meeting and knowing many of the political leaders who would occupy places of power in the national government for a generation after the war. In these and in a score of lesser ways Whitelaw Reid lived and moved at the center of the greatest events of his century. He saw the unfolding drama with a clear eye and understood it as well as most of the intelligent Americans of his generation and far better than did many.

Not only in his public and professional life but also in his private affairs the Washington years were crucial for Reid. In 1862 his only brother, Gavin, and his sister-in-law, Nettie, both died. Nine years older than Whitelaw and without his intellectual bent, Gavin had been more like an uncle than a brother, while Nettie had been a close friend and companion. In the last year of the war R. C. Reid died, and two years later the only daughter of the family, Chestina, was married. Thus in a brief span of four years Reid's position was changed from that of the family's youngest male to that of its head. He was not only left with all responsibility for his widowed mother, then in her sixties, but he also became the guardian of Gavin's two adolescent daughters, Ella and Caroline. Mrs. Reid remained at the house in Greene County while Ella and Carrie were sent to boarding schools; sometimes one or both were near their grandmother, but more often they were with their uncle and guardian. The increased family responsibilities were somewhat offset by inheritance. R. C. Reid's modest estate consisted principally of the house and farm at Xenia, where Mrs. Reid remained throughout her life in comfort but not in luxury. Her son's roots were in Ohio, in the *Gazette* in Cincinnati and in the farm at Xenia, and he would not sever the ties. Yet he would never return to Ohio except to visit, for the break with his home state was complete by the end of the war. It was symbolized by his southern experiment.

3

The Search for Identity

For three years after the war ended Reid responded to an opportunity that made its appearance during a trip in May 1865. After Andrew Johnson's inauguration, Salmon P. Chase decided to make a personal inspection tour of several southern cities. He invited his young friend and longtime supporter to accompany him, and the *Gazette* correspondent eagerly accepted. Although southern influences in the Miami Valley were heavy and Ohioans of that section were culturally almost as much southerner as northerner, Reid had been in the area of the Confederacy but once and then briefly. With some difficulty, he had gone to Richmond soon after the confederates evacuated the city. Transportation had been difficult, even hazardous, and at one point his wagon driver had refused to proceed farther in the dark because of danger from mines. In addition to physical obstacles encountered, the trip had been made over the objections of Assistant Secretary of War Charles A. Dana, who had gone to the confederate capital to gather up such papers and documents as the fleeing government might have left and who wanted no rivals there.[1]

The journey with Chase was a far different experience and unlike anything Reid had done before. It was more vacation than work, the first complete separation from routine and responsibility he had had since his much less enjoyable and unsatisfying trip to Minnesota five years earlier. Chase's party left Washington early in May and traveled in revenue cutters put at his disposal by the secretary of the treasury. The president and the secretaries of war and of the navy ordered civil, military, and naval officials along the proposed routes to give Chase full cooperation and to afford him every facility to make his journey a success. The pass Reid carried was a kind of which newsmen often dream but seldom see. Signed by the president of the United States, it authorized Reid to travel from Washington to New Orleans and return and to visit any place en route within the military occupation lines. Reid said he was offered a thousand dollars for the pass.

As the party proceeded to Fort Fisher, Charleston, Savannah,

Fernandina, and Key West, its members heard bands, saw parades, and reviewed troops, rode in fancy carriages, ate rich food, and drank fine wines. All these things were supplied in response to the executive orders for cooperation and in celebration of the still recent victory of union arms. The ruined and desolate Charleston, cradle of the rebellion, did not sadden Reid. He was disappointed in Savannah, having pictured it as a southern Cincinnati or St. Louis. Florida, he thought, offered some opportunity for investment (John Hay's orange grove speculation near St. Augustine interested all his northern friends who knew of it), but he felt that the state had little future and would be a poor place to live.

At Key West, thanks to a fortunate coincidence, the officers on Chase's vessel found it necessary to delay the trip for a few days, and the party found its work caught up. A trip to Havana was easily arranged, and for two eventful days all enjoyed the delights available in the capital of the Pearl of the Antilles. They did not omit the traditional visit to a bullring where Reid saw three bulls killed and a horse disemboweled. It was his first visit to foreign soil, and his reports betrayed his unfamiliarity with this Latin land. He could not fail to note the antagonism between the Creole and the Spaniard, and he correctly predicted eventual revolution, but his comments on slavery and predictions that its extinction in Cuba was imminent were wide of the mark.

After leaving Havana, the junketing tourists went next to Mobile and thence to New Orleans. The entertainment was lavish, the food and the drink of the best, and the talk stimulating. If New Orleans was not originally the real goal of the trip it became so, for the party stopped there ten days. Reid found New Orleans a city that he thought could be compared with New York: a rich harvest field for miscellaneous adventurers, hundreds of whom, he thought, had accumulated fortunes during the occupation of the city by union forces. In Mobile he had begun to think of the possibilities of large profits from cotton, and in New Orleans he pursued the idea further. Others were not averse to learning, and after leaving the Crescent City the party moved up the river, stopping at Davis' Bend below Vicksburg. There they drove in a fine equipage through spacious fields of young green cotton to Davis' house, where they heard optimistic accounts of plantation economics. From Vicksburg the party continued up the Mississippi to Cairo where, Reid reported, slaves waited on them at dinner, the last slaves he saw in America. On this last leg of the journey he relaxed fully and spent a whole day reading *Vanity Fair*. When he returned to Cincinnati he was determined to make some speculation in southern recovery.[2]

Possibly the glamor and excitement of the bands, and parades, and entertainment threw a rosy glow over the southern scene for Reid in the late spring of 1865. If there had been such a glow, it was completely dispelled during a second trip the following November.[3] Rather than on a fine cutter, he traveled by train in old and creaky coaches or decrepit boxcars over worn-out rails and on uneven roadbeds. His traveling companions were rough and often dirty Yankees as well as unrepentant and often uncouth southerners. Rather than bustling port cities filled with high-priced cotton where eager speculation on the future was everywhere, he saw ruined buildings, desolate fields, and listless, suffering people. Only in Atlanta did he find the energy and striving for recovery that he had seen on the earlier journey.

Both of Reid's trips into the South were, of course, fully reported in his letters to the *Gazette*. Characteristically, he told the whole story as he saw it, omitting no side and offering occasional generalizations about southern intransigence and northern cupidity. Always analytical, he saw some patterns, and these he lined out cautiously, sensing the shifting nature of emotions and the uncertainties of the postwar southern scene.

His experience with Negroes had been slight, for although the Xenia population included enough members of the race to have a church of their own, he seems not to have known any. He was not a proponent of universal suffrage, but while at Miami he had opposed the extension of slavery into Kansas and later had strongly criticized Stephen A. Douglas' advocacy of squatter sovereignty. He supported Lincoln in 1860 and approved of the Emancipation Proclamation when it was issued. He was sympathetic toward the plight of the ex-slaves, and found them to be orderly, respectable, and intelligent; he thought they were probably capable of caring for themselves. He also thought they could profit from schooling although he had some reservations as to their ultimate capabilities. The sea island Negroes, he felt, lacked the ability to be skilled workers; as farmers in the lower south, Negroes could support themselves but might not be able to produce exportable surpluses. The progress made by Negro children in the New Orleans schools was encouraging in reading, writing, and geography but their potential in what the onetime grade school principal thought of as the higher skills such as arithmetic raised his doubts about the intellectual capacities of the race.

The former rebels he found still rebellious; otherwise the ex-confederates did not seem to conform to any pattern. Well-bred southerners of intelligence felt that the rebel armies had suffered no disgrace from defeat by overwhelming numbers of northern hirelings. They refused to admit that justice had triumphed. They not only had no love for their conquerors, ex-Captain Reid thought, but they did not even understand that Jefferson Davis, William L. Yancey, Robert Toombs, and their fellow hotheads were alone responsible for the bloodbath of the war. In short, the Ohio reporter found that his opinion of the South's wartime leaders was not shared by all southerners. Even with the rebel predominant in the South, Reid believed the problem of the South's status in the weeks following the destruction of the Confederacy was not inherently complex or even very difficult, but that it was made so by northern failure to comprehend the situation as much as by southern intransigence.

To his surprise, Reid did not find a Union party in any southern state. The North, he thought, had erred grievously in thinking there was such a party in the South and that its members would be able to construct sober and loyal state governments. Further damage was done to the prospects of reunion in the summer of 1865, when northern members of the House and Senate and other leaders abandoned the new president, while southerners dinned their grievances into his ears. Johnson took a wrong course because he was weak and lacked good judgment, and his party did not give him proper guidance. "The history of our politics shows no graver blunder," Reid told the North. He came to believe that the dividing point between the possibility for smooth transition from rebellion to loyalty on the one hand and a widened division between the sections on the other had come at the end of May. Johnson's proclamation prescribing a mode of political reconstruction for North Carolina, Reid thought, gave stubborn southern leaders too much support in their defiance and discouraged the few who might have developed union-minded parties. Before the end of 1865 he discerned with some alarm the threatened dual danger of former slave-owners legislating for freedmen and of men having legislative responsibility for a debt created to subjugate them.

Not only was there no Union party in existence in the South, the *Gazette* reporter found, but the future of unionism there was seriously handicapped. Many union officers had fostered friction by carting away more than trivial booty, he found, and noted that one had collected for his walls an entire set of family portraits from an old South Carolina home. Rural Ohioans had simply bored Reid, but some rural southerners disgusted him. He referred to them as poor whites, saying that for dirt and utter ignorance of all the decencies of civilized life they had no equals in America. He added that to his grief they were almost the only Unionists. Not quite the only, for the Negroes would become Unionists, of course. He had some doubts about their qualifications for suffrage, but thought the ones he saw in the port cities as orderly, respectable, and intelligent as many New York City Democrats.

While the discovery that the South held neither a Union party nor a sound basis for one was a surprise and something of a disappointment to Reid, he was a reporter and no reformer, a critic rather than an advocate. When he returned to Washington in December to report the all-important organization of the Thirty-ninth Congress his mind was made up. His misgivings as to the shaky foundations for a Union party in the South were outweighed by his doubts about the wisdom of restoring power to the ex-rebels, with their opposition to Negro advancement and their tendency to think in terms of ultimate repudiation of the national debt. As he watched the drama in Congress on December 4, 1865, he felt no apprehension at the radicals' ruthless seizure of power through excluding the southerners and establishing the Committee of Fifteen. Reid believed it was right that the Congress was organized by the Unionists, made up of Republican, loyal Democratic, and independent leaders, elements fused in the heat of patriotism and dedicated to the privileged task of making permanent the results of a righteous war.[4]

Early in 1866 Reid once more set his face to the South, this time to join hundreds of other financial adventurers in get-rich-quick expeditions to the plantation country, where they hoped to make cotton king again—at least long enough to become princes. Some kind of investment in the South had been in Reid's mind since his trip with Chase. He had thought once of sugar. Later he gave at least a passing thought to the possibilities of gold, iron, or coal mining, but returns from investment in these industries would develop slowly at best. More important, his background in an agricultural section of Ohio enabled him to assess with more confidence the possibilities in a farming enterprise. The availability of land in Alabama at seven to fourteen dollars an acre and in the rich bottoms of Louisiana and Mississippi at prices almost as tempting nagged constantly at the mind of the young capitalist. Farm bred, he understood the risks inherent in attempts to make profits by farming in the lower South, despite the cheap land: "I should judge it a splendid opening for a careless man to lose money."[5] Still, the prospects were too tempting for him to take his own advice; he did not intend to be careless. Nor was he. When he went back to New Orleans early in 1866 he spent more than two months visiting both small and large plantations along both sides of the lower Mississippi in one of the richest cotton-producing regions of America. Hoping to gain broader understanding of the problem he might later meet in using Negro labor, he looked over sugar plantations as well as cotton-growing areas and studied the strength and weakness of the gang system. Nor did he overlook white labor as a possibility, but early decided it would be uneconomical.[6]

Had Reid considered a partner as carefully as he looked over laborers he might have remained longer in the cotton business. When he began his venture as a planter he had as an associate an Iowa adventurer, Francis Jay Herron, widely believed to be the youngest major general of the union army. The new partner was just Reid's age. A lawyer and would-be statesman, Herron, like Reid, was in Louisiana in 1866 to make his fortune. It is to Reid's credit that the enterprise did not end in disaster after he became involved with the general, for everything the Iowan had attempted had ended in failure. The two twenty-nine-year-old Yankee cotton planters bought land near the Mississippi River. The acreage made two large farms, which they called Fish Pond and Scotland Plantation. They cultivated something less than a thousand acres and worked as many as two hundred Negroes in the picking season. As cotton came out of the fields, it went into gins on the place, two small ones powered by mules and two somewhat larger ones run by wood-burning steam engines. Reid's investment totaled more than twenty thousand dollars, twelve thousand of which he borrowed from a Washington bank. The remainder represented his own funds or money secured on a short-term basis in Cincinnati. The Louisiana venture was not an outstanding success, but the high prices of cotton made it just remunerative enough to convince Reid he should try again, this time without Herron. For the next growing season, 1867, he went to Alabama, where he lost what profits he had made in Louisiana. He then renewed the decision he had made eight years earlier in Xenia, to live by the pen rather than the plow.[7]

Reid's poorly conceived and executed attempt to become a southern planter earned him little money and less reputation, but it did give him some experience he could use later. In contrast to these small gains much enduring literary output came from his pen in the two southern years. He completed his first book while putting in his first crop and finished a second as he closed his accounts on the planting experiment. *After the War* was easily done. It was little more than a chronicle of what he had seen and of his impressions during his earlier trips through the South. Much of the book was drawn from his letters to the *Gazette* and the rest he took from his notebooks. He had hardly sent the last of the manuscript to his publishers when he was deep in the writing of the far more pretentious and much more difficult *Ohio in the War*.

This work had been in the making since the summer of 1863, when William H. Moore approached the young journalistic hero of Shiloh and asked him to undertake the task of recording Ohio's already impressive and potentially decisive role in suppressing the rebellion. Modest in words but never in attempts, Reid was willing, especially since William H. Moore and his partners, Charles F. Wilstach and F. H. Baldwin, were ready to collect all the materials the author would need. The publishers were as good as their spokesman's word. They, or their agents, visited armies in the field, interviewed veterans of all ranks after the war, and collected thousands of documents. Reid's own acquaintance with Ohio's soldiers and their confidence in him was an invaluable aid, enabling him to secure information not included in official reports and not obtainable through publishers' interviews. Even with these advantages, *Ohio in the War* might easily have been no more than a compilation of testimonials bound together with a thread of narration. Such it was not.

Reid's account of Ohio's war effort is highly impressive. While he selected much documentary material for inclusion in the two fat volumes, his chief contribution was in his interpretive accounts. The bulk of the work consisted of sketches of most of Ohio's principal soldiers and some "near Ohioans," a striking array of more than a hundred generals, many of whom were the most outstanding figures of the union armies—Buell, Garfield, Grant, McClellan, McDowell,

Rosecrans, Sheridan, and Sherman. That Reid as Agate knew many of these personally, some of them well, hardly made his role of impartial historian easier. Yet he played the role with impressive skill. In almost every instance his analyses of his subjects' strengths and weaknesses coincided with the judgment scholars would hold a century later. If his style made some comments seem overlaudatory, they were balanced by Reid's temperament as critic and the blunt frankness of other comments.[8]

After the War and *Ohio in the War* occupied most of the spare time Reid had while in the South, but he took an extended trip north between the Louisiana and the Alabama experiments. Early in 1867 he went to Ohio, to Washington, and to Boston. In Xenia, he made some repairs on the house and had a marker set for his father's grave at a cost of more than a thousand dollars, eloquent testimony to his regard for the family name and to his belief that his father's standing in the community required a substantial stone as a memorial. The Washington trip was purely a business one, but his journey to Boston was to attend and help to manage the wedding of his twenty-two-year-old sister Chessie.[9]

At the end of 1867 Reid was once more in the *Gazette* offices in Cincinnati; from there he traveled when important news summoned him. Johnson's impeachment proceedings called him to Washington the following year, and he reported that political travesty in full. Throughout the trial he stood squarely against the president. As March passed and April wore on, despite increasing evidence that the vote would be close, he predicted that Johnson would be destroyed. In the first and second weeks of May he realized that many of the articles of impeachment would not be supported, but he still hoped for conviction on at least one or two. By the time the final vote was taken, the realistic reporter no longer believed the president would be impeached but the partisan observer remained convinced that justice had been thwarted.[10]

Notwithstanding his disappointment at the outcome of the trial, Reid enjoyed his sojourn in the heady atmosphere of the capital. While there he determined not to return to Ohio but to remain in the more stimulating air of the East. He accepted a long available offer from Horace Greeley to join the staff of the *New York Tribune*.

4

Greeley's Assistant

WHEN Reid walked through the Nassau Street doors of the *Tribune* office on Printing House Square in September 1868, he was nearing the end of his thirty-first year. His appearance was much the same as when he began his career with the *Cincinnati Gazette*. He was "tall and slender, with a drooping mustache and 'intelligent eyes' under a sweeping mass of dark hair worn in the 'Rebel cut.' "[1] His interests and experience had by this time plainly marked him for a career in journalism, but had indicated less clearly whether writing or editorial work would provide the greater opportunity and offer more satisfaction. The *Tribune* could open the way to these and to related endeavors, for the New York papers were multi-sided enterprises. The *Tribune* Association, housed in its own building and owned by the holders of its hundred shares of stock, was a million-dollar-a-year business. Samuel Sinclair's advertising, circulation, and business departments with a staff of some thirty people took in nearly a hundred thousand dollars a month. The business paid out that much to paper makers, type founders, printers, press services, reporters, special writers, to a host of other contributing persons and companies, and to stockholders. More than three hundred thousand subscribers and an unknown number of readers saw each issue of either the daily, weekly, or semiweekly *Tribune*. These citizens were enlightened with political information, discussions of scientific problems and discoveries, literary comment, documentary material, poetry, plain gossip, and whatever else Horace Greeley felt was good for the country. Regular and occasional reporters, notables in every field of activity, special correspondents, travelers and hacks, all scattered from coast to coast in the United States, from Canada to Panama, and from London to Vienna, sent a steady stream of matter to Nassau Street. There was something in the *Tribune* for nearly everyone. Greeley's chief contribution was in setting the tone of the Great Moral Organ, implictly in the news columns and in the choice of articles and explicitly on the editorial pages. He identified Republican principles with truth and justice, reserving to himself in the final analysis the sole right of defining the bases on which the party had been established and might continue to flourish. Greeley's truths frequently seemed to others to include "fictitious dangers which in the *Tribune*'s fancy" threatened Republican policies.[2]

For six months Reid sat near the center of the institution, writing and learning in Greeley's shadow and under John Russell Young's guidance. Four years Reid's junior, Young, the managing editor, was more experienced in newspaper work although his general outlook was less broad and his talents less diverse. The new staff member was expected to pull a share of the load with a minimum of jostling. The instructions Greeley and Young gave him were usually broad. He was asked to do "something on the fur seal trade," or to do an article "on this ten percent business," taking the ground that it was a mistake—"be firm but kind," or to prepare a statement on the Interior Department reorganization, "make any suggestions you like."[3] Where Greeley had set a tone and an approach, Reid frequently wrote at will on related topics without the editor's suggestions and sometimes without his knowledge. Greeley was deeply suspicious of Indiana's Union Republican Sen. Oliver Hazard Perry Morton, considering him an inflationist and therefore of doubtful honesty at best. Reid's editorials on Morton's speeches about resumption were sarcastic and patronizing, yet showed he had not forgotten what he had learned about finance while selling bonds for Jay Cooke a few years earlier.[4]

Young also had confidence in the new writer and on at least one occasion, too tired after a full day to work longer, he sent one of his own editorials to Reid for revision. Within four months of his arrival both Greeley and Young were willing to leave much responsibility in Reid's hands while they left the city for days at a time.[5]

Some journalists thought less of Greeley's assistant than did the *Tribune*'s managers. Before he joined the fraternity in Printing House Square, the *New York Sun* had portrayed him as Romeo Reed, an undermining influence on his *Cincinnati Gazette* partner, the virtuous Deacon Richard Smith.[6] A year after this dig the *Sun* was the unwitting instrument of "Romeo Reed's" engagement to the *Tribune*. For the *Sun* was directly responsible for John Russell Young's removal from the "old rookery," as the overcrowded building at Spruce and Nassau was sometimes called. Young's departure followed a dramatic exposé by his journalistic enemies. The *Tribune*'s managing editor had used his position to send Associated Press news items to a nonparticipating Philadelphia paper in which he had an interest. Contrary to association rules though it was, the practice was fairly common. In this instance it was known to Greeley, who took no action. But Young had a powerful enemy in Amos Cummings, a former *Tribune* city editor, brilliant but rough and profane. Greeley had had Young discharge him. Now managing editor of the *Sun* and abetted by his employer Charles Dana, Cummings mercilessly exposed Young as a "sneak news thief." At the same time he laid bare some of Young's private opinions of his fellow journalists, accomplished by publication in the *Sun* of four columns of Young's private letters and by subsequent comment. Because of the public manner in which Cummings and Dana struck at Young, Greeley could not protect him, but he tried to soften the blow as best he could by eliminating the managing editorship rather than by discharging the incumbent. The *Sun*'s first blow fell on April 27, 1869, and Young was out by mid-May.[7]

The same order that terminated Young's position gave the work to Reid, leaving him in possession of the managing editor's portfolio but without the ministerial title. Greeley's new right arm was not fully prepared for the task at hand. Reid was primarily a writer and at this he was excelled by few other newspaper people even in New York. He was also an editor of considerable ability and some experience. In the area of business his chief successes had been in investment rather than in operations. The place that was thrust upon him demanded the full use of all his talents. Unfortunately writing was the least of Reid's duties in the new position. Nothing in his experiences had prepared him for many of the tasks that now confronted him or the problems he had to solve in the weeks and months that followed his accession to Young's chair. Never a shirker and no stranger to stretches of sustained effort at a desk, he nevertheless had not previously experienced the pressures and frustrations of the month after month grind of office work for long hours without relieving change.

Nor had the plantation venture, his only previous experience with a large-scale enterprise, prepared him for a responsible role in managing and directing the *Tribune*. This intricate and rapidly moving organization had to collect the news, write it, edit it, set it up in type, print it, and distribute fifty thousand papers by breakfast time six days each week. The final stages of the process required time tables that had to be rigidly adhered to, "at any cost to individuals." A three o'clock deadline for going to press was so stringently enforced that slight delays were cause for consultation between managing editor and publisher. In one instance Reid sharply reprimanded Franklin J. Ottarson, the city editor, for "drifting along until 6 minutes before 3 trusting to luck" and threatened that action would be taken in case of another failure to go to press at the required time. Reid's assiduity was partly due to his own perfectionist attitude and partly to a desire to keep clear of a clash with Samuel Sinclair who dominated the circulation and business departments of the paper and who, next to Greeley, was the most powerful member of the *Tribune*'s staff.[8]

After two and a half years of this with hardly a break, Reid was as much relieved as dismayed when he was virtually forced out of the confining tedium of office work and thrust into the exhilarating atmosphere of a national political campaign as manager of a presidential candidate. Neither Greeley nor Reid had been enthusiastic Grant men. The *Tribune*'s expression of approval of the soldier-president at the time of his election was sincere but not effusive. In effect the paper said "amen" to Grant's "Let us have peace." Even this much support waned, and by 1870 Greeley was privately saying that Grant was impossible. Reid found the general too small a man for the presidency, disliked his principal advisors, and was repelled by the "coarse use of the civil service."[9] Yet neither Greeley nor his assistant was ready for the radical step of a party bolt at the halfway point of Grant's first term. More completely alienated Republicans met in Cincinnati and cast about for a program and candidate with which to oppose Grantism. The movement found no support in the *Tribune*. At this point Reid was revealing his political naïveté by expressing doubts about Grant's renomination. "I don't believe [it] either assured or very probable," he told Garfield in mid-July, a year before the convention would meet.[10]

As 1871 passed and the time for nomination came closer, Missouri defectors who knew the impossibility of stopping Grant from within the party, sent out a call for a convention to meet again in Cincinnati and name a Liberal Republican candidate. The call was made in January. Greeley hesitated, but by the end of February Reid not only believed that a Liberal Republican could be elected but also was thinking of the *Tribune*'s editor as a possible nominee. In March Reid sought the attitudes of national Republican leaders toward the political heresy of a party bolt. In this he was moving in the same direction as were many editors of both parties including Joseph Medill, Joseph Pulitzer, Horace White, Murat Halstead, William Cullen Bryant, and Samuel Bowles. The Republicans, especially Bowles, Reid, and White, were concerned about Sen. Charles Sumner's attitude, and they were all sensitive to the role that Sen. Carl Schurz might play. If Sumner, no friend of Grant, could be persuaded to give active support to a third party movement, its chance of success would be greatly enhanced. Reid and many others wrote to the senator in March and April and urged him to let his position be known. Reid also thought that "Schurz is immensely strong" and "is contemplating a bolt." By April, these considerations evidently resolved to their satisfaction, Reid was saying that the Cincinnati movement was the only one gaining strength, and Greeley was supporting strongly a New York "response" to Cincinnati. Most of the new-fledged statesmen and would-be president makers believed that Charles Francis Adams could become the strongest opponent for Grant. But the editor of the Great Moral Organ had a mystic faith in his own chances, and Reid seems to have been mesmerized into sharing the same belief.[11] Their hopes were not publicly revealed, and a week before the convention met the *Tribune*'s Samuel Sinclair expressed astonishment that Reid was going to Cincinnati to support Greeley's nomination.

Even though some of the greatest names in American journalism beat the drums for honesty, integrity, and responsibility in government, it quickly became clear that there was little more than principle behind the anti-Grant noise. Professional politicians were conspicuous by their absence from the Liberal bandwagon, and wealthy contributors did not crowd around the war chest. In mid-April the *Tribune* printed, probably from Reid's pen, advice on how to organize a national convention. Anyone may go, dissidents were advised. Those present, after arrival, might want to organize as delegations; voting would probably be on a basis of representation in Congress; the convention might or might not nominate a candidate.[12]

Tariff theorists, disgruntled intellectuals, journalists, civil service reformers, Frémont Republicans, old Whigs, and a few professional politicians converged on Cincinnati from all points of the compass during the last days of April. Reid, personifying several of these elements and professing to have "reasonable confidence" in Greeley's chance of success, left New York on April 25. After a stopover in Xenia, he arrived in Cincinnati on a Sunday.[13]

By the following day most of the participants had arrived, including more than a hundred and fifty from New York. Reid met with the New Yorkers on Monday morning long enough to make his presence known, then hastened to enter into alliance with the journalists. Bowles, White, Halstead, and Henry Watterson had "organized a fellowship . . . which went by the name of the Quadrilateral." This bastion of liberalism resisted Reid's entrance at first, but could neither exclude so powerful a journal as the *Tribune* nor risk alienating one that might influence so numerous a body as the sixty-eight-vote-strong New York delegation. It was the avowed purpose of the four journalists to limit the consideration of candidates to the strong but indifferent Adams and the weak but willing Lyman Trumbull against all opposition. The Greeley forces, if converted to Adams, might well decide the issue. The Quadrilateral was broken before the battle began, and Reid had established himself at the convention's principal information and operations center.[14]

From this vantage point Greeley's representative was able to keep close watch on the jumble of developments of Tuesday, Wednesday, and Thursday, when platform planks were shaped, groups of individuals made into state delegations, the delegations organized, and committees appointed. These arrangements were made formal as the loosely organized mass meeting named itself a convention at noon on Wednesday and chose its officers. Schurz became permanent chairman, and committees struggled to set on paper the general understandings arrived at in hotel rooms.

As the self-enfranchised delegates gathered at the Music Hall and discussed the principal contenders for a majority of the 700 available votes, Reid could count less than 150 ballots for his principal, and few delegates conceded Greeley more than an outside chance, if that, of gaiṇing the nomination. Yet he had but one serious opponent. Adams, despite his departure for Europe, his refusal to send even a message of interest to Cincinnati, and his disdain for the whole affair, remained in the forefront of the candidates. His strength was so apparent that by late Wednesday the Missouri delegation was wavering in its devotion to Gov. B. Gratz Brown, the state's leading political organizer and Schurz's chief rival in the state. Some of the Missouri delegates were leaning toward Adams, who had Schurz's backing. When Brown learned of the threatened treasonable defections, he boarded a train and hastened to the scene of conflict. Not only was an eastern conservative anathema to many western reformers, but nomination of a Schurz-supported candidate for a national office would enhance the German's already powerful position in Missouri politics.[15]

Brown arrived at midnight on Thursday and conferred hastily with representatives of the principal contenders. His main concern was to defeat Schurz, and he believed that the most direct way to accomplish that was to support Greeley against Schurz's candidate. He therefore agreed to accept second place on a Greeley-Brown ticket. Reid's role in these maneuvers was important but not crucial. He encouraged the New Yorkers to remain united and kept Greeley's name before the delegation, emphasizing his national reputation and insisting that he was exceptionally available because he had no enemies.[16]

With Schurz in the chair, the first trial of strength on April 3 resulted in the votes being divided between the reluctant Adams and the eager Greeley, 203 and 147 respectively. Four other candidates had to be content with smaller portions—Trumbull with 100 and Brown, David Davis, and Andrew G. Curtin with slightly under 100 each. As these results were being announced and without regard for previous tacit agreements to eschew nominating speeches, the red-bearded Brown gained the platform. Once before the leaderless Liberals he astounded the assemblage by urging Greeley on them. On the second ballot the *Tribune* candidate edged Adams, but by less than 10 votes. The New Englander regained the lead on the rapidly taken third and fourth ballots and on the fifth was only 50 votes short of success, but his strength was very nearly at its peak.

Reid had avoided being designated as an official delegate to gain greater freedom of movement. He remained on the floor of the Music Hall throughout the balloting, holding the Greeley men in line and halting desertions. When Adams came in second again (fewer than ten votes divided the two principal contenders) on the sixth ballot, Reid and the other New York leaders and the Brown men gave the signal for an all-out effort to stampede the assemblage. The New Yorkers and the Missourians responded by milling about, shouting, standing on chairs, crowding into other delegations, creating enough pro-Greeley noise and confusion to convince the doubtful. The battle plan was successful, the

Pyrrhic victory complete. Greeley was nominated after less than five hours of voting. Schurz was dumbfounded, the Quadrilateral was in ruins, and the regular Republicans of the nation were filled with astonishment and delight. Reid attempted to maintain an appearance of harmony between the Adamsites and the *Tribune* candidacy by having a victory dinner for the erstwhile statesmen-journalists. The company hardly touched the food, and none lingered at the board. Half a century of later experiences at political dinners did not dim Henry Watterson's memory of the meal. "Frostier conviviality I have never sat down to than Reid's dinner," he recalled.[17]

In New York, professing surprise at the unexpected outcome of the convention, the Liberal Republican candidate publicly withdrew from the editorial management of the *Tribune*. "The *Tribune* has ceased to be a party organ, but the unexpected nomination of its Editor at Cincinnati seems to involve it in a new embarrassment," Greeley told the nation, saying he would exercise no supervision over the columns of the paper until further notice. Reid assumed full control of the journal.[18]

The campaign was uneventful. The journalist-statesmen stuck to their bargain, albeit without enthusiasm. Schurz tried to escape. He suggested to Greeley that he could refuse the nomination and to Reid that the matter might be reconsidered. Sumner was willing to attack Grant but could not bring himself to do more than announce his support of the Native Philosopher. He would not campaign. It was the Democrats who saved Greeley from quick political oblivion by making him their candidate.[19]

As Democratic conventions in state after state instructed their national delegates for Greeley and Brown, Reid grew more optimistic. By the end of June his list of doubtful states that could be won included Pennsylvania, Indiana, and North Carolina. He thought Maine, Connecticut, and Rhode Island could be held and that New Hampshire was a toss-up. With these and the normally Republican states, Greeley could win. After the Democratic convention the *Tribune* spelled it out: the Democrats could carry fifteen states with 135 electoral votes; Greeley could take enough of the doubtful ones from the twenty-two normally Republican states to have more than the needed 183 electoral votes.[20]

Accomplishment of these ambitious objectives was beyond the capacities of Augustus Schell, chairman of the Democratic National

Committee, and Ethan Allen, the Liberal Republican campaign chairman. With neither adequate funds nor a well-organized Liberal party, the campaign was never a serious threat to the regular Republicans. Not even the Credit Mobilier sensation, which Dana's *Sun* exposed in September, could slow the march of Grant to another victory. The careful diligence of hardworking Chairman E. D. Morgan and Secretary William E. Chandler of the Republican National Committee more than offset the loss of a few reputations in the railroad scandals. Morgan and Chandler drew on the Pennsylvania iron manufacturers, the national banks, the House of Cooke and scores of lesser financial establishments, the Whiskey Ring, and on innumerable smaller enterprises dependent on favors and protection. Perhaps never before had political assessments on officeholders been greater.[21]

The entire expenditure for the Greeley campaign was estimated by the *New York Times* at no more than three hundred thousand dollars, a sum hardly more than a tenth of that available to the regular Republicans. Supporters not influenced by monetary considerations also upheld the regular cause. References to "Whitelie Reid" in *Harper's Weekly* bolstered the more effective Nast drawings in the same journal. The pro-Grant cartoonist pictured Reid before the door of the Democratic headquarters as an organ grinder. His instrument was labeled "This is not an organ" on one side and "New York Tribune" on the other. Organ-grinder Reid held Greeley on a leash; Greeley was represented as a monkey with a white hat and long white coat and carrying a tin cup labeled "votes."[22]

While opposition journalists struck at Reid, some of his own best writers gave him little support. John Hay was quite unenthusiastic about Greeley's candidacy and John R. G. Hassard went on an extended wedding trip during the campaign.

The Grant forces were moving so strongly by mid-September that Horace White looked for an alibi in case of defeat and easily found one in potential Democratic perfidy. The philosophy of the campaign is just here, he wrote Reid: if the Democratic vote can be held for Greeley then there are Liberal Republicans enough to elect him. But White feared Democratic defections. For his part, the acting editor of the *Tribune* deluded himself for a few more weeks, but by election time Reid was ready to agree that White was right.[23]

Greeley won in six states. None that his manager had considered doubtful in June went for the editor, who lost his own state by more than fifty thousand votes. Afterward Reid recalled that as the voting began he and Samuel J. Tilden assured themselves that the issue was in doubt only because each was trying to keep the other in the fight. To George Smalley, Reid confided the belief that gross inefficiency among the Brown managers and lavish use of money by the regular Republicans "in the wards . . . through the polls and through the returns" had counted heavily in the outcome. Greeley survived the defeat less than a month. Reid denied assertions that the unsuccessful candidate died of political disappointment. He ascribed the death to years of overwork, culminating in the strain of a long western trip during the campaign, from which he returned to be with his wife, who was dying.[24]

Greeley had little to do with the paper after the Cincinnati convention. Although he announced his resumption of the editorship on November 7, he did not take hold after the election, and his death had slight effect on Reid's day-to-day work of getting out the *Tribune*. The long-range fate of the paper was another matter, however. Ultimate control lay with the stockholders, and many of them were aware that circulation had dropped somewhat during the campaign and that revenues had suffered. The stock was reportedly worth less per share than the eight thousand dollars Reid paid for his first share.[25] The paper without Greeley might not be successful; many considered it editorless after his death. He had long been known as the voice of the *Tribune*, and the extent of his young assistant's contribution was known to few people. Horace Greeley's benign, whisker-fringed face and homey personality were nationwide symbols of journalistic integrity and popular wisdom. Reid had no such standing. Further, he himself did not consider that the position he had held under Greeley might be his without Greeley. He meant little to the Republicans of New York, chief supporters of the *Tribune* in ordinary circumstances. In short, Reid had neither the name to replace Greeley's nor political patrons to uphold him. Nor did he have sufficient financial resources to bid for the million-dollar property.[26]

He did, however, own shares in the paper. From the time of his connection with the *Cincinnati Gazette*, Reid had believed that a financial stake in an enterprise was necessary for maximum benefit to both employee and organization. He had had some difficulty, however, in acquiring his first share of *Tribune* stock. When John Russell Young left the paper he tentatively offered a share to Reid for eight thousand dollars, but when Reid tried to get it for less, Young disposed of it elsewhere.[27] Reid soon discovered that in some quarters ten thousand dollars was not considered too high a price. The new managing editor then turned to Greeley, who he knew felt that the paper's chief editors and writers should also be part owners. Appealing to the editor's idealism, Reid took a high moral stance and told the financially naïve Greeley that the stock was worth only seventy-five hundred dollars when Reid joined the paper and that the owners had no right to charge him for his own services by exacting a top price for a share of the enterprise in which he was a contributing member. Greeley succumbed to the argument and in April 1870 sold Reid a share for eight thousand dollars, which the purchaser thought was perhaps two thousand dollars under the true value.[28]

Within a week the stockholders decided to pay three hundred dollars per share in dividends, and Reid could have sold his for ten thousand dollars within a few months. But he had not bought for speculative purposes. As in other investments, well understanding the direction of the American economy, he refused to dispose of one good investment even to acquire another. Instead he borrowed the eight thousand dollars giving the Adams Express Co. eight shares of *Gazette* stock as collateral.[29] The following November he acquired another *Tribune* share, also through Greeley's good offices and at the same figure, again borrowing through Gen. E. S. Sanford of Adams Express. Further acquisitions included the purchase of five shares during the 1872 campaign on William Walter Phelps's advice that it was a good investment and to strengthen his position. Reid owned no more than fourteen of the hundred closely held shares by the time of Greeley's death, a respectable holding but not one sizable enough on which to base a bid for the paper.[30]

It was not Reid then, but Samuel Sinclair and William Orton, president of Western Union, who moved to gain control of the *Tribune* in December 1872. Sinclair was not the publisher, but with twenty shares he was the largest stockholder. He might have acquired more and named anyone he chose to succeed Greeley, but financial straits made him decide to liquidate some property, including the *Tribune* stock.[31] He offered them to Orton, neither a friend of Greeley nor an admirer of his policies, who gladly took the proffered shares. Orton then obtained, by mid-December, options on enough stock to control the *Tribune*

Association. Sinclair had already approached Schuyler Colfax as a national figure whose reputation might restore the paper's primacy, and the "Smiler" had indicated his willingness to be drafted as Greeley's successor. The scheme was well conceived, and most Republican papers considered it advantageous for the party.[32] Reid, Hay, and their cohorts unhappily prepared resignations and set about clearing their desks for departure when the new regime arrived.

At the moment of apparent success, however, the plan fell apart. Colfax was willing but not enthusiastic; his wife was reluctant; the Credit Mobilier revelations pointed to hazardous days for numerous friends; the options might prove difficult to renew or extend. Colfax bowed out. Orton turned to Reid, who had not fought but who had refused to cooperate in the earlier plan. The astonished managing editor did not hesitate. He borrowed money from William Sprague and from the wealthy young William Walter Phelps. Sprague was Salmon P. Chase's son-in-law, a heavy contributor to Greeley's campaign and an old Washington friend of Hay's. Reid had met Phelps a year earlier; the latter admired the editor and wanted to see him gain control of the *Tribune*. With this support, with his own shares plus those of Hay and a few other small holders, and with the reluctant collaboration of Sinclair and Orton, Reid was ready to bid. He secured a loan of never divulged size from Jay Gould and was able to acquire control of the paper. The financier needed a friendly voice among hostile press people as he faced the wrath of Erie stockholders. Reid was eager to gain control of the paper to which he had given more of himself, through more than four years, than to anything he had previously undertaken. The fortuitous combination of the financier's need and the journalist's ambition made this unlikely alliance possible. Once in control Reid quickly demonstrated his determination to retain his advantage, and he moved at once to forestall any change of heart by the stockholders. He exacted their acquiescence in a five-year agreement with heavy penalties for reneging, making him proprietor as well as editor.[33]

Reid got the *Tribune* but with it a heavy cross. Although Jay Gould was not active as a stockholder, the fact that he was one was no secret, and this cast a shadow over the paper. Charles Dana's *New York Sun* called the *Tribune* a "stock jobbing organ," Reid "Jay Gould's stool pigeon," and characterized the editor as a young fop, a hireling with a brilliant mind but without business competence or practical sense. Reid was hardly a fop, he was certainly not without business competence, and he was no stool pigeon for Gould. But he was worried about the connection. In 1874 he had a note from Phelps saying that Reid's controlling interest in the *Tribune* was rumored to be in danger. The editor told his friend that "The 'controlling interest' is locked up in my safe. I have . . . absolute control of it. . . . There is a possibility, of course, of my needing a great deal of money suddenly, some day, to hold on [but] I see no present danger." A year and a half later Reid discussed with Hay the possibility of the purchase of Gould's interest by Amasa Stone, Hay's wealthy father-in-law. Had Reid's situation been in real danger this arrangement might well have been made. As it was, the Gould shares were acquired in 1881, after Reid's marriage, by members of his wife's family. Gould, whose work Reid had characterized three weeks before acquiring the loan as outrageous and disreputable, was no longer criticized in the *Tribune*'s columns. This editorial policy was the basis of the *Sun*'s charge that Reid was Gould's "hireling."[34]

5

Proprietor of the *Tribune*

THE events at the end of 1872, Horace Greeley's death, Reid's near loss of his position and his unexpected triumph, were decisive for his career and for the future of the *Tribune*, but his routine was little altered. As John Russell Young's successor the details of management had crowded in upon him so that he could do little writing himself. A perfectionist in a loosely run office, he had seen waste and lost motion on every hand, for Greeley's zeal on the firing line of the editorial page had contrasted sharply with the slipshod practices permitted in other branches of the organization. To his dismay Reid had found that, although he was responsible for expenditures in the editorial department, the cashier paid out money on verbal instructions or informal memos from various staff members. To Reid, signing a check for unknown expenditures by sometimes unidentified persons was intolerable, and he had taken control of all such payments soon after succeeding Young.[1]

When he became proprietor of the paper Reid found that the business offices under Samuel Sinclair's control had been no better run than the financial side of the editorial and news departments under Greeley's management. Too many papers were sent out as exchanges or given away with no return at all; advertising accounts were poorly kept, and some had not been collected for many months; too high prices were being paid for ink and paper. When Reid gained control and Sinclair left, the new editor put the capable Gordon L. Ford at the head of the business office, and more efficient practices appeared at once.[2]

In other aspects of the *Tribune* establishment the new proprietor sometimes continued but more often changed earlier arrangements. The most important single source of news available to the *Tribune* at the time Reid joined the paper was the Associated Press wire service, a fourteen-thousand-dollar-a-year item, the heaviest single payment made by the *Tribune* for services. Much of the material could be used twice, for the semiweekly was largely made up by condensing the less perishable features of the daily. The small but vigorous AP had seven members, who bickered constantly among themselves as they sought to keep outsiders out and insiders in lines. It was Young's lack of respect for the AP's rules and his diversion of its news that had resulted in his forced separation from the paper. Less than a year later Reid discharged George H. Stout, able and longtime employee, for his efforts to build an organization that might someday rival the AP.[3] The cases of Young and Stout only illustrated the point that almost as much effort seemed needed to guard the news until it could be printed as to collect it. All member papers kept files on violations of the rules by others.[4] Occasionally, some made more or less formal charges, and once the *Sun* led an attack on the *Tribune* for withholding news from other members and called for an investigation, but no serious rift developed. In addition to the AP service, to speed dispatches of his own reporters and correspondents, Reid arranged for flat-rate monthly payments to Western Union Telegraph. The contract gave the *Tribune* as many as sixty thousand words a month at a sixth of the regular commercial rate.[5]

Reid also kept a watchful eye on any new development that would permit more efficient operation of his paper. In 1875 the first of Richard Hoe's new web presses to be seen in New York was installed in the *Tribune* basement. Three years later Reid ordered press attachments that "have switches, enabling us to fly the paper flat carrier size or five folds and a cutting and packing attachment, enabling us either to paste the paper along the line of the second fold . . . or not, as may be preferred." He revived the practice, which Young had abandoned, of indexing the paper as an economical investment, a time-saving device.[6]

Greeley had made the *Tribune* great despite inattention to good business practices, and Reid proposed to make it greater by increasing efficiency. But he did not neglect the basis of the paper's appeal to the people it served, nor confuse strength and influence with circulation figures. Despite varied views of his competitors, he believed the *Tribune*'s readers to be more intelligent and substantial thinkers than were the followers of most papers, and the editorial pages reflected this idea. At the same time he believed that the heads of other great dailies were also responsible journalists. "There is not an editor in New York who does not know the fortune that awaits the man there who is willing to make a daily as disreputable and vile as a hundred and fifty thousand readers would be willing to buy," he told a gathering of New York editors at Rochester in 1879.[7] He also told them that news gathering had succeeded white paper as the costliest item in producing a newspaper, but that he looked forward to a time when the greatest expenditures would be for brains and literary skill—if a Stanley is sent to Africa, a Macauley will go to tell the story for him, Reid predicted.[8] While he did not always follow all the ideals he expressed, he was consistent in seeking material from the pens of skilled writers.

In the editorial offices he owed much to the brilliant and versatile John R. G. Hassard, de facto managing editor when the proprietorship took most of Reid's time. He thought Hassard "good at almost anything." The worldly John Hay was Reid's first important addition to the staff of the *Tribune*. The Illinois poet and former secretary of Lincoln had an unassailable position among both literary and political figures that was invaluable to Reid, who was much less highly regarded in the first years of his move to Greeley's chair. Hay joined the paper at fifty dollars a week and was soon raised to sixty-five, a high salary for writing on any paper.[9] Reid paid his regular reporters thirty to forty dollars a week, but there was no established scale. Occasional or special contributors received varying pay. John Russell Young had accepted Mrs. Jane Cazneau's offer to write letters about San Domingo. He had offered the able wife of Grant's agent to the island ten dollars a column in gold for all the letters the *Tribune* printed. As interest in annexation mounted and as Mrs. Cazneau did not respond enthusiastically, Young raised the offer to ten dollars per letter and made what amounted to an informal three-month contract for six letters. The competent lady soon produced forty dollars' worth of annexationist literature, only to have Greeley decide that annexation of the island was not in the national interest. The *Tribune* cancelled the arrangement after paying for the letters at the agreed rate, and William L. Cazneau's chief publicist promptly moved to the more hospitable pages of James Gordon Bennett's *Herald*.[10] In a similar situation Young contracted with Henry George to act as *Tribune* correspondent in California, agreeing to pay him five dollars a column. After Young's departure Reid and Sinclair paid George for the articles he had sent but did not print them and cancelled the contract.[11]

The rates offered Jane Cazneau and Henry George were average. Reid was willing to pay fifteen dollars a column to William Dean Howells for book reviews and a special rate of twenty dollars each for fortnightly letters from Boston. The editor wanted clever "not too gossipy and yet not too stately" discussions of forthcoming books and authors and literary chitchat. These payments were exceptional, and most work, even that written by figures of similar stature, was for less money. Reid considered that some kind of matter should not require payment. When he heard that Howells' *Atlantic Monthly* had received a sensational Harriet Beecher Stowe article, he promptly asked the editor for advance copy ahead of the ordinary sheets sent to the press, promising extensive publicity.[12]

At Reid's request Bayard Taylor did book reviews regularly for whatever the editor thought they were worth. Unsolicited writing was considered on its merit. When *The Gilded Age* was about to appear, Samuel Clemens suggested Ned House as the reviewer. Not a great admirer of Twain, Reid believed that the author had subsidized House to puff the work and thought of printing the evidence, but did not go that far. Others approached the *Tribune* in varied ways. When Custer was killed, Walt Whitman sent a poem, "A Death Sonnet for Custer," and asked ten dollars for it, but he was more interested in its speedy appearance than in the money. Custer himself a few months earlier had offered to take a *Tribune* reporter on his next expedition, partly as a gesture of friendship to Reid and perhaps partly to assure prompt and friendly treatment of the mission.[13]

When Reid took over the paper he inherited experts in most areas of foreign correspondence, although he found one reporter inept and a source of irritation. He is "a most sincere and willing soul," but utterly unfit for the Foreign Department, "having no capacity for editing and no special knowledge of European affairs," Reid told George Ripley, adding that a grievous and afflictive desire to imitate Carlyle made the man's work even more dubious.[14] He felt that the reporter's salary of fifty dollars a week should command greater talent and a surer touch, but he found no replacement for some time.

Reid paid persons outside the United States rates similar to those given contributors in the country. Early in 1870 he agreed to pay Thomas Marshall five dollars a week in gold, in addition to regular rates for letters used, for representation in Ottawa during a session of Parliament, but balked at Marshall's request for designation as the Canadian correspondent of the *Tribune*. Marshall, however, as a mark of his special position, was allowed free copies of the paper.[15] Of greater interest to Reid in the following summer was the possibility of gaining articles from the pen of George Bancroft's nephew, J. C. Bancroft Davis. Davis, then assistant secretary of state, was asked for unsigned letters of Canadian separatist activities which were not to include discussion of annexation. The anonymous feature of the arrangement was necessary because of Davis's official position. There was another aspect: the unsigned letters would be cheaper. Doubtless you would not expect compensation, but we would prefer to pay regular rates, he told Davis on July 12. The assistant secretary was willing and said so promptly, but Napoleon III had declared war on Prussia between Reid's offer and Davis's acceptance, and Canadian separatism had to wait until the fighting in Europe quieted.[16]

In the Caribbean, a correspondent served the *Tribune* from Panama. Reid paid him on a column basis and regularly sent him three copies of the semiweekly and three of the weekly for exchange purposes. The editor hoped to build a subscription list in Central America and on the South American west coast as well as to procure news and interpretive matter on an exchange basis.[17]

From Europe scores of occasional and special correspondents, travelers, legation officers, and consular agents, both American and European, sent a steady stream of paper through London or directly to Spruce and Nassau streets. Reid sent Bayard Taylor to Vienna in 1873 to introduce the *Tribune*'s readers to the exposition. "What I want specially from you . . . is simply the brilliant descriptive work at the outset on which I hope you will lay yourself out," he told Taylor. Later J. W. Stillman was sent to do some letters on artistic and scientific features of the exposition and to secure illustrations. Reid used Eugene Virgil Smalley to take care of general and routine reporting from Vienna. At other times Smalley roamed Europe, usually sending his material through the London office, for which he was paid fifty dollars a week.[18]

On the continent, only Paris had a regular correspondent; John Russell Young had sent Clarence Cook there to write a weekly letter, for which he received a thousand dollars a year. But Reid found Cook without "journalistic tact" and lacking in a sense of news values, and he looked for other talent. When Hay considered going to France, Reid thought his services would be worth fifteen hundred dollars a year (as a replacement for Cook) but encouraged him to stay in the New York office of the *Tribune* instead.[19] When Hay decided to remain in New York, William H. Huntington took over coverage of regular news in Paris while Arsène Houssaye wrote on artistic and intellectual topics at thirty dollars per letter. It fell to Hay to translate these, and perhaps it was this onerous task that partly influenced Hay to urge Houssaye's replacement by Henry James. Reid made the move at Hay's urging and with James's willing cooperation. He wrote a score of letters before his verbosity and lack of interest in news matters caused Reid to terminate the arrangement. He told James that the letters were more magazine than newspaper material. The novelist elected to misinterpret the journalist's point and "agreed" that the products of his pen were perhaps too good for a newspaper.[20]

For *Tribune* readers the continent, and even Paris, was of less interest than Britain, especially London, and there the paper's greatest news-gathering agency outside Manhattan was ruled by George Washburne Smalley. Like Reid, Smalley had made his name as a war correspondent with the union armies. In 1866, sent from New York to report the Austro-Prussian War, he was frustrated by the speed of von Moltke's regiments, and the reporter never saw a battle. But he succeeded in interviewing Bismarck and so in enhancing his own reputation. More important for the *Tribune*, Smalley recognized the significance of the Atlantic cable, first permanently connected in 1866, and convinced Greeley and Young that an office should be set up in London at the end of the cable as a sort of European drawer of the *Tribune*'s New York desk.

After Greeley's death the new managing editor found his chief European representative a more satisfactory aid than any other *Tribune* worker with the possible exception of Hassard and Hay, and if forced to choose would probably have found Smalley more nearly indispensable. With Smalley, Reid discussed policies even after he became proprietor, while to others he suggested, usually regarding the suggestions as orders. Indeed, in at least one instance, more than a decade after he gained full control of the paper, Reid permitted Smalley to present his own views on Irish affairs although they were opposed to those of the *Tribune*, a privilege shared by no one else on the staff. In this Reid differed from Greeley, whose views no writer was allowed to ignore and who had sent specific instructions as to what Smalley should write on (crops, the pneumatic tube, London underground railroads) and discouraged what he thought to be of lesser importance ("mere political letters"). Yet Greeley's confidence in his London representative had sometimes resulted in Smalley having almost a free rein in the use of *Tribune* funds, another privilege shared by none. Most of the $128,000 Reid (with Greeley's approval) had spent on coverage of the Franco-

Prussian War had passed through Smalley's hands or was paid to his authorization.[21] But Smalley could be an expensive luxury in routine operations, and Reid expected careful bookkeeping. Less than six months after he took over the proprietorship he had Smalley's account checked back to the beginning of 1872 and complained, "While I have not the remotest disposition to urge any retrenchments where we get the worth of our money I cannot see in *The Tribune* for the last 15 months $36,000 worth of correspondence." Smalley's expenditures were cut promptly and drastically, and Reid forbade him to make drafts on the paper, preferring to send checks at Smalley's request and to exercise more control over the finances of the London office. At the end of the 1870s, Smalley was regularly receiving $1,250 a month for his office expenses.[22]

Reid's concern about the cost of Smalley's office was a reflection of his approach to all financial aspects of the *Tribune* operation. From the beginning of the Washington period, early in 1862, he had never for long been unaware either of the monetary side of any activity or of the relations between the money and the activity as a whole. The capital involved in the conduct of the *Tribune* was then approximately what it had been under Greeley's direction, but the arrangements were somewhat changed. At the time Reid joined the paper, Greeley thought the *Tribune* received and paid out a million dollars a year in regular transactions of business.[23] Three years later, at the time of Greeley's death and after a year of steadily deteriorating revenues, Samuel Sinclair reckoned the paper worth $713,000. This was somewhat less than the valuation of eight to ten thousand dollars put on each of the hundred shares of stock at this time. In 1878 Reid still thought of the paper as a million-dollar enterprise, which he felt was not altogether a blessing.[24] "The fact that enormous capital is now required for the conduct of a first-class newspaper does bring some advantages [and possibly] also serious disadvantages," he reflected after six years of experience.[25]

The estimates were closely related to solid facts. The daily circulation of forty to forty-five thousand copies at ten dollars a year for subscribers or four cents per copy in street sales brought in nearly half a million dollars a year. Sales of the weekly were less satisfactory. The rate was two dollars a year, and the circulation dwindled from nearly two hundred thousand at the time of Reid's arrival to approximately half that number of subscriptions a decade later.[26] Sales of the semiweekly at three dollars a year were comparatively unimportant; they shrank gradually from some twenty-five thousand under Greeley's management to less than ten thousand by the end of the 1870s. Thus *Tribune* income from sales was between three-quarters of a million and a million dollars a year at the end of Greeley's career, but fell by 25 percent during the following decade, although advertising revenue changed little.

Reid recognized that he did not have Greeley's appeal for readers of the *Weekly Tribune*. This and the growing strength of western papers made him decide soon after he gained control to devote his principal attentions to the daily.[27] Nevertheless, he worked constantly in the seventies to recapture subscribers, or at least to halt the decline in circulation. These needs, plus his growing fears of inflationary tendencies, brought him to seek a reconciliation with machine politicians in New York as a means of increasing sales of the paper. Such a step was made possible by the election of Rutherford Hayes in 1876 and the accompanying elimination of much of the odium of Grantism from the party.

Early in December of 1877 Reid prepared a circular that openly aligned his paper with the national party for the first time since he had taken over the *Tribune*. It read in part:

> The Republican Party is now in a struggle for its very life. The union of a Solid South and Tammany Hall threatens to grasp the Government & plunge us into repudiation or bankruptcy. The duty of the hour is to unite & strengthen the only party which can resist this danger. . . . You are therefore frankly asked to make a practical effort . . . to extend the circulation of *The Tribune*.[28]

The editor sent this and similar notices by the hundreds to postmasters in the northeast and northwest over his own name and accompanied by letters from appropriate local Republican committee chairmen.

The plan developed further after Reid got in touch with Thomas C. Platt, principal lieutenant of Sen. Roscoe Conkling, the head of the New York Republican organization. Reid asked for hints and discussion about plans for the 1878 campaigns. Platt replied warmly and offered to cooperate in an effort to increase the circulation of the *Tribune*. His willingness was not, however, without conditions, implicit and explicit. He assumed the paper would abandon the posture of independence it had taken since it broke with Grant, and he said flatly that he would not be a party to "the formation of *Tribune* clubs to be used in beating out [Conkling's] brains." Reid was willing, and the two met early in 1878 to plan a campaign that would strengthen Reid's paper, Platt's political position, and the Republican party. In the following weeks Platt went to Washington and into Indiana, Ohio, Michigan, and upstate New York enlisting the aid of party leaders. The program was largely one of having local Republican leaders act as agents to push the circulation of Reid's weekly.[29]

The weekly was available at a variety of reduced rates if taken in bulk quantities. The $2.00-per-year rate for individual subscriptions would be reduced to $1.80 each if five papers were sent to one address, to $1.50 if ten, to $1.25 if twenty, and fifty papers to one address could be had for $1.00 per subscription per year. Reid constantly urged the use of the "club plan," as the bulk rate was called. At election times he made the paper available on a monthly basis, or even "from now until one week after the election." In 1879 he offered copies of the weekly to James G. Blaine for a five-month term at thirty-three dollars per hundred—a figure equivalent to less than eighty cents for a one-year subscription.[30]

Platt asked county chairmen to subsidize the program under some circumstances by paying out of party funds the twenty-five-cent difference between the club prices of the *Times* and *Tribune*. Platt himself agreed to pay club rates for some subscriptions out of party funds and to supply Reid with the names of new "subscribers."[31]

These efforts slowed the shrinkage of readers but could not restore the old circulation of the weekly. They were accompanied by more friendly treatment of Platt, which opened the editor to the charge of having made his paper a party organ in exchange for a subsidy. The charge had some truth. In order to strengthen his paper's financial position, the editor was willing to soften his criticism of the New York bosses and to accept some of their suggestions. But this did not mean that the *Tribune* became a mouthpiece of the Republican machine in New York. In contrast with the weekly, the daily paper gained, and its average circulation reached fifty thousand copies by the mid-seventies.[32]

Despite the decline of the weekly, advertising did not suffer during Reid's first decade of proprietorship. Rates remained at the old two- to five-dollars-per-line level, the cost depending on the position in the paper. This compared with a twenty cents to one dollar rate for advertising in the daily. The semiweekly offered less flexibility—twenty-five and fifty cents. A ten-line insertion for one month could be placed in the daily for $78, in the weekly for $38, and in the semiweekly for $9.50. Rates for advertising in the *Sun* were slightly higher, for the *Times* considerably lower. Like many of his colleagues, Reid deplored the necessity for accepting advertisements and looked forward to a time when the better papers could omit the practice altogether—one of his rare departures from the realm of reality.[33]

Undaunted by the loss of circulation that accompanied Greeley's disastrous political campaign and that continued after his death, and unworried by frequent predictions of his imminent failure, Reid expanded his operation. Six months after gaining full control of the *Tribune* Association, the new publisher showed his independence by moving the *Tribune* to temporary space, tearing down the "old rookery" and beginning on the same site what he thought of as the "best newspaper office in the country." At the time he had two hundred thousand dollars in hand and a profit-making, debtless organization. Having full control he intended to put all profits into the building. We will be able to make a handsome dividend, he told his friend John Bigelow early in 1873 and added, "I don't propose, however, to divide a cent."[34] He borrowed only when necessary; his major loan was secured from the Mutual Life Insurance Company and amounted to four hundred thousand dollars. To give the *Tribune*, at Spruce and Nassau, frontage on a third street, Reid paid forty-six thousand dollars for property on Frankfort, mortgaging it for five years at 7 percent per year. The Tall Tower was ready in April 1875, two years after it had been begun, and the first *Tribune* rolled off the new presses on the tenth. Besides the paper itself, lawyers, engineers, architects, real estate agents, advertisers, and a restaurateur moved in at once, paying at the outset a thousand dollars a month into the coffers of the *Tribune* Association, and the sum increased as the remaining space in the building was rented.[35]

Reid began his expansion six months after gaining control of the *Tribune* Association and less than six months after that the fall of the house of Cooke signaled the panic of 1873. If Reid did not foresee the financial debacle, his careful preparations for expansion and his natural financial conservatism had readied him for the constricted economy of the ensuing five years. He did know that Jay Cooke and Co. was concerned about the price of gold two months before the company closed its doors with an unexplained shortage of currency in the vaults. Even before he learned this, he had severely pruned the *Tribune*'s exchange list, saying the move was necessary because of postal increases.[36] This action was in keeping with his general policy of cutting back expenses as exemplified by the termination of Smalley's financial usurpations. In an unusual move, at the end of his second year in charge, Reid had raised the salary of his nearly invaluable cashier, Nathaniel Tuttle, to two thousand dollars a year, leaving all other salaries unchanged because of bad times, he told his employee. Four years later, Tuttle's salary was still two thousand dollars.[37]

After four years of paring costs where possible, Reid still felt that expenses were too high. In June 1877 he discussed wage reduction with his printers, who had already suffered two cuts in the preceding four years. In the ensuing clash with Typographical Union No. 6, "Big Six," Reid was aided materially by a new employee. William P. Thompson was a hard-driving foreman, outspokenly antiunionist, who had experience on several papers and asked to join the *Tribune* because he admired it. With the editor's approval he worked out a money-saving agreement that he felt the union compositors would probably not accept and began to assemble a new labor force even before the new agreement had been rejected. His analysis was accurate and more than eighty men struck, but Thompson's plans were well made and in a few hours all essential operations of the *Tribune* had been resumed. Reid thought the change saved him thirty-five thousand dollars a year. Most salaries were also lower or unchanged, as the general level of wages in the nation fell by 40 to 60 percent.[38]

For one with money in hand and a ruthless attitude toward wages, the depression years of falling prices were an ideal time to put up a building. Fully understanding this, Reid signed few contracts when he began construction, preferring to bargain as he went. When, in mid-May 1874, more than fifty unskilled laborers refused to continue at Reid's scale he replaced them with Italians at no change in rates. A month later the bricklayers struck, but progress on the building continued without interruption. By the end of 1874 Reid estimated that his wage costs were some seventy-five dollars a day less than the rates that prevailed when construction began.

That his labor policies established him as a leader of anti-union sentiment troubled the editor of the *Tribune* not at all. He argued in the editorial columns that employers had the right to hire workers at lowest possible cost, whether or not they belonged to unions.

The completion of Reid's Tall Tower symbolized the recovery of the *Tribune*'s ancient glory, but it left the Association's shareholders little more than pride and vague hopes for the future. A 30 percent dividend had been paid in July 1869; five hundred dollars had been paid on each share at the end of that year; a hundred thousand dollars was divided among the hundred shareholders in the first six months of 1870; seventy thousand dollars was divided in 1872—all on stock valued at eight to ten thousand dollars a share. These handsome returns abruptly ceased when Reid gained control of the *Tribune* Association. Construction of the great new building absorbed all resources.[39] In his ruthless pursuit of every available dollar, Reid, seeking to collect a two-hundred-dollar debt owed him by a member of the *Philadelphia Times* staff, asked the editor of the *Philadelphia Press*, "What lawyer is there in Philadelphia who has some grudge against the Philadelphia *Times* . . . so that he would be prompted by his special personal feeling to take a personal interest in prosecuting a case?"[40]

Reid's revenues were such that he was privately well satisfied with the financial position of the paper at the end of the seventies. In the fourth year of his new building, the *Tribune* made a profit of eighty-five thousand dollars, but stockholders still received nothing. More than eight years passed after Greeley's death before profits were again divided.[41]

6

Editor in Politics

WHEN Reid joined the *Tribune* staff, Horace Greeley's paper was firmly behind the Congressional reconstruction policies. Charles A. Dana's *Sun* took a somewhat similar position. Henry J. Raymond's *Times*, however, considered Greeley's policies harsh, his course too severe, and accused him of inventing "fictitious dangers which in the *Tribune*'s fancy threaten the negro and its own party policy of reconstruction."[1] In the fall of 1868 Greeley told his readers that Grant would bring peace, make prosperity all but universal, encourage industry, and cause a rise in stock values, not just in paper but in gold. On the other hand, should Horatio Seymour triumph, "we inevitably enter upon the first phase of a counter-revolution. . . . [In the South] outrages and murder will be rifer than ever. . . . Anarchy and strife, terrorism and assassination, will pervade that section where the fires of Rebellion still smolder."[2]

Reid could accept the attack on the Democrats, but he would not write in this vein unless instructed to, even on the eve of an election. The young assistant differed in outlook from his chief on some matters. "This eternal assumption that the late Rebels are 'the South,' 'the Southern people,' etc., is at the bottom of all our remaining troubles," Greeley thought, and went on to say that less than a fourth of the southerners were rebels.[3] Reid thought differently. He had said plainly, in detail, and at some length in his perceptive and penetrating report on the South, *After the War*, that virtually all white southerners had been rebels and remained so after the war was over.[4] Such contrary views did not prevent Reid from cooperating fully and working closely with Greeley. Of course, the views of the apprentice were not expressed in print while the master lived. The difference was no small thing. Reid knew more about the South than Greeley did, as he knew more about politics, money, foreign affairs, and literature. The older man's advantage as an editor was that he had a feeling for the common man. He genuinely liked people and could become enthusiastic about them even though he was mistaken at times. The younger man only liked some persons.

At the time of his move to New York, Reid's knowledge of political affairs was national in orientation. He had less basic training and less standing in New York than in Washington and had much to learn about his adopted city and state. Few of the friends he had made outside of Ohio and Washington were New Yorkers, and he had great difficulty in finding leaders in New York who both espoused the policies he supported and were politically respectable, that is, who had Republican backgrounds and some following at the polls. His lack of rapport with New Yorkers made it difficult for him to foresee future trends in the state and kept him from feeling at home among the politicians. During his first few years in Manhattan he still felt more at home in Washington than in New York, and more comfortable in Ohio than in either. He had a feel for Ohio that he did not yet have for New York.

Reid's first friend of national position was Salmon P. Chase, who was thirty years Reid's senior. The older man was an Ohio senator and governor while the younger was in college, and they did not know each other until the war years when both were in Washington. Reid's attitude toward Lincoln may have been in part a reflection of Chase's coolness, and his southern trip in Chase's party strengthened the influence of the older man on the youthful writer. Early in his New York years, Reid regretted that Chase's physical infirmity prevented him from being a potential rallying point for an anti-Grant movement.[5] Less prominent, but nearer Reid's age and more similar in background, was James A. Garfield. Former teachers, both possessing respect for intellectual attainment, the two became friends during the war. Garfield later went to the House of Representatives and was emerging as a prominent conservative Republican leader as Reid searched for integrity in the party. The two were frequent correspondents, and the journalist felt he could be frank with Garfield.

Outside Ohio, Reid knew and admired Charles Sumner and privately deplored Greeley's critical editorial treatment of the Massachusetts senator in the *Tribune*.[6] He also was a friend and frequent correspondent of James G. Blaine. He recognized the Maine orator as a superb political craftsman and liked him personally, but thought of him as a winner in politics rather than as a statesman.

In his adopted home state the editor of the *Tribune* had difficulty in finding men of political standing that he could support wholeheartedly. He could not like the pompous, vain, and boastfully anti-intellectual

Roscoe Conkling, the chief political figure in New York at the time of Reid's arrival. The aversion extended to Conkling's cohorts and followers to such an extent that at times, in search of honorable political figures, Reid found himself consorting with Democrats, especially Samuel Tilden and Abram Hewitt. His first preference, however, was for Republicanism, and he found more of the qualities of a statesman in William M. Evarts than in any other leader of either party.

Reid's relation to New York Republican politics and his earlier Washington experiences made him view New York politics in a national mirror. He saw the principal state Republican leaders primarily as Grant men, and his opposition to Grantism dated from the general's first year in office, increased in 1872, and continued unremittingly through the second term. It was in part a measure of Reid's intensity of feeling about the general and his supporters, perhaps of his desperation, that he leaned for a short while toward Tilden. In addition, Tilden and Reid were at ease with each other, while the editor did not enjoy Conkling's company at the table. The Democrat's candor and his moderately liberal political position also made him attractive to Reid, who shared many of Tilden's views. Seeking to influence Greeley, Reid once showed his own political naïveté when he praised Tilden by saying that he was unquestionably anti-Grant and that he was withdrawing from Tammany Hall influences. Tilden shared the first trait with nearly every Democratic politician in the country, but no Democrat could back away from Tammany and succeed in New York politics in 1871.[7]

It was partly in an attempt to establish his own independence from New York regulars and the national party dominated by Conkling and Grant that Reid had undertaken the gloomy task of supporting Greeley's candidacy in 1872. His difficulties multiplied with the approach of the New York gubernatorial and congressional elections in 1874. Greeley was no longer standing near, and Reid was unsure. He could not go with the regulars, but the memory of the monumental failure of 1872 made him hesitant about deserting. As late as the end of October he still stood on the fence, unable to commit himself or the paper. The two parties were pretty much the same, he averred, and he thought the third term an issue that transcended the state as well as the national interests of both. He saw himself as one of the original Republicans, a Frémont supporter, unionist in the war years, who had been betrayed when greedy, coarse, and unscrupulous men had gained control of the party that saved the nation.[8] John Hay shared his friend's disgust at the low state to which the party had sunk and actually voted for Tilden, but immediately drew back from his heretical act. Reid could not go to the other party. He made only a tentative response to Tilden's bid for *Tribune* support after the Democrat defeated John Adams Dix by thirty thousand votes for the governorship in 1874. However, he did not completely close the door to Tilden as an alternative to Grant until Rutherford B. Hayes was nominated two years later.[9]

In Ohio, Reid could not do other than back the Republicans, and he helped persuade Carl Schurz to go to the aid of the party there in the gubernatorial race of 1875. That Hayes was the candidate made it easier for Reid to support the ticket, although Ohio leaders did not take the stand against Grant that Reid demanded as a price for his support in New York. There he made a determined effort to persuade Evarts to become a candidate for the governorship in 1876. Evarts was no purist in politics, but he belonged to a Republican faction that was burdened by the excesses of the Custom House rings, and the distinguished jurist had brought a number of petitions on behalf of New York Republicans who wished to see Conkling and his machine regulars displaced and who were, therefore, considered to be independents. Reid's effort was without avail. Evarts was reluctant to come out flatly in opposition to the party organization, and when the tide seemed against him in the nominating convention he pushed Edwin D. Morgan forward. Reid made the best of the situation. He tried to show that Morgan was Evart's choice and that Morgan would not be dominated by Conkling, hoping that his words would prove to be true.[10]

In the months preceding the national nominating conventions Reid was certain on only one political aim, opposition to a continuation of Grantism. Two years earlier he had argued that three terms constituted virtual treason against unwritten American law, only to have the charge boomerang. The Grant forces had replied that the whole people were fully capable of determining what was treasonable and what was not, and that only those who were unwilling to trust the people's judgment feared a test. A year before the conventions the *Tribune* moved closer to Tilden as a counterweight to the third-term movement.[11] Six months prior to the conventions Reid was asked whether Blaine might make a better show than some westerner. He was frankly skeptical; Blaine's fondness for bloody shirt speeches and his vulnerability to attack by scandalmongers were serious adverse factors. Reid's doubts were not even dispelled by his friend Hay's espousal of Blaine's cause.[12]

The work of the Republican national convention of 1876 further emphasized the extent to which Reid was separated from the party organization. He had no idea who might emerge as victor and stood ready to adopt the nominee or to condemn him. Blaine's first-ballot strength was more than twice that of his closest rival but was little more than a third of the total vote. Robert Ingersoll's famous speech extolling the Plumed Knight with the shining lance only underlined the lack of unity in the party whose delegates voted with Conkling while they applauded Ingersoll. While these factions contended, Hayes, fifth on the first ballot, gained in the trading and won the nomination on the seventh vote. The nomination of the Ohioan ended Reid's doubts and hesitancy. He thought Hayes not a great man, but a gentleman, clear of scandal and honest. Also, with the Grant element defeated at least temporarily, he had no more need of Tilden. Yet he had endorsed Tilden once, albeit gingerly, and he felt that he should give reasons for his decisions and actions. He seized upon the nomination of Thomas A. Hendricks as Tilden's running mate and provisions of the Democratic platform, which the *Tribune* called a shameful compromise with inflationist elements, as excuses to condemn the ticket.[13]

Reid did not establish communications with Hayes at the time of the nomination. Perhaps he thought it unseemly inasmuch as he had not given his support before the convention. A month later, however, he told Schurz that Hayes's nomination was an excellent one and at the same time assured the nominee of the *Tribune*'s unqualified support. The occasion for these announcements was Hayes's letter of acceptance, a document that rivaled the party platform in importance in Reid's view. When the Republican nominee struck at the spoils system, Reid hastened to express his approval in a personal letter. At the same time he revealed his inner anxiety about his own position. He did not do himself justice as he boasted of his relations with the great. "For instance," he wrote Hayes, "there is no reason why I should not mention to you, confidentially, . . . that when I was dining a few days ago with Mr. Abram S. Hewitt, the Chairman of the National Democratic Committee, he told me . . ." that the Democrats expect to carry Ohio. If Hayes was ignorant of Hewitt's position, the Republican party was doomed. In the same letter Reid casually mentioned his personal association with Tilden, calling him "the most sagacious political calculator I have ever seen."[14]

Reid's anxiety to impress and to please Hayes was one expression of his pleasure and relief at having an Ohioan as national leader of the party. He knew the state and felt comfortable with its leaders, their friends and supporters. Although Grant was born in the state and spent his youth there, it was not his political base and he was not an Ohioan in the sense that Hayes, James A. Garfield, and William McKinley were. Reid's account of Ohio's contributions to the union victory in 1861–65 was a political encyclopedia as well as a war history and gave him a status in the state he did not have in New York. "I have found your 'Ohio in the War' of the greatest use to me in writing my life of Hayes," Ohio's William Dean Howells told Reid a few weeks after the nomination.[15]

Notwithstanding his pleasure at Hayes's candidacy and his desire for victory, Reid was unsure about the election. His real respect for Tilden's sagacity and his unwillingness to accept the claims of Conkling, Blaine, and other regulars made him doubtful. When the returns came in on election night, he was prepared for failure, and on the following day the *Tribune* reported 188 votes for Tilden, 141 for Hayes and 34 undecided. Only the size of Tilden's victory, not the fact, was yet to be determined. Reid's gloom and defeatism vanished, however, when he learned that George Jones had printed a different set of figures in the *Times* and had claimed that the race was still undecided. The *Tribune* quickly adjusted and used the *Times* analysis the next day.[16] The editor brushed aside suggestions that he accept Tilden. He "must not be counted out," Reid's Democratic friend W. C. Whitney urged. In unconscious support of Whitney's view, John Hay, a week after the election, felt that Tilden had won and recommended that Reid make the best of it.[17]

Reid, however, had no intention of seeing Ohio deprived of her first president in his time and, besides, there was more good copy and greater circulation in a disputed election than in explaining the results of a close race. Having quickly adjusted its position, the *Tribune* remained certain that Hayes had won the election. Reid played no part in and apparently was unaware of behind-the-scenes negotiations that resulted in the Compromise of 1877 and allowed Hayes to enter the White House without a senate fight.[18]

Late in February, a few days before the time for inauguration, Reid wrote to the president-elect. The editor said that he wanted nothing for himself and did not ask anything for anyone else. He had not been consulted, his advice had not been sought, he reminded Hayes, but he offered his services as a source of information about "Eastern politics and politicians." He went on to suggest half a dozen worthies as good cabinet material, at the same time disclaiming any desire to influence the new administration and urging the president-elect to make his own cabinet selections.[19] Reid closed his letter by giving Hayes permission to use the advice or to drop the suggestions in a waste basket. Hayes chose the latter course. Reid's next effort was closer to the mark, but it still fell short and clearly indicated that he did not yet stand close to the seats of the mighty. On March 1 he wrote Evarts, thanking him for a recent note. "We are going to say something in the morning as to the proper head for Gov. Hayes' cabinet," the editor said, and offered to go to Washington "if it should seem necessary to reinforce our views by my personal presence." The editor's personal presence was no more needed than his nomination of Evarts as secretary of state, for the New Yorker had already been offered that department.[20]

Notwithstanding Reid's lack of intimacy with the incoming administration, he felt comfortable about the people in Washington. He was still not in the family, yet he was kin but once removed. The sense of kinship had been missing since the early war years in Washington, when the presence of Chase and Reid's feeling of rapport with John Nicolay and Hay had given the young reporter a sense of belonging. Reid respected Hayes, he had broken bread with Evarts, and he felt that the people in power had respect for him. After Evarts entered the cabinet, Reid's approving comments emphasized his own hopes: Evart's secretaryship will "rally to the administration a great many independents whose sympathies have always been with the Republican Party, but who have been able to give its recent management only a halting and uncertain approval."[21] In New York those who rallied to the banner Reid waved lost the first engagement. Six months after Hayes was inaugurated, Conkling administered a stinging rebuke to the new administration by defeating in the Senate an attempt to replace Chester A. Arthur with Theodore Roosevelt, Sr., in the patronage-rich New York customs house. Arthur remained in the post nearly a year and a half longer.[22]

Conkling's victory was of less significance for Reid than two other developments in the first half year of Hayes's term. In the summer of

1877 the *Tribune*'s columns carried a series of attacks on the administration which presaged a rapprochement with the New York party machine that took place in the following winter. The same summer saw widespread railroad strikes, and Reid's treatment of the events pointed to a new position for him in New York.

The attacks on the administration were made in a series of letters by Gail Hamilton, for which Reid paid the regular ten dollars a column rate. Gail Hamilton was a pseudonym for Mary Abigail Dodge, a cousin of Mrs. James G. Blaine and a close associate and admirer of the Maine leader. No one doubted where the inspiration came from for the articles. The letters were headed "Civil Service Reform," but the attacks were not limited to that area nor to reform leaders in the administration. Special attention was given, however, to Carl Schurz, secretary of the interior, who was lampooned as an overzealous reformer with little common sense and poor judgment who had done more harm than good over the years while collecting thousands of dollars from his own party for making campaign speeches. Schurz was portrayed as an inept bungler, hurtful to the president. The articles moved the *Tribune* closer to Blaine and away from the liberal elements Reid had supported in the preceding five years.[23]

While Gail Hamilton's articles were running, more ominous matter flowed into the *Tribune*'s newsrooms. The great railroad strikes of 1877 began in July. These resulted from a series of wage reductions beginning in 1873 and culminating in a horizontal 10 percent wage cut in July 1877. On the seventeenth some Baltimore and Ohio employees quit work and called on fellow laborers to join them in stopping the trains. The strike spread rapidly, the militia was mobilized at strategic centers, riots broke out, and the disorders took on the characteristics of a general strike. The struggle continued for two weeks, and the *Tribune* became more critical of the workers as violence spread.[24] By the end of July order had been established in most affected cities, and some basic elements of Reid's social philosophy had been set down clearly in comments on the editorial pages of his paper. Wages were not as low as the unions alleged, he contended; in fact the purchasing power of the worker was higher than in 1860. It was the inflationists who threatened the country by trying to steal from creditors and raise costs. Disrespect for law was also a characteristic of the unions, the *Tribune* thought, because they sought to rob the citizen of his right to work at his own level by trying to force him into a labor organization. These and similar tactics supported by some self-seeking and irresponsible Democrats, Grangers, and a few Republicans led to such excesses as strikes, violence, and bloodshed, as the nation had recently witnessed. Reid's solution was a firm insistence on the authority of law and the perfect freedom of the individual, both backed by such force as might be necessary.[25]

Reid was also discouraged by the fraud charges that the Democrats made against the Republicans, especially in New York. In the months following the election of 1876, committees of both House and Senate had investigated the returns. Witnesses were called, evidence heard, and telegrams were subpoenaed in response to demands for explanations of the charges of fraud. Little came of the investigations, but much curiosity was aroused by the large numbers of code messages found among the subpoenaed telegrams. Republicans derived small comfort from disclosures made by *Detroit Post* reporters who had broken a simple code and exposed illegal acts by the opposition party in Oregon. There, a Democratic agent had offered an elector ten thousand dollars for his vote. While Tilden's nephew, Col. W. T. Pelton, had been interested, the deal had not been consummated before the electoral commission's decisions about Hayes's victory became final. This was known early in 1877, but the knowledge was lost in the larger decisions of those weeks. Undaunted by the Oregon disclosures and confident that the fraud issue would be a useful one in the approaching election, the House of Representatives, dominated by the Democrats, in May 1878 appointed a special investigative committee with Clarkson N. Potter of New York as chairman. Potter's committee held hearings during the summer, and fraud charges became a constant element in the political atmosphere.

At this juncture some Republican leaders came upon a large bundle of old telegrams stored in a committee-room closet. These had been subpoenaed in the postelection investigation a year and a half earlier and had somehow not been returned to Western Union for destruction. Thoughtfully recalling the Oregon disclosures, Third Assistant Postmaster General Thomas J. Brady, Representative Eugene Hale of Maine, and the astute William E. Chandler looked over some of the papers and decided that at the very least they could be used to divert attention from anti-Republican fraud charges. Chandler secretly deposited copies of some of the telegrams on the desk of Gen. Benjamin

F. Butler, Republication member of the Potter Committee, who had long boasted that he could break any code if given enough data and time. Chandler could supply the data but he feared that Butler might not be able to make good his boast in the time left before the election. Chandler, therefore, wrote to Reid early in August, sending him seventeen pieces of paper embracing twenty-seven dispatches. Chandler suggested that the *Tribune* might print some uncoded messages side by side with cipher dispatches sent to the same addresses and demand the translations from the Democrats, if they had nothing to hide.

Reid accepted the role of needler with alacrity. His skillful handling of the material brought in more dispatches and suggestions from various sources, chiefly from Republicans on the Potter Committee. Soon hundreds of telegrams had found their way from the Senate committee rooms on the Potomac to the Tall Tower in Printing House Square. Unlike the Oregon messages, many others, mostly from South Carolina and Florida, were in complex and difficult codes. Translation would require long and concentrated effort, but the game seemed worth the candle. Reid set two of his ablest lieutenants at the task: John R. G. Hassard and Col. William M. Grosvenor.[26]

Less than two months after Chandler sent the seventeen pieces of paper, the *Tribune* was ready to treat its readers to the most dramatic exposé since the Credit Mobilier. The stage was well set. Reid easily maneuvered Democratic leaders not only into further charges of Republican corruption but also into self-righteous and wholly untenable claims of Democratic purity. At their convention in Syracuse early in October, the Democrats resolved that by force and fraud high officials and unrepudiated Republican leaders had reversed the national choice for president in 1876. On October 3 Reid called attention to this resolution and promised a full exposure of Democratic activities in 1876. To underline the point he printed, as a hint of what was to come, a few telegrams with translations.[27]

Reid waited four days to build suspense, then raised the curtain and the drama unfolded. The chief players were Tilden's nephew, Pelton, who had received offers from John C. Coyle, C. W. Wooley, Manton Marble, and others involving the purchase of votes. The script was taken from four hundred–odd telegraphic messages, enough of which were in cipher to provide dramatic highlights for every character and every scene. The first scene was laid in Florida. After a five-column introductory explanation, on Saturday, October 7, the *Tribune* ran on the following Monday more than nine columns of plain-language telegrams and cipher dispatches, together with translations of the latter and running commentary on all. A few days later a sequel in a South Carolina setting involving some new characters was presented to the *Tribune*'s readers. Without question Tilden's nephew had been involved in purchasing electoral votes at very high prices.[28]

The Democrats were undone. They had left themselves wholly vulnerable and had no line of retreat. Reid knew from the beginning that the story would end Tilden's political career, even though the Democratic leader was never accused of personal complicity. Pelton was his nephew and lived in his house, the address to which the fateful telegrams were sent. "No matter whether Tilden's card [denial] is believed or not," Reid predicted soon after he broke the story, the cipher revelations "have made an effective end of any political future he may have had."[29]

The exposures continued for months, although the main story was told in October 1878. Shortly after the first of the year the matter was quietly dropped, lest accumulating small errors and inaccuracies obscure the general impression already created.

For Reid the opportunity offered by the cipher dispatches came at a critical moment, and it was decisive. The presence of a man he could support in the White House had already put the editor in touch with the principal figures in a national administration for the first time. The cipher exposé made the *Tribune*'s editor a major figure on the national scene as well as in New York. The destruction of Tilden and consequent removal of the largest figure in the Democratic party was but one aspect of the victory. The moral triumph in discovering and proving that the Democrats were as guilt-stained as was the party of Grant added to the editor's stature in the eyes of the Republican bosses and allowed liberal elements to feel less self-conscious about political crimes in their party's past.

Reid's new status was soon reflected in administration attention. His disclaimer of interest in political appointment made in his letter to Hayes ten days before the inauguration was neither pretense nor hint for a job, although it strained at the truth to some degree. In contrast to Reid's view, Hay thought his friend should accept an appointment, and that one should be offered. This he told Reid at the time of the inauguration.[30] The new president apparently thought otherwise, for no offer was made during the first half of Hayes's term. After the full impact of the cipher exposé became obvious, however, the administration offered the *Tribune*'s editor a place commensurate with his contribution. It was the legation in Germany, made vacant by the death of Bayard Taylor, Reid's close friend and a former *Tribune* contributor.[31]

Reid did not hesitate. Less than a week after Secretary of State Evarts offered the appointment, Christmas intervening, Reid declined. He said, in effect, that he could serve the nation better and support Republican principles more effectively in Printing House Square than in Berlin.[32] Hay tried to persuade his friend to accept the offer, and Reid sought the place for Hay but neither intercession was successful. Evarts admired and respected Lincoln's former secretary but thought his standing as a national party figure was not significant enough for the appointment. Hay agreed. Andrew D. White succeeded Taylor in Germany.[33]

In a confidential and remarkably frank letter to Hay, dated March 20, 1879, Reid revealed his real reasons for declining the post.

> I declined it because it seemed a needless abandonment of a position in wh. . . my chances are at least as good as ever; and in wh my independence is greater than ever. If I had gone, the paper wld. hv. slipped away from me, inevitably;—or, if it did not, the profession wld. At the end of two years, I shld hv. had as much political preferment as the public wld. think I deserved & that career wld be ended. Without a miracle, I cldn't resume my professional career at anything like the same height. In a word, at 43 I shld. hv reached the climax. Whatever followed wld be inferior.

He added that the situation would be different if he were pecuniarily independent, "I mean if I absolutely owned all that I control."[34]

At the end of the year Evarts, Reid, and Hay again discussed a high appointment. Evarts wanted Hay for his first assistant secretary of state, as replacement for the retiring Frederick Seward. It was a measure of Reid's new stature, as well as of his close friendship with the persons concerned, that Evarts first broached the matter to the editor in October 1879. It was also a measure of Reid's new stature that he was able to persuade the reluctant Hay to take the place even after he had turned it down once.[35]

The fifteen months between Chandler's note to Reid enclosing the seventeen pieces of paper embracing twenty-seven dispatches and the talk with Evarts about Hay's appointment marked Reid's coming of age as a national political figure. It would not have come at this time had the president been a native of Massachusetts or of Missouri; it could not have occurred without Reid's destruction of Tilden in New York. It was also important that Reid insisted on being his own man, despite his moving closer to the New York machine. The editor of the *Tribune* could not claim independence from political partisanship for himself and his paper, but he had established his position as a major independent force within the party that governed the nation.

Reid's movements in the political and fiancial areas of New York in the seventies paralleled and to an extent reflected changes in the locations of his residences. When he went to New York in 1868 he occupied rooms for a short time at 667 Second Avenue. He soon moved to 226, later to 228, on East 18th Street, where he remained until after he took over the paper.[36] In the summer of 1873 he tried to buy "a small compact tasteful" place on Park Avenue and looked at numbers 11, 32, and 34. Nothing that suited him was available at a price he was willing to pay, but a few months later he was able to rent the handsome house at 23 Park Avenue. He paid two thousand dollars the first year but persuaded the owner to accept eighteen hundred dollars thereafter. Here he remained for six years before purchasing a brownstone home at 271 Lexington Avenue on the southeast corner of Lexington and 36th Street. He found McDonald's Livery Stable on 41st Street a convenient place to keep his horse. In these years he frequently walked down Broadway in the mornings. When he and Hay dined together they liked to walk back for dinner at the "Brigands," an Italian place on Third Avenue above Cooper Institute.[37]

The purchase of the Lexington Avenue house was perhaps less indicative of Reid's interest in social life than of his ability to afford it. His two nieces, Gavin's daughters, Reid's wards since his brother's death, moved into the Park Avenue place where the older, Caroline, died in the summer of 1876. Ella might have become a person of consequence in New York society as her uncle's hostess had she been strong and forceful, for he entertained frequently, but she was not suited for the role. As a hard-working bachelor Reid's chief social activities consisted of dining and talking with friends and occasionally attending the theater. Other pleasures were as simple. He once wrote Blaine for a special formula. What, he asked, is "the correct composition of that bath mixture, whose virtues you praised so persuasively. Was it one part alcohol and two parts spirits of ammonia, or vice versa?"[38]

At forty, Reid was five feet ten in height and kept his weight under 160 pounds. A slight droop to his shoulders led detractors to refer to his bent form. He brushed his hair back, and if it became disheveled one noticed that he wore it long, as he had since early youth. A high forehead, a thin and somewhat aquiline nose, and slightly prominent cheekbones gave his face an appearance of fragility when he was tired or pale. His friends frequently worried about his health, while less charitable observers noted his "frenzied look."[39]

The personality of the *Tribune*'s editor was seen in more varied lights than was his appearance. Introverted and withdrawn, married to the *Tribune*, he had no close personal friends of either sex after he left college until he was married unless Hay and William Walter Phelps could be called intimates.[40] He was distant in manner and slow to accept advances. Men found him exceedingly formal, too polite. On his side, Reid complained of being run down by the crowd and wanted few first-name relationships. When they were all thrown together at Cincinnati in 1872, neither Samuel Bowles, Horace White nor Murat Halstead liked Greeley's assistant as a person. Henry Watterson was more tolerant and later came to think of Reid as a man of the world and a person of charm, in contrast to Charles Dana's opinion of the *Tribune*'s editor as a young fop with a brilliant mind but no practical sense.[41] Hay, Reid's age, was closer to him than anyone else in the years from the beginning of the war, when both were in their twenties, until Hay's marriage and move to Ohio. Hay admired Reid as a journalistic craftsman, as a manager and businessman, and deferred to his judgment of political figures and trends. Despite their close association on the *Tribune*, there was little warmth or personal involvement in Hay's attitude toward his friend in the seventies, but both feelings developed as the years passed.[42]

While Reid established positions for himself in the fields of journalism and of politics in the first decade of his arrival in New York, he also strengthened the foundations for a position of financial substance. When he joined the *Tribune* he had neither debts nor financial obligations of consequence. The *Cincinnati Gazette* stock he owned provided a small base on which he hoped to build. The farm in Xenia took care of his mother's needs and remained her home; Gavin's daughters, his wards, were undemanding. Because he had carefully conserved his assets and had added to them steadily he was in a sufficiently strong position to take advantage of the completely unexpected opportunity to acquire financial as well as editorial control of the *Tribune* at Greeley's death.

From this new base Reid prospered by virtue of hard work, close attention to the business management of the paper, friendship with brokers E. C. Stedman and H. C. Fahnstock, with Jay Cooke, and help through Hay and Amasa Stone. A certain amount of luck had aided him when Gould lent him a large sum of money in December 1872 and then permitted him to repay it in his own time and in his own way. But these were less important to Reid personally and financially than the friendship, advice, and counsel of "WWP," as Reid usually addressed his friend.

Two years Reid's junior, William Walter Phelps was an easterner, a Yale graduate with a law degree from Columbia, and a witty speaker. He liked literature and literary talk as did Reid. An active Republican, elected to the national House of Representatives in 1872, Phelps shared Reid's interest in the party and its leadership. The two agreed on almost every basic issue if not always on detail. Unlike the editor, the financier was the son of a man of much wealth, John Jay Phelps. He was accustomed to dealing with large sums and properties and was a part of the business and financial community of the eastern seaboard. "WWP" helped Reid finance the *Tribune* purchase, advised him on its business operations, and helped him clear up the problems he inherited from Samuel Sinclair's mismanagement. More important, Phelps was always available and always willing to advise his friend about investments he had made or was considering, a privilege that Reid fully appreciated and of which he took full advantage.[43]

In the main, however, Reid's prosperity came as did that of scores of others in the postwar period of national economic growth and financial readjustment. For safety he had bought first-mortgage bonds from time to time as funds were available. In the deflationary years after the panic of 1873 these bonds enabled him to improve his position steadily.[44] He also traded freely on margins in stocks and was sometimes short, sometimes long, in a market closely watched by Phelps and other trusted friends among the brokers of Manhattan. "I see Erie seconds have had a tumble to 72½," he said in a note to E. C. Stedman, who handled much of Reid's trading. "I think it would be safe to buy 10,000; and if they go down to 72, 10,000 more; and 10,000 more at 71⅝—selling out either or all of these purchases immediately if possible at an advance of ¾ percent. My object of course is merely to mark down the line we now have." Had Reid's judgment been at fault Stedman would have held the orders.[45] On occasion he was in effect an insider and benefitted by knowing in advance of stock manipulation by others.

While growing rapidly in wealth, Reid had not lost the keen concern for pennies he had developed as a boy in rural Ohio, where he had never felt want but where money was scarce. When moving into the house on Lexington Avenue, on which he had paid some eight hundred dollars for repairs, he not only went to considerable trouble to show that the bill for sodding was $12.01 too much, but also suggested that the nurseryman might be liable for damages because, Reid alleged, he had "over-pruned the wisteria."[46]

7

Broadened Horizons

REID watched closely and with growing interest as it gradually became clear that Rutherford B. Hayes would neither be nominated for a second term nor take a significant part in the convention of 1880. As the candidacies for the nomination developed, Reid kept in touch with friends and political allies from Ohio to Maine, with John Sherman and John Hay, with Thomas C. Platt, with James G. Blaine, William E. Chandler, and William Walter Phelps. Grantism had come alive after long quiescence on the general's arrival at San Francisco in September of 1879 from his protracted round-the-world trip. By the end of the year Reid thought the boom was declining, although in fact the regular party workers were steadily fastening delegates in county and state committees. Early in the nomination year party machines from New York, Pennsylvania, and Illinois succeeded in electing delegations to the national convention that were pledged to support the nomination of Grant, and other states followed the lead.[1]

The *Tribune* opposed Grant and all his supporters consistently and forcefully. Beyond this the editor was unwilling to go. The opposition must be a party matter, not a factional effort in behalf of any specific candidate. In this Reid refused to join two of his closest friends. Phelps and Hay had long been and remained staunch supporters of Blaine, who they felt was not only the strongest potential opponent of Grant but also the best qualified Republican to lead the nation along the paths of prosperity and progress. Nor was Reid willing to forward the ambitions of the third outstanding contender, despite his long admiration for John Sherman and that Ohioan's policies as chairman of the Senate Finance Committee and as Hayes's secretary of the treasury. Thus when the editor of the *Tribune* joined scores of other journalists in Chicago at the end of May to report and interpret the convention, neither he personally nor his paper was committed to anything except the defeat of Grant. He thought Blaine would be nominated, and he would be satisfied with that, but primarily he was seeking a winner. Others had the same objective but with more positive preferences. By the time the convention assembled and before it was organized, a deadlock was plainly indicated, but any Republican nominee seemed sure to go to the White House the following March.

At the convention Reid stood in uncompromising opposition to boss Roscoe Conkling. That New York leader, with Sen. John A. Logan of Illinois and Simon Cameron of Pennsylvania, led the fight for Grant's nomination. The lines were so clearly drawn that Reid's paper could forecast the results of the first ballot with considerable accuracy ten days before the vote was taken. On May 28 the *Tribune* gave Grant and Blaine 315 and 272 votes respectively and on June 7 the convention gave them 304 and 284; other candidates' strengths were also well understood before the convention met.[2] Lines held firmly through the first day of activity when twenty-eight ballots were taken without changing the relative strength of any significant candidate, and the day ended without revealing new strength in any area.

A reasonably objective *Tribune* reader could easily feel that the editor passively assumed the nomination would go to Blaine, and that he was willing to put forth positive effort to assure changes in the leadership of the New York Republican organization. Proof of the willingness came when Reid gave front-page prominence to a news story describing the bolt of New York state senator Judge W. H. Robertson and sixteen other delegates from the state at the convention. These, "the Chicago seventeen," defied Conkling and refused to support Grant. Reid rightly considered Robertson's move a crippling blow against Conkling's control of the New York Republican party organization and used the power of the *Tribune* to support Robertson's move and to protect him from Conkling's wrath.[3]

If Reid had any inkling of the final result of the convention he concealed it from the *Tribune*'s readers. In a special dispatch from Chicago summarizing the results of the first day's balloting, he indicated that Blaine was the most likely candidate on whom anti-third-term elements at the convention would unite. The editorial pages and news stories, however, remained neutral in tone as the one-time Great Moral Organ stood ready to support any good Republican who could defeat Grant in the convention and at the same time break Conkling's hold on the party machinery in New York.[4]

The *Tribune*, therefore, was in no way embarrassed when a dark horse triumphed. Nor was there need for false effort or a search for laudatory phrases when the paper elatedly reported James A. Garfield's nomination on the second day of the convention. The nominee was not only an Ohio compatriot but an old personal friend whom both Reid and Hay had long admired and respected. Reid had given him such high praise a dozen years earlier in *Ohio in the War* that he could fairly be accused of some bias, although the volumes showed remarkable objectivity in treating other Buckeye heroes.[5]

None of these factors made Reid lose sight of the danger of party division and weakened enthusiasm on the part of the defeated candidates, who still were the powers in the Republican organization. The paper paid tribute to Blaine's and Sherman's patriotism and unselfish devotion to the party and recognized the need for Conkling's help. The editorial columns on the day following the nomination praised Blaine and Sherman for breaking the back of the Grant movement and making possible the nomination of a man who could unite the Republicans. Reid thought the Maine orator the strongest unsuccessful candidate and gave him most of the credit, but did not slight the others.[6]

As his newspaper promoted party harmony and sought support for Garfield from Republicans of all ranks, Reid sent a steady stream of advice to the nominee. He urged Garfield in peremptory phrases to remain at his home, Mentor, and to avoid speeches. Others should take the stump and bear the burdensome parts of the campaign, he advised. Again and again the editor warned the nominee against making compromises to gain support.[7] Reid was especially anxious that Garfield not overestimate Carl Schurz's influence on the German vote. His attitude indicated small interest in the liberal element in the party. The editor thought the secretary of the interior would be useful on the stump but that he had been a constant source of injury to Hayes, and that Garfield should not bargain for Schurz's support.[8]

Reid's first concern was that Garfield be elected. His unhappy experiences in the campaign of 1872 had taught him, had he had no other political knowledge, the necessity of having professional and machine support. Despite his bitter contests with Conkling, Reid was aware of the importance of Conkling's role in the campaign and was willing to accept his aid, but not at the price of giving him control of the patronage in New York. The editor told Garfield with relief, when the New York boss agreed to help, that "he is undoubtedly of great value on the stump . . . and we shall now have him as active as can be."[9]

Reid's concern for organization support and for enthusiastic party activity in the campaign extended beyond the confines of New York. Soon after his return from the convention he relayed to the nominee the anxiety of an old Xenia newspaper associate, now Sen. Preston B. Plumb of Kansas. Plumb felt, Reid told Garfield, that "the working politicians" would be alarmed if a new Republican administration should follow Hayes's civil service policies too closely.[10] When Hayes took office he was pledged to reform in that area. His appointment of Carl Schurz as secretary of the interior and Schurz's adoption of civil service policies for the department was Hayes's first step toward the promised reform. The move brought savage criticism from many party regulars. Plumb and others felt that these critics wanted some assurance that the advice of members of Congress would not be ignored by the administration when it made selection for political office. Reid, therefore, suggested that Garfield make "some intimation, either in the letter of acceptance or . . . through a known friend . . . that you have no idea of conducting the administration without reference to or independently of the leading men of the Republican party, and that you would naturally consult with the men whom the people have selected and put forward."[11]

Garfield recognized the political soundness of Reid's suggestions, and he also understood the unique position occupied by his friend who controlled the news and editorial columns of a great newspaper in a doubtful state. Garfield understood that Reid was, by virtue of this position, at the center of an information net made up of regular reporters and scores of contributors and had privileged access to nationwide wire services. More important, the nominee respected Reid's judgment, his knowledge of men, and above all his relative disinterest in appointive office or political payoff. If Garfield's course was not laid on the basis of Reid's advice, at least it moved toward Reid's objectives, and in the civil service matter Garfield's statement in his letter of acceptance closely followed the language of Reid's note. The candidate assured his party that he did not intend to scrap the spoils system as far as congressional control over offices was concerned.[12]

The New York editor was also able to help the Ohio statesman by introducing him to men he would need to know, men whose support and confidence was important. Reid arranged for the candidate to meet William E. Dodge when Garfield was in New York early in August. On the same trip east, Garfield and Phelps went to Reid's house on Lexington Avenue where they discussed the campaign with Jay Gould, who agreed to help. Reid was also privy to the collection and distribution of funds from other sources, and he helped plan the effective use of various sums with Blaine and with Marshall Jewell, chairman of the Republican National Committee.[13]

These relationships were, of course, general knowledge. A cartoon of the period showing Garfield as a bride, on the arm of the prospective groom, Uncle Sam, has Reid close behind in elegant bridesmaid's dress; Schurz and Murat Halstead are also in attendance, while Conkling, Logan, W. H. Barnum (the chairman of the Democratic National Committee), and "Credit Mobilier" are at hand in various roles.[14] The bridesmaid of the cartoon was indeed an intimate of the bride and more than once was at Mentor where the two discussed problems of the campaign.

One indication of Reid's position of influence came in the second week in December, when Garfield turned to him for support in a delicate quest. The president-elect needed a trustworthy person who was reliable, discreet, tasteful, and sound of judgment to serve as a private secretary. Such a position, Garfield thought, should be held in higher esteem than the secretaryship of state. The ideal person, he felt, was none other than one of Lincoln's secretaries. Reid was asked to approach John Hay. Reid knew Hay well enough to be able to guess his answer; nevertheless, he wrote to his friend. Hay knew exactly what Garfield wanted: a man who would keep job-seekers and other unwanted visitors away from the president without offending them, a role extremely distasteful to Hay. He said so to Reid, assuming that the word would be tactfully passed to Garfield so that a direct offer and refusal could be avoided.[15] But the *Tribune* editor's usual tact and his usual readiness to take part in inner-council planning had deserted him. He did not tell Garfield of Hay's answer. In the second week of December Whitelaw Reid was engaged in a delicate and difficult negotiation of his own. He was deciding to propose to Lizzie Mills.

Reid had met Darius Ogden Mills's daughter two years earlier while visiting at Millbrae, the palatial Mills home near San Francisco, and he was attracted to Miss Mills almost from the beginning despite their highly dissimilar backgrounds. During a visit that her family made to New York early in 1880 Reid's interest increased markedly. In February he gave two consecutive theater parties to have the needed excuses to see her. Although interested, he had not declared himself, and so when the family left New York the two corresponded with some difficulty, there being few proper subjects available for cross-continental discussion between the forty-two-year-old New York editor and twenty-two-year-old San Francisco belle. Nevertheless, occasional circumspect letters served to keep interest awake without arousing too much parental curiosity. When the family returned to New York late in 1880 Reid's and Miss Mills's relationship moved rapidly toward a climax.[16]

Reid's attention had strayed so far from politics in December that he failed to discover that Garfield, on November 27, had offered the State Department to Blaine. On the twentieth of December Blaine accepted the chief post in the incoming administration, carefully guarding the politically explosive news from friend and critic alike by enclosing his letter of acceptance to the president-elect in a note to Mrs. Garfield to assure that no unfriendly eye would see the message.[17] The secret was carefully kept. Nearly a month after the offer and four days after the acceptance Reid, writing of Blaine and the State Department, told Phelps, "I can get it offered to him the day I can convey the assurance that he will certainly take it."[18] This information was not only out of date, it was inaccurate, since the place had been offered without such assurance. But Reid's lapse is easily understood, for his note to Phelps was sent on Christmas Eve, while his thoughts were on an engagement to take Miss Mills to the opera that night. Next day she sent him a Christmas card featuring a painted sprig of mistletoe with the printed message, "I surmount All Difficulties."[19]

Shortly after Christmas the Millses went to Washington attend the traditional New Year's reception, the last formal affair to be given by President and Mrs. Hayes. Miss Mills was a guest at the White House.[20] With his still unacknowledged fiancée out of town, Reid turned most of his attention to political developments, and it was in the last few days of December that he learned from Blaine of his acceptance of the State Department. The two, sometimes with Chauncey Depew and other leaders, discussed other appointments at length, giving especial attention to the cabinet, to the open New York senatorship, and to eligibles for appointment as ministers to foreign countries.[21] In these, as in earlier discussions, Reid was always on guard against Conkling's control of appointments of New Yorkers, and with this attitude Blaine was in full sympathy. The mutual feeling was so strong that Reid printed in his paper on January 3 a statement, actually prepared by Blaine but without his name, indicating that the incoming administration would not interfere in the New York senatorial contest. The real meaning of the announcement was plainly set forth. The influence of the national party would not be used against "the men from New York and other states" who had voted for Garfield at the Chicago convention in defiance of boss-imposed unity rules. Patronage would not be denied the independents. The *Tribune*'s readers, knowing its owner's relations with Garfield, had no doubt that the editorial was an official policy statement. Reid reinforced the editorial by going to Albany to assure Robertson's cohorts of Garfield's good will.[22]

While Garfield in effect promised not to use his influence against the bolters in New York, Reid sought to bring that influence to bear against the regulars, at least against Conkling. With Blaine's aid, Chauncey Depew was persuaded to become a candidate for the vacant seat in the United States Senate. Other politicians, seeing Conkling's hold threatened, sprang into the race. The issue became confused, and the legislature was unable to settle on one candidate. At this juncture, Platt decided to move far enough toward the incoming administration to gain its support. He convinced Blaine that he would cooperate with Garfield. He agreed to help confirm any of the bolters who might come before the Senate, even including Robertson, and he promised to try to keep Conkling "reasonable." These and other assurances satisfied Blaine, Reid, and their friends, who then helped Platt round up enough votes, including those pledged to Depew, to gain the Senate seat. Reid would have preferred Depew, but he believed Platt would stick by his agreements, and at least Conkling had suffered another blow in not being able to take credit for getting Platt into the Senate.[23]

From this point, although neither seemed to him to proceed without ever-present danger, both of Reid's major undertakings moved smoothly. On January 2, writing from the White House, Lizzie Mills had addressed Whitelaw Reid by his first name for the first time, saying she felt it was time they ceased to be formal with each other.[24] The step symbolized their determination to overcome, possibly even to ignore, parental opposition to their marriage. Two weeks later she seemed herself to be almost on the verge of the cabinet-maker's circle when she spoke to him about her father as a possibility for the Treasury post in the new administration. But her approach was unlike Reid's. She had little interest in the matter, her father seemed reluctant, and her mother was opposed, she told her future husband. At the same time Reid was urging Garfield to keep Mr. Mills in mind as a highly satisfactory solution to the difficult problem of finding a secretary of the treasury who would not increase partisan warfare within the party. Hay also supported Mills for the Treasury post and actually suggested him to Reid, unaware of the developing Reid-Mills relationship.[25]

Mills resisted the urging of his well-wishers and showed no interest in a place that, though not beyond his capabilities, was considerably beyond his political standing. He also resisted Reid's suit for his daughter's hand, albeit with less success than he resisted the Treasury, for the pressure was much greater.[26] Parental objection was an embarrassing matter for a time, however. In the latter part of January, a month after Whitelaw had proposed and Lizzie had accepted, he had to ask both Hay and Blaine to deny that there was an engagement. Hay responded by lecturing his friend on the beauties of married life and by urging him to make up his mind and propose.[27]

Early in February Mr. Mills capitulated to his daughter. Father has finally consented to our engagement, she told Whitelaw; she continued, "Of course I can not flatter myself that my parents are wildly delighted, but we will make them so in time." The successful suitor at once expressed to his future father-in-law both his gratitude and his understanding of Mr. Mills' hesitancy. He then told Hay and Blaine, and both expressed their delight with enthusiasm.[28]

This climax was soon followed by a second. Reid went to Washington at the end of February; the Garfields arrived on March 1 and took rooms at the Riggs House. For the first time the president-elect was under full pressure from the politicians, and the cabinet was made, unmade, and remade with the inauguration little more than seventy-two hours away. Reid's most specific contribution to Garfield's cabinet making was in helping select a New York man for one of the posts. He seconded Blaine's suggestion of Thomas L. James, who would satisfy the regulars but who might be brought in without Conkling's prior knowledge and hence would not be beholden to the boss. Reid discussed the appointment with Garfield, made the first overtures to James in New York, called him to Washington for a few days later, took him to see Blaine, and finally had the heady experience of introducing to the president-elect a man he had never met but was about to appoint as postmaster-general.[29]

In these hectic days Reid was a frequent visitor to the Riggs House, at Blaine's residence, and at the White House. He occupied a peculiarly strategic position, and he could help the incoming administration measurably, for he had a unique combination of qualifications. Not only would his *Tribune* approve, explain, and justify everything that Garfield did, but knowing of decisions as they were being made, the writers of editorials could prepare in advance their comments on each new development. Reid's close personal relations with both Garfield and Blaine, and the mutual trust among the three added strength to the editor's role. That the communications facilities available to the *Tribune* offered quicker and safer means of exchanging messages between Washington and other centers than were available elsewhere increased Reid's importance to Garfield in the fluid situation of the inaugural period. Of especial importance was the fact that there was no other New Yorker of stature whom the incoming president knew as intimately or could trust as fully as he could Reid. Further, Reid neither sought an appointment for himself nor demanded one for any friend, unless Mr. Mills be counted, and he owed no political debt. As evidence of his appreciation, Garfield offered his friend the legation in Germany, but after consulting his bride-to-be, Reid declined.[30]

Through the whirl of preinaugural preparations, Reid was more frequently near the chief figures of the incoming administration than were any of the New York politicos. At the inaugural ceremonies on the east portico of the White House, Reid sat within arm's reach of the outgoing and the incoming presidents. All of this was so distressing to Conkling that he protested about the treatment accorded him and complained to Garfield of Reid's interference. Reid happily described the boss's discomfiture to Miss Mills and added, "G. told me of it with a chuckle."[31]

Conkling's displeasure did not decrease, and his fight for appointments for his followers reached a climax in the weeks following the inauguration in the most dramatic political development of Garfield's short presidency. Again Reid was privy to events behind the scenes, and this time he played a major role himself. The affair involved Judge Robertson, who had led the revolt against Conkling's control of the state delegation to the Chicago convention and who was a central figure in the defeat of the Grant drive.[32] In January and February following the election, Reid reminded Garfield of Robertson's contributions at Chicago and sent some of Robertson's general comments on the New York political situation to the president-elect. Later Reid secured more specific information from the New Yorker for Garfield, who did not know Robertson personally.[33] Near the end of March, with Reid's support and Blaine's urging, the president appointed Judge Robertson collector of the New York Custom House.

Conkling correctly interpreted the move as a smashing blow at his control of the New York party organization. Aided by Platt he tried desperately to get Garfield to change his mind, to persuade Robertson to decline the nomination, or to block confirmation. But Garfield would never have challenged the boss without wide approval or with any thought of retreating. Not only had Reid's *Tribune* long been Conkling's implacable enemy, but many other leaders were restive. Of ominous import was the circumstance that Jay Gould, Chauncey Depew, and other wealthy New Yorkers were quite willing to see him displaced. National figures such as Blaine and John Sherman had found him unpleasant to deal with. Conkling's frantic efforts to avert the humiliation of seeing the man he considered a traitor and a renegade get one of the richest and most powerful posts in the state resulted in but one major gain for the boss. Reid, Depew, and their friends thought they had secured Platt's aid or at least his friendly neutrality in exchange for their decisive support of his candidacy for the United States Senate. But Platt remained loyal to Conkling and actually sent a follower to ask Reid to persuade Robertson to give up the collectorship! Reid, of course, had understood the significance of the situation from its inception. "I wish to say to the President," he had told Hay four days after Robertson's appointment in a private message intended for Garfield's ear, "that . . . this is the turning point of his Administration—the crisis of his Fate."[34] In a letter to Reid a few days later Garfield agreed that the matter was a crucial test for his administration. In April Reid continued to urge Garfield to stand firm. The end of the story came on May 16 when Conkling and Platt, misjudging the power of their opponents, resigned from the United States Senate in protest against Robertson's appointment. Robertson was confirmed and the senators were not reelected.

But Reid was not there to see. On April 26 at the Millses' Fifth Avenue home, some 250 friends saw Elisabeth Mills become Mrs. Whitelaw

Reid. Early in May, after a brief trip to Xenia to see Reid's mother, the bride and groom sailed for Europe on their wedding trip.

With the Garfield administration safely established and the New York political situation well in hand, there seemed to be nothing on the horizon to mar the couple's European travels. Reid was also unworried about leaving the *Tribune*. He had been able to persuade Hay to take the editor's chair, and he could trust his friend to make judgments and decisions that were usually almost undistinguishable from Reid's own. As a convenience to both, Hay lived in the house on Lexington Avenue during Reid's absence. Hay charged himself a dollar a day for breakfast, the only meal he ate there, and paid half the servants' wages during his five-month stay. John Russell Young thought the *Tribune* was "never so fierce" as under Hay's editorship. Reid's rule was one of whips while Hay's was that of scorpions, and the staff members welcomed Reid back with relief, Young said later.[35]

Two months after the newly married couple had said goodbye to Garfield, the shocking news of the "attempted assassination" was given to Reid on the day it happened by his London correspondent, George W. Smalley. Two days later Hay wrote to the absent editor of "the hideous subject of the day" and averred that "it is far more horrible than the one 16 years ago."[36]

The President was shot on July 2 and died September 19. Reid and his bride were in England and Scotland in July. Later they went to the Continent, visiting Paris, Amsterdam, and Brussels and going into Switzerland, Italy, and Austria. They were in Salzburg when Garfield died, and they remained abroad for another six weeks. Thus Reid, out of the country and preoccupied with other things, took little part in the political maneuvering that followed the assassination.

The new president, Chester A. Arthur, was quite unlike his predecessor and represented a different element in the party. He soon replaced most of the cabinet members. As Garfield's secretary of state and one of his most influential supporters, Blaine was one of those most badly hurt by the new situation. Reid's position was different from Blaine's, but he, too, found himself among the outsiders. The experiences of having been very close to the White House and then almost completely shut out brought the Maine leader and the New York editor closer together than they had been before Garfield's election.

"Arthur means death and destruction to every Garfield man," Blaine told Reid.[37] Writing to his friend from London at the end of October shortly before returning to New York after his wedding trip, Reid advised Blaine, then still in the cabinet, about the future. It would be a mistake to remain in the cabinet without being its real head, the editor wrote. With Grant standing at Arthur's elbow and with men hostile to Blaine in the cabinet, his position would be a weak one. Therefore he should resign, Reid advised. You are the greatest independent political force in the country, the "residuary legatee" of Garfield's popularity, the editor said. He advised Blaine to return to Maine, support the party, and wait for 1884 when he could be chosen by the electorate to lead the nation.[38]

Blaine did resign. He and Reid assumed the roles of loyal critics of the new regime in public, although their private exchanges were less restrained. Reid was especially critical of the administration when it was in conflict with Blaine. In the spring of 1882 the *Tribune* attacked Arthur for permitting the new secretary of state, Frederick T. Frelinghuysen, to cancel the Latin American conference that Blaine had arranged and for which invitations had been sent out.[39]

Blaine's and Reid's situation was a matter of interest to many people outside of politics as well as to the politicians. A somewhat extreme, yet nevertheless indicative attitude was expressed by the caustic Clover (Mrs. Henry) Adams early in 1882. "The rat Blaine" is finally cornered, she thought, and all the papers oppose him except the *Tribune*, whose editor is "a scheming tramp from Ohio," owned body and soul by Blaine.[40]

Reid, however, now had other resources. On his return from Europe, late in the fall of 1881, he found himself in a situation in which politics took second place to vastly increased social activity. For more than a decade his membership in the Union League Club, the Century Club, and especially the Lotos Club, over whose regularly held dinners of a hundred to two hundred men Reid had presided as club president since 1872, gave him easy access to prominent people from most of the business and professional classes in New York. He had acquired a house at a good address where he could entertain as many friends as could engage in what he called "good talk." These relationships, heavily weighted with men interested in public affairs, had satisfied bachelor Reid's need for social activity.[41]

But Lizzie Mills had been accustomed to a different life, both in one of the finest country houses on the west coast and in her parents' elaborate establishment at 634 Fifth Avenue. D. O. Mills, Reid's senior by twelve years, had left his New York birthplace at the age of twenty-three and had taken enough capital to Sacramento in 1849 to begin a banking business. His success in this led to investment in other enterprises, and he retained extensive interests in California when in 1878 he returned to New York to retire as a person of great wealth. Among the properties he retained in the West was his California home, Millbrae, situated on a six-thousand-acre tract in San Mateo County near San Francisco. The house was lavishly furnished and the grounds had been landscaped by Frederick Law Olmstead. Mills had given Olmstead a free hand, even when he decided to bring in trees from the Sandwich Islands for a special effect.[42] Lizzie Mills Reid did not wish to do with less for her house or grounds. Her husband's Lexington Avenue home, even with summer trips to a cottage in Wave Crest Park beyond Far Rockaway, or to the Adirondacks, was insufficient. Five years after their marriage and after the birth of a son, Ogden Mills, and a daughter, named Jean Templeton for Mrs. Mills, the Reids moved from Lexington Avenue to 451 Madison.

The house they bought had been designed for Henry Villard by the firm of McKim, Meade, and White. It was built on land Villard acquired from Columbia College, which stood across 50th Street from his plot. Stanford White designed a courtyard structure to incorporate six separate residences, and the architectural features were provided by the talented young Joseph Wells who based the design on a Florentine model, the fifteenth-century papal chancery palace. Not content with one palace, "Madam insists it is time for the children to have a country home," Reid told Hay when Ogden and Jean were four and two.[43]

The summer home the Reids had in mind and soon acquired was on a seven-hundred-acre estate in Westchester County some three miles east of White Plains; it was called Ophir Farm. The place had been developed and named by Ben Holladay more than a decade earlier during the period of his great financial successes in western transportation. In his last years the estate, including Holladay's great stone mansion with its splendid appointments, was sold to John Roach, "the father of iron ship-building in America," who continued to develop it.[44]

Reid learned in the summer of 1886 that the estate might be purchased.

91

He estimated that the previous owners had spent almost a quarter of a million on the house and grounds, but thought the place might be had for a third of that sum. Before the end of the year negotiations resulted in a transfer, and Mills, in his daughter's name, gave his son-in-law a hundred and twenty thousand dollars. At the time of the purchase Ophir Farm was assessed for taxes at eighty-five thousand, and the amount was raised to a hundred thousand when the Reids commenced extensive renovations.[45]

They employed Frederick Law Olmstead to make changes and additions in the grounds involving streams, trees, road alignments, terraces, walls, and some small buildings. The planning involved much stonework, partly because of Reid's liking for the material, partly due to the terrain, and partly as a result of the existence on the estate of a large quarry from which the bulk of the needed stone could be taken.[46] Olmstead made plans and began work on the basis of the Reids' suggestions, but before he had made much progress, in mid-July 1888 a fire of unknown origin almost totally destroyed the main house, leaving only the kitchen wing, the foundations and some of the masonry walls in usable condition. Much of the furniture was saved. Reid and his wife with her father's approval and promise of help decided to rebuild on Holladay's foundations, and employed Stanford White's firm to plan and supervise the reconstruction. After the fire, as the rebuilding got under way, Reid insured the property for a hundred and fifty thousand dollars.[47]

When Reid bought Ophir he did not abandon Wild Air, the camp developed from a cabin in the Adirondacks he had acquired in 1882. Located near the princely establishments put up for men of great wealth by the fabled Paul Smith, Wild Air with its sleeping and living quarters in a main cabin, its detached kitchen and dining rooms, its icehouse, boathouse, and connecting walks was relatively unpretentious. The camp was cared for by one Fred Barnes, who performed similar services for others in the vicinity.[48]

Reid almost never took his wife and children to Xenia, but he visited his mother at his boyhood home regularly. He kept the house in sound condition, gradually improved both it and the farm, and occasionally bought up small adjoining tracts when the prices were attractive. He employed local people, long resident in the county, to look after his mother and the properties.[49]

92

The editor of the *Tribune* moved as easily in the Mills circles as he did among the political figures, journalists, and literary people of New York. Never awed by power since his days as a wartime reporter, the self-made head of one of the great newspapers of the country recognized no superior in his own field and no calling higher than that of journalism. A man who had acquired moderate wealth by his own efforts, now allied with one of the country's great fortunes through a wife who enjoyed spending it, he could afford more luxury than his first forty years had taught him to want. As a newcomer to New York his associates had been drawn from the more fluid circles of the city. The fortunes owned by the people whose society he had frequented were no older, nor were they larger, than that of D. O. Mills.

Reid's positive, vigorous, and aggressive yet carefully shielded personality struck the people who knew him in many different ways. Some of the most widely held notions about him were expressed in an anonymous novel of 1885 in which Reid and Hay figured prominently, the former as Horatio Blackdaw and the latter as his friend Hilliard. Blackdaw appeared as one of the phenomenal journalistic successes of the day, who ruled his lieutenants on the *Atlas* with a martinet's vigor, tempered by simplicity, and who expected no more than he cheerfully gave. What Reid's friends saw as a withdrawn and reflective personality became profound calculation and a self-engrossed nature in Blackdaw. He was portrayed as the narrow and provincial product of a small society, yet one who possessed the aplomb of Gulliver and the confidence of Pertinax. Hay and Phelps saw Reid's open search for profits from his paper and from his investments as an indication of his desire for security, comforts, and pleasure. In contrast his fictional counterpart was described as a worshipper of money who panted for the recognition it gave in a new society and as a self-made man who secretly adored the prestige that he thought wealth alone could bring.[50]

8

Business and Politics

WHILE the machinations of Horatio Blackdaw and his friends were titillating some and angering others, Reid was involved in more serious problems than literary criticism. In the eighties the systems of cooperative news-gathering that had developed in the United States were growing rapidly. Foremost among these agencies was the Associated Press, a New York-based wire service with national coverage that supplied the *Tribune* with most of its straight news. The AP had been developed and was owned by the *Tribune* and six other New York papers, the *Herald*, *Times*, *World*, *Express*, *Sun*, and *Journal of Commerce*. These gathered news, exchanged it among themselves, and sold it to some 348 clients, paying a quarter to a half million dollars a year to Western Union for the needed wire services.[1] Other organizations also developed, and in the eighties the New England Associated Press and the Chicago-based Western Associated Press were the principal regional groups that bought news from the New York organization.

As Reid arrived in New York late in 1881 from his extended trip abroad, he found the restive westerners challenging their eastern colleagues' almost exclusive control of the systems. Negotiations and compromises undertaken during the year following Reid's return resulted in the establishment of a joint committee of five under the chairmanship of Charles A. Dana, editor of the *Sun*. Dana, Reid, and James Gordon Bennett of the *Herald* were joined in the group by two members of the Western Associated Press, Walter N. Haldeman of the *Louisville Courier-Journal* and Richard Smith of the *Cincinnati Gazette*. They agreed on a five-year contract, which became effective January 1, 1883. It left substantially unchanged the business relationships that had prevailed with respect to news exchange and controls in the eastern and western territories. William Henry Smith, who was general agent in the western cooperative, became general manager of the new organization at an annual salary of seventy-five hundred dollars. After a little more than a year of operation, profits averaging more than twenty-five thousand dollars a year were being divided.[2]

The joint executive committee directed news-gathering and distribution in the United States with very little interference from rival groups. The AP's exclusive contracts with Reuters, Havas, and Wolff assured the American organization of a near monopoly on foreign news entering the United States.[3]

Further expansion and consolidation came in the mid-eighties when the joint executive committee made agreements with the newly organized United Press. Established in 1882 as a private commercial venture by papers unable to buy Associated Press service, the UP had expanded so rapidly that the older cooperative took steps to avoid duplication of effort and expense and to avert possible future conflict. A union of the two agencies was effected early in 1885. At first it was only an agreement for a reciprocal exchange of services between the two organizations, but the connection was made more binding in October. Reid and his four colleagues on the joint executive committee, together with William Henry Smith, secretly gained control of the United Press by acquiring a substantial amount of stock.[4] The shares were purchased, but very shortly afterward a 100 percent dividend was declared so that in fact the stock was simply transferred to the new owners without cost to them. The move both strengthened the news coverage of all member papers and held down ruinous rivalries.

The arrangement, however, did not put an end to all worrisome problems, for the needs of the rapidly growing West soon made it expedient to establish a still newer and more flexible United Press. This was accomplished under an Illinois charter in 1887, and Reid and the other members of the joint executive committee again acquired substantial shares of stock in the new organization. In a short time Reid, Dana, and William F. Laffan, manager and publisher of the *Sun*, held 725 shares each, Haldeman and the Smiths, Richard and William Henry, held 500 each; the total of 3,675 shares was enough to control the corporation. Further agreements between still intact regional news-gathering agencies were made through the eighties.[5]

Each individual associated with the reorganization and consolidation of these agencies was a prominent figure in his own right. Together they exercised powerful influences on the nation. Despite intensive rivalries between the separate papers and frequent exchanges of criticism, the editors avoided personal attacks on each other and were usually on excellent terms as individuals.

Reid was no less concerned with handling news than with gathering it, and he constantly searched for more speedy and efficient ways of getting it in his paper and on the streets. Early in the eighties he was using three Barr-patented typesetting machines in the *Tribune* rooms. Most of the editorial page was set on a Barr brevier model, and the bulk of the foreign letters on a minion model. Nearly all the local miscellany, the eighth page, was also machine set, as was special matter for the weekly and the semiweekly. Reid thought, in the summer of 1883, that his was the only daily paper in the country using such machines. That they used special type and broke a good deal of it, were subject to frequent breakdowns, and were centers of labor discontent troubled the *Tribune*'s editor very little. They saved money in the composing room.[6]

Reid's success with the Barr machines made him more receptive to the idea of mechanical devices for speed and efficiency than were some of his competitors. He was more realistic in appraising its possibilities, therefore, when he first saw the complex and cumbersome invention of Ottmar Mergenthaler. The inventor's backers, a Washington group led by James O. Clephane, Lemon G. Hine, and Stilson Hutchins, had more faith than money, and their National Typographic Company needed stronger financing than they could give it. Through mutual acquaintances the Washington promoters interested Melville Stone in the enterprise, and he enlisted the powerful support of William H. Rand, William Henry Smith, Victor Lawson, and others. The editor of the *Tribune*, already interested in the possibilities of the machines, readily joined the group when invited.[7]

Reid has been credited with naming the linotype when he supposedly said, "Why, it's a line of type," on seeing the product of Mergenthaler's machine. Whether he named it or not, and Stone thought Rand responsible for the label, is less important than that from the time he first saw one, the second built by its inventor, Reid assumed a central place in the development of Mergenthaler's revolutionary device. In March 1885 he sent W. P. Thompson, foreman of the *Tribune*'s composing room, to experiment with the machine and to try it under conditions of cold, heat, continuous operation, and at varying speeds to discover its strengths and weaknesses. After satisfying himself that the contrivance would really work, Reid took the first twelve linotypes constructed into the *Tribune* Building. On July 3 his paper was made up in part on the machines. Within the year Stone had another twelve in the *Chicago Daily News* rooms, where their poor performance caused Lawson to complain bitterly. By the first part of 1888 some sixty machines were in use in the composing rooms of members of the syndicate that controlled the linotype company.[8]

Reid dominated the group of individuals who had joined together to promote the development of Mergenthaler's inventions, and he was the central figure in organizing the corporate body that owned and controlled the machines. By the end of 1886, before the company was producing "linotypes" commercially, Reid's more than 7,000 shares gave him the largest single voice in the organization. These, plus Clephane's 3,900 shares, the second largest holding, and the 1,000 each held by Rand, Stone, and Mergenthaler, plus a total of nearly 2,500 more held by William Henry Smith, Haldeman, and three others, gave the syndicate a voting strength of over 16,000 shares. Holders of another 7,000 usually could be relied on to support the syndicate, and when they did the combined vote of more than 23,000 shares was decisive.[9]

Reid held tenaciously to his central position in the 'group that controlled the machines. Gradually D. O. Mills and Mills' son Ogden invested in the enterprise. Five years after Reid first saw the device, his brother-in-law was director and vice president of the Mergenthaler Linotype Company, Mr. Mills was a director, and the three were the principal influences in the organization. The operations of the company were profitable and increased Reid's growing fortune considerably.[10] The use of the machines to print the paper was also profitable but this damaged his reputation in labor circles.

Nearly ten years before the linotype machines became a part of the *Tribune*'s operation, Reid's wage-cutting policies, a part of his response to the depression after the panic of 1873, had caused more than eighty compositers and substitutes, all members of New York Typographical Union No. 6, to walk out of the *Tribune* offices. Reid had thereupon blacklisted members of that or any other union in his composing rooms, and exacted from new employees pledges similar to the yellow dog contracts in use in some other industries.[11] He ran the *Tribune* as an open shop without apparent friction from 1877 to 1883, when new difficulties brought on a strike. This was followed by negotiations, mutual charges of bad faith, flare-ups, and a widening rather than a narrowing of the split between the paper and organized labor. The typographical union made a serious and extended effort to damage the *Tribune* through boycott, while Reid remained indifferent.[12]

The arrival of the linotype machines changed neither Reid's attitude nor that of Union No. 6; it merely added new differences. At the *Tribune* Building immediately, and soon across the nation, the same questions arose that had bedeviled master and man from the beginning of the machine age. The union held that a linotype operator was a compositor and should be paid compositor's wages. The typefounders and newspaper proprietors contended that the product of the machines was not that of the compositor's stick and sought low-cost labor, sometimes women, to operate the linotypes. Victor Lawson, with the second twelve machines found that despite breakdowns his composition costs were little more than a third as expensive as with hand work.[13]

At the beginning of the eighties printers on the big-city dailies received thirty-five to forty cents per thousand ems for setting type, while a decade later the machine could produce a thousand ems for twelve or thirteen cents. When the first machines were brought into the *Tribune* building, the union condemned them as only another attempt to destroy labor. The machines did indeed make all the members of the syndicate less concerned about the compositors. There was no settlement of the differences with the union through the eighties.[14]

Reid's wage policy, viewed as antilabor by the union, was no different in his mind from his efforts to keep down the cost of steam for power, lower the price of paper, and reduce the expense of distribution. He was more successful in these attempts than in increasing circulation, and the figures remained stubbornly constant. The weekly had lost heavily, as more than half its subscribers abandoned it in the campaign of 1872 and in the months after Horace Greeley's death. It never recovered and in the eighties had less than half the 190,000 readers who saw it in Greeley's day. The daily's losses were not so great, but its circulation fell below 40,000 before the damage done in 1872 was repaired. Sales gradually increased during the middle and late eighties, reaching a peak of some 80,000 copies, but they were usually nearer 50,000. The Sunday edition, launched at the end of 1879, had about the same circulation as the daily paper.[15]

The price cuts that Joseph Pulitzer forced on the New York dailies in 1883 disturbed Reid very little. He did not change until George

Jones on September 18 dropped the price of the *Times* to two cents. Reid came down to three cents the next day and circulation of the rival papers fluctuated for a short time, but the *Tribune* neither gained nor lost circulation in the long run, which meant that the editor lost income because of the lowered price. Through the seventies, the number of *Tribune* readers exceeded those who preferred the *Times*. Bennett's *Herald* and Dana's *Sun*, however, were more widely circulated. After Joseph Pulitzer took over the *World*, it too outsold Reid's paper.[16] Henry Hall of Reid's business office reflected a significant *Tribune* attitude about circulation in the mid-eighties when he proudly informed Reid one July that his paper was selling better than the other city dailies at all the resorts in New York state. On its first trip of the season the Saratoga Special had borne no fewer than 1,942 copies of the *Tribune* and only 1,000 of the *Herald!* Furthermore, the *Tribune* could beat the *World* to Newport by three hours and so would capture more of the clientele of that mecca.[17]

While circulation remained steady and Reid held costs down, the constant increase in New York's population pushed property values up; the *Tribune* Building, assessed at four hundred thousand dollars at the beginning of the decade, had to pay taxes on a valuation of six hundred thousand dollars five years later. The amount was not exaggerated, for it was income from the Tall Tower that enabled Reid to resume paying dividends on *Tribune* stock in the early eighties. These had been cut off when the building was begun and were again paid despite the losses in revenue following the price cut.[18]

The resumption of dividend payments gave little indication of the value of *Tribune* stock, since the closely held shares rarely came on the market. When Bayard Taylor's widow sought to sell two or three shares in 1883, she hoped to get ten thousand dollars for each of them. Reid discouraged her. He estimated that the shares were worth half of that figure, and that at five thousand dollars they were bringing a 7½ percent return.[19] Shareholders' confusion about the value of the stock stemmed not only from the long period when no dividends were paid, but also from the doubling of the capital stock from 100 shares to 200 in 1878. By that time Reid felt strong enough and sufficiently secure in his position to issue the additional stock. The fact that the move reduced the stockholders' equity in the *Tribune* Association was of less importance to him than his desire to strengthen his hold on the organization. There was little diffusion of the new shares, although, in line with principles established from Greeley's time, Reid wanted the *Tribune* employees to hold some investment in the association. In order that all old hands would appear to have as much of the new stock as they had of the old, Reid issued a proportionate number of the new shares in their names. However, few of the employees could buy the additional stock outright, and they signed it over to Reid, so that in fact most of the new shares remained in his hands.[20] At the end of 1883 Reid owned 75 of the 200 shares. Mrs. Reid owned another 48 and her brother Ogden had acquired 20, a total for the family of 143, including those once owned by Jay Gould. The remaining 57 shares were held by more than a score of employees, estates, or other small investors.[21]

In the world of politics during Arthur's administration, Reid's path paralleled that of Blaine, and the editor looked forward confidently to his friend's nomination for the presidency in 1884.[22] The assessment of the trend proved accurate, as the Plumed Knight became increasingly popular through the Arthur years. Reid and Blaine spoke frankly to each other in the scores of letters they exchanged through this period. Blaine did not hesitate to send notes and suggestions for the *Tribune*'s editorial pages, and Reid used or rejected them as his judgment dictated. In these exchanges it was Blaine who pressed and Reid who held back. The Maine orator felt that his New York friend was too slow to pick up issues and struck too gently against the wicked. "I wish you would agonize more and more for the tariff," Blaine implored Reid.[23] The tariff and the bloody shirt were Blaine's main concerns. Reid was in full agreement about the tariff, but he was more skillful in presenting that and other issues to the people. Blaine's bludgeoning frontal attack became a more subtle campaign in the hands of the journalist, who also advised others on tactics. When William E. Chandler at the end of 1883 proposed making a campaign document of Horace Porter's letters on the tariff, then running in the *Tribune*, Reid read him a lesson in politics. Let the letters continue to run in the paper, he told the administration strategist, because people think a newspaper is news, and a campaign document is tainted.[24] A few months later Reid printed a speech that William Walter Phelps had made at Trenton to the New Jersey State Board of Agriculture on the value of protection to farmers. The editor thought the speech was a particularly effective argument for the tariff and a telling campaign document "because obviously not designed for it."[25]

101

Reid's handling of the tariff issue was matched by his skillful penwork in the intraparty struggle between Blaine and the administration on the southern question. The editor of the *Tribune* cared nothing for Chester Arthur. "All in the world we want out of him is to die with reasonable decency when the necessity of his political death at last dawns on his vision," Reid told Phelps early in 1884.[26] The *Tribune* constantly sniped at the President and thereby alienated many regulars. But Reid considered that to oppose Arthur was an isolated action and did not mean opposition to the party.

A different approach was needed when Blaine's attitudes conflicted with those of William E. Chandler. In 1882 the administration endorsed William Mahone's independent movement in Virginia, hoping to build new strength in the South. Blaine led resistance to what he was convinced was a departure from traditional Republican policy; it seemed to be a desertion of the Negro and an alliance with the former rebels. When Reid supported Blaine, Chandler tried without success to convince the editor that an alliance with southern independents was the soundest plan the Republican party could adopt. The dissension continued through 1883, Blaine and Arthur each seeking to gain advantage and to build his own influence in the party. At the end of the year Reid renewed a Blaine-inspired denunciation of the southern independents, and Chandler again urged him to reconsider. This time the *Tribune* found something creditable to say about Mahone. The New Hampshire leaders and the New York editor continued to work together, and Chandler recognized and appreciated Reid's significant position as a mediator of differences within the party.[27]

In less public areas of political activity Blaine worked with little help from Reid but with the latter's knowledge. The candidate made agreements with John A. Logan of Illinois, who would be Blaine's running mate, John Sherman of Ohio, and with Thomas C. Platt and the New York regulars. Reid was not happy about the bargain with Logan, an old antagonist from the Grant years, but could not offer a satisfactory alternative. Despite his displeasure he was firmly committed to Blaine as were a majority of the party leaders when the Republicans met at the Exposition Building in Chicago on June 3, 1884. The Plumed Knight was put in nomination by an Ohio orator and the seconding speeches were delivered by four carefully selected leaders. One of these was Platt, whose role at the convention completed his alienation from the now thoroughly discredited Conkling and put Platt and Reid on the same side for the second time in a national endeavor. The preconvention planning, supported by floor work at Chicago in which Reid took part, proved adequate. Blaine was nominated on the fourth ballot and Logan's nomination followed.

Carl Schurz, George William Curtis, Horace White, E. L. Godkin, Theodore Roosevelt, and other conspicuous Republican reformers had vainly opposed putting a regular at the head of the ticket. Some of them were ready to leave the party, and they let the Democratic leaders know that they would support Cleveland against Blaine if the New York governor should be nominated. This unnecessary support probably had little more effect than did Tammany's solid opposition to Cleveland who was nominated on the second ballot.[28]

As the campaign developed the reformers were joined in New York by one of their bitterest enemies and Reid's oldest opponent in the state. Unlike Platt, Roscoe Conkling had never forgiven Blaine for his support of Garfield in the Robertson affair and its aftermath. Now, his machine in other hands and his political career over, the former boss worked to destroy Blaine. Conkling also met with and advised Democratic leaders on state and national levels and, over various names, wrote letters for newspapers. Many papers were available to him, including most of the outstanding ones in the East. In New York City only the *Tribune* and the *Commercial Advertiser* continued as Blaine partisans; all the other papers opposed the Republican nominee. The situation caused Reid to warn the sometimes indiscreet Smalley to be extremely careful in his letters from London on English attitudes about the election, "since the interests of the party are so largely in our hands in this city."[29]

Reid worked closely with Blaine during the campaign as confidant, adviser, and shield against demands from importunate ward and district leaders. The two saw most issues alike, but disagreed on one point of strategy. Blaine urged Reid to make some kind of adjustment with the typographers' union, with which he had never made peace. Blaine believed they had voting strength, and when they asked his intercession he approached Reid. Reid, however, was adamant in his refusal to negotiate and positive in his view that the union had little strength and would be against Blaine in any event.[30]

Reid also worked with the other party leaders, and important sums passed through his hands into those of Stephen B. Elkins in the national

103

headquarters in New York City. Summing up the situation in mid-October, Reid felt that the national committee's sixty-thousand-dollar debt, which they did not seem to be liquidating, indicated a general weakness. He also complained that the committee did not seem able to get contributions from the Custom House, the subtreasury, or the Post Office. On the other hand such men as Collis P. Huntington and Jay Gould, who had already contributed five thousand dollars each, could be approached again if a real emergency arose, Reid thought. In details the editor was pessimistic, in general he was conservatively optimistic as election day approached.[31]

Reid's relation to the campaign was seen as very close and his effectiveness of a high order by the opposition. Cartoons of the period frequently included him among the party leaders. One of the best known portrayals was Bernard Gillam's second "tatooed man" cartoon, which appeared in *Puck* on June 4. It showed Reid as a slave dealer stripping a cloak from Blaine and revealing him unclad. Although Blaine was tatooed with Corruption, Antilabor, Northern Pacific Bonds and other scandals, Reid assured the admiring Republican leaders assembled to view prospective nominees, "Now, Gentlemen, don't make any mistake in your decision! Here's Purity and Magnetism for you—can't be beat!"

Even more effective and probably the best known drawing of the campaign, was Walt MacDougall's cartoon in the *World* on the eve of the election. On Blaine's return from his triumphant western tour, some two hundred wealthy and prominent Republicans including Cyrus Field, Jay Gould, Russell Sage, D. O. Mills, and Jesse Seligman attended a dinner for the nominee at Delmonico's Restaurant. The opposition press promptly labeled it "the millionaire's dinner," and MacDougall's drawing of "Belshazzer Blaine and the Money Kings" had Reid hovering at Blaine's shoulder in the center of the scene. Earlier the same day the Rev. Samuel D. Burchard, a Presbyterian minister speaking for several hundred Protestant clergymen gathered at the Fifth Avenue Hotel to greet Blaine, spoke the alliterative phrase that immortalized him. We are your friends, Mr. Blaine, he said, and we as Republicans don't propose to identify ourselves with "the party of rum, Romanism, and rebellion." A reporter recognized the importance of the words, which Blaine did not (if he heard them at all), and on the following Sunday Democratic strategists had ward leaders distributing handbills carrying the phrase to Catholic churches all over the country.[32]

Reid knew the election would be close and had warned Blaine two weeks before the polls were opened that "the work has not yet been done that would make experienced politicians content."[33] Nonetheless he believed Blaine would win and was reluctant to accept the results as they came into the *Tribune* office where he sat in deepening gloom, with Phelps and his daughter, through election night. As the count mounted, despite growing doubts, he fired off wires of encouragement to inquirers, telling one that "we have and can hold" New York, but admitting that New Jersey and Connecticut were in doubt. But the year was 1884 and not 1876, and New York, New Jersey and Connecticut were not susceptible to the pressures exerted on South Carolina, Florida and Louisiana in the earlier year. New York could not be held, New Jersey and Connecticut were lost, and Cleveland was elected.[34]

Privately Reid thought the results a calamity, and in fact he had stood to gain as much in power and position as any man in the country save Blaine himself by a victory. On the other hand he had to admit that the campaign and close election had pushed the *Tribune*'s circulation and advertising to such heights that the paper was in better shape than it had ever been. This satisfaction did not prevent him from flailing Burchard so mercilessly for causing the election to be lost that Hay begged him to desist. The minister was a very old and not very wise man, heartbroken at what he had done, Hay said, and reminded Reid that it really *was* rumsellers' money, Irish Catholic machines, and rebel votes that put Cleveland in office. All Burchard did was tell the truth, Hay went on, but admitted it was told at the wrong time and place. Another view was that of the typographers who loudly advanced the claim that their organized opposition to Blaine in New York had tipped the scales.[35]

When Clevelend was elected Reid had been in New York sixteen years. Only in Garfield's half year had the *Tribune*'s editor been wholly in sympathy with the administration in power. During the rest of the time his position had varied from that of the bitter uphill battler against Conkling and Grantism, culminating in the ill-conceived bolt in 1872, to the mild attitude of a loyal critic of Hayes. He therefore slipped easily into his normal role of opposition to the president as the new administration took shape.

In the new cabinet, Reid could approve only Secretary of the Navy William C. Whitney, a personal friend of long standing. The others he found mediocre or worse. He directed his heaviest fire at Attorney General Augustus H. Garland, who was castigated as a secessionist from Arkansas who could never be expected to administer the office fairly and was certain to discriminate against Negroes. Cleveland's veto of the Dependent Pension Bill early in 1887 was condemned as a concession to rebel influences. Later in the year the administration suggested the return of captured confederate battle flags. The *Tribune* interpreted this gesture as an insult to all union veterans and a first step toward assumption of the confederate war debts.[36]

In considering the administration's foreign policy the *Tribune* was no less partisan than on other measures. On February 20, 1888, Cleveland sent to the Senate a fisheries treaty with Great Britain, one carefully worked out by Secretary of State Thomas F. Bayard in tedious negotiations. On the twenty-third Reid said that the treaty marked "the lowest point of degradation which American diplomacy has ever reached." When the treaty was rejected in August by a purely party vote, the *Tribune* was loud in its praise of the Senate for casting out the "senseless and un-American treaty."[37]

Reid's most telling stroke during the Democratic quadrennium was a point-by-point denunciation of the administration that he printed in the *Tribune* on March 4, 1887, under the title "Half Way Through." This effort so pleased the party leaders that they issued it as a campaign document.

In the Cleveland years Reid watched Blaine's popularity remain at a high level as the editor aided his friend in the columns of the paper. Yet he shied away from discussion of 1888. Blaine's special personal friends should not push him again, Reid warned Hay, because "It is too big a responsibility to take." At the same time he thought Blaine would be nominated and could be elected.[38] In the mid-term races Blaine campaigned not only widely and effectively but with such fanfare that one critic opined he only needed a red bandwagon to be classed as a circus. As in the earlier years, Reid's relation to the party and program was assessed with partisan forcefulness if not with flattery by opposition cartoonists. C. J. Taylor, F. Opper, and J. Keppler, especially, lampooned the *Tribune*'s owner as an enemy of progress and an associate of the wicked. A common theme was illustrated in a drawing in 1886 of Reid, Blaine, Sherman, and others viewing a happy, prosperous, highly employed American labor force under Cleveland. In the cartoon the Republican leaders gloomily warned the people that ruin and devastation were about to overtake the nation; the caption read: "They are out of office." Reid was always portrayed by the opposition as thin and slightly stooped, almost gaunt, with long and usually unkempt hair, a drooping mustache, and sometimes a hint of an imperial.[39]

As the time for the convention of 1888 neared, the central position that Reid and the *Tribune* held in the party was reemphasized. At the end of 1887, when Cleveland named L. Q. C. Lamar to the Supreme Court, William E. Chandler at once sought Reid's aid in opposing confirmation of the southerner. It is a party matter, the Republican chieftain said, and a duty to resist; the *Tribune* should persuade William M. Evarts to denounce Lamar and should demand that senators Don Cameron of Pennsylvania, Dwight M. Sabin of Minnesota, John H. Mitchell of Oregon, and Philetus Sawyer of Wisconsin, all reportedly pro-Lamar, do the same. Reid, having no reason to resist the policy laid down by Chandler, followed it. In a series of editorials he appealed to the senators Chandler had named, asking them to oppose Lamar. The effort was not successful and the Mississippian was confirmed.[40]

In the same weeks the *Tribune* was responsible for putting a more far-reaching issue of vastly wider popular appeal before the country. When Cleveland chose to devote his message to Congress of 1887 to a severe indictment of the protective tariff and to make this the chief issue of the coming campaign, Republicans generally hooted about free trade foolishness. One, however, considered the message a personal challenge. Blaine, who had given half the space in his seventeen-page letter of acceptance in 1884 to the same issue, sounded a war cry that echoed from the Atlantic to the Pacific.

Cleveland's speech was abstracted in the European press on December 7. Blaine was in Paris at the time, and at the Hotel Binda there he gave Reid's London agent, George Smalley, a statement in the form of an interview. The Republican chief began with assertions that he knew would assure close attention to his words from a widespread anglophobic audience in the United States. The London papers, Blaine announced, were saying that Cleveland's program would admit more English goods to the American market, and Great Britain was solidly behind the policies announced by the president. The Plumed Knight then attacked the low tariff at length, with all his skill, and none of the force of his words was lost as Smalley prepared the statement for the cable. He sent it all, and Reid printed it in full on December 8.[41]

Publication and wide copying of "Blaine's Paris Letter" or simply the "Blaine Letter" at once established him as the country's leading opponent of Cleveland and made him the outstanding contender for the Republican presidential nomination, still six months away. This quickly became apparent to Blaine despite his distance from the scene and, this time to the consternation of his supporters, he sent another message from abroad. Writing from Florence in January, he told the party leaders through the chairman of the national committee that he did not intend to run for president again.

In the early months of 1888 the Florence letter was interpreted in the United States in accordance with the aspirations of the individuals who considered it. Reid contended that Blaine was perfectly sincere in refusing to volunteer to run, that the letter was no mere maneuver. At the same time, he argued, no man is "so big that he can refuse the greatest office on earth" if it is thrust upon him. Conflicting views about the Florence letter had already reached Blaine, and when Reid's interpretation became public, Blaine wrote to him stating flatly and finally that he would not run. After holding it for several days, Reid reluctantly printed the letter.[42]

Publication of the disclaimer gave heart to supporters of favorite sons including Reid's friends William Walter Phelps, Sherman, and Chauncey Depew, as well as to anti-Blaine elements. Joseph B. Foraker thought that Reid, Phelps, and their friends were so committed to their champion that they were left desperate after the Plumed Knight refused to do battle. They "are hurriedly striving to form combinations that will place them and their fellows in supporting relations to the coming administration, whoever it may be," Foraker thought.[43] He was right. Phelps, Thomas C. Platt, Depew, Frank Hiscock, Stephen B. Elkins, and others visited Reid at his Madison Avenue house. They agreed that Blaine was still the most effective possible nominee even after publicly stepping out of the race. If he could not be drafted, however, they thought that Benjamin Harrison, a native of Ohio and a graduate of Miami University, but a citizen of Indiana by adoption, would be an acceptable candidate.

Three weeks after Blaine's final refusal removed their most prominent political figure from contention, the Republicans convened in Chicago to choose an opponent for Cleveland, who had been nominated by acclamation in St. Louis on June 5. Blaine's withdrawal had opened the field to all; seldom if ever had a convention distributed its votes among so many. Even Phelps received a few votes through the first three ballots. Sherman held some 230 delegates through seven ballots but could not add to them. Harrison, beginning with eighty supporters, gained steadily and on the eighth ballot cast on the sixth day won the nomination. Blaine urged Phelps for second place on the ticket, but Harrison and the other party chieftains felt that New York was more important than New Jersey, and the convention named Levi Morton.[44]

The tariff was the gauntlet bravely thrown by Cleveland and boldly seized by Blaine that became the central issue of the campaign, but it was not decisive. Tammany's refusal to support Cleveland, the successful use by the Republicans of the Grand Army of the Republic, and the availability of more than four million dollars for Harrison's backers had greater influence on the outcome. In the campaign the Republicans carefully avoided the kinds of errors they felt had cost them the election four years earlier and skillfully exploited a series of damaging mishaps that befell the Democrats. The most dramatic of these was a letter written by the luckless Sir Lionel Sackville-West, British minister to the United States, advising a naturalized Anglo-American to vote for Cleveland. The *Tribune* led scores of Republican papers in spreading the news throughout the last fortnight of the campaign. Cleveland was un-American, a British-dominated free trader and not fit to govern Americans, Reid's paper proclaimed. On election day the almost evenly divided voters chose Cleveland, but the Republicans carried New York state and in the Electoral College the New York vote gave Harrison the victory.[45]

9

Minister to France: General Policies

REID's relations with Harrison were not as close as had been those with Garfield. Yet the continued power of the *Tribune*, the editor's increasing support of the party in the paper and with financial contributions, his alliance with the strongly Republican D. O. Mills family, the disappearance of Roscoe Conkling and a closer association with New York political leaders, even including Thomas C. Platt, had strengthened Reid's position in the national party. He did not hesitate to advise the new president. Soon after the election he joined Stephen B. Elkins, Murat Halstead, and others in urging an immediate offer of the State Department to Blaine. A feeling was widespread that the man Mrs. Blaine contemptuously referred to as "the Indiana accident" needed a figure with the Maine idol's stature and magnetism to give the incoming administration strength and national prestige.[1]

To facilitate communication with the president-elect's headquarters, the *Tribune*'s editor sent one of his ablest young reporters, William McPherson, to Indianapolis early in December. McPherson took with him letters of introduction to Harrison and to his chief aides emphasizing the young man's discretion in the event they needed a channel for special communication.[2]

In the same weeks Reid also sent advisory opinions on a variety of topics to Indianapolis. Because of the diffusion of power and divisive factionalism in New York, Harrison from the beginning was more inclined to listen to Reid and a few others who spoke sincerely for party unity than to the professional politicians. At least one appointment, that of Benjamin F. Tracy of Brooklyn to head the Navy Department, was made on the recommendation of Reid, with support from Elihu Root. They had put Tracy forward, among others, as one who had ability and who would be acceptable to all factions.

Although he disclaimed interest in holding office, Reid's financial and political position, his wide connections, and especially his association with James G. Blaine made it almost imperative that he be offered something. The only problem was that of finding a place both suitable

111

and not preempted by a stronger claimant. The editor's background and interests clearly pointed to the cabinet or to one of the principal diplomatic posts as appropriate possibilities. Blaine was to have State, the Treasury was not suitable, War would not be attractive, the attorney generalship called for legal training, and the postmaster general's office was not a proper place. However, the rapidly growing Navy Department offered a real opportunity, and it would be no comedown for Reid to follow William C. Whitney in the secretaryship. At Elkin's suggestion Platt mentioned the possibility to Harrison, and the matter was dicussed at high levels, but Harrison chose Tracy, leaving a foreign appointment the only remaining possibility.[3]

Reid had refused offers from both Garfield and Hayes to represent the United States in Germany, a post considered to be in the middle range of prestige appointments. Berlin was looked upon as about equal to Rome or The Hague and a cut above St. Petersburg, Madrid, or Vienna. Only Great Britain or France could be thought of as fitting for the editor of the New York *Tribune*, and of these London was without question the more desirable.[4]

Speculation about Reid's place in the Harrison administration began among his friends soon after the election and increased and spread as the weeks wore on. As early as November 13 John Hay asked his friend flatly if the English mission had been promised him, and when Reid remained silent continued to hint at the topic. Hay and William Walter Phelps were not overlooked as possibilities, although their political standings in Ohio and New Jersey were not equal to Reid's in New York. Perhaps in part at his instigation and certainly with his knowledge, early in February both Elkins and Phelps put Reid's name forward and urged a decision. But Harrison kept his own counsel, and when Reid went to Washington for the inauguration, he was still in the dark as to his fate. By this time an overriding interest in the London post was attributed to him by an enlarging circle of commentators, and he was increasingly embarrassed as appointments were made and he had not been approached. Two weeks later, although Harrison had given no hint of his intention, Blaine still assumed that Reid would be sent to London in due time.[5]

A number of factors had stayed the president's hand. One of these was Blaine's own record. The British press had called the Plumed Knight the "Irish candidate" for the presidency in 1884. Blaine's famous Paris letter printed prominently and in full in the *Tribune* of December 7, 1887, had opened on an inflammatory anti-British note. With Blaine as secretary of state, Downing Street might well be reluctant to accept Reid, long a strong supporter even if he were not Blaine's "Chief henchman," as some politicians charged. Another circumstance unfavorable to Reid was that the *Tribune*'s London correspondent, George W. Smalley, had been highly critical of widespread English disapproval of Republican tariff and civil service policies. At other times the *Tribune* had championed Irish home rule, had been a stern critic of the incumbent Salisbury ministry, had helped defeat the fisheries treaty in the Senate, and had been very harsh in the Sackville-West incident. Whether these circumstances influenced Harrison decisively or not, he used them as a reason for his reluctance to send the *Tribune*'s editor to London.[6]

A decision as to Reid's fate was made late in March. At that point, Blaine, Hay, and Phelps, as well as Reid, felt that the appointment would not be withheld much longer. Hay especially, but Elkins and others as well, were convinced that the only possibilities were London or Paris and believed they had persuaded Harrison that Reid would refuse the lesser post if offered. Elkins talked to the president at length on Wednesday, March 12, and reported that Harrison saw some difficulties in appointing Reid but could not think of a more suitable person for Great Britain. At this juncture Elkins and Hay separately, at Reid's request, told the president in positive terms that they were certain the editor would refuse the French mission if it were offered. Instead of bowing to this ultimatum, Harrison sent Vice-President Levi Morton to New York to explain to Reid how the *Tribune*'s position on British affairs, while of great value in supporting and explaining American policies and attitudes, militated against sending its editor as the nation's official representative.[7]

The message came as a bitter pill. Reid's position was now highly exposed because of the months of speculation about his relationship to the administration. If the English mission were not offered, he felt, an immediate offer of France (which he could refuse) would save his face to some extent. But Harrison did not relish the prospect of four years in Washington with a disgruntled Reid in New York. He summoned Hay and convinced him, while Hay protested, that it would be impossible for Reid to go to England without creating friction that would make the appointment a very costly one; if he would accept Paris he would put the president under obligation to him and he would have Harrison's personal good will; a refusal of the Paris post would be interpreted as an indication of a breach between the *Tribune* and the White House. Would Hay help?[8]

Hay's first loyalty was to the party. He saw Blaine in Washington on Sunday afternoon, March 16, converted him to Harrison's view, and took the New York train the same day. When the president's second emissary to Reid arrived at 415 Madison Avenue at midnight Sunday in the wake of Morton's icebreaking trip, Reid had few defenses left. Without Hay's or Blaine's political and moral support he could no longer hold out against the president's wishes. Hay wired Blaine that Reid had acquiesced and later told Harrison of the midnight discussion.[9]

There remained the problem of finding a minister for Great Britain whose appointment would not offend Reid and his friends; the president was not unequal to the task. He sent the one figure in the Republican party who was above criticism from any individual or faction, American or British, Robert Todd Lincoln. That the political pot still simmered, however, showed in Blaine's note to Phelps about the diplomatic appointments. The secretary was sorry France was not available, but Reid was not likely to want to stay a full term, and Phelps could probably succeed him; meantime, would Phelps join John A. Kasson on the Samoan mission? Reid and Hay, on the other hand, had the impression that Blaine would see that Hay replaced his friend in Paris.[10]

Reid, however, was out of the turmoil for a while. Six days after the midnight conference at 415 Madison Avenue, the Senate confirmed him as Envoy Extraordinary and Minister Plenipotentiary to the Republic of France. Strong support from Frank Hiscock in the Senate and from firm friends in the newspaper world gave him some comfort in his new role in spite of his earlier reservations on going to Paris.[11]

The protracted negotiations about the appointment and the failure to get the London post left Reid with little pleasure or enthusiasm about the assignment, so that he felt he would be most pleased about the whole affair after it was over. As soon as the confirmation was made, it was arranged that Ogden Mills would go to Paris to look for lodgings. Meantime, Ogden's brother-in-law, the minister-designate, would divest himself of his responsibilities as editor of the *Tribune* and attempt to put the paper in safe hands. He would also arrange for the care of his house on Madison Avenue, the reconstruction of the Ophir Farm house and some development of the estate, the maintenance of Wild Air and of the properties at Xenia, the protection of his interests in the Associated Press and Mergenthaler directorships, and the finding of a suitable successor to the presidency of the Lotos Club. From his comfortable study on the ninth floor of the *Tribune* Building the coming period of the mission to France seemed far less complex and difficult in its Paris than in its New York aspect. The matter of the *Tribune* was quickly resolved by making Donald Nicholson, a kindly, bearded Welshman of long service, the editor. Other matters would have to be handled by Reid at long range or by Ogden Mills.

The Lotos Club presidency involved relationships of long standing that would be interrupted as a result of Reid's extended absence from New York. He had held the office by virtue of repeated reelection since 1872, except for a two-year interim, despite a frequently announced desire to bow out. It was a place that he had thoroughly enjoyed but that had filled a decreasing proportion of his needs since he had married and as his place in public affairs had expanded. The club elected Frank R. Lawrence to succeed Reid and gave the old president a farewell dinner a week before he sailed. The hundred and fifty diners included New York's most prominent political leaders, journalists, financiers, and churchmen, and two French consular officers. The guest of honor had no cause to regret that the affair coincided with a memorial dinner to General Grant at Delmonico's.[12]

Delmonico's tables later bore a dinner for the newly appointed minister when some forty gentlemen of the *Tribune* staff met to speed their chief on his way. Col. William M. Grosvenor presided and William Winter spoke for the assembled persons who would operate Reid's chief enterprise during his absence. None of the highly laudatory remarks made at the Lotos Club or the *Tribune* dinner reflected the attitude privately expressed elsewhere by Theodore Roosevelt that, while Reid as an individual was a good choice for the Paris post, newspaper editors should never receive political appointments.[13]

After Ogden Mills agreed to go to Paris to look for servants, a house, and to make other living arrangements, the minister-designate put such matters out of his mind for the time that remained before departure. Robert M. McLane, the retiring minister, wanted to retain his position through the first week in May to participate in long-planned festivals at

115

Versailles, an arrangement quite satisfactory to Reid, who was in no haste to leave New York. A month after his appointment he put a brief statement in the *Tribune* announcing his retirement from the editorship and direction of the paper. On May 4, with Mrs. Reid and their two children, he sailed for France on the *Bourgogne*. Eight days later they docked at Havre and proceeded at once to Paris, where they were met at the St. Lazaire station by Ogden Mills and his wife together with the legation staff. Since a suitable house had not yet been found, the new minister's brother-in-law had engaged rooms for the family at the Hotel Meurice, and the party proceeded there at once.[14]

The situation at the chancellery was somewhat more encouraging. Four years earlier Reid's predecessor, Robert McLane, had replaced the then inadequate offices with comfortable quarters in the Rue Gallilée, and Reid found no fault with these.[15] Here he met Henry Vignaud, the highly capable first secretary of legation. A confederate agent in France with journalistic responsibilities at the time Reid was a war correspondent in union areas, Vignaud had remained in Paris after the war and later obtained a place in the legation. Through his talents and efforts he had made himself almost a fixture on the staff, gradually becoming more French than American in speech, appearance, and manner. Augustus Jay, the second secretary, possessed talents that complemented those of Vignaud, so that Reid felt he would have few problems with the normal conduct of the mission. He was not much concerned with other staff people and replied in very general terms to a request from Chauncey Depew asking special consideration for an incumbent. His own first recommendation for an appointment was rejected by the secretary of state. Reid had neglected, or chose to ignore, the point that the individual could not speak French. Nor had he given much thought to Franco-American diplomatic issues. He considered that the post, which had to an extent been thrust upon him, would provide opportunities for travel and for stimulating social life. He felt that after a year and a half, possibly two, he could return to the *Tribune* and Ophir Farm with added prestige and honors.

In his first weeks in Paris Reid's expectations seemed well founded. He was received by the minister of foreign affairs, on May 16 and on May 21 presented his credentials to President Sadi Carnot at the Elysée, accompanied by Vignaud and the legation staff.[16] By this time a house had been found at 35 Avenue Hoche, and the family moved into adequate quarters, for which they paid seventeen hundred dollars per month. The place had been in the family of a French consul-general in Egypt and was full of mummies, bronze, pottery, statues of Isis, Osiris, and lesser figures, and a wealth of other mementos. The Reids removed most of the art (leaving, however, marble sphinxes at the balustrade ends of the grand staircase) and redecorated the whole. They paid special attention to the grand drawing room, furnishing it in crimson brocaded satin, giving it a painted ceiling that represented a cloud-flecked sky, and placing a life-sized statue of Helen of Troy in front of the central window.[17]

Reid's first official duties were hardly more than extensions of his social activities. On July 14 he attended the usual Bastille Day displays that, despite rain, seemed appropriately brilliant to the American minister. Earlier festivities on July 4 had featured the unveiling of Bartholdi's statue on the Ile de Cygnes opposite the Pont de Grinelle. The bronze statue was made from the original that had served as a model for "'Liberty Enlightening the World" and was a gift from American residents to the city of Paris. Even the first instruction from the State Department had social overtones. A Miss Fanny Van Nostrand with two friends, all of the highest respectability and social position in America, had departed Nice without, it was alleged, paying a dressmaker's bill. The three had been arrested and imprisoned on arrival at Mentone. Their friend Secretary of the Navy Tracy was much concerned. Secretary of State Blaine instructed Reid to secure their release and see that the functionaries responsible for the outrage were fired forthwith.[18]

These being his most serious problems at the outset, Reid could tell Nicholson that things were going extremely well, that his first worries about a house, furnishings, and servants were over, the family was comfortably settled, and all were in the best of health.[19]

Reid, however, did face serious problems in the following months, and he was equal to the occasion as each task arose. When he was named to represent the United States in France, he knew more about European and world politics than any of his predecessors since the Civil War with the possible exception of Robert M. McLane. The new minister's early education in foreign affairs had been gained only from reading; it had been little stimulated by his first trip outside the country, the visit to Havana in May 1865. In the ensuing quarter century his familiarity with international questions was broadened principally through the foreign news that came to the *Tribune*, through his brother-in-law Ogden and other friends who traveled abroad, and slightly by his six-month tour of Europe in 1881.

At the time of his appointment Reid's most strongly held convictions about outside affairs related to the western hemisphere rather than to Europe. In Havana he had been less interested by the bullfights and the gored horses he saw than by the existence of a slavery issue and of antagonisms between native and Spaniard.[20] He knew that years of unwise Spanish rule had increased the desire of the creoles to govern themselves, and he felt that Spanish dominion over the island was well-nigh ended. He would have liked to see Cuba free, but the possibility of annexation and statehood disturbed him, for he was not an expansionist.[21]

Similar reluctance tempered his sympathy for San Domingo's people under Spanish misrule, but he thought the United States should move slowly in support of separatist movements. A big question for American statesmanship would soon be "how to get rid of these incarnate revolutions" in adjacent tropical countries, he told Schuyler Colfax, and he asked how the nation could keep them from swarming in "and clinging to our skirts?"[22]

In Horace Greeley's day Central America held no issues on which the *Tribune* needed to take a position. The problem was to find news worth printing. At the beginning of the eighties, however, circumstances made the Isthmus a matter of more immediate interest. Late in 1879 a number of enterprising Americans organized the Provisional Interoceanic Canal Society, obtained a concession from Nicaragua, and later gained Grant's public support. This activity, plus rumors of Ferdinand de Lesseps' impending operations in Panama stirred press interest in America's position in the Isthmian area. Reid had few doubts that the item of principal importance was Great Britain's position, and that the Clayton-Bulwer Treaty was a feature central to the issue. The treaty had long been forgotten, he told the *Tribune*'s readers; it was dead of inanition. Yet technically it still lived and must be put to rest by some positive act. From this position the *Tribune* could support Blaine with vigor and with consistency when he became secretary of state and sought to abrogate the Clayton-Bulwer Treaty. Reid's argument was that only one power could be guardian for a canal, and that one had to be the United States. He also pointed out that a no-fortification agreement meant handing the Isthmus over in a crisis to the nation with the largest navy. This was and was likely to remain Great Britain.[23]

At the time he took over the *Tribune*, Reid's attitude toward expansion anywhere was similar to his position with respect to San Domingo. His views about Hawaii reveal that he was not among those who advocated outward movement of the country. Annexationist discussions about Hawaii in the early seventies included talk of reciprocity and of a naval station as well. Reid opposed adding "a Kanaka state" to the country, which he thought would be a positive evil. He also regarded reciprocity with a dubious eye and was relieved when the Hawaiian king cut off discussions at the end of 1873. The naval station idea so strongly urged in Maj. Gen. John M. Schofield's report to the secretary of war in May 1873 was less easily dismissed, Reid thought. Yet he could see no need to add Pearl River Bay to the lengthening number of stations held for a small and listless navy. More than a decade later, while expansionist sentiments grew elsewhere, Reid's position was unchanged.[24] When the Senate approved the reciprocity treaty with Hawaii in January 1887, the *Tribune* looked darkly on the prospects. The abrupt disclosure of imperial projects in the Pacific, making reciprocity dependent on Hawaii's agreement to the exclusive use of Pearl River Bay by a power with practically no navy, unable to defend the station from attack, was a grotesque plan, the *Tribune* said. "It is a novel proceeding . . . on the part of the United States, to solicit territorial rights outside the national domain."[25]

Not only should relations with Caribbean islands and Hawaii be free of commitment, Reid also believed that the United States should steer clear of European affairs. His ideas about America's political relations with the Continent seldom found cause for expression, but when an occasion arose the expressions were clear and unequivocal. At the end of 1884 Secretary of State Frederick T. Frelinghuysen accepted an invitation to send a representative to Berlin to discuss the situation in the Congo. The secretary emphasized the point that the meeting was not a congress, but was only a conference. He named the minister to Germany, John A. Kasson, as the American representative, warned in his instructions that the United States was not to be pledged to any course contrary to its well-known independent policy, and said that America reserved the freest liberty of action after the conclusion of the conference. The instructions seemed to Reid to be too liberal. The Monroe Doctrine forbade United States participation in European affairs, the *Tribune* said, and by sending delegates to the Congo meeting, the secretary of state had virtually repudiated the Doctrine. Even worse, the basic and underlying principles of American diplomacy as laid down in Washington's Farewell Address had been violated when Americans were sent to involve this country in European problems. Whether the meeting was a conference or a congress was immaterial, it was a gathering of foreigners, and attendance was not in the interest of the United States.[26]

Reid's stated attitude about his own relation to the making of American foreign policy as a participant rather than an observer and critic was in line with these judgments. When, midway through Hayes's administration, the offer of the German legation came to the editor of the *Tribune*, Reid had promptly refused on the ground that he could contribute more to party and country in Printing House Square than in Berlin.[27]

When a decade later he accepted the Paris post, it was without enthusiasm and as much for the social rewards as for the experience in diplomacy. Much of his work in France was routine. Passport applications, consular appointments, and favors for fellow citizens were constants in the routine. More unusual duties included accepting in the name of his country a pair of eyeglasses once owned by George Washington, given by a descendant of LaFayette. On another occasion he negotiated on behalf of the secretary of the interior with a group of Sioux Indians visiting in Paris.[28] These and scores of other matters of little significance came to Reid while he served as minister, broadening his view of the problems of diplomacy without overly taxing him, for he left most of the routine work to Vignaud, Jay, and the clerks.

In the area of international affairs as distinguished from purely Franco-American relations, the minister saw fleetingly two developing situations that involved decisions about the future of United States foreign policy and that were of considerable significance. The first of these concerned a contest for European oil markets.

Some time after Reid arrived in France he learned for the first time about some of Standard Oil's European operations. In the eighties the expanding activities of the Standard in Reid's native Ohio were accompanied by intensified efforts on the part of the company's export divisions, which resulted in increased foreign sales. In the same decade Russian oil production, skillfully managed by the Nobel brothers and others, outstripped Russian demand, and by 1881 the producers were in a position to exploit the European market.[29] Americans were concerned, and John H. Flagg, attorney for the United States exporters, complained that France discriminated against American oil in favor of Russian oil. He said that the discrimination was not done openly but resulted from improper classification of oil imports into France. Russian distillates, he alleged, paid the same low tariff rates as U.S. crudes, while American distillates were assessed at prohibitively higher rates.[30]

The general situation was revealed to the *Tribune*'s readers as a matter of news in 1887 when the paper described the rapidly developing Baku fields and pointed out that Russian expansion had revolutionized the petroleum trade in Europe. Russian producers were elated by the rapidity of their successes and boasted that they would soon drive American petroleum out of Europe. The American consul at Baku gloomily agreed that the United States had lost or was losing southern Europe and parts of Asia but hoped that the French, English, and some of the German markets could be held. Reid first took notice of the problem in the summer of 1890 after he was informed directly by private shippers that the Chamber of Deputies was about to recommend an increased duty on mineral lubricating oil. The changed tariff would discriminate against American in favor of Russian oil, the complainants said and cited statistics to support the point. Reid forwarded the information to the French foreign office and reported the matter to the State Department.[31]

France's Foreign Minister Alexander Félix Joseph Ribot denied the oil shippers' charges. The proposed increase would not benefit Russian crude oil, he said, since France did not import it, and would only amount to a one franc per barrel differential on refined oil, twenty-six francs for American and twenty-five for Russian. This, he pointed out, was not intended as a discrimination but was due to the unfortunate fact that the United States did not have most-favored-nation clauses in its treaties with France, while Russia did have such privileges and for that reason would benefit from the tariff change. He did not deal with Flagg's earlier allegation that petroleum imports were improperly classified. Again Reid reported the exchange without attempting to challenge Ribot's position. The State Department was more concerned, and in Blaine's absence Acting Secretary William F. Wharton sent a stiff protest insisting that Ribot had not stated the facts correctly. But Reid felt he had no sound basis for further remonstrance and did not pursue the matter.[32]

At the end of 1891 some effort on Reid's part was made necessary when the Chambers again took up the tariff. Under the pressure of growing protectionist sentiment in France, especially in the Senate, higher rates threatened United States petroleum sales. Reid's influence had little effect on the decision to leave the old petroleum rates unchanged, while duties on most other items were increased. In his assessment of the situation he emphasized the point that no satisfactory Franco-American commercial treaty existed. He also reported that some members of the French government had pressed for a higher petroleum duty on the grounds that such a change would put pressure on the United States to negotiate a new commercial treaty, which Reid believed many influential elements in France wanted. After passage of the new French tariff, separate discussion of petroleum was dropped, but the American minister was instructed to endeavor to get French assurance that new adjustments of petroleum duties would not discriminate against United States oil.[33] On the whole, during Reid's mission the deterioration of the market for American oil in France received scant attention.

The other international, rather than Franco-American, matter that Reid brushed against while abroad was of a different order. While Russian expansion worked against America's economic position in Europe, other rivalries offered opportunities for American expansion. At the time Reid went to Paris, Portugal was attempting to protect and enlarge her interests in Africa by uniting Angola with Mozambique to make a continuous trans-African colony. The consequent encroachment on territory Great Britain was interested in brought on conflict, and Portugal approached the United States for aid indirectly through the French Society for Arbitration. Early in 1890 a representative of the society handed Reid a letter addressed to Secretary of State Blaine, asking the United States to intervene with Great Britain to bring about arbitration of the British-Portuguese African dispute. The society's representative pointed out that the United States was a signatory of the "Congo Act of Berlin" and insisted that it was America's duty to press for arbitration.[34]

Despite his earlier denunciation of American participation in the conferences about African affairs, Reid forwarded the proposal without adverse comment. Blaine, however, took a strongly negative position. After pointing pridefully to his country's long record of support for the principles of arbitration, he vigorously denied that the United States had any obligations in the dispute or any interests in Africa. The matter was adjusted after the appearance of a British fleet before Lisbon and a British ultimatum. Portugal would suffer no loss of territory but her pride was hurt by the threat of force. Smarting under this harsh treatment, perhaps fearful of future disputes, and despite the earlier rebuff, the Portuguese again approached Reid in the summer of 1891. This time the move was direct rather than through an intermediary, and the Portuguese minister of finance, Marianno de Carvalho, called on Reid in Paris. The minister explained that his country wanted to discuss the offer of far reaching commercial and navigation privileges in Portugal's ports and harbors in return for special advantages for her exports to the United States. The arrangement, he said, would be much more advantageous than the ordinary commercial treaty that the American minister in Lisbon was then attempting to negotiate. The suggestion was accompanied by a startling proposition. Carvalho offered, in the name of his country, bases in the Azores and in Portuguese Africa for American naval squadrons. The proposal was not a general feeler but was carefully drawn, named specific ports in Angola and Mozambique, and included provisions about garrisons, shops, workmen, construction expenses, and other details. Reid forwarded these proposals directly to Blaine at his Bar Harbor residence rather than to the State Department. The minister explained that the Portuguese had approached him rather than George Batcheller, minister to Portugal, because the latter was not well known. He added that Carvalho was regarded in Paris as the ablest man in the Lisbon ministry, but Reid made no comment on the proposals as such. He asked for an early reply and intimated that he hoped Blaine would authorize further exploration of the Portuguese offer.[35]

Blaine was ill in June 1891 and may not have seen the communication. After waiting nearly a month for a reply to his urgent letter, Reid wrote to the president. For safety he addressed the letter to Col. E. W. Halford, Harrison's secretary; he enclosed a copy of the earlier message to Blaine and asked for guidance.[36] Harrison was only slightly interested. He wrote his minister that the proposals about naval stations

123

were "entirely inadmissable," but thought that the suggestions as to commercial arrangements might be explored further. The president informed the secretary of state of what he had said to Reid, and Blaine answered that he was in complete accord that the naval propositions were "entirely inadmissable," adding that Hawaii, Cuba, and Puerto Rico were the only non-continental places that were important enough to the United States for acquisition of bases.[37]

Reid conveyed the rejection to Carvalho, and the matter was not considered further while Reid was minister. His final comments to Harrison, however, indicated the beginning of a change of posture on Reid's part and foreshadowed his most significant role in American foreign policy. He had abandoned the narrow, small-navy concept of America's world position that was implicit in his condemnation of the move toward acquisition of a base in Hawaii, in his doubts about expansion in the Caribbean, and in his disapproval of participation in the Congo discussions of 1884. "I knew . . . that the [Portuguese] propositions, as sent, could not be entertained," he told Harrison, but he had thought that "in view of the growing needs of our Navy" we might acquire coaling stations in Africa, somewhat as was once attempted in Haiti.[38]

Minister to France: Concerns at Home

WHEN Reid left the United States early in May 1889, he took with him a number of continuing tasks and responsibilities that he would have preferred to leave behind. Some were business matters, which could be delegated at least in part, but some were personal and could not be left to others. That he was willing to accept an assignment by the president to represent the country in an important foreign post while crucial and time-consuming affairs at home demanded much of his attention reveals much about his attitude toward the mission to France. He thought of it as an honor and as a deserved recognition of his services to his party and his country. Like most men of his generation who were similarly situated, he did not think of a diplomatic appointment as a position that might require his full time and energies.

Chief among Reid's personal concerns while he lived in Paris was that of the work at Ophir Farm; the minister and his wife devoted hours of time and scores of communications to directing all phases of the new construction there. They advised the unthrifty Frederick Law Olmstead, in a vain effort to keep expenses down, about the most minute details relating to terrace stonework, retaining walls, boundary walls, gates, roads, drainage, ponds, wooded sections, pasture areas, grading around the house, shrubbery, and greenhouses. From time to time Reid told James M. Logan, the hard-working but unimaginative overseer and manager of the farm and estate, to help Olmstead with some particular project. He also made Logan directly responsible for specific jobs such as constructing cisterns and icehouses, in addition to his routine duties such as maintaining the nursery, caring for the farm animals, and keeping constant watch over the pond, dam, and turbine that supplied the house with electricity.[1]

If the planning and work on the grounds seemed complex because of Olmstead's expensive approach, Logan's limited imagination, and Reid's distance from the scene, those operations seemed to be models of simplicity when compared with the problems encountered in finishing the interior of the main house. In contrast with the outside work, which was well advanced when Reid left New York, the interior was almost untouched.[2] The firm of McKim, Meade, and White, in charge of alterations at Ophir and also at the Madison Avenue house, was a large one with many specialists. Reid in Paris consulted by mail directly with individuals at all levels, including subcontractors, about details of both projects. His father-in-law made occasional suggestions, and Lizzie was as particular as her husband in matters in which she was interested.[3]

Mills' ideas sometimes offered great challenges. Early in January 1890, he suggested that the drawing room at 451 Madison Avenue would not only be quite appropriate at Ophir, but that if it were moved, the way would be open for putting a finer room in the town house. Reid sometimes argued with Lizzie but never with her father. He shivered at the thought of the expense, having discovered that Stanford White was no more economical than Olmstead, but he did not oppose the plan directly.[4] However, with his wife's cooperation, he found a suitable alternative in a Louis XIV room in a chateau near Paris. This was moved to Ophir as the drawing room at a cost of nearly ten thousand dollars, plus another four thousand for a small adjoining sitting room in the same style. The Reids located the Louis XIV room, purchased it through Jules Allard et Fils, and sent Allard to New York to install it, complete with lighting and yellow satin draperies.[5] Reid thought himself, he told his father-in-law ruefully, somewhat in the position of a man who bought a pair of fine new andirons and ended by building a new house to put them in.[6] From time to time the Reids acquired and sent to New York less elaborate art and decorative materials from Germany and Italy as well as from elsewhere in France. Once the decision was made not to move the drawing room, changes in the Madison Avenue house were slight. In general, Reid wanted the house to reflect his ownership and to diminish the Villard influence somewhat. To this end he planned replacement of some Latin inscriptions over doorways and in mantles with inscriptions in English.[7]

Reid's other real estate responsibilities gave little trouble while he was in France. Fred Barnes cared for the Adirondack camp, Wild Air, even to looking after tax payments. William Conley watched over the several small pieces of land in the Xenia and Cedarville vicinity, including the farm where Reid's mother lived. Two ten-acre plots in the Palisades area that Reid had bought as a speculation long before needed no care, and Nathaniel Tuttle paid the taxes from Reid's *Tribune* account.[8]

As he prepared to depart for France, Reid had anticipated less difficulty because of being away from the *Tribune* than from his houses. He had no John Hay to leave in charge this time, however, and he watched the paper more closely than he had on his less extended absence eight years earlier. Donald Nicholson, with Reid's firm backing, sought to keep the paper from losing ground in the owner's absence. The staff respected the kindly Welshman and cooperated with him; only Smalley attempted to take advantage of the proprietor's absence. When the paper's London representative extended his vacations and began using his letters to the *Tribune* to chronicle the goings and comings of his friends in a way that Reid would not have permitted, Nicholson complained. Reid told Nicholson to work it out himself, making it clear that Smalley would get no support from Paris.[9] In one area, however, Nicholson had very little room for judgments: the *Tribune* was not to be used as a vehicle for criticism of France.

Reid had been in Paris less than two months when one Félix Aucaigne, a French acquaintance living in New York, complained to him of anti-French articles in the *Tribune*. The editor told Aucaigne that when he accepted the post in France, he gave up all connection with the editorial policies of the paper. He then wrote to Nicholson, telling him flatly that Isaac Ford, who had written the offending material, should omit comments to which sensitive Frenchmen might object. Later articles by Ford contained adverse comments on Georges Clemenceau and other French leaders, and the American minister at once ordered that the reporter not discuss French politics at all—or even French topics.[10] On the positive side Nicholson did not lack for suggestions from Paris about subjects that were suitable. When the count of Paris visited New York, Reid warned against any sympathy for the count's political aspirations, but encouraged stories about the old soldier of the Army of the Potomac and historian of the Civil War; when the Marquis de Chambrun, husband of Lafayette's granddaughter, wrote a book about the United States, the *Tribune* was told to give it some attention; when a prominent American was barred from French tracks for having his jockey pull a horse, the American minister instructed his paper about how to handle the story. Nicholson attended to all instructions and suggestions. Nor did he miss the hints. He sent Ford to Brazil and replaced him with the more circumspect William McPherson.[11]

The editor's new position, his first public office, affected his perspective in other ways at times. Before he had been in Paris a year, Reid had extended his long-held objections to personal criticism of editors to exclude adverse comment about their papers. He emphasized to the *Tribune* staff that the *Herald*, *World*, and other dailies should not be identified as the sources of stories the *Tribune* castigated. Criticism of a scurrilous news item was proper, he said, but there was no need to offend the paper in which it appeared. Individuals, even including Democratic senators, could be treated as gentlemen although their words or actions might well demand critical attention. On one occasion Reid wired Nicholson peremptorily to stop publishing attacks on John R. McLean, a Washington journalist and an old Ohio compatriot.[12] At times he went to unusual lengths to avoid giving offense. On one occasion Max Seckendorff, head of the *Tribune*'s Washington Bureau, scored the Pension Office so severely that President Harrison became upset. He sent his secretary to demand the name of the person who had supplied the data for the article. Seckendorff in accord with well-established journalistic practice refused to reveal his source. Nicholson did not interfere. Russell Harrison, the president's son, thereupon wrote to Paris. Reid, in a move that once would have been completely out of character, recommended that Seckendorff call at the White House and, after fully explaining the nature of pledges given to news sources, reveal the name of the man who had furnished the information in question.[13]

These editorial policies and practices represented some departure from previous ones, but they in no way affected the circulation or income of the *Tribune* during Reid's term in France.[14] At the end of 1889 the paper showed a profit that was more than 25 percent above that of 1888. Most of the increase was from savings on Reid's salary, which was not paid during his ministry, and from an increase in government advertising. However, general advertising was also increased, and rentals in the *Tribune* Building were improved.[15]

The pleasant sound of his news was marred by only one ominous note, but that fell on Reid's ear without noticeable effect. In April 1891 the *Tribune* celebrated its semicentennial anniversary at a meeting at the Metropolitan Opera House with appropriate speeches and ceremonies. Henry Hall reported to his employer the peculiar feeling he had while standing at the entrance to the Opera House and actually seeing three thousand *Tribune* readers in the flesh enter the auditorium. He was struck by the elderly complexion of the crowd. The only young men who came, he said, were especially invited. The situation boded ill for the future of the *Tribune*, Hall thought, but Reid was not bothered. He was pleased at the dignity of the occasion, with its advertising value, and at the treatment accorded the event by the *Herald* and *Sun*.[16]

Of a different order of importance and of far more concern to the absent editor than Hall's thoughts on the celebration or even the favorable financial reports was the perennial problem of the *Tribune*'s friction with New York Typographical Union No. 6. The conflict that had begun in the mid-seventies had continued with few periods of peace and with little real possibility of solution. But discussion, never completely broken off, continued after Reid left for France, and early in 1891 the union president set down what he considered a reasonable basis for settlement. Reid considered the terms quite droll.[17] He was willing to pay union wages and he was willing to employ union printers. But he flatly refused to countenance a closed shop with the *Tribune* rooms open only to members of "Big Six." This to Reid meant turning the management of his printing over to inexperienced and irresponsible persons and his desertion of long-faithful employees who would be forced into the union whether they wanted to join or not. Reid also held steadfastly to the position he had taken when he first acquired the Mergenthaler machines: that the *Tribune* employed linotype operators and not printers in the composing rooms and that the union scales for printers were, therefore, inappropriate. It was his considered opinion that his position was unassailable and that the union was asking for unwarranted and undeserved rights and privileges. Yet he understood the difficulties in the way of a meeting of minds in the atmosphere of mutual distrust. This thing has always been "as ticklish to handle as nitroglycerine" he told Nicholson.[18]

It was especially ticklish after Reid's appointment to an important government post. As on previous occasions, John E. Milholland of the *Tribune* staff acted as mediator. In this instance the astute and versatile Milholland worked with Reid by correspondence, with the union leaders through Nicholson, and with New York politicos. By the end of September 1891 negotiations had progressed so satisfactorily that Milholland sailed for France to try to persuade Reid to put his signature on an agreement that would bring peace between organized labor and the national administration's chief voice in New York.[19]

But a memorandum from Nathaniel Tuttle, the *Tribune*'s cashier,

129

reached Paris before the mediator did, and it nullified whatever concessions Milholland might later have been authorized to make. For Tuttle's analysis indicated that an adjustment on the union's terms would burden the *Tribune* with six hundred dollars a week in increased costs at the outset. Reid thought the figure would go to a thousand dollars a week before the proposed agreement with the union had been in effect six months and that discussions on this basis were out of the question.[20] Milholland returned to New York, and Reid warned Nicholson to be ready for any emergency, pointing out specific dangers that might be imminent. The untrustworthy Thomas C. Platt was in communication with the union leaders, he said. The *Tribune* should prepare for a strike by stockpiling miscellaneous matter, perhaps a hundred columns, and if necessary the paper could be reduced to eight pages for a time. Subscription room and business office clerks, even the younger editorial and city men, ought to be trained to operate the machines in an emergency. There was to be no surrender, whatever the cost.[21]

At the same time Reid wrote in what he considered a conciliatory tone to William J. Brennan, president of No. 6. The union had left the paper of its own free will fifteen years earlier, the editor said. The *Tribune* held no grievance and in employment policies had followed the precepts of the first president of Typographical Union No. 6, the revered Horace Greeley. Reid went on to tell Brennan that they were in agreement on the union's chief objective, that of keeping wages up, but the paper could not turn over the management of a large number of complex machines to men who not only could not operate them properly but had already denounced them as failures. Reid entrusted a copy of this letter to Milholland, now back in New York, along with further arguments against the union proposals.[22]

The impasse reached in the fall of 1891 did not halt discussion. Political leaders were increasingly concerned. In October Sen. Frank Hiscock sent Reid a note asking for a contribution to the Republican campaign fund, and he used the occasion to urge Reid's acceptance of the union's offer. Hiscock's note by chance juxtaposed points that Reid had come to associate in his thinking: campaign contributions, wage levels, and the high costs to him of buying union support for the Republican party. He sent Hiscock fifteen hundred dollars, increasing his previous year's contribution by half, and at the same time used the opportunity to make his point to the New York senator. The union plan, he told Hiscock, would cost the *Tribune* thirty thousand dollars a year for an indefinite period. What other person in New York, he demanded, was expected to make such a contribution?[23] Reid's unwillingness to accept the burden was strengthened by his conviction that the real political influence, in votes, of the union was of little significance.[24] Negotiations continued throughout Reid's term as minister to France without a settlement.

A lengthy controversy of another kind came to a head while Reid was in France. It paralleled his conflict with the typographical union and illustrated the point that the ramifications of the uncooperative relationship extended beyond controlling the composing rooms. A month after Greeley's death a committee with W. W. Niles as chairman, E. C. Stedman as secretary, and Reid as one of some sixty-five members had been established to collect funds for a memorial. Nearly three thousand dollars had been sent to Reid in 1873, more had later been sent to the *Tribune* office, and some to the committee, but the fund had grown slowly. With the depression following the panic of 1873, contributions had virtually ceased and the committee gradually dissolved. Reid held the sums he had collected and those sent to the *Tribune* at interest. He renewed the project in 1879 and 1880 but did not revive the committees. In 1881 he commissioned John Quincy Adams Ward for a fee of $13,500 to design and model a suitable statue to be completed in two years. Others also chose the popular sculptor for various art projects, and he received half a dozen major commissions and some minor ones while he was designing and executing the Greeley statue. For reasons of his own, Ward gave this assignment a very low priority and work proceeded at a snail's pace.

The statue was still unfinished in November 1887 when W. W. Niles undertook to revive the old committee of 1873 and to renew the effort to provide a memorial for Greeley. He seemed unaware of the Ward project, but Reid soon informed him that plans to make and place the statue were far advanced. In the following year officers of Typographical Union No. 6, apparently oblivious that anyone had thought seriously of a tribute to the union's first president, decided to correct the oversight. Early in 1889, their preliminary plans well under way, the union's officers learned of Reid's project and of Niles's committee. When approached, the latter readily agreed to cooperate with the printers, and the combined groups contracted with Alexander Doyle to execute a statue of Greeley, ignoring Ward's work. The printers now suggested that the combined groups take over the funds Reid had been holding, which they seemed to think had been gathering dust for some time. The scheme became known to Reid early in January 1890, when George Jones printed the union version of a fair method of uniting Doyle's vigorous but weakly financed plans with Reid's seemingly stalled but monetarily solid project. Added strength and interest had accrued to the proposal when Big Six was joined in its program by Brooklyn Typographical Union No. 98 and by Horace Greeley Post No. 577, GAR, a veteran's organization composed of union printers.[25] Reid, not embarrassed but under some pressure, was grateful when James Gordon Bennett came to his aid. Bennett offered Reid the *Herald* as a medium for replying to the printers. The minister simply said that he had been acting for a group of Greeley's admirers, had long held the statue funds at interest, that after some delays excellent progress was being made on a worthy memorial, and that he wished the printers success in their own undertaking. Bennett, at his friend's request, left the report out of his Paris and London editions, printing it only in his New York paper. Nicholson copied the report in the *Tribune*.[26]

At this juncture Reid expected Ward to have his model cast in bronze and ready for unveiling in time to be included with observances of the *Tribune*'s fiftieth anniversary, and the minister intended to go to New York to attend the ceremonies. He had been anxious for some time to visit his mother, then eighty-six, who had had a fall both painful and distressing. Of another order of importance was the urgent need to confer with Stanford White, Frederick Law Olmstead, James M. Logan, and others about the progress of work at Ophir Farm. And, of course, a visit to the United States would provide an opportunity for talks with the president and secretary of state about Franco-American relations.[27]

Early in the year the minister announced his intention of visiting the United States in April. He pressed Ward for progress reports on the statue, on the design of a pedestal to be done by Richard Hunt, and on the placing of inscriptions. The sculptor assured him that all went well.[28]

Mrs. Reid preceded her husband to New York to have a longer visit, arriving late in February. The minister followed a month later, only to find that problems involved in making a bronze cast of Ward's model were so complex that the project had to be postponed for an indefinite period. Reid was nettled and wondered if other unsuspected mishaps had occurred. He asked Nicholson to work up a full history of the Greeley memorial project, including agreements, penalties, committee members' names, work of chairmen, and financial statements.[29] He was further disgruntled when the printers attempted to exploit this new setback and again approached him about uniting their memorial plans and his funds. This, Reid said, he was perfectly willing to do. He told Murat Halstead, who had presented the printers' suggestion, that the union had only to accept Ward's design for "the finest sitting statue yet made in America," Hunt's pedestal, and Reid's inscription. He would even give the printers a voice in selecting a site, he continued, as long as it was in or facing Printing House Square and if Ward and Hunt approved. Reid then wrote to Ward and told him, without mentioning Halstead, about the correspondence. "I take it for granted neither you nor Hunt" will agree to any site other than the one already selected, he said. "I write you confidentially. . . . Please do not give anyone the idea you have consulted with me."[30]

Reid's tactics were not necessary. The union's errors in assuming that Ward would not complete his figure and that Reid could be persuaded to help finance the Doyle statue were enough to assure failure of the attempt to unite the two memorial projects. Thus Greeley, perhaps because he had bequeathed some of his own inability to cooperate both to his followers in the composing room and to his successor in the editor's chair, had two important statues in his memory. The *Tribune*-sponsored memorial was unveiled in September 1890. In his absence Reid put the arrangements in Nicholson's hands, making few suggestions beyond selecting the date for the occasion. He chose September 20, the date of the first issue of the weekly *Tribune*.[31] As the day approached, fearful of another last-minute hitch, he cabled his brother-in-law and requested that he supervise the final plans. There was no hitch. John Hay, acting for Reid, presided and introduced Chauncey Depew, the orator of the occasion. Gabrielle Greeley, the founder's daughter, pulled a string that removed an American flag and at long last revealed Ward's work to the public.[32]

Four days before the ceremonies in front of the *Tribune* Building developments in the West threatened more trouble than the union had caused. The danger came suddenly and with little warning. When Reid left for Paris in May 1889, the *Tribune*'s connections with wire service news sources were the strongest and most productive in the paper's history. This situation was a result of the effective working of the New York Associated Press and the Western Associated Press under the direction of the Joint Executive Committee, an arrangement begun in 1882, and of agreements between the committee and the United Press made in 1885, 1887, and 1888.[33]

The arrangements were highly valuable to Reid, Dana, Haldeman, and others of the Joint Executive Committee, but some directors of the Western Associated Press, because of territorial overlapping, felt that their best interests were not served by the UP contract. They called on their general manager, William Henry Smith, for a detailed statement of relations between the UP and the other associations. Smith's report, submitted September 16, 1890, was seemingly complete, but the directors felt that important factors remained unrevealed. They appointed a committee, headed by Victor Lawson of the *Chicago Daily News*, long prominent in the Western AP, to confer with the directors of the New York AP and with those of the UP and to recommend modifications in the contract if it seemed necessary.[34]

Reid quickly learned of Smith's report and later heard of the appointment of Lawson's committee. Early in February 1891 he became aware that Lawson was not friendly toward the AP-UP alliance, but it was not until April that he learned of the depth and extent of the investigation.[35] Lawson seemed to be bent on destroying the Joint Executive Committee as the directing force in the cooperative efforts of the press associations, on ousting the general manager of the Western AP and replacing him with Lawson's old associate Melville Stone, and on breaking the connection between the Western AP and the other organizations.[36]

Far away and involved with many other matters, Reid at first was unconcerned about the developments in Chicago, but as he learned of the strength of Lawson's movement he became disturbed. He queried Dana, also in Europe, about the possibilities. Dana was very pessimistic. He had been in touch with Haldeman and Richard Smith and found them ready to throw in the sponge. Dana recommended that they not only return the UP stock obtained from John Walsh when the original arrangements had been made, but that all dividends the members of the Joint Executive Committee had received over the preceding seven years also be returned. This action would dissolve the trust, Dana thought, and clear the way for him to resign, along with Reid and the others, before they were all turned out. Melville Stone, Dana continued, had shown that Lawson's group was strong enough to force all of these moves if it so chose.[37]

Reid thought Dana too timid. He sent the pessimistic estimate to Nicholson, who was acting as Reid's representative on the Joint Executive Committee, and cautioned him to take no steps unless forced to do so. Reid had little sympathy with the notion of surrendering the stock or the dividends. Nor did he relish relinquishing his place on the Joint Executive Committee. Above all he objected to the replacement of his old and trusted colleague William Henry Smith as general manager of the powerful press association by the "Venomous Mugwump" Melville Stone. Nevertheless, knowing that Dana was no alarmist and respecting his judgment, Reid wrote out a letter of resignation and sent it to Nicholson to be used only if necessary. He also instructed his deputy to calculate the exact amount of the dividends that would have to be repaid in the event of total defeat.[38]

Victor Lawson and his committee worked diligently for nearly a year and submitted their report at the annual meeting of the Western Associated Press at Detroit, August 18, 1891. As foreseen, he recommended that Haldeman and both Smiths resign, that the UP stock and accrued dividends be recovered, and that the tripartite contract among the New York Associated Press, the Western Associated Press, and the United Press be abrogated. Lawson carried the day in his own organization, and a new board of directors, one that he headed, was chosen to govern the Western AP.[39]

When Reid learned of these developments his attitude remained unchanged. He again consulted Dana, urging caution, while indicating his willingness to consider a *Sun-Tribune* alliance, to include the *Herald* or *World* or both, to continue the essential elements of the old AP arrangements minus Haldeman and Richard Smith but retaining William Henry Smith in a responsible office.[40] The *Tribune*'s editor plainly wanted to eat his cake and have it too. He did not intend to leave the AP. The odium of stepping out of that highly respected organization that he had been instrumental in developing to enter the newly organized, second-class United Press was distasteful. He predicted that secession would mean a long and costly war, with the risk of great loss and with nothing to gain that the Joint Executive Committee did not already have. Finally, he believed that political considerations motivated some of the interested individuals. Bennett, Joseph Pulitzer, Stone, and George Jones, he thought, were partially if not primarily interested in removing the staunchly Republican William Henry Smith.[41] In short Reid opposed surrender and favored some sort of compromise.

His fears did not convince Dana that to come to terms with the new status quo was the lesser evil, and in December the *Sun* withdrew from the New York Associated Press, and Dana left the Joint Executive Committee. Had Bennett been willing to go with Dana, Reid would have added the *Tribune* in a three-paper effort to establish a new association, which could have taken over most of the services and clients of the old one. But he was unwilling, though strongly tempted, to join in a *Sun-Tribune* venture without the *Herald*. The move seemed too hazardous to make without careful analysis on the ground. He could not go to New York, and Ogden Mills, who was there, would not recommend a positive move.[42] Reid therefore did nothing. When Lawson and his friends forced the abrogation of the old contracts and reconstituted and enlarged the Joint Executive Committee, they retained Reid as a member, albeit with considerably less influence than he had enjoyed under earlier arrangements.

Having lost the battle, Reid adjusted his position to conform with the new alignments. The *Tribune*, he told Nicholson, was now to cooperate with the new committee in all ways and should make no objections to new policies except on strictly legal grounds. At the same time he warned that a careful watch must be kept on the ways in which the changed circumstances affected the *Tribune*.[43]

Reid's most important business interest in New York, after the *Tribune*, gave him less bother while he was in Paris than any of his other affairs in America. During his ministry to France the Mergenthaler Printing Company was reorganized, new stock was issued in exchange for the old, a new general manager was appointed, and changes were made in the operation of the company. Reid watched with interest but without concern, even when he disapproved of some moves, for the company was now being directed by D. O. Mills, his son Ogden, and their friend William C. Whitney, men so prestigiously talented financially that few would care to challenge a decision they made. Reid readily gave them the support of his voting strength but he bowed to no man or combination of men in his confidence in his own judgment. Among the extensive changes made while he was away, he opposed only the appointment of a general manager from the Washington group of stockholders in the company. "Washington is a sort of village, where everybody knows everybody, and is under all sorts of personal obligations," he warned his father-in-law. They are more interested in finding places for each other than in sound business, he thought, and they try to make money by roping in other people, holding stock on thin margins, and trusting that some clever scheme will send the price up. Reid wanted a shrewd and driving New York or Boston man in charge but had no candidate in mind, and when the Millses gave the general managership to P. T. Dodge of the Washington group Reid acquiesced without further protest.[44] His only other concern about the company was that his side not be outvoted. He took to Paris, besides his own stock, certificates representing some five hundred shares registered in various names, mostly those of *Tribune* staff members. This was de facto Reid's stock. He held proxies for voting it, and he saw to it that when calls were made, the shares that stood in others' names were paid for in the registered names but at varied times to avoid giving the impression that one office handled all the transactions. Reid also instructed Tuttle to pay the calls a little later than due, "after the fashion of our Washington friends."[45]

A special stimulus for Reid's interest in the growth of the company was provided by Jacob Bright, the English industrialist, who became interested in the linotype and formed a company in 1889 to introduce the machines on his side of the Atlantic. This enterprising group at once sought testimonials from those who had developed the company, including the American minister to France, as to the efficiency and performance of Ottmar Mergenthaler's invention. The Englishmen first asked for an extraordinarily sweeping endorsement that Reid peremptorily refused. Then they sought a statement that would demonstrate the great savings made in the *Tribune*'s composing room, to be shown only to the English board of directors. When this was denied, Jacob Bright himself asked Reid for a private estimate that would never be made public. Reid still balked. He recalled that he had exposed in the *Tribune* fifteen years earlier the misfortunes that had befallen Gen. Robert C. Schenck, a fellow Ohioan and Miami University alumnus, whose connection with the Emma Silver Mine venture while minister to Great Britain had caused a scandal. While the linotype was no Emma Mine stock jobbery, Reid feared that his English friends had prepared a situation for him that included too many elements of the earlier disaster. He therefore cautioned his lieutenants in New York to give the English group needed information only as long as his own position was not compromised and the *Tribune*'s profit and loss columns were not exposed to outside viewers.[46]

II

Minister to France:
Franco-American Diplomacy

REID'S main accomplishments while American minister to France were almost completely separated from the routine administrative duties of the legation as well as from the potentially more exotic negotiations for naval bases in Africa. While in Paris he succeeded in settling a long-pending controversy about American pork, in making a reciprocity agreement, and in concluding an extradition treaty. The most pressing problem and the one of most concern to the Harrison administration was the unhappy position of the American hog in French markets. No situation with which Reid had to deal as minister was more trying or difficult than that of France's prohibition against imports of United States pork, an American export of growing importance in centers of strong Republican leanings. The discrimination had existed for ten years and had been the subject of unsuccessful negotiation by Levi Morton and Robert M. McLane, who served as ministers to France from 1881 until 1889.[1] Secretary of State James G. Blaine called Reid's attention to the matter soon after the latter's arrival in Paris. Blaine sent a resolution of protest against the prohibition from the Chicago Board of Trade, suggested that Reid review the correspondence in his legation in order to appreciate the magnitude of the question, and pointed out that American packers were lobbying for retaliatory legislation against France. At the same time the secretary warned that, while justice was expected from France, the minister was not to threaten retaliation.[2] As Reid viewed the matter on his arrival, it was fairly simple. In 1881 a series of scares about trichinosis had resulted in France's prohibiting all imports of American pork on the ground that it was unsanitary. Similar prohibitions soon followed in Austria-Hungary, Turkey, Germany, and Greece, lending strength to the French position.[3] Nevertheless, proof that Frenchmen had been infected by the disease was nebulous, and Reid believed the allegation had virtually no foundation. He had no doubt that he could persuade the French to lift the decree of prohibition.

Further resolutions and communications from American packers and shippers were soon added to those of the Chicago Board of Trade, and during the fall of 1889 Reid discussed France's policy with the French minister of foreign affairs. The talks convinced the American minister that France was favorably inclined toward removing the prohibition. At the same time Reid came to understand that exclusion was no longer on purely sanitary grounds but that French protectionism had become a significant factor.[4]

While Harrison's appointee undertook the task of increasing Franco-American good will and improving commerce, Harrison's party undertook the task of preparing legislation that was to have far-reaching repercussions on American relations with all countries. For the first time since the election of 1874 the Republicans had majorities in both the House and Senate and controlled the executive department. The new administration interpreted the election of 1888 as a mandate to revise the tariff schedules upward and to enlarge the list of protected articles. To this end Congressman William McKinley, high priest of protectionism and chairman of the House Committee on Ways and Means, began active work on legislation that came to be known as the McKinley Act. The committee commenced its work in December 1889 and prepared both an administrative bill and a new set of tariff schedules. The committee completed the first of these in the spring, and the president signed it on June 10, 1890. The administrative act established a board of appraisers, which it empowered to classify and appraise imported goods. McKinley reported the tariff bill proper on April 16, 1890, and five days later the House passed it by a party vote of 164 to 142. The Senate considered the legislation at some length, and passage was delayed there until September. President Harrison signed the bill on October 1.[5]

Reid, during a quick trip home early in 1890, was in Washington in March and April as the tariff bill was being put in final shape for reporting to the House. While he was in America, a new French minister of foreign affairs was appointed. Alexander Félix Joseph Ribot, like his predecessor, was friendly toward policies favorable to a well-developed Franco-American trade. Like the American minister, he was a staunch protectionist. At the same time, both Reid and Ribot deplored the work on both sides of the Atlantic of extreme enthusiasts for protection, that might result in a lessening of trade. In France some chambers of commerce, a number of commission merchants, and a few deputies had become alarmed even before the new American tariff was out of committee, and a clamor arose for retaliation against American goods because of the drastic schedules in the McKinley bill. Under these circumstances Ribot asked Reid's personal good offices to bring about amendments to the McKinley bill, and Reid, while in Washington, urged his friends in Congress to consider France's position. At the same time the House moved to put works of art on the free list, and Reid's friends in the Senate promised to help. The possibility of these concessions led Ribot to move toward dropping the prohibition against American pork.[6]

Thus when Reid returned to France in late April 1890, several influences not previously present affected the pending discussions. The gains he had made while in Washington were only beginnings, and he found the French highly disgruntled. The rates in the tariff bill as passed by the House were held to be injurious to French commerce. In addition the administrative (Custom House) bill, supposedly designed to prevent fraud, was so framed that it penalized the honest merchant and insulted French traders by imputing fraudulent intent to all French exporters. If further proof were needed to convince wavering French legislators of American perfidy, Congress provided it by acting adversely on a bill long desired by European intellectuals to respect foreign copyrights in the United States. Reid, then, found the French skeptical about American commercial policy and prepared to use the American desire to be rid of the pork prohibition law as a lever with which to pry obnoxious schedules out of the McKinley bill. When Reid mentioned pork, Ribot talked of the McKinley bill.[7] It was also clear to the American minister that French protectionists would use the high American rates, especially those on pork, to justify high French rates on United States pork, which would make meaningless a removal of the prohibition. He hoped, however, that the protectionists would not have their way, and in the late summer of 1890 he believed that a low duty of perhaps twelve francs per hundred kilograms was a distinct possibility. Therefore his objective became the speedy removal of the prohibition.[8]

Reid attacked the prohibition per se, as economically harmful to the French consumer. He sought to block French use of the McKinley bills as weapons by working through Blaine, McKinley, and friends in the Senate to lower some rates applicable to French products. He combatted French indignation over the duties on art and statuary by persuading Frank Hiscock, William E. Chandler, William M. Evarts,

John Sherman, and other senators, that the duties should be removed.[9] Nor did he fail to play upon French pride and patriotism. If the excuse for exclusion of American pork was indeed a fear of trichinosis, such a stand was unworthy of Frenchmen, he said. "If it were a question of importation among a nation of savages where pork is eaten raw, there might be a valid reason for its exclusion, but not in the nation that marches at the head of the civilization of Europe."[10] Besides, the Germans had seen the error of prohibition and would soon end their exclusion. Did France intend to permit Germany to lead in ending the injustice done France's historic friend? He next looked for some ground on which to stand in order to bargain more effectively with French legislators who might not be moved by pride or logic, and found it in a principle Blaine was urging. Blaine's Latin American trade and friendship program was also threatened by the McKinley bill. The secretary was pressing for a reciprocity clause in the McKinley bill that would exempt American countries from some of the new duties.[11] Without entering the lists for or against reciprocity, an exceedingly touchy subject within the administration, Reid seized upon the idea of granting special concessions to France in exchange for special treatment. He avoided use of the word "reciprocity," referring instead to "permissive legislation" giving the president power to raise or lower duties in response to foreign tariff practices. The minister coupled this soft approach with its obvious counterpart—a hint of retaliation, preferably against French wine—if the pork prohibition were continued. These considerations were backed with hard facts of economic analysis. The minister argued, and supported his arguments with figures, that the prohibition had cost France heavily. The treasury had lost revenues by not collecting duties on the importation of pork, shippers had been deprived of freight, grocers and country peddlers had been deprived of useful trade, laboring classes had been deprived of a cheap article of food. These losses were not accompanied by better health, higher prices for farmers, or lower prices for consumers. The only gains had gone to the French butcher, or merchandiser, who was generally regarded, Reid thought, as a wealthy plutocrat whose further enrichment was not essential to French progress.[12]

Reid put these arguments, considerations, and hints in a carefully written twenty-five-hundred-word dispatch, addressed to Ribot but intended for a far wider audience. He expected Ribot to show it to Jules

Roche, who was minister of commerce, to the ministers of the interior and of agriculture, to Félix Jules Méline, president of the commission on the budget, and to other officials. As a matter of routine the minister sent a copy of the dispatch to the State Department with a covering letter. In addition Reid sent to Blaine a second copy, enclosed in a private letter, and asked that Blaine show it to President Harrison. Reid further suggested that Blaine send the dispatch to the Senate, partly to promote the idea of favorable tariff rates for French products but chiefly in order that it might become public and so be given to the press. To make certain that the press handled the matter properly in Washington, Reid sent a third copy of the dispatch to M. G. Seckendorff, the *Tribune*'s Washington correspondent, "in strictest confidence." Warning Seckendorff not to utter a whisper until there was distinct authority from the State Department, Reid explained the purpose of the dispatch and told his correspondent to use his copy to gain wide, prompt, and correct publication.[13] Donald Nicholson was the recipient of a fourth copy of the dispatch for use in the *Tribune*. Reid instructed Nicholson that on receipt of information that the dispatch was available to the press, he was to take pains with it and have it conspicuously and correctly printed—"minion lead for the first half column or more and minion lead after every cross head." The proprietor of the *Tribune*, always thorough, did not neglect to include hints for use in editorials.[14]

Reid carefully explained to Blaine that the time was ripe for gaining a definite commitment from the French government. He mentioned several minor tariff amendments and administrative regulations which might be employed as means of persuading France to cooperate.

The plan worked as its author had intended. In the State Department assistant secretaries Alvey Adee and William F. Wharton sent copies of the dispatch to the secretary of the treasury, the Tariff Commission, the Senate Committee on Finance, and to McKinley's House Committee on Ways and Means.[15] With Blaine's encouragement, the Senate called for the pork correspondence. The resulting public release included most of the written exchanges relating to pork and to the tariff between the two governments from July 1889 to July 1890. Thanks to Reid's preparations, Seckendorff and Nicholson did not wonder how to handle the mass of papers or which of Reid's many letters to Ribot to emphasize. When the *Tribune*'s eighty thousand readers picked up their papers on August 16, they found Reid's dispatch in two full columns, beginning on page one. Turning to the editorial page the readers were treated to a half-column appreciation of "Minister Reid's Strong Letter." The factual report and the editorial were followed the next day by Seckendorff's interpretative account of the developments. In his account Seckendorff turned Reid's gentle hint of a duty on wines into a prediction of retaliation against wines, silks, sardines, and other French products if France persisted in prohibiting American pork.[16] As Reid had foreseen, French papers took the story from America. The *Journal des Debats*, *Paris*, *La Lanterne*, *Figaro*, *Le Moniteur Universel*, *XIXe Siècle*, *Le Temps*, and others considered the pork prohibition and opposed its continuation.[17]

Reid felt at the time and believed later that the battle against French prohibition of American pork was won by September 1890. The French government was convinced that the policy should be abandoned; leading French newspapers agreed with the *Tribune*'s judgment that the prohibition was unwise. American leaders were ready to make some concessions to regain entrance to French ports for the product. Only a slight push was now needed, and to furnish it Reid put forward the pending American Meat Inspection bill. The legislation, if passed, would destroy arguments that American pork entering France was impure. For the act provided a special sanitary inspection system in the United States that would examine all outgoing pork for trichinosis and other diseases. Ribot considered this act of crucial importance to the success of a recommendation, which the government was now ready to make, that the Chambers permit the prohibition to be dropped. The recommendation would be accompanied by a proposal that a low duty be placed on American pork entering France.[18]

Any victory celebration, however, was premature. On October 1 the McKinley tariff went into effect. Its repercussions in France were not immediately disruptive, for the new rates on wines, textiles, and other French exports were known in advance and had already been condemned in all quarters. Nevertheless, knowledge that the obnoxious schedules were actually in effect weakened Reid's carefully built-up position as a friend of French commerce. As the Chambers considered the government's recommendation against continuance of prohibition, the McKinley tariff became a center of attention. French protectionists found it the perfect tool needed to fashion a high schedule of rates for French products.

France first felt the McKinley bill directly through a United States Treasury circular, issued October 17 under Section 20 of the new act, forbidding the importation of French hides unless accompanied by certificates of disinfection. Various diseases among French cattle were alleged. The circular did not make any new French friends for Reid. In November another blow was dealt the minister's hopes for an early resumption of American pork exports to France by American voters, for the Republicans were soundly beaten at the polls. As the tariff had been an issue, Frenchmen seized upon the results of the election as an indication that the hated tariff would be repealed.[19]

The Chambers then made it clear that it would not act on the pork bills before Congress met. The American minister took advantage of the opportunity for a vacation. He made an extended trip through the Middle East, visiting Vienna, Constantinople, Jerusalem, Cairo, and other places of interest and making an ascent of the Nile. The trip was mainly for relaxation and pleasure rather than for reasons of health. He had had a flare-up of his asthmatic trouble in the preceding summer. His doctors put him on a restricted diet for several weeks, under which he lost weight and had "spells of suffocation." The difficulties were largely over by October, and he suffered no further serious attacks during his mission to France.[20]

On his return from Egypt early in 1891 Reid found that the McKinley tariff had become a major obstacle, one that threatened to halt the progress of his negotiations. "You are right," he told John W. Foster in July 1891, "as to my having been fearfully handicapped" by the bill.[21] A survey of French sentiment in the spring of 1891 convinced him that removal of the prohibition, an objective he had thought certainly attainable a year earlier, was now endangered by increasing opposition. But the American minister had convinced the French government, and he was certain that Ribot could take the step. His principal fear was that the French Cabinet would hesitate to press for removal and fail through simple caution. At the same time and more ominously, the possibility of a low duty was becoming fainter. The Méline tariff commission, in its new schedule of rates, had recommended a duty of twenty-five francs per hundred kilos on pork, double the figure Reid had considered the highest possible levy that would still permit imports from the United States.[22]

In opposing the high rates, the American minister intensified his earlier appeals and emphasized especially the new Meat Inspection Act. This legislation received Harrison's signature on March 2, 1891. Reid believed that if it had come six months earlier it might well have turned the trick, but resentment against the McKinley Act was too strong in March of 1891. The Congress also finally passed a copyright bill in March, the first effective American law of its nature, one embodying some principles long desired by French literary and artistic groups. If the Meat Inspection Act was too late, the copyright bill was too little—it did not provide for artists' rights to painting and sculpture, nor for free entry of art works.[23]

When the Chambers acted on the new budget proposals, it set a 20-franc tariff on pork, thereby tacitly approving the removal of the prohibition. When the Senate took up the matter, it quickly accepted the new tariff in principle and immediately raised the figure on pork to 25 francs, despite strong efforts by Reid's friends to keep the duty down. The Chambers accepted the higher rate, and the new tariff was formally promulgated at the same time that the prohibition against American pork, after ten years of negotiation, was dropped. The American hog could move freely in the markets of France—if he could clear the tariff wall.[24]

Whitelaw Reid won his battle, but William McKinley had in effect collaborated with French protectionists and lost the war. The prohibition of American pork imports, originally a matter of sanitation, had come to be a protective device. Reid's success in bringing prohibition to an end was no mean feat. His further achievement in persuading the French government to propose a duty low enough to permit American pork to enter had been an equal triumph. The McKinley bills, however, had so alienated French legislators that they set their tariff rates too high to permit importation and so nullified the American minister's long and skillful effort to reopen trade in this product.[25]

McKinley's bills affected Franco-American commerce in areas other than the pork trade, and some of Reid's last efforts in France were concerned with the problem of making a workable reciprocity arrangement for the two countries. French procrastination made his task more onerous. It was not until late in December 1891 that the Foreign Office belatedly realized that France needed to take positive steps to protect certain of its products from ruinous competition in United States markets in 1892, when the McKinley tariff would become effective.

Taken with previous legislation, this hotly debated act, signed by President Harrison on October 1, 1890, enlarged the list of protected articles but provided for the free admission into the United States of sugar, molasses, tea, coffee, hides, and some other products. Section 3 of the act empowered the president to establish punitive duties against countries exporting these items to the United States if he considered that they did not properly reciprocate by giving American products special privileges.[26] France's concern about the possible effects on her commerce had been much lessened by the results of the voting in the United States on November 6, 1890. The election was considered in France to be virtually a popular referendum on and condemnation of the McKinley Act. Democratic strength in the House of Representatives increased from 159 to 235 as the Republican membership shrank from 166 to 88. William McKinley, author of one of the most unpopular bills his party had ever passed, lost the seat he had held for seven terms. To the pragmatic French all this strongly suggested that some of the provisions of the bill might never be put into effect.

The Foreign Office was caught unprepared, therefore, when it learned in mid-December 1891 of Harrison's intention to raise duties on the articles covered in the McKinley Act for all countries not having reciprocity agreements with the United States. Two days before Christmas the minister of foreign affairs hurriedly approached Reid, hoping to stave off the threatened blow to France's exports. Deeply involved in their own tariff rulings then before the Chambers, the French were reluctant to discuss reciprocity in December. Could France be exempted from the effects of the impending presidential proclamation, at least for a few weeks?[27] The State Department, through the voice of John W. Foster to whom Blaine had entrusted the responsibility for agreements about reciprocity, expressed its willingness to cooperate. It accepted, on December 31, a Reid-Ribot exchange of notes as evidence that "negotiations" were progressing satisfactorily. The proclamation, effective the following day, did not raise rates on French products. The Chambers passed a tariff bill in January and set February 1 as its effective date, climaxing a twenty-year effort to establish a maximum-minimum system in France.[28]

In the first ten weeks of 1892 Reid sought to complete a reciprocity agreement before the end of his mission, Ribot worked to make good his commitment to apply minimum rates to enough American products to justify continued exemption from the rates set in the McKinley bill. No major obstacles stood in the way of finding enough French exports to fulfill the requirements, yet the task of selecting specific items was no overnight exercise. Foster considered that the value of American exports entering France at a low duty should have as close a relationship as possible to the value of French goods entering the United States under the provisions of Section 3 of the McKinley bill. It quickly became apparent that French and United States figures on the values of various items in Franco-American trade in 1891, the year selected for comparison, differed markedly in some instances. Nor were matters made easier when questions were raised as to whether the reciprocal arrangements were to include the French colonies. Despite these and numerous minor irritants, the will to find a formula overcame the difficulties of projecting a trade balance, and in mid-March, nine days before he was to sail for New York, Reid reported success. The commercial agreement had been closed, he said, and only the expected approval of the Chambers was needed to make France's commitment final.[29]

In the weeks preceding his departure, as he worked desperately to conclude the reciprocity arrangement, Reid also was concerned about a pressing need to correct the unsatisfactory nature of the existing Franco-American extradition treaty. The problem had received wide attention, and progress had been made in many places. In the eighties arrangements with several countries were rewritten and some new ones were made. Treaties with Belgium, Great Britain, Italy, Spain, and the Netherlands were improved, while Columbia, Japan, and Luxembourg were added to the list of nations with which the United States had extradition agreements.[30] In the spring of 1890 Reid received instructions and full powers to begin negotiations for bringing the Franco-American accord, then more than thirty years old in its most recent form and applying to only ten crimes, more in line with the newer agreements in force with other countries. He broached the matter to the foreign minister but did not pursue it in 1890.[31]

Late in November 1891, as he was deciding to terminate his mission within a few months and in order to complete the major projects that were pending, Reid prodded the French about extradition. Ribot agreed to serious discussion of a new treaty and at once received a draft of the American proposals. Even at this stage, with a beginning barely made and notice that he would resign in February already in Harrison's hands,

Reid felt no urgency. He planned a trip to Spain and Morocco for December; Henry Vignaud and H. C. Hall, counsel of legation, could work out details of the treaty with members of the French Foreign Office during his absence, he thought.[32]

Using the existing extradition treaty with France and similar agreements with Great Britain, the Netherlands, and Spain as guides and precedents, Reid's and Ribot's assistants arrived at a memorandum of agreement. In general, the French sought to broaden the treaty provisions and lengthen the list of crimes, while the Americans wanted renewal along more conservative lines with fewer changes. Late in January Reid sent the State Department a detailed commentary on the progress of the negotiations, including a list of the departures from the first American draft. None of the thirteen articles in that draft had escaped some alteration.[33]

Negotiation moved more rapidly in February. Reid planned to sail on the twenty-seventh, but differing views about the treaty that had seemed small in the early discussions now loomed larger. Because of this and unexpected delays in the unfinished reciprocity discussions, the sailing date was put off a month, and the pace of the negotiations increased markedly as Reid and Ribot became personally active in attempts to complete the treaty. Letters and telegrams sped between Paris and Washington as Reid anxiously tried to persuade the State Department to agree to more liberal articles and the French to accept less so that he might take a signed extradition treaty home when he left France. Harrison and Blaine gave him much leeway and expressed the hope that the French minister would be expeditious enough "to give you the gratification of completing the treaty." At the same time they indicated plainly that Reid should not feel he had to remain in Paris at the expense of his own needs and plans.[34] The minister felt that his need was for a successful arrangement. In the latter stages of the negotiations he was borrowing clauses and sometimes entire articles from United States treaties with other countries in his now feverish effort to find a formula acceptable in both Washington and Paris. The final version of the extradition treaty was completed less than thirty-six hours before Reid's departure, and even then at the cost of permitting the French and English versions to differ somewhat. The treaty was signed at the French Foreign Office on March 25, and the American minister sailed on the *Gascogne* from Havre the following day with the treaty among his papers.

Reid had served his country well in France. When he went to Paris he did not expect that he would be called on for much serious work, but when he became aware that important matters in Franco-American relations needed adjustment, he moved to resolve the differences between the two countries. His work resulted in the signing of three important agreements. The minister worked easily with officials of the French Foreign Office and was highly regarded by ministers and ambassadors to France from other countries. When he returned to New York at the end of his mission he was praised by Henri de Blowitz, Paris correspondent of the *Times* (London), as one who had brought the intelligence and flexibility of the journalist to diplomacy, who combined "the useful and the ornamental," and who could discuss with the French in their own language the matters of issue between the two countries.[36]

When Reid arrived in New York, his availability for the second position on the Republican ticket in the approaching campaign had already been established. Two weeks before the minister's departure from Paris, his paper had reprinted suggestions, from the *New York Herald* and from the *Chicago Inter-Ocean*, that the *Tribune*'s owner would be a proper Republican vice-presidential nominee. A week later the *Tribune* printed items from New York, New Jersey, and Pennsylvania papers endorsing Reid's suitability as a candidate and predicting support for him if New York advanced his name in the convention. At one of the farewell banquets for the departing minister, in Paris on March 24, a speaker told the three hundred assembled notables that Reid was being called home to accept higher honors, but did not specify the nature of the coming responsibilities.[37] Much of this talk was inspired by John E. Milholland. Reid's lieutenant had worked quietly, but his efforts in the eleventh district of New York, Vice-President Levi Morton's own political district where Platt's organization was strongly entrenched, attracted the attention of Morton supporters.[38]

In the meantime, in its news stories and editorials the *Tribune* praised Harrison, ignored Morton, and portrayed Reid as a citizen of the world who was a distinguished and distinctive Republican asset. The paper reported fully on welcoming dinners given for the returned diplomat and statesman by the Ohio Society of New York, the New York Chamber of Commerce, the Lotos Club, and other friendly organizations that were attended by politically prominent eastern Republican leaders.[39]

Reid made his first overt move in the political arena at the end of April at the New York State Republican Convention, where he accepted the offer, unanimously made, of the permanent chairmanship. In his principal speech he emphasized the achievements of the Republican party and repeated its widely held conviction that real Americans, regardless of party affiliation, could only support Republicans. At the convention the president's friends, especially Chauncey Depew and Benjamin F. Tracy, worked hard among the delegates with some success. However, on Hiscock's advice they did not press for an instructed delegation, fearing that such an attempt might bring on opposition from Blaine forces.[40]

During the weeks preceding his party's national convention, Reid privately expressed doubts that Harrison would be renominated. He was especially pessimistic about the New York vote and guardedly told Stephen B. Elkins that delegates from the state were unlikely to vote for Harrison on the first ballot. Under the circumstances, Reid confided, the *Tribune* was "going as far for the President as the condition of things" in New York permitted. In some way he could not explain, he said, since he had been in France during the preceding three years, patronage in the state had gone to men who had become Harrison's opponents.[41] As Reid saw it, the "condition of things" did not exclude consistent praise for Harrison and his administration. "Not since 1864 have there been three years more honorable to the country . . . than the last three, or more fruitful in wise legislation," the editorial columns proclaimed. Harrison could easily defeat any Democratic nominee, the paper insisted repeatedly. At the same time Reid's organ refrained from recommending that the president be renominated, then piously told the nation that the selection of a candidate was in the hands of the delegates who would represent the party at its national convention. More revealing was the absence of any reference to Morton. If readers of the *Tribune* had not known who Harrison's vice-president was, they would not have learned it from the editorial pages of Reid's paper from the time of his last weeks in France, early in 1892, to the opening of the national convention in Minneapolis in June.[42]

While Republicans from over the nation, including New York's seventy-two uninstructed delegates, converged on Minneapolis, Blaine resigned his position as the head of Harrison's cabinet. The possibility of major realignments at the convention loomed with the news of the event.

151

Various and conflicting speculations about Blaine's motives arose at once. He was in poor health. Possibly he wished to retire from public life; this was one rumor. Or perhaps his partisans were anxious to place his name in nomination at the convention, and so he wished to dissociate himself from Harrison's administration. Since Blaine had offered no reason for leaving the State Department, the rumors flourished. Privately, Reid blamed ill-treatment of his friend by "the bosses who so wickedly defiled Blaine's name by their sordid use of it, not because they loved it or cared to protect it but merely because it was the handiest club for wreaking their revenge on Harrison." Col. E. W. Halford's impressions confirmed Reid's view. If Blaine's motives were clearer to himself than to his friends, he did not enlighten them. Disputes about patronage early in Harrison's term, the crippling attacks of what Blaine called lumbago, the deaths of his three oldest children in 1891 and early in 1892, all undoubtedly influenced him.[43] The *Tribune* attempted neither explanation of the resignation nor predictions of its consequences but was content to summarize, without emphasis or names, some of the more reasoned comments that had been offered.

As the delegates arrived in Minneapolis, Reid reiterated advice he had given earlier. "Throw No Bricks," the *Tribune* pleaded. Without mentioning Blaine by name, the paper suggested that recent events might cause complications and excitement in some quarters. Yet "this is a Republican year," it insisted, and the party's nominee will be elected, it assured the country.

At the opening of the convention and through the developments of the two following days, the *Tribune* held to its aloof position as the voice of the party and refrained from committing itself to the president's renomination. Some of Harrison's supporters in Minneapolis, fearing defeat if their candidate showed any early weakness, sought to stave off a vote until they could secure enough delegates for a first ballot victory. Others believed victory was certain. Reid's editorial writers continued to say only that Harrison could be reelected, an opportunity they thought was open to anyone named by the convention. Morton was not included in these assurances, and there was no speculation in Reid's paper about the second place on the Republican ticket.[44]

After the morning session on the third day of the uninspired meeting at Minneapolis, Thursday, June 9, delegates who were committed to or who favored Harrison, gathered at Market Hall. The 468 individuals who attended represented or could speak definitely for 521 certain Harrison votes, enough to nominate. The caucus chose Chauncey Depew as its strategist and agreed to follow his lead in the convention. The unanimity and strength displayed at the Thursday meeting caused the *Tribune*, in its Friday editions, to predict Harrison's nomination on the first ballot, to call for party unity throughout the country, and to condemn factionalism. The paper still was silent on the subject of a running mate for the presidential nominee.

The estimate was not premature. Midway through the Friday session the delegates cast their first ballots, and the result was a clean victory for Harrison, whose 535 votes eclipsed the total votes of the opposition. Blaine's and McKinley's 364 supporters were evenly divided, while Thomas B. Reed's 4 votes and Robert Todd Lincoln's 1 vote were only gestures. The result seemed clear, but analysis revealed fatal flaws; the president had failed to secure a majority of the votes in New York, Ohio, or Pennsylvania.[45]

As Harrison's supporters cheered their victory Friday afternoon, and while numbers of delegates prepared to depart for home in various states of elation or disgust, the New York leaders passed the word that the state's representatives would convene at seven o'clock. Convention chiefs had assumed from the beginning that Harrison's running mate would come from the Empire State, and the president's failure to secure a majority of its votes strengthened the assumption. When the New Yorkers, their dinners hastily disposed of, met at seven, Horace Porter took the chair in the absence of Warner Miller, one of a dozen from the state who had departed for home or who chose not to attend. Most delegates seemed to assume Morton's renomination, but none urged his name, and when it was reported that the vice-president had said he did not want a place on the ticket no one rose to deny the allegation.

In this situation, in the absence of a consensus, divided among themselves and distrustful of each other, the apathetic New York delegates named Reid as their choice for vice-president. His name, once offered, had support from prominent members of the delegation; his great wealth made his active participation in the campaign of utmost importance in a year when apathy was widespread; no one cared to oppose openly the owner of the powerful *Tribune*. As a clinching maneuver the astute Milholland dramatically produced the president of the New York Typographical Union. That worthy told the state's delegates, orally and in writing, that the union's difference with Reid and his paper had been resolved, thus making the capitalist acceptable to labor. Finally, many of Blaine's supporters, who made up half of the New York delegation, viewed Reid as a friend of their champion and his nomination as a sure way of securing the Maine orator's support for the ticket and of retaining his influence in the party. Shortly before the national body reconvened at eight o'clock, the New York group unanimously approved the *Tribune*'s owner as its choice for Harrison's running mate. Less than an hour later state senator Edmund O'Conner of Binghamton placed Reid's name before the convention, and the delegates, anxious to be home for the weekend, approved New York's choice by acclamation.[46]

Among those who left at once were Thomas C. Platt and his cohorts, whose rumored approval of Reid, neither affirmed nor denied at the caucus, had been one small factor in the New York decision. On the other hand "Harrison's selection . . . caused a chattering of teeth among . . . Republicans of the East," Platt recalled later, and he added that when Reid was put on the ticket, "many of the New York delegates, including myself, wrapped ourselves in overcoats and ear-muffs, hurried from the convention hall, and took the first train for New York."[47] Platt's reaction to the nomination was an indication of his political acuity. Blaine's soon-issued call for party harmony and an end to rancor was not unheeded, but it was unnecessary. There was not only an absence of bitterness, there was an absence of interest in the campaign. Mark Hanna's preconvention prediction that if Harrison were nominated, "it would be the most lifeless campaign for half a century," was a sound assessment of political realities.[48]

The campaign moved as Platt, Hanna, and numerous others had foreseen, haltingly and without enthusiasm or excitement. The Republican party's two most outstanding figures took little part in the canvass. Harrison's extraordinary talent for extemporaneous speaking was not used. Although it was not usual for a president up for reelection to go on the stump, circumstances in 1892 might well have caused some change in the practice. However, Mrs. Harrison was declining and her husband spent most of the campaign weeks with her at Loon Lake in the Adirondacks in a vain attempt to restore her health. Nor were the erstwhile Plumed Knight's acid tongue and forensic skills available. His health was poor, his spirits low, and his enthusiasm for Harrison nearly nonexistent. In mid-October Reid persuaded him to visit Ophir Farm, and there Blaine made his only speech of the campaign. He contributed an article to the *North American Review*, but neither the speech nor the essay was more than a mild endorsement of Harrison's term in office.[49]

In these circumstances Reid became the principal spokesman for the party and the foremost attraction at political rallies in the East and Midwest. He began early, speaking at a Fourth of July celebration at Rye, New York, but his extensive tours did not commence until mid-August. On the eighteenth he opened his campaign with a major speech at Springfield, Illinois. After appearing in Chicago he moved to Ohio. At Cedarville he attended a "nonpartisan" gathering with his 89-year-old mother at his side and later visited an orphanage at Xenia, accompanied by his wife. His major efforts in these early weeks of the campaign came at the end of the month. It was not a speech, but more in line with his proven abilities than was political oratory. With aid from Elkins and others, Reid arranged a meeting of Republican chieftains at Ophir Farm, ostensibly to discuss Harrison's letter of acceptance. The president was persuaded to leave his Adirondack retreat to be present, and Platt was induced to attend. Reid had talked to the New York boss earlier, and Harrison had written him a lengthy conciliatory letter, but the meeting at Ophir Farm marked the beginning of Platt's open and active cooperation in the campaign.[50]

The vice-presidential nominee's other major attempts at conciliation were not as successful. Despite Milholland's best efforts, Reid's antiunion reputation was too well established to be brushed aside or quickly forgotten. In the campaign his position was that his quarrels with the typographical union had all been settled, that relations were satisfactory, and that differences had been due to misunderstandings about the nature of the linotype in publishing rather than to his hostility to labor. Most of the dissatisfaction, he said, resulted from efforts by Democratic elements in the union who wanted the controversy to remain open for political reasons. Late in the campaign the *New York Times* gave two columns to a letter from a former *Tribune* compositor alleging unfair treatment. Reid could only reiterate what he had said earlier and print letters from three employees supporting his position.[51]

Nor did Harrison's running mate make any headway in an effort to end a strike at Andrew Carnegie's Homestead Steel plant, which coincided with the presidential campaign and which was thought to be more damaging to the Republican cause than to Cleveland's. Reid sought to mediate at the outset of the strike and secured an offer from union leaders in mid-July, but it was not acceptable to the plant's managers. Later, with Harrison's and Carnegie's approval, he attempted to work out a settlement with Henry C. Frick, Carnegie's lieutenant, but this also failed.[52]

As the campaign progressed, Reid stepped up the pace of his speechmaking. In September he returned to Ohio for an appearance, and he spoke several times in New York. On the twenty-eighth he sat on a platform while Platt made the principal address at a great rally in Cooper Union. In October the citizens of Boston, Indianapolis, and Jersey City saw and heard the Republican vice presidential candidate as he attended parades and rallies and visited political clubs. The greatest turnout of the campaign occured on October 24 in Indianapolis, home of the president, when Reid and Depew were seen by twenty-five thousand citizens, according to the *Tribune*'s estimate.[53]

On the tours they made together Depew bore most of the burden of speechmaking; when Reid was on the stump he was only slightly less the editor than when at his desk. He had never liked the emotionalism of such sure arguments as the bloody shirt message, either in content or in style. He was at his best in the Lotos Club, at college commencements, or at gatherings elsewhere among his intellectual peers rather than before the general public. In the campaign of 1892 he touched the same themes wherever he went, changing the emphasis to suit the occasion. The Republican party, he told a rally in Boston,

> freed the slave, it saved the Nation. It paid the debt, it pensioned the soldiers. It protected labor as well as freed it. It fostered our manufacturers, built our continental railways, gave every man who would occupy it a homestead, developed and admitted our new States, began our new navy, began our new merchant marine, extended our commerce, opened new markets for our industries and made the McKinley tariff.[54]

At every step, Reid said, the Democrats resisted this magnificent march. While the Republicans have been in power the country has been peaceful, contented, and prosperous, he proclaimed. And he asked why anyone should want to make a radical change from all this.

His formal letter accepting the vice presidential nomination was published October 19. In it he developed the same points he had made in his speeches, sometimes using the same words. He paid particular attention to the tariff, and contended that it should cover the differences in the costs of domestic and foreign products caused by the difference between wage levels in the United States and foreign countries, a common argument in later years but only beginning to appear in 1892. Reid concluded his letter with a eulogy of the Harrison administration and a warning that a Democratic victory in the election would mean a disastrous shock to business. Hay thought the letter could not have been improved and that it gave a lift to the campaign. "How can any honest or rational man be against us this year?" he asked Reid. And, yet, blind to Republican faults as Hay frequently was, he could not like Harrison, he didn't think New York safe, and he was unable to foresee victory.[55]

As election day drew near Reid made a final swing through upstate New York by train, accompanied by Depew. They passed through eight counties, making a score of stops and nearly that many speeches and ended the three-day trip on November third. Reid made his last appearances of the campaign at Cooper Union and at Albany where, in Bleecker Hall, he addressed a large gathering of laborers in a final attempt to persuade them that their best hope lay with the Republican party.

Reid thought that the campaign of 1892 was a dignified one, free of the calumny and abuse common in the political wars of the day, and he noted that he was treated with great courtesy by newsmen of both parties. These factors made it easy for him to follow his natural inclinations and to avoid using the gaudy embroidery on speeches that was available through the use of personal attack and invective. At the same time many observers agreed with former-President Rutherford Hayes, who thought, all in all, the campaign was "the most lethargic canvass ever known in a contest."[56]

Had money alone been able to lift the campaign it might have been one of the most dynamic canvasses rather than one of the most lethargic, for Republicans spent nearly six million dollars trying to reelect Harrison, a far greater amount than had been spent in any previous campaign.[57] The expenditure was of no avail, and the Democratic victory was a great triumph for the party. The *Tribune* could only allege that the result of the election was as great a surprise to the country as to the paper. It had confidently expected a Republican victory, but it had relied on fallacious information, the editorial writers proclaimed defensively. They thought that the Democrats were totally unprepared for their victory and that "the election of Tuesday [was] the greatest surprise in recent political history." Reid believed the tariff was a major factor in the voters' decision and observed that many Americans had shown they still felt that the McKinley tariff had gone too far.[58]

A week after the election Reid attended a New York Chamber of Commerce dinner at Delmonico's. There, before business, commercial, and professional leaders, he apologized for the ineffectual results of his speechmaking during the preceding months and called on the Democrats to make their purposes clear. If they planned to reverse the course the nation had pursued for thirty years, they should announce their intentions plainly, he said. This should be done without delay, so as to avoid uncertainty, a condition of affairs more hurtful to business than any other.[59]

Writing to Harrison three weeks after the disaster, Reid repeated his thought that the Democrats were as surprised at the results of the election as the Republicans were and predicted that the coalition that won could not be maintained. Your position is of immense importance, he said. "You will be the first American private citizen, and will have a degree of esteem among the people such as no man, similarly placed, has enjoyed in our time," Reid told his erstwhile running mate.[60]

Disappointments and Withdrawal

IN THE years immediately following Reid's failure to gain the vice-presidency of the United States, the defeated candidate virtually retired from public life. He seemed to think his career was over and that only empty years lay ahead. Even if this were true, his accomplishments to 1893 had given him a place in American history. In that year Henry Adams thought that among the educated men of his time and in his circle, men born in the thirties and professionally trained, three were examples of success.[1] He named John Hay, William C. Whitney, and Reid. Reid certainly belonged in the group. His position was not far below that of Hay in the field of literature, broadly conceived, and was higher in political standing. Adams thought Whitney the most popular type, and perhaps he was, but he controlled no more wealth and had no greater power than did Reid. Among other figures of the same generation that Adams might have mentioned having professional training and with eastern bases, were Charles A. Dana and James Gordon Bennett in journalism and Chauncey Depew and Joseph H. Choate in political and capitalist circles. Reid's position and influence in the worlds of journalism, business, and politics equalled that of any one of these. Indeed, few Americans of his generation held stronger positions in as many areas of influence as did the owner of the *New York Tribune*.

Despite his successes, the dominant note in Reid's career in the years immediately following his defeat in 1892 was one of pessimistic withdrawal. "My old friend the *Tribune* is too gloomy," the editor's friend H. C. Fahnstock said of the paper in the summer of 1893. Fahnstock thought the editorial pages of the paper were misleading its readers by overemphasizing the faults of the Democratic leaders, exaggerating the effects of the depression, and seeing little likelihood that the country would survive.[2]

Reid was inactive politically, he ceased to manage his financial affairs, and he left the paper to subordinates. From the end of 1892 to the spring of 1896 he was more withdrawn than at any time since he entered Miami University. During the four years following his defeat for the vice-presidency, he spent nearly twenty-four months away from New York, and when he was in the state he was frequently out of the city. Most of this self-exile was spent in Arizona and California; half a year was spent in Egypt with stopovers in Europe; the rest was at Ophir or Wild Air. Nearly three years after the defeat of 1892 Hay spoke to Henry Adams of Reid's unhappiness. He is far from gay, Hay said, but "does not worry his friends except by his [asthmatic] wheezing, and his pathetic attempt to talk jauntily of next year."[3]

The sojourns that Reid took in the West and in North Africa were for reasons of health. As in earlier times of discouragement his physical difficulties flared up. A year after the defeated Harrison administration left office, Reid was at Millbrae. Press reports from the East about his precarious condition became so insistent that he authorized his father-in-law to make a statement. Mills admitted that when his son-in-law had arrived in California, he was suffering from asthma and bronchitis. The climate and outdoor exercise, including horseback riding, however, had greatly increased the editor's strength. The asthma had disappeared, Mills told the press, and Reid's paper printed the good news on page one.[4] Reid, back East in May 1894, reassured the *Tribune*'s readers: his throat complaint and catarrh had yielded to treatment while he was on the west coast. He was stronger and better than for many years, he said.[5] If indeed Reid had regained his strength, the recovery was temporary. He was well enough to take part in a July 4 celebration at Rye and he stayed in New York into the fall, but he feared to face the winter there.

In October 1894 he departed for North Africa in search of a warmer and drier climate. The quest took him across the top of the continent from Morocco to Algiers to Tunis and then to Egypt. After some sightseeing he arranged an expedition from Cairo into the Sinai Peninsula with a score of camels, somewhat more numerous retainers, and equipage for all. Completely separated from news sources and other cares, he enjoyed the active and invigorating outdoor life despite some severe storms. Thinking it would protect his face from wind and sand, he grew a beard, which he wore the rest of his life. After seeing Jerusalem he went to Paris and London in May and sailed from Southampton on June 1, 1895. He arrived in New York feeling stronger than he had since the political campaign. But the bronchitis lingered, the asthma remained a threat, and the doctors thought a New York winter might bring both maladies back in force. The illness depressed him. Victor Lawson recalled later that Reid had advised him not to have asthma and had said that smallpox and typhoid fever were lesser evils.[6]

Reid left the East at the end of October 1895 and went to Tucson, remaining there or in Phoenix nearly six months. The combination of the climate and the stimulus of an approaching political campaign gave him the energy to take a personal hand in the *Tribune*'s day-to-day news coverage and commentary. He even telegraphed editorials at times, and told a friend he had not done as much regular work on the paper since beginning the mission to France. He also spent much time out of doors. He often rode twenty or thirty miles in a day and sometimes drove as much behind a pair of horses he kept. Frequently he was accompanied by fourteen-year-old Ogden and twelve-year-old Jean, and Lizzie was also in Arizona some of the time. Occasional visits by friends provided social recreation.[7]

In late April 1896 the Reids moved to Millbrae for six weeks and were back at Ophir in the first week of June. Almost exactly a year had passed since the editor's return from Africa and Europe, and he had spent more than half of it away from New York. This time he remained in the East from the time of McKinley's nomination until after the election of 1896. But the pressure of the campaign and his fears of the New York winter once more drove him west. Traveling in a private railroad car supplied by Chauncey Depew, he was in Phoenix on December 1.

In these years of semiretirement no crisis arose in *Tribune* affairs. The paper lost the valuable services of George W. Smalley, who left the *Tribune*'s London Bureau to head the London *Times*'s offices in Washington. He was succeeded by Isaac N. Ford. On the credit side, Reid's frequent absences from New York may have contributed to better labor relations in the Tall Tower in Printing House Square. The patched-up truce made with Typographical Union No. 6 at the time of the Republican convention of 1892 was incomplete and did not prevent friction between the paper's management and some of its employees. Early in January 1894, the Committee on Allied Printing Trades announced that the *Tribune* could not be considered a union office. A brief strike ended inconclusively. All the while, John E. Milholland persevered in peacemaking efforts, and both sides made concessions. On November 24, while Reid was in Egypt, the *Tribune* Association signed a formal agreement with Big Six, finally ending the twenty-year-old dispute.[8]

A much less satisfactory situation developed in the matter of the *Tribune*'s relationship with the wire services. Competition among the United Press, the New York Associated Press, and the Western Associated Press, the most important news gathering agencies in the country, increased in the early nineties. The friction had been alleviated but not eliminated when the Joint Executive Committee was reconstituted and enlarged late in 1891. Reid's position was weakened, although he had been retained as a member of the committee. His influence was probably lessened further when his old and close friend William Henry Smith retired from the general managership in the following year.

The bickering worsened in 1893 after the old Western Associated Press went out of existence and a new Associated Press was chartered in Illinois. It soon became evident that the new organization and the United Press would not cooperate in the old way. The differences were accentuated by disastrous losses in revenue brought on by the effects of the widespread economic depression of 1893. In the following year open war broke out, and financial problems were further heightened by a news-war tax that the associations placed on member papers. At the time the *Tribune* and other principal United Press papers, the *Herald*, the *Sun*, and the *Times*, were each paying more than seventy thousand dollars a year to make up the annual UP deficit.[9]

The depression and the expenses of the conflict contributed to the collapse of the *Times*, making it nearly impossible for that paper to continue the struggle. Bennett, in Paris, was greatly annoyed by the constantly shifting situation and was ready to end the fight. Reid, away from New York much of the time, with his vitality lowered, did not want to give up but had little stomach for continuing a losing fight. Only Dana was adamant; he would not surrender. Faced with the alternative of quitting or of attempting to operate a *Sun-Tribune* press association, Reid gave up. On March 27, 1897, the *Tribune*, the *Times*, and the *Herald* were taken into the Associated Press. Two days later Dana, as president of the UP, filed bankruptcy papers for that association and on April 7 it ceased to exist as a news service.[10]

Reid's defeat in the news agency war was offset by the earlier Republican triumph at the polls. An Ohio Republican was again in the White House, again with considerable help from the *Tribune*. As had been the case with previous Republican administrations, Reid felt that he deserved a reward and thought that the expected appointment should be commensurate with his view of the size of his contributions. But a dark shadow lay across the path to a prestigious place in the incoming administration.

Reid's truce with Thomas C. Platt, made during the campaign of 1892, had proved to be even more fragile than that made with the typographers at the nominating convention earlier in the same year. The editor and the politician had little in common other than that both were tall, thin, New York Republicans, somewhat frail in appearance, with strong desires to minimize each other's influence. Their differences were far from secret, and newspapers frequently reminded readers that no love was lost between the two. In the mid-nineties the *Albany Evening Journal* and the *New York Sun*, both friendly to Platt, sniped at Reid for abusing the party chief. The *Tribune* fired back, and the *Buffalo Courier* and other papers advertised the feud.[11]

On his part Reid had never forgotten that he had been on the winning side in the conflict that destroyed Roscoe Conkling in 1881 and that the boss's lieutenant, Platt, had gone down to defeat in the same fight. Conkling had never recovered his position of dominance, but Platt slowly rebuilt his political strength. In the early part of the ensuing decade he shared power in New York with Chauncey Depew, Warner Miller, and Frank Hiscock, all but Platt more or less friendly to Reid. This circumstance, with his recollection of his part in the Conkling-Platt fall, his increasingly substantial financial position, and the *Tribune*'s central place in the Republican party led Reid to believe that Platt could be ignored, or even antagonized, without great danger. He did not even seem to be alarmed after the election of 1894, when Levi Morton captured the governorship and Platt's dominance of New York politics became nearly complete.[12] Further, Reid's attention was directed away from New York in the four years of his extended absences. As the time for the convention of 1896 approached, his attention was more and more fixed on the national scene and the efforts of the various aspirants to gain leads in the presidential race.

Mark Hanna's work for William McKinley had been well done. Early in 1896 it was widely apparent that he was the outstanding candidate, and by March the professionals were publicly predicting his nomination, even those who preferred other candidates. The *Tribune* had given cautious but effective aid to the Ohioan, and in March the major expressed his "very great appreciation" for Reid's support.[13] However, the editor did not yet come out openly in favor of him. At the end of April, with the convention only six weeks away, reporters cornered him at Millbrae and asked about his preferences. "I am heartily in favor of the nominee at St. Louis," he said, and added that he would support as well as approve the party choice. Pressed further, Reid would only say that he thought McKinley "certainly seems to have a long lead."[14] He was not as reticent about the issues in the coming race. He believed that the people wanted to get back to protection and sound money, that the tariff and opposition to free coinage were the great issues.[15]

By the end of May Reid was ready to commit himself publicly. When he was again approached by reporters, he predicted McKinley's nomiation without equivocating and named Speaker Thomas B. Reed as his choice for the vice-presidency. The interview, distributed by the wire services, was prominently displayed on page one of the *Tribune*.[16]

Reid made his statement as he boarded a train for the East. On June 4 he was in Cleveland, where he talked to Mark Hanna and repeated to newsmen that, "My big namesake from Maine" should have second place on the Republican ticket. During a stopover in Ohio he went to Canton to have lunch and an afternoon with the major. There was no announcement about the conversation, but Reid was hardly back in New York when he received from McKinley a draft of a monetary plank for the Republican platform. It favored "sound money" and the "existing standard." Reid was to circulate it, without revealing the author, among eastern financiers. He showed it to J. P. Morgan and others and quickly learned that the bankers wanted a stronger statement. When he relayed his findings to McKinley, the candidate moved closer to the single standard forces.[17]

By the time the Republican convention opened in St. Louis on June 16, Ohio's favorite son was ready to campaign on a platform with a gold plank, a plan the *Tribune* could support with enthusiasm. Reid also approved of the other principal planks that were shaped as the convention began its work: sympathy for the Cubans, the annexation of Hawaii, expansion of the navy, and continued protectionism. As there were no surprises in the platform, there was none in the selection of a candidate. McKinley was nominated on the first ballot. With 453½ votes needed, his 661½ overwhelmed all opposition. Reed, McKinley's choice for a running mate, refused to take second place, as did Levi Morton, and the party then named Hanna's choice, Garrett A. Hobart, a wealthy New Jersey businessman.[18]

Although Reid had less part in the decisions made at this convention than in any since he bolted from the regulars in the fall of 1872, the candidates and the platform were as agreeable to him as any preceding combination the Republicans had produced. If he had any objections, the Democrats erased them when they convened three weeks later in Chicago, nominated William Jennings Bryan, and wrote free silver into their platform.

The editor watched the campaign from New York, spending much of his time at Ophir or Wild Air. The *Tribune* staff could be trusted to say the right things about both candidates and all the issues without close supervision. Reid made no formal speeches, but early in September he sent a letter embodying some of his views to a meeting at Canton of the Republican Editorial Association of Ohio. The letter was read aloud to the journalists in McKinley's presence.

Writing from Wild Air on September 4, Reid began with the matter that disturbed him most. The American people, he said, had had their fill of the incumbent administration and were ready to return to Republicanism as a normal reaction to mismanagement by the Democrats. This, in an orderly election contested on reasonable grounds, would not have been especially unsettling for the country. "Then burst forth the Adullamites." The unscrupulous, the unthinking, the debtors, and other undesirables had captured, humiliated, and disgraced the Democratic party. They demanded a vote against the Eighth Commandment, for free silver was nothing less than stealing forty-seven cents from every dollar. The American people do not have the right to overrule Mt. Sinai at the polls, Reid continued. "Many of our opponents are as sincere as we are and mean to be honest, but the thing they have done is the wickedest and most immoral public act since Secession." The editor next accused the opposition of attacking the Constitution and the judiciary by protesting the use of federal power to suppress riots and by proposing to pack the Supreme Court. On the positive side he expressed approval of the principle of protection, suggesting that attacks on the tariff struck at the foundation of the nation. Let us be considerate "of our erring countrymen, who may have been honestly misled," he suggested, "but let us indulge in no disguises as to the unpatriotic, un-American and revolutionary character of this whole programme." McKinley's presence at the meeting meant the editors could accept Reid's letter as a

165

statement of party doctrine and use it accordingly. But he deprecated their efforts. What we write and what the editors say will not have a determining effect, he concluded. The best speeches "are coming from the porch of a little, two story wooden cottage in Canton; and they make us as proud, in this crisis, of our leader as we are of our cause."[19]

Reid was in New York City on the day of the election. The next morning the *Tribune*'s reports were headlined: "Uprising of a Great Republic" and "Anarchy-Repudiation Trampled Under Foot." Someone headed the editorial comment on the election results, "Thank God."[20]

That evening Reid gave a dinner for the Hannas and included Abram S. Hewitt, Bourke Cockran, Edward J. Phelps, and other prominent conservative Democrats in the guest list, seeking to build a bridge between the incoming administration and the "gold wing" of the other party. He wrote to the president-elect the following day to tell him of the affair and added, "I think you have the greatest opportunity since Lincoln, as you have made the greatest campaign and have had the greatest popular triumph." The editor thought so well of this sentence that he printed it in the *Tribune* a few days later along with congratulatory notes to McKinley from former President Harrison and other notables.[21]

Reid left New York three weeks after the election and arrived in Phoenix on December 1 for the winter. Even before he left the East, rumors were circulating about the place the ex-minister to France, vice-presidential candidate of four years earlier, longtime party supporter, and old friend of the new president would have in the incoming government. As early as November 11 the *Tribune* denied *Sun* reports that Reid had told his friends he could have anything he wanted and that he wanted the State Department. Despite the denial the *Sun* was at least half right. A week later Reid admitted to Hay that he did indeed want the State Department. He had already given the matter much thought, he told his friend. Several factors, Reid thought, would have some bearing on his chances. Hay stood high on the list of possible appointees, Depew had a claim on the place, and Platt was unfriendly.[22]

At this point, three weeks after the election, it seemed to interested analysts that Platt was the principal obstacle between Reid and the secretaryship. "I told Hanna to tell McKinley if he wanted Hell with the lid off . . . to appoint Reid," Platt was reported to have said. If the words were not exact, the attitude was correctly interpreted, Reid thought.[23]

To counter the threat, as he had warned Garfield after his nomination a quarter of a century earlier, Reid now warned McKinley to avoid the mistake of trying to conciliate the New York bosses.[24] In 1880 it had been Conkling who stood in Reid's path; twenty-six years later it was Conkling's one-time lieutenant, Platt, who obstructed the editor's course.

En route to Arizona late in November Reid had stopped in Canton, where he had his first quiet talk after the election with McKinley and Hanna. They were warm and friendly but gave him no feeling of assurance. He judged that no firm decisions had been made and that the principal places were still open. On the train west from near Louisville, he wrote to Depew, to Hay, and perhaps to others asking them to warn the major that yielding to Platt would be a grievous error.[25]

From Arizona, a week after he had seen McKinley in Canton, he presented his case to the president-elect for a place in the cabinet and for preference over Platt in a painfully long letter. In it he emphasized his early and continued support of McKinley and charged that Platt had called the president-elect an erratic, mortgaged, flabby, and weak candidate. He warned that Platt must be handled firmly and without fear and asserted that the New York senator could do no harm if met resolutely. Reid told McKinley flatly that the appointment of Cornelius Bliss, a Platt lieutenant long rumored to be a candidate for the Interior Department, would be unacceptable to him. The editor couched further comments on cabinet organization in general terms, but he left no possible doubt that he wanted a prominent place, felt himself entitled to one, and expected McKinley to appoint him whether the New York senator objected or not.[26] A month later, on being asked, he told Bliss he would accept the embassy in Great Britain if it were offered. In his view, for a former minister to France and vice-presidential candidate in 1892, the only suitable places left were the State Department or the mission to Great Britain.[27]

Reid's friends responded to his lightly concealed requests for aid. Joseph B. Foraker, newly elected senator from McKinley's own state who had nominated the major at the St. Louis convention, and John Hay were the aspirant's most influential supporters. In a conference at Canton in December, Foraker strongly supported Reid as one fully

167

qualified to head the cabinet, but the president-elect was unresponsive. Hay did not see McKinley for some time after the election. He talked seriously with Hanna, however, at about the same time that Foraker saw McKinley. Hay straightforwardly advanced Reid as the best possible choice for secretaryship of state. He went further and said that he would not accept a place in the cabinet himself if it meant that Reid would thereby be excluded. Hay thought that Hanna's manner indicated that the idea of Reid as a cabinet member was new to him. McKinley's manager gave no indication of his reaction to the proposal other than to ask whether Reid's health would permit the close confinement of so exacting a position. Hay could only say that he had no doubt Reid would accept the State Department if it were offered. Reid was grateful to Hay, but urged him not to refuse the cabinet post if McKinley offered it.[28]

At this point Hay felt that the situation was a fluid one, and that final decisions depended largely on whether Hanna, who wanted a Senate seat, would withstand McKinley's urging that Hanna himself enter the cabinet. For his part the president-elect gave few overt hints about his plans except to say plainly that he did not intend to be hurried. At the end of the year Reid was quite resentful and admitted he could not be philosophic about being left out. He still felt that no final decisions had been made about the State Department, but he thought that John Sherman, William B. Allison, and Andrew D. White were the strongest possibilities. Sherman, who had already been approached, was offered and accepted the post early in January, leaving his Senate seat available for Hanna.[29]

A month later the situation had not improved for the *Tribune*'s editor. Late in January Hay went to Canton, where he found forbidding political obstacles blocking an appointment for Reid. Platt's hostility was much more damaging than Reid wanted to believe it to be. The one-vote margin the Republicans held in the Senate gave McKinley and Hanna much concern. Nor was Platt the only problem. Reid, as a New Yorker, needed strong support in his state, but no important element there worked for him. When Hay told his friend how the chief members of the incoming administration felt, Reid was so discouraged that he agreed to take the Navy Department if he could get it. He could not.[30]

Hay's message was a preparatory warning. It was soon followed by a warm, carefully composed, face-saving communication from the president-elect, written with Hay's cooperation. McKinley told Reid that he would like to appoint him to a place commensurate with his contributions and talents. But his long illness made either the miserable climate of London or Washington or the onerous duties and the confining nature of the work in the State Department or in an embassy too harsh a threat to impose on the editor, McKinley said.[31]

A few days later "an excellent authority" in Canton released a statement. Reid had been favorably considered for a cabinet post or an important foreign embassy. It had recently been decided, however, that his health would not permit him to undertake such a place at this time. When Major McKinley learned of this decision he expressed deep regret that he could not have the benefit of Reid's services in the administration, the statement concluded.[32]

McKinley's long-standing admiration for Hay was increased by the latter's forbearance and sensitivity during the protracted consideration of the appointment of Reid to a place that Hay wanted but would not accept as long as his friend was eligible. As soon as the announcement of Reid's "withdrawal" was reported, McKinley named Hay as his ambassador to the Court of St. James. Reid was quite bitter. His reply to McKinley's dexterously diplomatic letter was cool and formal. More indicative of his feelings was an instruction to Donald Nicholson about Hay's appointment. "The public will consider this as my nomination," he said, and for this reason and because of long association the *Tribune* should "speak well" of it. But after that, the editor concluded, "no more gush."[33]

Reid's note to Nicholson was a reflection of his own frustration rather than of his opinion about the appointment. Hay had been Reid's most trusted friend since the war years. They shared the same beliefs and philosophy in most areas and each respected and admired the other as a person. In the seventies Reid had been willing to turn the *Tribune* over to Hay, if it became necessary, to avoid a possible move by Jay Gould to threaten Reid's control. In 1881 when the editor left the country on his extended wedding trip, he had no hesitancy in entrusting the paper to Hay. In the following years Reid confided in his friend about his inner feelings and ambitions. For his part, Hay was quite aware of Reid's self-seeking nature, his inordinate desire for recognition, and his frequent lack of concern about others. At the same time Hay felt comfortable with his friend, possibly because Reid put so much confidence and trust in him. "I feel nowhere such a sense of perfect confidence and repose as in your house," Hay said after a visit. On another occasion, referring to their relationship with each other, Hay spoke of "the old love, the old confidence, the old trust."[34]

While Hay was a better choice than Reid for Great Britain, Sherman was a far worse one for the State Department. McKinley, of course, as did all careful observers, understood that his seventy-four-year-old fellow Ohioan was completely unable to direct a cabinet department. To protect the aging secretary, the new president persuaded his friend Judge William R. Day of Canton to move to Washington and assume the position of first assistant secretary of state. This well-meant arrangement in no way offset the appointment of Sherman. The reticent and retiring Day was an able lawyer but had no experience in foreign affairs and little knowledge of other countries. The second and third assistant secretaries were able and experienced, especially the almost totally deaf but nearly invaluable Alvey Adee, but both were career workers who followed instructions, kept the files in order, and attended to the correspondence. They did not initiate policy or action, and they rarely made decisions about major matters, although Adee's hints and suggestions were frequently adopted. One foreign diplomat summed up the situation with the remark, "The head of the Department knows nothing, the First Assistant says nothing, the Second Assistant hears nothing."[35] As a consequence, when situations arose that did not seem urgent to Day, they were simply set aside.

One such matter, through a series of fumbles, misunderstandings and half-starts, provided an opportunity for Reid to get an appointment, albeit a short one, that was not subject to Platt's veto and that carried with it a title and an entrée to the homes of world figures, including that of Queen Victoria.

As the sixtieth anniversary of the queen's accession to the throne approached, the British decided to hold elaborate celebrations and to invite chiefs of state to send messages of greeting by special embassies. Accordingly, late in March Sir Julian Pauncefote, the British ambassador in Washington, inquired unofficially whether the United States intended to send a special mission to London in June. Sherman replied affirmatively and said that Ambassador Hay would soon have further information for the Foreign Office.[36]

If McKinley was aware of the exchange of notes, he was much less interested in the arrangements that would soon be needed than in the pending selection and appointment of a special commission of bimetal-lists to attend an international silver convention in Europe. More distracting were problems growing out of the special session of Congress that had begun March 15 and was considering tariff legislation and conditions in Cuba. Most distracting of all were the nearly continuous streams of office seekers that poured into the White House, where the president's secretary, John Addison Porter, was frequently unable to dam the flow, and the president was hard put to find time to do his work.

For two weeks after Pauncefote's query neither he nor Hay heard anything about American representation at the Diamond Jubilee. In mid-April Sir Julian again brought up the matter and asked whether the United States would like to send a warship flying an admiral's flag to the celebration.[37] This query also lay unanswered, as the ailing secretary of the Navy, John D. Long, seemed to be no more active than the somnambulant State officials. The first move came in late April when Long was out of Washington for a few days. Acting Secretary Theodore Roosevelt, along with many other maneuvers he performed during Long's absence, informed Sherman, Pauncefote, and Hay that the United States would indeed send a vessel with an admiral's flag. He added as many details as seemed safe, but even Roosevelt did not have the temerity to name the admiral who would be aboard the ship.[38]

Sherman and his assistants, however, continued to ignore the Jubilee, and six weeks after Sir Julian's first inquiry, Hay, still without instructions, sought to help things along. He suggested, following the precedent made at Victoria's fiftieth anniversary, that the United States ambassador be designated as the envoy to represent his country. Silence greeted this message, and two days later, May 14, Hay, evidently pressed by the Foreign Office, requested telegraphic instructions.[39]

By this time the *Tribune*'s able Washington representative, Max Seckendorff, had become aware of the administration's inactivity and had learned something of the nature of the Jubilee celebration. Knowing of Reid's interest in a foreign appointment, Seckendorff investigated carefully and got in touch with his employer. From mid-May Seckendorff was actively seeking a place for Reid in the special embassy. As a result, on McKinley's instructions, Sherman told Hay on May 21 that the United States would send Adm. Joseph N. Miller, Gen. Nelson A. Miles, and "two eminent civilians" to London in June and that Hay would head the mission. Miller's selection was routine; Miles wanted to go and his wife was John Sherman's niece. The choice of the civilians was more difficult. Reid's claims to preference, strongly advanced by Seckendorff, gradually persuaded McKinley. Twenty-four hours after the message listing Miller, Miles, and "two eminent civilians," Sherman relayed to Hay McKinley's new thought. He had decided to send one civilian, he to bear the president's message to the queen, and he named Reid. Hay was still to be at the head of the mission.[40]

Doubtless relieved to have the question settled, McKinley prepared to go to New York for ceremonies connected with the interment of General Grant's remains in the elaborate mausoleum on Riverside Drive. But neither the naïve president nor his advisors had understood the complexities of European diplomatic protocol. Hay now had to inform Washington that the queen would receive only one envoy. Reid might bear the message across the Atlantic but only Hay, as head of the mission, could go before Victoria. Mindful of Reid's sensitive feelings and aware of McKinley's difficult position, Hay magnanimously urged that he be omitted from the special embassy and that Reid be made its head.[41]

The president's immediate reaction was to refuse. If a mission were sent, Hay should head it, he thought. More conversation with Seckendorff and more reflection, however, convinced him that Hay had shown him the only way out of a corner into which, without advice from Sherman or Day, he had in part strayed and in part been guided by Seckendorff. He gratefully accepted Hay's suggestion.

On May 27 Reid jubilantly left New York for Washington to accept the appointment as ambassador extraordinary on special mission. At the moment he received the president's summons, Reid was about to pack for another summer at Ophir Farm and was in the process of deciding whether to pay thirty-five cents a yard for king's windsor plaster for his chicken house or the thirty cents that ordinary mortar would have cost.[42]

Next day the secretary of state formally notified the new ambassador of the president's decision, and on the twenty-ninth McKinley sent Hay the longest letter he had ever written as president; he expressed his approval of Hay's conduct and help and emphasized his appreciation of Hay's course in the matter of Reid's appointment.[43]

After some conversation with McKinley at the White House, the special ambassador-designate returned to his rooms at the Shoreham, telegraphed Lizzie about the talk so she could begin to make preparations to go with him, and mentioned that he had asked for the appointment of Ogden Mills to a place in the mission. She replied at once, "Father would be much pleased" if this could be arranged.[44]

Reid was determined to use his unexpected opportunity to the maximum degree possible and planned an early departure. He cabled Ogden in Paris, mentioned the request for an official appointment, and asked his brother-in-law to go to London. Much time would be gained if Ogden would see Hay about details and requirements of the mission, find a suitable house (no easy task in a city swollen with Jubilee celebrants), and inquire about the problems involved in getting dresses for Lizzie in London. Reid later borrowed $15,000 from Ogden. For his part Ogden only begged, "Don't forget to bring my wife's green bag" containing her jewelry.[45]

As Reid was cabling Ogden, Sherman was telling Hay formally that Reid, Miller, and Miles would make up the special mission, and McKinley was composing the message that his ambassador would bear across the sea and hand to the queen. In a separate cable later, the secretary of state sent Hay more details, including that of Ogden's appointment as secretary of the mission with the rank of attaché, and said that the president was confident of Hay's and Reid's willingness to cooperate during the Jubilee period. Further instructions would follow, Sherman added.[46]

Reid first learned of his appointment on a Thursday. On the following Wednesday, June 2, he sailed on the *Majestic*, accompanied by Lizzie, their fifteen-year-old son Ogden and thirteen-year-old daughter Jean, and their private secretaries.

While the Reids were on the North Atlantic, Ogden Mills was active in England. He found a house surrounded by those of earls, dukes, countesses, former ambassadors, and wealthy Americans. The Earl of Lonsdale's London place, at 14–15 Carlton House Terrace, could be had for two hundred guineas a week, and after gaining Reid's approval, Ogden rented it for an unstated number of weeks.[47]

In London, established in regal splendor in Lonsdale House, the Reids plunged into a social maelstrom of a kind found only at international gatherings in great capitals. When McKinley sent a new Hawaiian annexation treaty to the Senate in mid-June, Reid almost ignored it, only noting that the people in London were concerned about nothing but the Jubilee. When Nicholson and Henry Hall raised questions about

173

Tribune problems, the editor brushed their queries aside; "everything not imperatively demanding an answer has gone unacknowledged," he said at the time.[48] This attitude was in striking contrast with the long, minutely detailed letters on a score of topics, many written at times of great diplomatic activity, sent to New York during Reid's ministry to France.

His calendar was crowded with widely varying events from the moment of his arrival to that of his departure. He entertained American visitors and his English hosts and hostesses as well as friends and associates he had known in France six years earlier. He was, as head of the special embassy, present at court functions and was also included on numerous invitation lists because he was a wealthy American and editor of the *Tribune*. Reid enjoyed the royal atmosphere. Hay reported to Adams that, "the sight of a worthy human being happy is comforting to the soul, and I have seen my friend Whitelaw sitting between two princesses at supper every night, a week running. . . . His rapture had the *aliquid amari* that the end must come, but the memory of it will soothe many an hour of ennui at Ophir Farm."[49]

A more mundane note in Reid's movements in official circles was occasioned by his dress. As had been the case with almost all American envoys since Secretary of State William L. Marcy's famous "dress circular" nearly half a century earlier, "the republican simplicity of [Reid's] attire was in startling contrast with the brilliancy of the uniforms" of other envoys attending the various functions. The difference was particularly emphasized when the black-clad Reid rode in a carriage with the brilliantly accoutered French and Spanish ambassadors in the magnificent procession before scores of thousands that wound from Buckingham Palace to St. Paul's on June 22. The *Tribune* managed a reportorial triumph of a sort when it noted that the only personages in the entire cavalcade who wore black were Victoria and Reid.[50]

The official purpose of Reid's visit and the reason for his appointment came on the day before the procession, when he went to Buckingham in the afternoon. Preceded by the ambassador from Spain and followed by the Papal envoy, McKinley's representative presented the president's message of good will and congratulations to the queen.

As the sixtieth year of Victoria's reign ended, the social activity in her capital ran on undiminished. The Reids attended luncheons, dinners, balls, opera parties, and yachting parties and continued to have guests at Lonsdale House. The special embassy ended July 2, and the ambassador's commission expired, but the entertainment did not cease for him until he departed three weeks later.

Reid did not make public statements while he was special ambassador, but two short speeches after the mission ended were widely reported. Since July 4 fell on Sunday, the American Society of London held its Independence Day dinner on Monday. Reid and Hay spoke to the three hundred men present; all were American residents in England or visitors. Reid's short talk was replete with references to the unity of the Anglo-Saxon race, the responsibilities of great nations, and British-American solidarity. Later in the same week the two Americans attended a banquet given for the Colonial Premiers by the Cordwainers Company. Reid responded to the toast, "To Our Visitors." He said that, although visitors, we "must pinch ourselves" to keep from thinking we are at home. He went on to emphasize the cultural unity of Britain, the United States, Canada, and Australia. Despite criticism by some American papers of the strongly anglophile tone of the talks, Reid thought well enough of them to have the two printed and bound. He gave McKinley and Victoria special copies and less handsome ones to less notable figures.[51]

The Reids left London on July 24 and sailed from Southampton on the *St. Paul* after six weeks of more constant activity than he had engaged in since the campaign of 1892. In a final published statement, an interview with an Associated Press reporter, he reiterated his belief in Britain's strong desire to continue on good terms with the United States but declined to comment on any bearing the Jubilee might have on the international situation. The astute and frequently critical Henry White, then first secretary in the London embassy, thoroughly approved of Reid's appointment to represent his country at the Jubilee.[52]

13

War With Spain
and the Peace Commission

REID returned to the United States early in August and after a brief visit
to Washington went to Wild Air and then to Ophir. For the first time in
four years he spent the winter in New York. As he surveyed the
reporting of the news after returning from the Jubilee, he found public
interest in Cuba building rapidly. At this juncture he favored an
independent Cuba, but opposed intervention, immediate recognition of
independence or of belligerency, and above all, opposed annexation by
the United States. Thirty years earlier, after his postwar trip to Havana,
the young reporter had believed that Spanish rule in the island was
doomed but that admission of Cuba to the United States would be a
great error. American rights should be defended, but the United States
should not press outward, he held.[1] Reid felt similarly about moving into
the Pacific. In 1873 he opposed annexation of the Sandwich Islands (the
adoption of "a Kanaka state") or even the lease of a naval base in Pearl
River Bay; he was still against Hawaiian treaties in 1887.[2]

In the late eighties Reid's views began to change slightly. His
comments on Secretary of the Navy William C. Whitney's naval
expansion plans in 1885 were more critical of the administration's
methods and techniques than of the expansion itself. Five years later,
when, as minister to France he was approached by Portuguese officials
about the establishment of American bases in Africa, he seemed to favor
the possibility. In 1892 he gave the Republican party full credit for
beginning "our new navy."[3] The party platform on which vice-presidential candidate Reid stood in that year called for an adequate navy and the
construction and control of a Nicaraguan canal by the United States, but
went no further in expansionist recommendations.[4]

In the mid-nineties Reid was still doubtful about expansion but felt
that a strong stand in the western hemisphere was a correct policy.
Secretary of State Richard Olney's bold letter of July 1895 in the
Venezuelan boundary situation was "uncommonly well done," Reid

said later. He characterized Cleveland's message to Congress the following December on the same subject as "splendidly American." While the Cleveland-Olney stand on Venezuela gained much popular support in the United States because of its anti-British tone, Reid's attitude was not all anti-British. In general he approved Britain's policies in the rest of the world. But he was an American nationalist and believed that the Monroe Doctrine gave the United States special rights, duties, and privileges in the western hemisphere. Yet he was ever cautious, and a year later Cleveland's temperate policy in Cuba gained Reid's favor. "I thought better of Mr. Cleveland's remarks on the Cuban question than of almost anything else he has ever done," he said.[5]

By the end of 1896 Reid's views had changed on one important point. He was still fearful of adding new states, but was now willing to hold populated areas permanently as territories. Some day the United States will have Cuba and the Sandwich Islands, he told McKinley after Bryan's defeat, and he added, "To that extent I believe in Manifest Destiny." If we get them in your administration, he continued, you should make it plain that we will hold them like territories, with some self-government but never permit them to become states.[6] Reid did not express any opinion on foreign policy while special ambassador at Victoria's Jubilee but called for Anglo-American amity and good will at the end of his mission in London.

In the following fall he stood behind McKinley's cautious Cuban policy and praised the president's call in his annual message for Americans to give Spain "a reasonable chance" to restore order. His convictions that this was the proper course were strengthened by recommendations from the *Tribune*'s London bureau that great caution be used in editorial comment about Cuba.[7] While publicly Reid talked of a peaceful solution of the Spanish problems, privately he was fearful. By now ready to accept the annexation of Hawaii as inevitable and even as desirable because it would be a popular move, he hoped that annexation could be accomplished early in 1898 before the Cuban volcano erupted.[8] When the *Maine* went to Havana late in January, the *Tribune* called it a routine movement and reprimanded alarmists. Six weeks after the vessel went down, the naval inquiry court published its view that the ship had been sunk by an external explosion of a submarine mine, and McKinley sent his ultimatum to Spain. The *Tribune* still refused to join in the hysterical demands for immediate action made by some other papers.

Reid opposed war and demanded that the "so-called war party" prove that its ends could not be gained peacefully. At the same time he warned Donald Nicholson that if war came the *Tribune* must not be the last to assent and must not seem to be dragged into support of it. If war did not come but if the United States should intervene, Reid would support McKinley's plan to move without recognition of Cuban independence.[9]

The editor was not always fully informed of the president's plans. On April 5 McKinley completed a message to Congress recommending forcible intervention, and the next morning the *Tribune*, claiming to speak for the American people and the civilized world, thundered its approval of the president's decision to act. But McKinley withheld the message to allow evacuation of Americans who were in Cuba. Reid's paper had to tread water for nearly a week before it could move to support the published message.[10] Even then the support was for a strong stand, not for war. On April 19, two months after the *Maine* went to the bottom, the *Tribune* editorialized that it was nonsense to talk of war with Spain over the sinking of the battleship. "In the first place this nation is not going to war with Spain at all if it can help it honorably and if Spain does not force war upon it."[11] On the same day Congress adopted a joint resolution declaring Cuba independent, authorizing United States intervention, and disclaiming any intent to annex the island. From this time Reid's public position was that war had been thrust upon the United States and that, after long and patient forbearance in the face of continued Spanish provocation, McKinley had been forced to intervene to restore peace and order in Cuba. Four years later Reid told Max Seckendorff that the war against Spain might have been and ought to have been averted.[12]

Privately at first and later publicly Reid predicted that serious difficulties might well grow out of intervention. The Teller Amendment to the joint resolution of April 19, he thought, could prove to be embarrassing if the United States were forced to occupy Cuba for an extended period after the expulsion of Spain. He was also disturbed about the cost of the conflict. He preferred excise taxes on tea, coffee, beer, and similar items to borrowing, and he believed a draft would be more economical than the Civil War practice of trying to stimulate enlistments through bounties.[13]

In the critical weeks before the break with Spain, McKinley had asked for Reid's views, and the editor sent them in full in letters marked "personal." Not content with this caution he warned Seckendorff when an important communication was en route to the White House, directing him to be sure that Addison Porter, the president's private secretary, saw to it that the message reached its destination. In special cases Seckendorff received résumés of the editor's ideas for guidance.[14]

In the same weeks Reid sought Seckendorff's advice about the organization of *Tribune* war news, particularly with reference to exchanges with other papers. Isaac Ford sent full reports from London about the Spanish situation and included private estimates of personalities and their probable effects on negotiations.[15] Seckendorff's and Ford's reports, together with those of C. Inman Barnard of the *Tribune*'s Paris office, gave Reid a perspective on developments available to few men inside the administration or out of it. After the war began, Reid gave Barnard's office increased funds and authority to secure news and information, as the *Tribune*'s owner considered Paris more favorably situated than London for this work. Barnard also kept his friends in official places informed as to Reid's views of probable American demands after the war, in order that these not come as a surprise to France.[16]

Contrary to the apparent situation, Reid's freedom of expression in the two years following the election of 1896 was restricted by several factors. While he was America's representative at Victoria's Jubilee, his paper could hardly speak critically about Anglo-American affairs or even about United States relations with other nations. It was time for harmony and good will. A more constant, although less obvious, restraint was the ever-present possibility, as Reid saw it, that the president might ask Reid to go to London or to head the cabinet.

Soon after the election, in advising McKinley about cabinet appointees, Reid had recommended himself in plain terms. You need, he told the president-elect, competent men worthy of your confidence with staying power for two, three, or four years, useful in storm as well as in fair weather, who can bring strength to the administration when it needs the powerful support of public opinion and whose aid was given when you needed their friendship.[17] His interest in a position was no secret, and few believed his repeated denials that he sought office. The *Sun* pictured the *Tribune*'s editor as the personification of patient merit standing in the door at Ophir Farm dreaming of a job, "something in the plush breeches line"; or, later, as fairly itching for John Sherman's place.[18] Rumors that Reid might get into the cabinet were made more plausible by Sherman's obvious weakness and lack of fitness for the position he held. When Reid called on him after returning from the Jubilee, speculations broke out. Sherman told reporters that the call was not about the secretaryship and complained that he was tired of repeating denials that he planned to resign.[19]

When the final break with Spain was imminent and the doddering Sherman's presence in the cabinet was no longer safe because of his lapses of memory, Stephen B. Elkins assured Reid of his support for the post. John E. Milholland talked to Thomas C. Platt and came out of the interview with the idea that the boss was ready to bury the hatchet. Milholland also thought that in the event McKinley considered offering State to Reid, Mark Hanna would be neutral and Addison Porter friendly and useful. In addition to these considerations, Vice-President Garrett A. Hobart was considered to be an active and influential friend.[20]

Reid, however, had been badly hurt in the melee two years earlier and had no stomach for another fight. The *Tribune* insisted that he had never sought public office and did not do so now. It reminded its readers that Reid had twice refused high office offered by two presidents and that he had given up his mission to France a year before his term was up. Privately, his chief complaint was of having his name publicly discussed with apparent administration support, only to be dropped at the last moment.

Reid did have support for a prominent place, but his backers were not in New York. He believed that no one would oppose him if McKinley simply sent his name to the Senate, but he feared trouble if the president asked for suggestions and so brought on discussions of other candidates. His forebodings were well founded. Platt told McKinley in no uncertain terms, during a visit to the White House on July 21, 1898, and in a twenty-two page letter three weeks later, that he considered Reid utterly unreliable. He is "selfish and unscrupulous . . . a fawning and unctuous friend while he is a friend," the senator said. "I have known Reid for a quarter of a century, and have never known the time when he could be induced to look beyond . . . his personal advantage," Platt wrote McKinley, and he promised that if an appointment were offered he would oppose it in the Senate.[21] When war came and McKinley had to replace Sherman quickly, he did the easy thing and appointed

William R. Day, which no one could criticize under the circumstances.

Despite Reid's disappointment about the State Department, the *Tribune* continued to support the administration's war program and at the outset made hints about a peace plan. In the first week after Dewey's victory in Manila Bay, Reid felt that the United States was obliged to hold the Philippines to the end of the war but that no commitment about the future could or should be made.[22] At the same time he was becoming increasingly conscious of the various courses of action that were offered by the Spanish war, as had been indicated in his skepticism about the wisdom of limiting American freedom of action by the adoption of the Teller Amendment. Nearly all the arguments for holding the Philippines that would be offered in the succeeding months were touched upon in the *Tribune* within a week of the battle of Manila Bay. The United States could not turn the Spanish out and leave the islanders to their own devices, they were not ready for self-government; Americans must administer them until a decision was made about their ultimate disposition. The United States had three possible courses. One was to retain the islands permanently. A second was to give them independence. A third course was to give them to another power.[23] The paper did not choose a course.

Privately, in the latter part of July, Reid wished to retain only a few coaling stations and give the islands to England or France, although he realized that such a course was politically impossible.[24] Publicly, through the *Tribune*, he hinted that the United States might have to retain the islands but asserted that it was important to avoid expressing opinions that would commit or hamper the administration in its future course of action.

From this time the *Tribune* moved steadily toward an openly imperialist policy. It condemned the "Little America" doctrine and gave warm praise to Richard Olney's attack on concepts of American isolationism, made in an address at Harvard two months before Manila Bay and printed in the *Atlantic Monthly*.[25] The conservative policies recommended in Washington's Farewell Address had been well enough for a young, poor, and feeble nation a hundred years earlier. But the United States was not to live forever in swaddling clothes, it must take its place as one of the great brotherhood of civilized states, the *Tribune* argued. The "fetich [*sic*] of isolation must be cut down" and in its place the standard of

182

humanity and worldwide human sympathy must be upraised.[26]

While Reid was advancing these thoughts through his paper, the military and political forces of the nation were moving in the same direction. In early July the fleet commanded by Adm. Cervera y Topete was destroyed and the city of Santiago surrendered, bringing the end of the war closer. In the same week Congress passed and McKinley signed a joint resolution providing for the annexation of Hawaii. By this time Reid had become recognized as a potent champion of "the large policy" and was widely regarded as a strong candidate for the leadership of the State Department when McKinley permitted Day to leave. In mid-July a chance conversation with Richard Watson Gilder resulted in further recognition of the *Tribune*'s owner as a spokesman for expansion. The editor of the *Tribune* and the editor of the *Century* talked about some of the opportunities and problems that would be involved in making peace with Spain. Gilder was impressed with Reid's views and asked him to write something immediately for the *Century*, although the next issue was nearly ready for the presses. Reid was reluctant but Gilder successfully played on his pride and prejudices by telling him that the forthcoming issue would carry an article by Carl Schurz opposing the acquisition of island territories populated by alien peoples and urging Reid to present the other view. Gilder wrote him, phoned him, and even went to Ophir to see him.[27]

Reid finally consented and hastily assembled *Tribune* editorials about policies, constitutional questions, and other problems involved in acquiring and holding noncontiguous territories. Schurz's article in the September *Century*, consisting of dark "Thoughts on American Imperialism," was preceded by Reid's "The Territory with Which We Are Threatened."[28]

Reid's article followed closely and expanded considerably the *Tribune* editorials that had appeared in the weeks after Dewey's victory at Manila Bay. While his reasoning was more deterministic than moralistic, he argued that the United States was morally bound in Cuba and could not evade its responsibility in Asia. "Humanity in the Philippine Islands is as important as humanity in the West Indies," he wrote. As he had done on earlier occasions, he compared the American relationship with the Cubans to that of England with the Egyptians earlier. The English went there to establish public tranquility, he said, and are still there after fourteen years, and we may have to remain in Cuba that long. He denied that arguments against acquiring territory made on legal grounds had any validity, citing Article IV, section 3, of the Constitution as explicit and unmistakable authority for complete freedom of action by the Congress in territorial matters. He pointed out that Jefferson did not ask the people of Louisiana, Monroe did not ask Floridians, Polk the Mexicans, nor Johnson the Russians and Aleuts, whether they wanted to become a part of the United States.

Reid's thinking about the settlement with Spain made strong impressions in many quarters. At the end of July, when Spain sued for peace, McKinley sent his postmaster-general and political adviser, Charles Emory Smith, on a hasty trip to New York. Smith and Reid discussed the question of how to handle the Spanish overtures, and Reid gave him a memorandum for use when the cabinet met to discuss the American reply.[29]

The *Tribune* policy continued to be one of bracing McKinley up, rather than of forcing his hand in efforts to establish the United States as strongly in the Philippine Islands as the American people would permit. The line that Reid now laid down for his paper was that the nation was faced with an inevitable duty and that to remain in the islands was the only practical solution to a situation this country had neither sought nor desired.[30]

When the Spanish-American armistice was arranged on August 12, McKinley decided to put Judge Day at the head of the Peace Commission, and the secretary resigned as head of the cabinet. Soon after, with an eye to the need for getting a treaty through the Senate, the president asked Cushman Davis of Minnesota, chairman of the Senate Foreign Relations Committee, and William P. Frye of Maine, also a member of the committee, to serve on the commission. They accepted at once. A fourth nominee, Associate Justice of the Supreme Court Edward D. White, hesitated at first and then accepted but later withdrew. He was replaced by George Gray of Delaware, a conservative Democrat, who was also on the Senate Foreign Relations Committee.[31] In the meantime, McKinley had asked Reid to serve, and the editor telegraphed his acceptance. In the same fortnight the president asked Hay to return to the United States to replace Day as secretary of state. Hay, after hesitating, agreed but Reid did not know of the appointment when he joined the Peace Commission.[32]

McKinley's offer of a place on the commission reached Reid at Wild

Air. He immediately instructed Nicholson to ask Gilder for permission to print the *Century* article in the *Tribune*. If Gilder were willing, Nicholson was to run it "in full . . . in minion solid" next to the editorial page. Either Gilder was not interested or Reid changed his mind. His paper ignored the article until after publication in the *Century*, when the New York *Times* gave it strong support. The *Tribune* then ran a full-column résumé of the *Times* editorial article.[33]

Reid returned to Ophir from Wild Air early in September to prepare for his work in Paris. He secured, through Henry Vignaud of the American Embassy in Paris, the services of M. Blanchard as his private secretary. Blanchard had served in the same capacity for Robert McLane and Jefferson Coolidge in their ministries in France as well as for Reid during his, and he would be of very great value. In mid-September Reid made a brief trip to Washington where the commissioners met to discuss problems and procedures among themselves and to see the president and members of the cabinet.

While in Washington Reid learned that Hay was to be secretary of state, but did not learn that McKinley had offered the English mission, as soon as it was vacant, to Sen. George F. Hoar. The senator's known opposition to an expansionist treaty made it advisable to get him out of the way. When he rejected the offer, the president decided to wait.[34] In a private session with McKinley, Reid unburdened himself on the subject of an appointment. He had never sought office. Three presidents had offered him high posts. He had refused the first two and, after accepting the third, had resigned a year before the term was up, one of the rare instances in American diplomatic history in which so high a position had been relinquished merely from a preference for private life. The vice-presidential nomination in 1892 was entirely unsolicited, he averred, but he gave so much energy to the campaign that he underwent three years of ill health after the election. Further, after the nomination, he had contributed perhaps double the amount of money that "any other candidate the Republican party had ever named" had given. Some of McKinley's public statements during the campaign of 1896 had led Reid and others to believe that he would be offered a position in the cabinet. Reid understood the problems involved in such an appointment. Now, however, there was a vacancy in London. The president publicly had intimated that Reid was well fitted for the post, and the country considered his nomination settled. But Platt's protest had made the president postpone any action. Reid was humiliated. McKinley replied that he understood everything perfectly, that there were some things he could not say, but he assured Reid of his affectionate friendship.[35]

In discussions with the president, along with the other commissioners, about the peace, Reid held the ground he had already taken in the *Century* article. Davis wanted coaling stations in the Ladrones and in the Carolines. He also wanted all the Philippines, possibly excepting Mindanao and the Sulu group, where Mohammedan populations might prove difficult. Frye wanted the Spanish West Indies and all the Philippines, and he had some interest in the Carolines and the Ladrones. Day thought the islands in the Caribbean were enough and wanted to abandon the Pacific adventure. Gray was not present during these discussions.[36]

The peace commission sailed on the Cunard liner *Campania* on September 17 with fifteen secretaries and consultants. All the commissioners took their wives. Jean, her governess, and three servants completed the Reids' party. On their arrival in Paris the commissioners went immediately to the Hotel Continental, where comfortable quarters had been reserved for them, although at the cost of relocating some regular patrons.[37]

The American and Spanish delegations were introduced to each other by Théophile Delcassé, foreign minister of France, at a breakfast soon after their arrival. Reid felt at the time that the mood and tone of the Spanish effort was discernible at this first encounter. The Spanish minister to France, Fernando de Leon y Castillo, reminded Reid, "You have had a great victory. . . . Now you must prove your greatness by your magnanimity . . . your victory will be dimmed by any lack of magnanimity to a fallen foe." Reid thought the tone "one of rather proud supplication." He understood the historic nature of what the Spaniards thought of as the final dissolution of their once glorious empire, and he was sympathetic. In the same days he was taking a cold, hard look at the values of Cuban bonds and at the nature of the guarantees behind them, whether of island revenues or of Spanish treasury funds, knowing that the Spaniards would press the Americans to assume the Cuban debt.[38] Delcassé's breakfast was the first of several occasions on which their French hosts entertained both commissions. Others included dinners, the opera, plays, and a horse race.

The working arrangements for the negotiations were quickly decided by Chairman Day and the others. No American spoke Spanish, and while three or four Spaniards spoke English, they were not facile enough to use that language; interpreters were necessary. The fact that Reid alone of the Americans used French with confidence and that several of the Spaniards spoke French put him in the position of being the only one present able to communicate freely and directly with both delegations.[39]

The Americans soon decided to gather each morning at ten to discuss the day's plans. For convenience they met in Reid's rooms. At two in the afternoon they frequently met there before going to meet the Spaniards in the sumptuous Salle des Conférences at the French Foreign Office on the Quai d'Orsay. Reid had his own landau and usually took Davis and one or two of the others to the meetings. The rest, including Secretary John Bassett Moore, went by cab. On the occasion of the first formal meeting, to create an impression and so that the American commissioners could arrive together, Reid borrowed his wife's Victoria, a more elaborate carriage than the usual vehicles for hire.[40]

Reid's language facility, the meetings in his room, and the use of his carriages gave him a place of prominence among his fellows that was more apparent than real. His position was somewhat unlike that of the others, but contrary to outside impressions such as James Gordon Bennett's thought that he held the balance of power between the expansionists and the conservatives, he was no more influential than Day, Davis, or Frye.[41] Gray, as though in silent protest against expansionism, was frequently late and sometimes absent from the meetings.

Reid had advantages beyond those of wealth and some facility in French that made him especially useful to the commission. While minister to France and when McKinley's representative at the Jubilee, he had met many of the diplomats who still represented their countries in Paris in the latter part of 1898.[42] Both the German and the Spanish envoys to France fell in this group. Moreover, Reid was the only American commissioner with an international reputation. When Wilhelm II wanted to convey information to the Americans about German interests in Spain's Pacific Islands, he instructed his ambassador in Paris to see Reid.[43]

Reid's usefulness to the commission was probably greater than his influence on the outcome of the negotiations. He had expert knowledge of sources of information, both historical and current. He was more aware than the others of the availability of materials in the American Embassy files. C. Inman Barnard, the able head of the *Tribune*'s Paris office, prepared daily reports for his employer. Products of both Reid's requests and Barnard's initiative, the reports consisted of press clippings about the peace conference, rumors (so labeled), unprinted news items, and hastily scribbled memoranda on persons and a wide variety of events related to the work of the commission.[44] Without doubt, Reid was the best informed member of either delegation about English and continental opinion on the results of the war and the negotiations in Paris.

The Spaniards, partly because of their overestimation of his position, partly because he seemed more sympathetic, and partly because his French made him more accessible, sought to influence the course of the negotiations through Reid. At a critical point in the peace talks, Castillo had a small dinner at which the Reids were the only Americans present. "You are the only diplomat" in either commission, the Spanish ambassador said, and it is your duty "to find some middle way, to avoid the absolute failure of the negotiation." On the same occasion Castillo told Lizzie Reid that her husband was a most able diplomat and that if he rather than Stewart Woodford had been sent to Spain as McKinley's ambassador the war could have been avoided.[45] Reid, of course, understood Castillo's motives and reported the discussions in detail to Day.

In the formal meetings of the two commissions Reid's special position all but disappeared. These began in midafternoon as soon as the two groups assembled at the French Foreign Office. The Salle des Conférences was almost ideal as a meeting place. However, despite its gorgeous chandeliers and appliqués it lacked both gas and electricity, so that on dark days or when meetings ran late the envoys were disturbed by servants bringing in lamps, an annoyance to the Americans. On the other hand the French hosts not only provided the visitors with ample writing materials and other conference necessities but also maintained, in an adjoining room, a buffet with wines, cold dishes, cigars, and cigarettes. From the beginning the room was fragrant with the aroma of tobacco, for most of the commissioners smoked during the sessions.[46]

Protocol for the meetings was brief and simple. There was no formal chairman, no precedence or rank. The press was excluded and all discussion was in strict confidence. Reid felt that from the beginning of the formal meetings the Spaniards were trying mainly to save face and protect their future public lives. Realizing that they must consent to the dismemberment of their empire, they wanted to delay the inevitable and to be able to prove later that they had fought for every inch of territory given up.[47]

The first moves were painful but rapid. The surrender of Cuba and the cession of Puerto Rico and Guam were made without argument. The first serious difficulty came on the question of the Cuban debt. The Spanish insisted that at least some of the amount should be assumed by an independent Cuba or by the United States or by both. The Americans flatly refused to accept that position. In mid-October Reid feared a rupture and foresaw a possible Spanish attempt to secure European arbitration of the entire peace arrangement. The Americans were so certain that a break was possible that they planned to force it on an easily understood issue such as the Cuban debt rather than let the Spaniards bring about an impasse on some abstruse point.[48]

In Reid's view the crisis came at the end of a lengthy session on Monday, October 24, when Day asked the Spanish commissioners flatly if they would reject any articles relating to Cuba and Puerto Rico unless they included in some form an assumption of the debt by Cuba, the United States, or both.[49]

The Spaniards did not reply, but asked for time to consider, and the next meeting was postponed until Wednesday. On Tuesday the Spanish ambassador made an urgent appeal to Reid and visited him in his rooms shortly before midnight. Castillo's call was made at the instigation of Eugenio Montero Rios, head of the Spanish commission, who feared and wished to avoid a rupture of the negotiations. Castillo and Reid discussed the problems at issue at length, particularly the Cuban debt. When the Spaniard left, he understood that the Americans would not accept any part of the debt, and both men felt that neither commission wanted a rupture. When Reid told Day of the talk, the latter reported it fully to McKinley, with the comment that the Reid-Castillo meeting had probably averted a break-off of the negotiations. John Hay thought that Reid's meeting with Castillo was clearly the turning point in the peace talks and that his position at the conference table was "where McGregor sits." Reid doubted the accuracy of the judgment, believing that Day would get most of the credit.[50]

When the two commissions met again on Wednesday, Spain agreed to the American position on the Cuban debt, that none of it would be assumed by an independent Cuba or by the United States, with the proviso that their acquiescence would be voided unless other points at issue were resolved and a treaty agreed upon.

Meantime, the Americans had discussed among themselves their position on the Philippine Islands question. From the beginning Reid and Cushman Davis had stood together. Both favored taking all the Philippines and additional islands from the Carolines and Ladrones, or Marianas, that might be useful for cable stations, naval bases, or other purposes. Senator Gray opposed acquiring anything in the Pacific, and Frye and Day fell between these positions. Reid and Davis sought to persuade the others but not to the point of antagonizing them. The differences persisted, and as the Cuban debt crisis approached, the commissioners decided to send their views on the Philippines question to Washington. If the debt crisis passed safely there would be need for instructions about the Pacific.[51]

On October 25 Day forwarded to Hay by cable a letter signed by Davis, Frye and Reid, one from Gray, and Day's own. The first was an argument for claiming all the Philippine Islands, because any division would be a "naval, political, and commercial mistake." If a division had to be made the three expansionists recommended that the dividing line run from San Bernardino Strait, south of Masbate, north of Panay, and thence to the northeast corner of Borneo, giving the United States Luzon, Mindoro, and Palawan, the principal northern and western islands. Day argued for taking only Luzon, in accordance with his existing instructions. If naval estimates required more cessions for strategic purposes (the defense of Luzon), Day suggested a dividing line that would give the United States slightly less than would the Davis-Frye-Reid line. Gray flatly said that it would be unwise to take the Philippines "in whole or in part" and argued that to do so would reverse the nation's historic continental policy, entangle it in Europe's Asian politics, and necessitate burdensome outlays for defense purposes. At the very least the commissioners should keep to their original instructions, Gray urged, and quoted McKinley's statement that "we had no design of aggrandizement and no ambition of conquest" when the United States entered the war with Spain.[52]

Day's cable was received in Washington on a Wednesday. McKinley did not deliberate long. He met with the cabinet, and on Friday Hay cabled Day that the president thought it his plain duty to accept the entire Philippine archipelago and that the cabinet agreed. Details of the cession were left to the commissioners, and it was made their responsibility to phrase the articles and persuade the Spaniards to accept them.[53]

Reid's principal contributions from this point were in the wording of the articles, although the main burden of that task was carried by John Bassett Moore. Occasionally a point was settled by an adamant yea or nay from Davis who, as chairman of the Foreign Relations Committee would have to take the treaty over its first hurdle in Washington. Hay's thought that Reid more than anyone else was responsible for the treaty was an exaggeration of the importance of his friend's role.[54]

In fact it was Frye who proposed a key to open a deadlock that seemed to be a greater obstruction than had been the Cuban debt crisis. The Spanish commissioners could not return to Madrid stripped of everything. Rather, they would have abandoned the negotiations and let the war begin anew. Frye told McKinley this and urged that the United States give Spain ten or twenty million dollars for debts incurred in making internal improvements in the Philippines. Frye thought a resumption of the war would be unpopular and very expensive and would further erode America's popularity abroad, already damaged by Europe's sympathy for Spain's plight. Reid thought twelve to fifteen million for the Philippines, Carolines, and Ladrones would be about right. The Spanish commissioners were silent at first, but Castillo was reported to have mentioned forty million dollars as a low figure for the islands.[55]

After much deliberation the figure of twenty million, which Reid thought was too much, was used in the draft article. The Spanish commissioners were informed of American intentions toward the Philippines in an ultimatum on November 21. They at once asked for time to consult Madrid. To make certain the Spaniards understood the American position and to avoid a hasty and unfavorable move, Day and others persuaded Reid to call on Castillo and tell him unofficially that the ultimatum meant exactly what it said. After two days the Spanish commissioners asked for a further extension of time, and their reply was delayed until the twenty-fourth.[56] In the meantime, the Germans had become concerned about the extent of American ambitions in the Pacific, and the Kaiser had told his ambassador to France, Count George Herbert Münster, to watch the Spanish-American meetings closely. In secret agreements made in September Germany had arranged to buy from Spain, depending on the outcome of the peace, several islands in the Caroline group. Soon after the negotiations in Paris began, Count Münster had the American commissioners to dinner at his embassy and learned directly of their interest in the Philippines.[57] This and other information led the Kaiser to send Münster to call on Reid on October 26 and again on November 8. The talks were long ones. Reid was left with the idea that Germany was interested in the Philippines but would not interfere with American acquisition, and Münster learned that Reid wanted the entire archipelago. At subsequent casual and social meetings the subject frequently came up, and Münster repeatedly tried to learn the extent of American interest in islands outside the Philippine group.[58]

As American pressure on Spain increased for small islands the Germans wanted, particularly Kusaie in the easternmost Carolines, the Kaiser again sent Münster to see Reid, this time to make a strong statement about long-established German rights in the Carolines. Alarmed, Reid sought out Day, who promptly cabled Washington for instructions to cover this new element in the negotiations.[59] In the following days Münster made several informal calls on Reid to seek or convey information. Meanwhile the Kaiser's ambassador in Washington had protested American efforts to acquire Kusaie, and McKinley dropped the project rather than chance involvement with German claims in Spanish possessions.[60]

Spain's reply to the American ultimatum on the Philippines came on November 24. It was neither an acceptance nor a rejection of the American proposals but an attempt to salvage something out of the wreckage of Spain's empire: a much larger payment for the Philippines, or retention of a part of the archipelago, or arbitration of responsibility for the Cuban debt, or a combination of these reservations. Reid thought the Spanish propositions frivolous and was irritated when others considered them seriously. A test vote showed that Davis, Day, and Reid were against consideration of any of the Spanish propositions, but Frye and Gray favored discussion. Day thought it necessary to cable Hay, and a few days later the commissioners had presidential backing for rejecting the Spanish proposals. The Spaniards had no choice. They were forced to accede. The negotiations were concluded.[61]

Next day the *New York Tribune*'s lengthy editorial comment on the completion of the negotiations was headed "Peace With Honor." The well-established *Tribune* position was repeated: the "expansion" and "imperialism" of America began with Jefferson; United States principles did not change with the Spanish war; the signing of the treaty was a time for congratulation and serious thought about the future. The editorial referred to McKinley's firm, generous, and farseeing statesmanship and concluded, "Our Commissioners will bring from Paris Peace With Honor as a holy trust committed to this Nation."[62]

In the same issue the *Tribune* printed an Associated Press correspondent's interview in Paris with William T. Stead, a prominent English editor and journalist, who had just completed a trip through six countries. "Outside of England I have not met a single non-American who was not opposed to the expansion of America," he said. "Nor through my whole tour of Europe have I met a European who did not receive the protestations of genuine sincerity with which the American people entered in the war with more or less mocking incredulity." Stead's opinion was news and however much Reid's editors disagreed with it they ran the interview on page one. Eight months earlier Hay had expressed privately much the same feeling. He told Lodge in April that England was the only country not openly against the United States in its quarrel with Spain.[63]

The essential points of the treaty were decided by the end of November but the exact phrasing of some of the articles required ten more days of anticlimactic and frustrating meetings. Minor questions proved to be so irritating that the Americans occasionally snapped at each other, something that had rarely happened in the long weeks of close association. They were also irritated by what they considered pettiness in some State Department restrictions on their freedom of action and by hints in some press reports that negotiations were fully controlled in Washington. On the other hand Davis and Reid, whose positions had been very close on nearly all issues and whose views had usually prevailed, congratulated each other privately on their mutual success.[64]

By December 9 all the words had been agreed upon and the last memoranda recording Spanish protestations and the American replies had been exchanged. The final sentences of the final American paper were complimentary references to the Spaniards' learning, thoroughness, and concern for their country. Reid phrased the sentiments at

Day's request to end the negotiations on a graceful note. The signing on December 10 was held up until after eight in the evening due to a shortage of parchment in the Spanish embassy, which almost seemed to be a final desperate effort to postpone the inevitable.[65]

The *Tribune* hailed the end of war and the beginning of peace but expressed regret that the treaty was not broader and did not include agreements on general commercial and other relations voided or put in doubt by the war. The London *Times* thought that America's treatment of Spain was no harsher than Germany's treatment of France in 1871 or Russia's treatment of Turkey in 1878. The Spaniards were polite to the end but were filled with gloom and felt that American demands had been excessive. Even Castillo would not dine with Reid the evening before the treaty was signed.[66]

The American commissioners left Paris December 16 and on the following day embarked from Southhampton on the American liner *St. Louis*. They arrived in New York on the twenty-fourth and went immediately to Washington. There the heady taste of satisfaction in a job well done turned to wormwood in Reid's mouth when he learned that McKinley had decided to send Joseph H. Choate to the Court of St. James. The topic had been touched on in Reid's correspondence with Hay in October and November. The possibility of Reid's appointment to the War Department following Russell Alger's impending departure from that office was also mentioned. But Reid wanted London and told Hay that if he was not wanted for that post he would return to private life and to politics but not to office holding.

Just prior to his departure from Paris, Reid had received a cable from Hay saying that the "tendency is to Choate for London."[67] But that preparation did not lessen Reid's bitter reaction to the definite news that he had been set aside again, as he viewed McKinley's act. He still protested that he had never sought the place, which was hardly accurate. He affirmed that an endorsement of his qualifications by friends and especially by his fellow commissioners sent to McKinley from Paris had been done without his knowledge, which was probably true. He was convinced that he deserved the appointment and that he was better qualified for it than anyone else who had been considered. As late as the first week in January, long after the decision to send Choate to England had been made, Reid's friends worked for him.

Abram Hewitt wrote to the president. He said he did not recommend appointments to public office but had heard that allegations that Reid was unpopular among the businessmen of New York were being used against the editor in his consideration as a possible appointee. Hewitt then told McKinley that no man in the city had the confidence of the mercantile class more than Reid did. He went on to mention the commercial treaty with France, Reid's great success as special ambassador at Victoria's Jubilee—especially in the two public speeches which were never-surpassed gems, and the recent outstanding work in Paris as highly favorable accomplishments in Reid's background. Henry Hall worked frantically, even after Seckendorff told him the case was hopeless.[68] Reid's most strident complaint was that the president had hinted that he, Reid, was a prominent possibility for the place, that there had been widespread approval of his probable appointment, but that he had suddenly been set aside. He attributed this not to Platt's animosity but to McKinley's weak-kneed bowing to Platt's shrill complaint that Reid's appointment would break up the Republican organization in New York.[69]

Once again the laurels Reid thought he deserved had been snatched away at the last moment to be placed on another brow.

14

New Activities and Successes

REID was only moderately active in public affairs from the time of his work on the Peace Commission to his appointment as ambassador to Great Britain in 1905. His relations with McKinley were friendly but cool during the remainder of the president's life. The *Tribune*'s editor did not participate in the political maneuvering before and during the Republican nominating convention of 1900 or in the election campaign, except to advise Donald Nicholson about the course the paper should take in some situations. The Reids were at Ophir or Wild Air from the end of June through late November except for occasional brief trips to the Madison Avenue house. After a visit to the west coast, to Millbrae, in March and April 1901, they returned to New York. Reid was at Wild Air when McKinley was assassinated.

Although he took little active part in political matters, the period was a turning point in Reid's political situation. Rather than working as a leading figure of the loyal opposition to the dominant faction in the Republican organization in his state, he became a leading supporter. This change occurred in a period of six months and developed as an element of Reid's relationships with Thomas C. Platt and with Theodore Roosevelt. The former connection was of long duration and had been a dominant factor in Reid's political past; the latter was new and helped determine his future.

Reid's battle with the New York Republican machine had lasted thirty years. He had fought it when Roscoe Conkling was the boss in the seventies and thought he had won. But Conkling's chief lieutenant was not defeated. Tom Platt reestablished himself in New York and blocked the appointment of the *Tribune*'s editor and owner to a prominent place in the cabinet or the diplomatic world for many years. When Joseph H. Choate, also an opponent of Platt's, was asked how it was that the senator was reconciled to Choate's appointment as ambassador at the Court of St. James, the lawyer had a ready explanation. "Only two were considered by the President for the position. One was Whitelaw Reid, and the other myself, and Platt supported me because he hated Reid worse than he did me," Choate explained.[1]

The end of the feud was anticlimactic. Platt was ill, he was losing control of the organization, and his wife was dying. Reid was no longer young, he was tired of fighting, and he had had many honors. Late in 1900 and early in 1901 intimations reached him that Platt wanted to "bury the hatchet." Reid's only requirement was the absolute withdrawal of the senatorial proscription, and he was assured that this was understood.[2] After some preliminary arrangements the ancient antagonists met in a private room at the Holland House with no one else present. They talked a few minutes, agreed to quit fighting, try to get on in the party together, shook hands, and parted. The words meant little. The fact that they shook hands in such circumstances was enough.

Platt informed President Roosevelt, Gov. Benjamin B. Odell, and the New York State Republican Committee of his peace with Reid. Reid told Nicholson, Hart Lyman, Roscoe C. E. Brown, James Martin, Nathaniel Tuttle, Henry Hall, and Max Seckendorff of his peace with Platt. An essential part of the Reid-Platt peace was the editor's decision to support Odell's leadership of the party in New York, a leadership based on the governor's control of the state machine. In this situation Odell would rule but would still respect Platt's requests. As Reid phrased it, he "won't wound Platt's sensibilities."[3]

In back of the changed relationship with the party and with the machine, including Platt and Odell, was Reid's relationship with Roosevelt. While governor, Roosevelt had thought Reid always delightful socially. "However, I am glad we have Choate as Ambassador," he told a friend shortly after Choate's appointment to England. Later the governor spoke of the editor as acting dishonestly through the *Tribune* because he had not been given the English mission or a place in the cabinet. Reid had attacked the appointment of staunch New York Republican Elihu Root as secretary of war maliciously, out of jealousy; he was trying to defeat the party because of bitter feelings toward McKinley and Platt, and he "has attacked me," Teddy complained and privately accused the *Tribune*'s editor of "mere personal vindictiveness and soreheadedness."[4]

On his part, Reid was not much more objective than the governor. As a member of the State Board of Regents Reid believed that the chief executive official of his state had to "run back and forth" between the executive mansion in Albany and Platt's Fifth Avenue hotel suite to find out what the governor's office could do in the matter of appointments in the state's educational system.[5] The sixty-two-year-old veteran sometimes felt that the forty-two-year-old recruit was not entirely mature. Reid had known and liked Theodore's father and had known the son as a young man. It disturbed him that the "unstable characteristics" that Roosevelt had as a youth seemed to remain with him. The governor's excellent intentions, Reid thought, were often thwarted or warped by a consuming ambition and "a heedless mode of action before thought," which delighted his enemies and confounded his friends. It also bothered Reid that Governor Roosevelt never asked his advice or consulted him in any way about political matters.[6]

These attitudes led Reid to believe that Roosevelt might have difficulty in gaining reelection in 1900 and would certainly lose without the full support of the *Tribune*. In April he privately wrote off Roosevelt's suitability as a vice-presidential candidate in the national elections.[7] Nevertheless, the *Tribune* gave full support to the McKinley-Roosevelt ticket. More importantly, through indirect means, probably via Seckendorff, Roosevelt learned of Reid's sincere concern about their relations and began to see the *Tribune* in a new light. The communication changed from occasional stiffly formal notes to more frequent, warm, and personal letters. Shortly after the nominating convention, the new vice-presidential candidate expressed a desire to have a political talk with the editor of the *Tribune*, and Reid invited him to Wild Air. The candidate could not make the visit, but relations between the two continued to improve.[8] At the end of the year the *Tribune*'s summary of Roosevelt's work as governor was very complimentary.[9] The following fall, the day after McKinley's death, the *Tribune* spoke of the new president's "exalted personal character," of his large experience in executive tasks, and predicted that he would be a great and good president.[10] The next day Reid went down to Washington to look over the situation and talk to John Hay and others. It was the only time during Roosevelt's first term that Reid was not at Wild Air or Ophir in mid-September. Exactly eleven months earlier he had found it impossible to leave Wild Air to talk to Governor and vice-presidential-nominee Roosevelt about political matters.[11]

While Reid's relations with the New York political machine were changing significantly, his already established position as a nationally recognized figure in the area of American foreign policy was being further developed and refined. Early in February 1899, the Senate approved the Treaty of Paris, 57–27, without amendment. Reid was pleased with the Senate's action, but he was not satisfied with the nation's lack of full acceptance of the settlement. In the next twelve months he made a dozen major speeches defending the work of the Peace Commission. In February he spoke in support of the treaty to a large gathering at a Lotos Club dinner, to the Marquette Club in Chicago, to an American Asiatic Association dinner at Delmonico's honoring Adm. Lord Charles Beresford, and to an Ohio Society dinner at the Waldorf-Astoria honoring the members of the Peace Commission.[12]

Later he wrote an article for the first issue of the *Anglo-Saxon Review*, an English magazine sponsored by Lady Randolph Churchill, to get his views before British readers and to promote friendly Anglo-American relations.[13] In June he made the commencement address at the seventy-fifth anniversary of his alma mater, speaking for an hour and a half. He talked of "Our New Duties," reiterated his support of the large policy and condemned the views of "Little Americans."[14] Appreciative alumni recognized his national stature with a poem in the volume produced to commemorate Miami's diamond anniversary.

> Another son who, with thought-sharpened pen,
> (Standing in front where only brains can lead)
> Has moved the hearts, and wills and minds of men—
> Those who love genius must admire your Reid;
> Where the Tri-color floats in freedom's name,
> He proved the truth of my contention here;
> Though empire was the stake, 'twas still the same
> Miami's son stood with the best, their peer.[15]

Reid liked the *Anglo-Saxon Review* article and the Miami address. "In these two I have pretty fully developed my own ideas as to our necessary policy," he told Isaac Ford, for the guidance of the *Tribune*'s London correspondent. Reid felt at this time that he was ahead of the country in his thinking, but that the public would gradually accept his views.[16]

In the article and the speech Reid had simply enlarged and amplified positions he had previously expressed. He touched on all questions about American policy that had been raised in Paris and brought up later by opponents of the treaty, and he justified the commission's course on each point. He emphasized especially the rationale behind the refusal to arbitrate, the refusal to assume the Cuban debt despite the risk of a break in the negotiations, and the basis for the twenty-million-dollar payment to Spain.[17]

One new element had appeared in the *Anglo-Saxon Review* article. The author's denial that American acquisition of territory in Asia in any way involved disavowment of the principles in the Monroe Doctrine was important but incidental. More to the point was his inclusion, in his defense of the constitutionality of the treaty provisions, of a carefully argued denial of the widely held view that the United States was inexorably bound to "fit our territories for statehood."[18]

Cushman Davis followed Reid's well publicized advocacy of the views they both held with close attention. He read the *Anglo-Saxon Review* article carefully, praised Reid's position on the Philippine questions, and approved his taking a. public stand on the issues.[19] McKinley's cabinet members felt that Reid's definitions of the constitutional relations between the United States and its new possessions were the clearest and ablest statements on the subject made by any spokesman.[20]

Reid continued to develop his line of thinking in editorials and speeches. In October he was invited to accept an LL.D. at Princeton, which surprised him, and he decided to use the opportunity to talk about the results of the war with Spain.[21] He may also have been surprised, but he was not abashed when the Princeton students greeted him with a "Rah! Rah! Sis! Boom! A-h-h-h! /Tiger! Reid! Reid! Reid!"[22]

In his speech Reid defended Commodore George B. Dewey's course in attacking the Spanish fleet and then remaining in Manila Bay, the subsequent conduct of the war, the work of the Peace Commission, the constitutionality of the treaty, and the American response to the "unprovoked attack on our troops" by the Filipinos. He recommended a gradual movement toward giving the natives self-government and autonomous status, except in foreign relations and financial affairs. He restated his view that the acquisition of the Philippines was in line with uniform policies followed by American presidents for a century, that the expansion of the United States had been done in the interests of civilization, Christianity, and justice, and that material interests had been subordinated to duty.[23]

After the Princeton address, which Reid thought of as a continuation of the Miami speech, his emphasis changed somewhat although his position remained the same. Addressing the Massachusetts Club in March 1900, he spoke out strongly against those who urged statehood for the newly acquired islands. Massachusetts, he told his audience of Boston business and professional men, should not be subject to neutralization by Mindanao in Congress. He thought it a "cowardly tendency" for public men to advocate admitting just any area to full partnership in the American union. If the Republicans tried to make states out of all the new territories, it would be the duty of every patriot to oppose the Republican party, he averred, while conceding that few members of Congress agreed with him. The islands should be given as much self-government as they were capable of taking, and the United States must provide them with the best civil service that the nation could devise. "My last word is an appeal to . . . stand all together for the Continental Union and for a pure Civil Service for the islands," he concluded. Later in the year while on his annual visit to Millbrae he spoke at the University of California on Charter Day and again at a formal banquet in San Francisco for the departing members of the Philippine Commission. In each case his theme was expansionism and his argument was in defense of the large policy. The *Tribune* also consistently supported administration policy within the islands. It was necessary to "smother out the last smouldering fires of insurrection," the *Tribune* said in February 1901. The Filipinos must return to peaceful ways and take advantage of the opportunities for progress offered by the United States. On Memorial Day in 1902 Roosevelt said at Arlington National Cemetery that the United States was fighting for peace and freedom in the Philippines and that American cruelties in the fighting had been shamelessly exaggerated. The speech was reported on page one of the *Tribune*, and in an editorial the paper praised the president's position.[24]

Reid's attitudes about the islands and the islanders were a part of a broader view about the direction and consequences of American growth. He was concerned about the moves to admit the remaining territories in the West to statehood. He believed privately that the Republican party had discredited itself, played low politics, and acted without statesmanship or patriotism when it admitted "mining camps" and "sage brush states" into the union early in Harrison's administration. He thought that Oklahoma perhaps would have to come in eventually, but that the applications of "wholly unfit territories" should be denied. Arizona and New Mexico, if admitted at all, should come in as a single state. He disclaimed approval of "demagogue resolutions" in the Republican national platform about the "right" of territories to admission, although in his campaign for the vice-presidency in 1892 he had boasted that his party had "developed and admitted our new states." In 1892 he had accused the Democrats of opposing the admission of new states; in 1903 it was the conniving Democrats who plotted to bring more into the union.[25]

As a corollary to his doubts about new states, Reid had his doubts about new peoples. He was alarmed at the "extraordinary change in character" of immigrants entering the United States at the beginning of the twentieth century. This is no longer a Puritan nor an Anglo-Saxon people, he told the New England Society at a celebration of the 283rd anniversary of the landing of the Pilgrims. For seventeen years immigration from the lands of our ancestors and their kinfolk has declined, he said. Croats, Slavs, Hungarians, Sicilians, Sardinians, Chinese, and Japanese will soon equal the number of the Indo-Germanic family in the United States, he warned. He recommended that immigrants be sifted by requiring evidence of intelligence, character, thrift, and literacy. He was also concerned that socialists, communists, anarchists, and outcasts "from every other civilized land" were moving into the United States in such numbers as to make the country "the common sewer for Christendom." He shed no tears for the past. "What is done is beyond recall," and with all our faults our achievement is colossal, he thought. But to continue indefinitely to weaken the country by admitting inferior people and unready states would be folly, he warned.[26]

Reid's concern about the mounting numbers of eastern and southern Europeans and the Asiatics who were entering the United States was paralleled not only by his already well developed anglophilism but also by a marked pro-German outlook. When the German acquisition of the Carolines, Mariannas, and other remnants of Spain's Pacific territories became public knowledge in June 1899, the *Tribune* approved and affirmed American friendship for Germany.[27] Later that year Reid proclaimed through his paper that God and nature meant for Great Britain, Germany, and the United States to be eternally at peace and amity with each other. Germans and Americans were of the same racial stock, Germany was the one great power in Europe with which the United States had never fought, American commercial relations with

Germany were greater than with any other country save Great Britain, and these facts were bases for exceptionally strong ties among these powers.[28] Late in 1901, countering criticism of German saber rattling in the Caribbean, the *Tribune* underlined and accepted the German ambassador's denial of newspaper reports that his country had ambitions in South America and the West Indies.[29] However, when Prince Henry, brother of the German emperor, was about to begin a visit to the United States early in 1902 Reid toned down one of Max Seckendorff's admiring dispatches in order to avoid having a "pro-German" label put on the *Tribune*.[30]

Reid wanted his paper to be neither "pro-German" nor "pro-British," but his strongest affirmation of American friendship with other peoples related to the English.[31] He not only defended their course in the Boer War but also carefully fenced off Dutch, German, and Irish criticism of the English position in South Africa. In speeches, in the columns of the *Tribune*, and in private correspondence he explained away past Anglo-American differences and emphasized that "irresistable forces of blood and history" would withstand all efforts to divide the two countries. Giving himself due credit for this happy situation, he dated the beginning of good relations between the United States and Britain from the time of Victoria's Diamond Jubilee.[32]

One of Reid's oldest and most consistent positions on American foreign policy was his strong belief in the principles of the Monroe Doctrine. He had opposed Grant's expansionist attempts in the Dominican Republic, but he had also opposed interference in the Caribbean by any non-American power. At the same time, he thought that the islands would inevitably come more and more under American influence. At the end of the century he felt that the United States sooner or later would "have the practical responsibility for the West India archipelago." Thus, while he did not approve, he could not protest when he thought the administration was encouraging revolutionary activities in San Domingo in the summer of 1899, with the objective of establishing a protectorate.[33]

Later, when the question of a canal came up, Reid was more realistic about the situation than the secretary of state. The *Tribune* supported the first Hay-Pauncefote Treaty and Hay was grateful.[34] But the editor privately thought that the terms of the arrangement would give much ammunition to the Democrats in the campaign of 1900 and told Hay that he had misgivings about the treaty and that he had been criticized for his paper's position. The essential thing, in Reid's view, was that "it must be an American canal." If the Clayton-Bulwer Treaty were in the way, it should be modified by mutual consent or if necessary abrogated, he thought.[35]

Reid's views about the doctrine closely paralleled those of President Roosevelt, an agreement that became plain in the spring and early summer of 1903. In April Roosevelt began a two-month, fourteen-thousand-mile tour of the West, on which he planned to make some seventy-five speeches.[36] He set a foreign policy theme in one of his first addresses before six thousand people at the University of Chicago, where he was invited to accept an LL.D. degree. He called for a larger and more powerful navy and a broader interpretation of the Monroe Doctrine, linked the concept of American primacy in the western hemisphere to a demand for the fighting strength to make the Doctrine respected, and told his audience, "There is a homely old adage which runs: 'Speak softly and carry a big stick; you will go far.'"[37]

The president's tone alarmed Reid. He thought Roosevelt was declaring his intent to bar all the world from interference anywhere in the western hemisphere, even when some interference might be justified. Reid had little respect for most governments south of the border. He agreed with the sentiments expressed by an anonymous writer in the *North American Review* in the spring of 1903 that the United States should not ally itself with the "banditti" of South America to resist the legitimate efforts of such great civilized powers as England and Germany to protect their citizens. Yet he hesitated to challenge extensions of the Doctrine lest such should seem discordant notes when the administration needed friendly support at home.[38]

Reid felt so strongly, however, that he decided to set forth his own interpretation of the Monroe Doctrine. He did so in an address to the graduating class of the Yale Law School in 1903. He traced the origin of Monroe's announcement and declared that the early bases for the principles no longer existed. He deplored the later extensions made by fervent patriots. He declared that the natural sphere of American interest and influence was in the Caribbean, the Gulf of Mexico, and the Isthmian areas. There the Doctrine should be applied stringently, he thought, but sparingly elsewhere. The United States, he said, has a special relationship with all nations in the western hemisphere but is not as directly concerned with the association between Europe and the more southerly countries as with the foreign relations of countries nearer the United States and the Isthmus.[39]

When Roosevelt read Reid's speech he praised it. "I am nearer your view than you think," the president told the editor. He added that he had first drafted a message saying essentially what Reid later said at Yale, but he felt that if he expressed himself that way it would have been "accepted abroad as an invitation to make aggression on the parts of America in which I said we had less interest than in the regions around the Mediterranean."[40] Reid replied that he also was aware that any effort to moderate the extravagant pretensions of the American people about the meaning of the Monroe Doctrine might furnish undue encouragement for European aggression. He assured Roosevelt that because of that fear he had been at great pains to avoid suggesting any connection between his Yale speech, calling for a limited definition, and administration policy. I did not even let Hay know what I planned to say, Reid told Roosevelt.[41]

Reid's established policy predetermined his position when the Panama revolt came in November 1903. He sent Nicholson a detailed memorandum about the line to take in editorial treatment of the situation. The United States had responded correctly to all the events. Colombia was to be blamed for the trouble in the Isthmus, and Panama should be recognized and supported at once.[42] Reid quickly congratulated Roosevelt on his "Panama coup" and repeated his view that the chief use of the Monroe Doctrine was that it gave the United States the right to assert its authority anywhere in the Caribbean Sea or the Gulf of Mexico.[43]

Reid's only formal diplomatic activity between his work on the Peace Commission in 1898 and his appointment as ambassador to Great Britain in 1905 came midway between the two assignments. A year after Queen Victoria's death, notices were sent from London to foreign offices around the world inviting them to send representatives to the coronation of Edward VII in the summer of 1902. Roosevelt decided to send a special embassy, and Reid was a natural choice to head the mission; military and naval officers were added.[44] Perhaps Lizzie Reid's decision to accompany her husband and to take Jean, now eighteen, was a factor in the decisions of the "female households" of the other

American embassy members to make the trip. In any event, housing problems developed at once for the Americans. When Henry White, first secretary in London, learned that ladies would attend, he hastily consulted the lord chamberlain and soon informed the State Department that the king planned to be host to the special embassies but that ladies were not included in that part of the invitations. "Please let us know *as soon as possible*" which members of the embassy would be the king's guests, White begged the State Department and added that they would probably be put up at the Buckingham Palace Hotel. Hay referred the matter to Reid, remarking that the special ambassador would undoubtedly be better satisfied in a private house than in the hotel.[45]

Reid had already made plans to lease a house in London. He had secured Brook House in Park Lane for four thousand pounds for the summer, planning to remain there for some time after the coronation to take part in social events of the season. One social triumph eluded him. The Reids had invited Alice Roosevelt to visit them at Brook House but the president, after first approving, decided that his daughter should not go to England at that time.[46]

After the usual farewell dinners Reid sailed for London, arriving on June 7. The occasion was less eventful than his previous official visit, for the king fell ill, the coronation was postponed, and the special embassy was closed three weeks after it had begun. The Reids remained at Brook House for another month until July 26, when they sailed for New York. Ten days later Reid lunched with the president at Oyster Bay and recounted his experiences in England. The coronation was held quietly on August 9 without Reid's presence.[47]

Reid's occasional work on the diplomatic front and his greatly enlarged interest in foreign affairs paralleled activities in other areas. Two decades earlier he had written part of a long article on newspapers for the ninth edition of the *Encyclopedia Britannica*. When the tenth edition was planned in 1900, he was asked to revise his previous contribution and to keep the article short. Reid sent in 4,130 words, only to have his manuscript returned with instructions to cut it drastically. He rewrote the account and returned 2,700 words, still a bit more than the editors wanted, but they used it.[48]

Always interested in education Reid was pleased when he was made a member of the Board of Trustees at Stanford University in 1902.[49] He was much more interested in the University of the State of New York, and he had been an active member of the State Board of Regents for many years.[50]

Supervision of the educational system of Reid's adopted state was, by an 1853 statute, vested partly in a Board of Regents, a nonpartisan body, and partly in a Department of Public Instruction, which was headed by a political appointee. In the late decades of the century the phenomenal growth of public high schools in New York created an area where rivalry between the two directing authorities of the state educational system developed rapidly. In 1900 Theodore Roosevelt, as earlier governors had, proposed that the legislature act to unify the system. Reid opposed the change. He believed that New York's educational development was equal to any in the nation and thought it unwise to tamper with the bodies that were responsible. His main fear was that administration of the system would, if changed, fall into the hands of politicians, and he feared Platt's influence as well as a possible future loss of political control to the Democrats. He was particularly jealous of the power and prestige of the Board of Regents.[51] He thought that ideally every youth should have all the education his capacity "and his circumstances" would permit. He felt that success in America should be measured by academic achievement as well as by the dollar mark. He did not believe that America would ever cluster colleges in any university "as circumstances that can never be reproduced" had grouped several, half a millenium earlier, "on the banks of the Cam and the Isis." However, he considered that the English model could be followed in spirit. Colleges of moderate size under university direction and inspiration, although not physically near each other, could vitalize young minds. He thought that collegiate instruction in the humanities, by which he meant a "classical education," plus modern languages, philosophy, mathematics, and science, opened the door to further studies at university levels for men. He thought the idea of coeducation was a controversial matter. Vassar, Smith, Wellesley, and Bryn Mawr offered greater opportunities than women had in other countries, he felt, but he believed that university coeducation was inappropriate since women and men led different kinds of lives.[52] He conceded that reformers, even those who advocated simplified spelling, had a place in the universities but not in the common schools. Nor should young scholars be subjected to educational fads,

208

"not even the metric [system] fad," he thought. The basic fundamentals of reading, writing, and ciphering were the concern of the common school, he believed.[53]

Reid's views on education probably had less to do with his positions on the Board of Regents and elsewhere than did his financial and political standing. He opposed the inevitably approaching changes in the structure of the directing bodies of the New York educational system, yet he was elected vice-chancellor of the University of the State of New York in December 1902 after twenty-four years of close association with the institution. He still opposed basic changes and believed that the fifty-year-old system should be continued, perhaps with some additional definition of jurisdiction.[54]

However, long-needed revision of the system could not be prevented, and early in 1904 the state legislature passed a Unification Act. The new law reduced the number of regents from 19 to 11, defined their powers, created a new office within the Board of Regents, that of a commissioner of education, and established lines of authority over elementary and secondary schools, as well as colleges, universities, professional and technical schools, museums, and other agencies. Reid was elected for a term of nine years as a member of the new Board of Regents and shortly was elected as the first chancellor of the University of New York to serve under the new system. Andrew Sloan Draper became commissioner of education, an excellent choice in the chancellor's view.[55]

Reid's foreign assignment to the Jubilee, his participation as a member of the Peace Commission, and his mission to the coronation seemed to stimulate him, and for a time he took a larger part in the operation of the *Tribune* than he had since his mission to France. In 1901 H. N. Kellogg replaced Henry Hall as circulation manager, director of the press, delivery, and mail rooms, and manager of the *Tribune* Building. Reid instructed Kellogg as to his duties in detail and informed and advised him about his relationships with other staff members. He also described the paper's special constituencies. He told Kellogg that the *Tribune* had more clergymen among its readers than any three or four of the other city papers. The readers also included large proportions of college people and of reformers, the editor thought. In general, Reid said, the *Tribune* constituency consisted of "people with rather positive ideas," and he warned the new circulation manager to be on his guard against antagonizing one or more of the elements.[56] Four years later circulation was down and advertising was down, but Reid only asked for explanations without blaming Kellogg for the declines.[57]

The change from Hall to Kellogg was of less importance than the loss of a reporter a year later. In 1902, after twenty years with the paper, Max Seckendorff left the *Tribune* to go with Frank A. Munsey. Reid was very sorry, for the highly capable Seckendorff had been treated with confidence by most Washington officials, including McKinley and Roosevelt.[58] Not since Smalley had left the London bureau to represent the *Times* of London in Washington had the *Tribune* suffered a greater loss. But Smalley was replaced by Isaac Ford, a highly capable journalist who had been with the paper since Greeley's days. Seckendorff was replaced by Richard Lee Fearn, a good reporter, but farther from his predecessor in ability than Ford was from Smalley.

It was an indication of Reid's relationships with many of his employees that he had no inkling of Seckendorff's intentions; the letter of resignation, effective immediately, came as "a bolt out of the blue."[59] Another indication of a somewhat different nature was revealed in a complaint that Reid made to Hall a year and a half before Hall left the *Tribune*. It is a good illustration of how not to conduct a business, Reid told his employee, for you and Mr. Tuttle to be sitting at adjoining desks and "writing letters at each other through me."[60] Hall and Tuttle had been on the *Tribune* since Reid had taken it over. The sudden nature of Seckendorff's move is not clear. He spoke of money, but not until he had resigned. Both Hall and Tuttle were unsure of their authority in areas of doubtful responsibility and each feared to appear to challenge the other directly. Even Nicholson was unsure. After a quarter of a century on the paper, much of it as Reid's second in command, the Welshman hesitated to make even a small decision. When he referred a question about a twenty-dollar-a-week expense to his employer, Reid complained that it was "like extracting teeth to get an opinion from you," not realizing that virtually all his employees who had any financial responsibilities felt as Nicholson did.[61]

Reid's paper was in a weak financial position at the beginning of the century. This disturbed him, but not to the extent that monetary problems had upset him earlier. From time to time Tuttle had to call for loans to meet expenses. These were made by Reid or Mrs. Reid, who received interest, but the principal was not recovered.[62]

Although Reid watched the paper carefully in all of its aspects and advised all and sundry in both details and general policies, he relied on Donald Nicholson until his retirement for the management of the *Tribune* and for its direction, always with Reid's guidance. At times he felt it necessary to remind Nicholson of some broad policy. Many people think the *Tribune* speaks for the Republican party and this must be kept in mind, he warned in the summer of 1901. Later, on a more specific point, he ordered that attacks on the Brooklyn Transit Company be dropped, adding that he and the Mills family were heavy investors in that enterprise.[63] Occasionally he addressed himself to small details. When he discovered that typewriters were being used in the editorial room he demanded explanations: "I utterly disbelieve in the practice of dictating editorials," he said, adding that it led to wordy, slipshod composition.[64]

While Reid's active participation in the direction and management of the *Tribune* gradually lessened, his interest in it continued unabated. As his son grew up, the father thought that Ogden might one day want the paper for himself. When the elder Reid was sixty the younger was fifteen. The father thought the son reckless, careless, thoughtless, and immature. He drove too fast; when away from home he wrote infrequently and then did not date his letters; he was unconcerned about his studies. The father was shocked when his son dropped Latin and Greek after one year in college. But Whitelaw Reid had complete confidence in Ogden's ability to overcome these weaknesses, and his criticisms were gentle and understanding. When Ogden finished his studies at the Browning School in New York in 1899 at seventeen, Reid told Mr. Browning that the boy had ability to pass the entrance examinations at Yale, but was too immature to go to college. It was arranged that the young man should go to Camp Pasquanay where his father hoped the boy might learn some confidence in himself. The results were not favorable. In the fall Ogden was sent with a tutor, E. H. Rudd, to Bonn for a period of study and to grow a little older.[65]

The following year Ogden entered Yale. In his first year he continued his carefree ways, made barely passing grades; he did not improve later. In his senior year he procrastinated so long about paying his fees that the bursar had to write to his father about the matter. Later in the same year he took his polo ponies to New Haven, a diversion his dismayed parents thought he could ill afford. He was no more seriously bent when at home.

211

After one of Ogden's weekend visits to New York in the spring of 1904, Reid lamented to his wife, who was in the West with her father, that their son had managed to stay up all night, go twice to the theater, attend a reception, and dance until four in the morning, "etc.," in a single forty-eight-hour period. Two months before commencement the dean feared that Ogden's graduation was in doubt. In Yale's grading system, a student needed a minimum average of 200 on a scale of 400 in each course offered for a degree. Ogden had 220 in American Social Conditions, 210 in Society, 215 in Philosophy, 0.90 in Elementary Statistics, and "unsatisfactory" in Organic Evolution. Reid discussed the situation with his son but in despair reported to his wife that Ogden's "invincible cheerfulness leads him to regard the Dean's statement with indifference, and he reminds me that the Dean was mistaken before!" Ogden graduated with his class.[66]

Had the possibility of Ogden's taking over the paper not existed, the *Tribune* might well have been sold, for offers to buy it occasionally came and Reid was less and less active in its operation as he grew older. However, he thought of his ownership as a sort of trust and would not have disposed of it to other than a person or persons he believed would uphold his own editorial policies, moral principles, and political convictions.[67]

After returning from the mission to France in 1892, the Reids spent less and less time at their Florentine palace on Madison Avenue. When he was in his sixties the two went regularly to the west coast for several weeks each year, spending most of the time at Millbrae. The trip west was usually made in late February or early March, and they returned in April or May. In June and part of July they were usually at Ophir. From late July to late August they enjoyed the quiet and peace of life on upper St. Regis Lake at Wild Air. After that they alternated between Ophir and Madison Avenue. In one twelve-month period Reid spent some four months in New York City and the rest of the year at Millbrae, Ophir, or Wild Air.

In their transcontinental journeys they frequently rode in D. O. Mills's private car, the "Idler," and in crossing the country on at least one occasion every railroad that transported them was one in which Mills was a director. Usually the trips were uneventful, but the family barely missed death en route east in May 1901 when the "Idler" was badly damaged in a collision. Several members of the train crew were killed but the family escaped with scratches and bruises.[68]

When in New York City the Reids did their entertaining at the Madison Avenue house, where they could seat fifty people with ease in the dining room. The tablecloths were reportedly especially woven for them in Ireland, and guests speculated that the huge coverings could only be hung out to dry after laundering in Central Park.[69] The guest lists for these dinners in the years between the Jubilee and the mission to Great Britain reflected Reid's interests. Early in 1903 he told his friend of more than thirty years, John Quincy Adams Ward, that he was sorry the sculptor had failed to appear for a dinner. The ambassadors were all there, and most of them brought their wives and daughters, Reid said, along with several former first assistant secretaries of state as well as John Bigelow, Andrew Carnegie, and Pierpont Morgan. The editor had tried to "balance the bloated capitalists" with Ward and literary people such as William Dean Howells, Richard Watson Gilder, and E. C. Stedman. Only Stedman and Gilder appeared. "It always happens that way," Reid complained and added that Howells would probably follow up by inveighing against New York society for worshipping Mammon and neglecting art and literature.[70]

As much as he enjoyed the luxury and nearness to the *Tribune* Building of the Madison Avenue house and the quiet isolation of Wild Air, both of which he continued to expand and improve, Reid's favorite abode in his later years was Ophir. Fifteen years after acquiring the farm Reid had begun to think of it as Ophir Hall. In 1902 he had the words "Ophir Farm" on the entrance gate replaced with "Ophir Hall." He instructed his agent to do this quietly lest the newspapers in New York City "chatter about it."[71]

The altered name reflected few differences in the character of the place. After the extensive work at the time of the mission to France changes were more in degree than in kind. Reid had a small herd of Kerry cows, some sheep, various kinds of poultry, three collies, and two French poodles. About half of the thirty horses and ponies were for farm use and the others were for the carriages or for riding.[72] Reid named one of the horses Agate, his Civil War pen name. He still enjoyed riding and went by horseback over much of the seven hundred acres that comprised Ophir Hall several times a week when he was there. In 1902, when over sixty-four years old, he occasionally rode "after the hounds . . . in spite of my old bones and gray beard."[73]

Although he was in what might be called semiretirement, the matter of a political appointment for Reid continued to come up from time to time. He never became reconciled to Choate's appointment to England. He thought of the ambassador as inept, not fitted socially or politically for his position; he saw him as a speaker with more wit than judgment.[74]

Such views, although privately expressed, were widely suspected and were frequently attributed to jealousy on Reid's part. The *Sun* and other papers as well as individuals, with just enough basis to make it seem plausible, had constructed an image of Reid as an insatiable office-seeker, lying in wait for every place that might become vacant at home or abroad.[75] The *Tribune*'s writers had defended their employer for years against these accusations, and Reid sometimes wrote in his paper in his own defense. In November of 1899 he repeated the often stated denials in an editorial he wrote himself. He said that Mr. Reid had never asked for an office; that each of three successive Republican administrations (Hayes, Garfield, and Harrison) had tendered him a place. When he finally accepted the third, he continued, he finished his work and resigned to return to private life before his term expired, a thing almost unheard of in such a post. The two temporary posts under McKinley were absolutely unsolicited and undesired.[76]

After mid-1899, however, with Choate firmly in London, Hay in State, Root in the War Department—in which Reid was interested because of its role in the administration of the new island possessions—Reid was less concerned about the gossip and rumors than at earlier times when they might have influenced an appointment.

The first possible opening after Choate's appointment came so unexpectedly and was over so quickly that speculation did not develop. At the end of McKinley's first term John W. Griggs left the cabinet, and the president offered the attorney-general's department to Choate. Thinking he would take the place and that Reid might then be given the embassy in London, McKinley summoned Reid to Washington. But Choate declined the offer.[77] Fifteen months later Roosevelt sent Reid to the planned coronation of Edward VII. The king's illness and postponement of the coronation were somewhat frustrating, but Reid renewed acquaintances he had made at the Jubilee and enjoyed the short visit to England. He also gained the usual ironic comments on his efforts and interests. In a conversation invented by Finley Peter Dunne, Hennessey asked Dooley what was going on. Dooley reeled off thirty or forty news items including one to the effect that "Th' Hon'rable Whitelaw Reid is havin' a cast of his knee breeches made, which will be exhibited in New York during th' comin' winter."[78]

Reid supported Roosevelt in his domestic policies as well as in foreign affairs. During the labor struggles of the first administration the *Tribune* stood to the right of the president. It favored his firm stand in the coal strike of 1902 and would have supported much stronger action. Reid seemed to be oblivious of the inequality in bargaining relations between the employer and the individual employee, whether in the *Tribune* rooms or in coal mines or in railroads. As industry grew larger the position of the worker became weaker, but changing conditions did not change his views, and in his economic philosophy he stood with the industrial capitalists of his generation. He held to the same position he had taken in the railroad strikes of 1877 and reiterated these in a speech at Carnegie Hall in Pittsburgh in 1902. Labor had a right to combine to seek better wages, hours, and working conditions, but the use of violence to attain such ends could not be tolerated. Respect for authority and the maintenance of law and order were among the principles upon which the country had been founded, Reid believed. The widest respect for individual initiative and the right of every man to sell his own labor without interference from unions were basic elements of this philosophy.[79]

In another area Reid's position was closer to Roosevelt's, even though the president's cause was not in line with the views of a majority of the *Tribune*'s readers. As early as 1890 Reid had recognized a distinction between "good" and "bad" trusts, between the legitimate growth of business on one hand and combinations that might endanger public welfare on another. The *Tribune* condemned the indiscriminate denunciation of every trust, whether it harmed the public or not, but held that combinations achieved by unfair practices designed to obtain monopolistic power could be regulated by the government. In line with this view, in March 1904 the *Tribune* pointed out that Wall Street's forebodings about Roosevelt's ruining the country by prosecuting the Northern Securities Company had been unjustified. The Supreme Court had agreed with the executive branch of the government, and despite dire predictions business was undisturbed, Northern Securities stock had risen in price, and the country was satisfied with the results, Reid's paper stated.[80]

At this time, on the whole, the New York press was hostile to Roosevelt. The *Tribune*'s position on his foreign and domestic policies virtually isolated Reid among the editors in the city. The *World* opposed the president's foreign policy, the *Sun* inveighed against his domestic program, and the other papers took similarly adverse stances. In February 1904 Reid told the president that he was lonely in the New York newspaper field in supporting the administration.[81]

Six months later Reid, while defending Roosevelt, showed a rarely exposed yet constant and integral element of his character. In August Joseph Pulitzer accused the president of trying to make himself a dictator. Reid hastened to warn Nicholson not to attack Pulitzer. For one thing, Nicholson was reminded, Pulitzer was blind, and for another, he had always personally liked Reid. Refute his accusation indirectly, Reid instructed, but without referring to the author.[82] Earlier the editor had learned that Hay had been invited to take a place as one of the original trustees of Pulitzer's newly established School of Journalism at Columbia College. Reid urged his friend to accept Nicholas Murray Butler's and Pulitzer's offer.[83]

The combined effects of continued support of the party, his careful treatment of and growing personal association with the president and members of his family, his greatly improved relations with the New York machine through the handshake with Platt and an understanding with Odell, and his heavy financial support of the Republicans finally gained for Reid the longwanted appointment as ambassador to Great Britain. Sometime late in 1904 Roosevelt decided to appoint the editor to the place, despite a long-standing aversion to having editors as ambassadors. There were still objections, but Roosevelt, unlike McKinley, would not be moved. He believed that Reid was fitted for the place and that he deserved the embassy. The matter was so well settled by the end of the year that the *Tribune* could print a summary of unofficial but probable changes in diplomatic posts and include Choate's and Reid's names.[84]

The Reids began to make plans at once to obtain a house in London, staff it, and to make provisions for their New York residences for what they thought would probably be a four-year period beginning in March when Choate was expected to return to New York. They had a longer planning period than they wanted, for Choate was not ready to leave London. Two weeks before Roosevelt's inauguration Choate secured the president's approval of his intent to remain in his position until he could dedicate a memorial window to John Harvard he had given to St. Saviour's Church, but which was not yet ready to be installed.[85] The Reids were furious. Lizzie Reid complained to her friend Anna Roosevelt Cowles, the president's sister. She could not believe the president intended to do such an unfair thing as to deprive her husband of a season in London.[86] Reid complained to Hay, labeling Choate's action unreasonable, discourteous, and trifling with the president.[87] But nothing could be done. Reid ruefully accepted the situation and even allowed Choate to extract a letter from him accepting as valid Choate's explanation of his longer stay at his post.[88]

Meantime, Henry White, first secretary at the embassy, worked to secure a house in London for the new ambassador. After much negotiation he leased Dorchester House, a palatial mansion and a fine example of Renaissance architecture, located directly opposite Hyde Park in Park Lane. The place was far finer than Brook House, which Reid had taken for the coronation, and much more sumptuous than Choate's comparatively simple residence in Carlton House Terrace. The task of making final preparations for Reid's arrival in London fell to John Ridgely Carter who succeeded White as first secretary when the latter was sent to Rome as minister. Carter's problems were more complex if less crucial than those of his predecessor. They involved the engaging of a staff, the acquisition of horses, motors, and other equipage, and the making of arrangements for the reception of the new ambassador and his family.[89]

In New York the paper was quickly cared for. Since Nicholson had recently retired, continuity of management and policy for the *Tribune* was provided by giving the titles of editor and publisher, held by Reid, to Nicholson's former assistant, Hart Lyman. James Martin, a trusted writer, was named managing editor.[90]

The Reids sailed for England on May 27.

15

Mission to Great Britain: I

THE REIDS landed in England June 3, and welcoming delegations greeted them warmly at Plymouth and at Southampton.[1] The embassy staff met them at Waterloo Station and escorted the family to Dorchester House, one of the most beautiful and impressive homes in London.[2] Two days later the ambassador and his family were driven to the palace in three royal carriages with an escort. After Reid had presented his credentials, the king received the members of the ambassador's family. The first duties of the newly arrived representative of the United States were social, and a long list of luncheons, dinners, balls, and other affairs had awaited his arrival.[3] On their side the Reids entertained in a style that made other ambassadors envious and awed many of their guests.

Despite its magnificence, Dorchester House was not a satisfactory abode for year-round living for them, partly because Reid feared that the London winter would affect his health adversely and partly because they wanted a retreat out of the city. They rented Wrest Park, a spacious place forty miles from Dorchester House or an hour and three-quarters in Reid's motor car, a saving of an hour over the time required by train. The mansion stood on a terrace surrounded by marble statuary. The grounds were wooded, there was a deer park, a lake for boating; there were seven miles of walks, and a fine dining hall stood in the woods. Unfortunately, there were no electric lights in the mansion, but Reid did not mind. He employed forty-four servants there and felt that these "important personages" were quite able to care for the oil lamps without being overworked. Guests invited to Wrest Park from London could make their own way or they could take a train from St. Pancras Station to Flitwick. If the latter, Reid's automobile, painted in blue with red lines and his monogram on the doors, would meet the visitors and drive them to the mansion.[4]

Besides being an ideal place to entertain, Wrest Park was a place where Reid could indulge in sports and exercise, especially horseback riding. As he had done during much of his life he rode in all seasons and all weathers and felt deprived when he could not go out. He also enjoyed shooting parties with numbers of guests or with a few intimates. At the age of seventy he and two friends spent a day in the field. Reid killed "over a dozen pheasants" and several hares and rabbits. He went out to shoot with confidence because, in that same year, he had acquired "some shooting spectacles" that made it possible for him to keep up the sport despite weakening vision.[5]

The magnificence of the ambassador's establishments in England, which together cost some fourteen thousand dollars a month to maintain, soon attracted the attention of critics. Reid felt it necessary to defend himself to the president and to advise his paper. He pointed out that his dining rooms in the Madison Avenue house and at Ophir were larger than those at Dorchester House and at Wrest Park, and that therefore his dinner parties in England were smaller than in New York. The rent he paid on Park Lane was little more than he could get for his New York house, and the upkeep on Wrest Park was much less than at Ophir. In short, he lived in London much as he did in New York. Nevertheless, the carping comments irritated him. One attack provoked him to remark disgustedly that he supposed the critic, a congressman from Louisville, would like to have the American ambassador entertain on the Kentucky plan—hog and hominy, corn pone and bourbon whiskey, with a subsequent séance at draw poker.[6]

A more generous commentator recalled that the ambassador seemed quite in place amid the sumptuous furnishings and costly pictures in Dorchester House and that he had a simple and sincere love of grandeur. Reporters, recalling Reid's journalistic background, hoped to find him a ready source of news. They found him courteous, friendly, and pleasant, but they were discouraged at having to run a gauntlet of "half a dozen liveried flunkies" before being able to see the ambassador.[7] The house was, however, more open on some occasions. Soon after his arrival more than three thousand persons attended a Fourth of July reception at Dorchester House. The crowds continued to be large at this annual Independence Day event and more than five thousand came in 1911.[8]

On a smaller scale, Reid invited scores of prominent Americans to visit his English homes. Henry Adams came for a week in 1907. Reid found him charming and easy to entertain. The two discussed Adams' work on the publication of John Hay's letters, and the visitor asked his host to look over some Reid-Hay correspondence that Adams thought would be appropriate for publishing.

One American who was not invited was Samuel Gompers. The English-born president of the American Federation of Labor visited his native land in the summer of 1909. His friends sought invitations for him, and the National Civic Federation asked Reid's aid in obtaining an invitation for Gompers to speak at the July Fourth dinner of the American Society in London. Reid could not recall any recent activities of the labor leader and asked the *Tribune*'s editor, Hart Lyman, for an opinion. Lyman sent a strongly adverse report, including the point that Gompers was then under an indictment for contempt of court. Using that point as a reason Reid prevented his countryman from having an invitation to the dinner.[9]

Of all the Americans who visited England while Reid was ambassador, none was more welcome than Theodore Roosevelt. After leaving the White House the ex-president traveled widely and, following his famed African trip, visited Europe and England. Reid kept in close touch with Roosevelt's plans from the outset. Even before the election of 1908 the ambassador had begun to collect information about game preserves in Africa, elephant guns, camping equipment, and other things that would be helpful on a hunting trip.[10]

For the visit to England, Reid became Roosevelt's host and chief planner. Roosevelt had originally intended to have a personal and informal visit to England with his old friend of Cuban campaign days, Arthur Lee, now a Conservative member of Parliament. Reid realized at once that Roosevelt's ebullient personality and world reputation made it impossible for him to travel as a simple private citizen. The ambassador foresaw that many great pressures both political and social would be exerted by those wanting to talk with, entertain, or just meet the ex-president. Only after much effort on Reid's part was Roosevelt convinced. He made Dorchester House and Wrest Park his headquarters, and Reid planned much of the detail for the English visit. An unforeseen event made the occasion even more important than expected. King Edward VII died a few days before Roosevelt's arrival and the funeral was held while he was in London. Partly at Reid's suggestion, Taft made Roosevelt a special ambassador to attend the ceremonies. Most of the crowned heads of Europe came. Roosevelt rode in the funeral procession with the new king, George V, the kaiser, and seven other European sovereigns, and later he was more sought after than any of them. Only Buckingham Palace, where the kaiser stayed, rivaled

Dorchester House as a social center during the ex-president's visit.[11]

Reid's only regret in all this was the necessity of wearing the "simple dress of an American citizen" as he had had to do at Victoria's Jubilee. The only concession to foreign custom was the substitution of black knee breeches and silk stockings for trousers, worn as a part of a full dress suit at court functions. Reid professed not to mind the contrast with the brilliant diplomatic costumes of other ambassadors in the evening. He complained, however, that evening dress with white tie and gloves gave one a very dissipated look at 11:30 in the morning.[12]

When he went to London in 1905 Reid expected to stay through Roosevelt's term in office, that is, until the spring of 1909. In the election of 1908 he supported Taft and the Republicans strongly in the *Tribune* and even more strongly than usual with contributions. He was credited by the Republican National Committee with a gift of ten thousand dollars, the same as that of J. P. Morgan. Reid told Charles Evans Hughes of the amount and remarked that he considered ten thousand dollars the maximum sum one might contribute without being suspected of dishonorable motives. However, he told Roosevelt that he gave the party more than twice that amount, and he believed that only Charles·Taft and Larz Anderson gave more.[13]

After Taft's election Reid lost no time in making it plain that he was in no haste to retire from his post. He denied that he was interested in election to the Senate or that he wanted to be secretary of state, as newspaper reporters had alleged. He placed his office at Taft's disposal, "as I suppose to be the practice at the incoming of a new Administration, even of one's own party." He asked only that if he were to be replaced he be advised "in time to retire with dignity." At the same time he made it plain to Taft that he would be willing to remain in London for the 1909 season.[14]

Reid expressed his wishes more strongly to men he knew better than he knew the incoming president and indicated that he thought it only reasonable that he remain as ambassador until after Roosevelt's visit. He asked support from Senators Henry Cabot Lodge, Chauncey Depew, and Stephen B. Elkins, from Andrew Carnegie, and most important, from Roosevelt. He sent Hart Lyman to see Taft. To remain until August was, for family reasons, so important that Reid said he'd stay in London whether he was replaced as ambassador or not. He felt that a new ambassador would be embarrassed to begin a term with the old one still in London. Beyond that, a new man could hardly cope with the complexities of Roosevelt's visit, and if Reid were replaced Roosevelt would be put in difficult situations while in London. The efforts were successful and before Taft's inauguration Reid knew that he was assured another season and that probably he would still be at his post when Roosevelt came.[15]

Taft had considered a new man for London, but the pressures and his desire not to antagonize Reid caused him to refrain from sending a replacement immediately. Shortly after his inauguration he offered to appoint Charles W. Eliot, then about to resign the presidency of Harvard University, to succeed Reid in the following year. After thinking it over the seventy-five-year-old Eliot declined, Reid did not again offer to leave, and Taft did not find a candidate for the place with enough influence to bring about a change.[16]

One reason the Reids were so anxious to remain in England was their daughter's situation. Late in April or early in May 1908 Jean startled her parents with the news that she planned to marry an Englishman, and at an early date. Further, he was twice her age. After his first shock, Reid found reasons to be sanguine about the match. He would not be subjected to the then common charge against wealthy Americans of buying a title for his daughter. The Honorable John Ward did not have a title; he was the younger brother of the Earl of Dudley. Further, he had independent means, a fortune of some half a million dollars, and he held a number of good posts. The difference in years, Reid reasoned, was less important than that Johnny, as he was called, had reached an age when stability and a settled life were important concerns.[17]

The family approved of the match. D. O. Mills gave Jean a hundred thousand dollars; the Reids gave her a like amount. The Wards then purchased a twenty-three-hundred-acre estate, Chilton Lodge, some ten miles from Newberry, for something less than half a million dollars, taking a mortgage for the difference between the cost and the Mills-Reid gifts.[18]

While enjoying their homes in England the Reids watched their American homes, not only the Madison Avenue house, Ophir, and Wild Air, but also the Mills' houses at 634 Fifth Avenue and Millbrae in San Mateo County, as well as the Reid homestead in Xenia. While abroad, as they had done when in France, they made changes in the New York houses. They enlarged the Madison Avenue house by building additions at the rear and by making renovations inside. The work was carefully supervised from London by Lizzie Reid, the legal owner of the house and the real planner.[19]

Expansion plans at Ophir were not extensive when the Reids first went to England, but the absentee owner kept a close watch on his manager. William C. Whipple, an amiable and honest but somewhat less than energetic person, did reasonably well in caring for the stock, the farm, and the main house, but the gate cottage and infrequently used equipment gradually deteriorated. In 1910 the Reids summoned William R. Mead of McKim, Mead, and White to London to discuss Ophir. They intended to spend most of their time there after leaving London and planned elaborate and extended additions. Reid thought of many of the additions as a library in memory of D. O. Mills, who had died early in the year. It is an indication of Reid's character that he insisted that the stone for the new walls and additions come from his own quarries, as had the bulk of the stone work for the other structures. He felt a deep sentimental interest in the integral relationship between the land and the buildings.[20]

The situation at Wild Air was similar to that on Madison Avenue and at Ophir. Early in 1906 Reid instructed Fred Barnes to make such repairs on the roofs of the cabins as to ensure their good condition "in our life-times."[21] Two years later McKim, Mead, and White were making drawings for a new building with many improvements in the main structure. The idea, again, was Lizzie Reid's and she planned much of the detail. The family had used the camp for a month during August and September of 1909 and had celebrated Mills' eighty-fifth birthday there on September 5. During the other years of the mission to Great Britain they found little time for Upper St. Regis.[22]

When on leave from his post Reid rarely visited Xenia, as no member of the family had lived there since his mother's death. However, he instructed William Conley, the farm manager, to keep "the family part of the old house" in constant order so that he could stop there at any time. He also ordered simple changes in the landscape such as the planting of cedar, black walnut, hickory, and oak, and the removal of some of the ash trees. Conley sent small sums annually as the owner's portion of the farm income after expenses had been paid.[23] Some of this money found its way back to Xenia or Cedarville. In his late years Xenia's wealthiest and most distinguished son could not refuse requests from old inhabitants for financial aid because of illness or other misfortune.[24]

Reid returned to the United States regularly during his mission to England. He crossed the Atlantic at least sixteen times after arriving in London in June 1905. When the family traveled together they usually took a three-room suite on a Cunard or White Star Line vessel and additional accommodations for several secretaries and servants.[25] The trips home were principally for personal and family reasons, primarily to see his son Ogden and Mrs. Reid's father and brother, to look over the houses, and to talk with friends. The ambassador always went to Washington at least once while in the United States. He spent little time in the *Tribune* Building.

When Reid went to London in 1905, Ogden Mills became president of the *Tribune* Association. Hart Lyman was put in charge of the paper as editor and publisher at a salary of ten thousand dollars. Then fifty-four years old, he had been with the *Tribune* since the mid-seventies and had been Donald Nicholson's assistant in the latter's last years as editor. Lyman was a Yale graduate, a thorough Republican, and a member of the University Club. He could be trusted to keep the paper on course as, in Reid's words, the most "trustworthy and the best family newspaper in New York—the one which a gentleman (at least one of Republican leanings) is better satisfied to read every morning himself and to have read in his family." After being away three years and despite watching the paper lose circulation and money, Reid still believed in aiming at a constituency which wanted "a paper written by gentlemen for gentlemen."[26]

When Lyman took the *Tribune* over, his managing editor was James Martin; a year later Roscoe C. E. Brown succeeded Martin and remained in the place until 1912. Lyman, Brown, and Reid's other lieutenants were under heavy pressure from Adolph Ochs's *Times*, William Randolph Hearst's *Journal*, and Joseph Pulitzer's *World* in a continuing battle for circulation and advertising accounts. Without Reid's presence and aware that they were only occupying their places pending his son's decision to take the paper, Reid's lieutenants simply kept it going.[27]

The effects of this policy were damaging. An article entitled, "Is An Honest Newspaper Possible?" appeared in the October 1908 issue of the *Atlantic Monthly*. The anonymous author described the woeful condition of the press and detailed the strengths and weaknesses of seven leading New York papers. None was given a high rating, and the *Tribune* fell near the bottom of the group. It was the last specimen left in the city of a newspaper operated for a political machine, the article stated. Its editorial policy was simply the endorsement of the Republican party. Its financial page was beneath contempt. The news columns were readable but commonplace in content; the best feature was the reporting of foreign news, which was sometimes above average. The author did not name any paper he discussed, but Reid easily identified all seven from the descriptions. He was angry and told Lyman to run a story on the article in the *Tribune* defending the press and describing the *Atlantic* as a once great literary magazine that had deteriorated in quality.[28]

The magazine's assessment was not entirely fair but it had some truth. The *Tribune* gradually lost readers, its income ceased to match its expenses, and it could only be kept going by subsidy. Bonds were issued to ease the burden but without avail. The small stockholders did not take them, and more than 90 percent of them were bought by the Reids or by Ogden Mills. The last ones went to Reid in 1911 and were transferred to his son, giving Ogden his first substantial ownership in the property. The few shares of *Tribune* stock held outside the family also gradually found their way into Reid's safe as small holders offered them. Reid always bought them, always anonymously, through his bookkeepers. One of the odd shares was reissued in Ogden's name early in 1909 so that, as a shareholder, he could be made a member of the board of directors.[29]

While Reid was in London a quarter to a half million dollars a year had to be pumped into the weakening paper. This expense, plus the cost of construction on Madison Avenue and at Ophir, when added to the expenses at Dorchester House and Wrest Park, put a strain on Reid's income. Less than a month before his death he sought a short term loan of four hundred thousand dollars to tide him over the cost of closing his English residences, returning home, and reestablishing himself in New York.[30]

Meantime Ogden remained in the United States while his parents and sister resided in England. Born when Reid was forty-five years of age, the boy had been his father's pride and his despair. The elder Reid taught the younger to ride, to shoot, and to swim and was pleased that Ogden was a better shot and a better swimmer than he. He worried about his son's poor academic performance and his irresponsibility. Ogden was not concerned. After graduating from Yale he went on to complete the requirements for a law degree. He then worked in a law office for a time and was admitted to the bar in 1908. In the summer of that year he decided to go on the *Tribune*. He began as a reporter, worked on the copy desk, served as assistant editor, assistant night editor, and in other places. In the spring of 1912 he took the position of managing editor. His father was pleased that the son wanted to keep the paper, but the carelessness was still a problem. When Ogden was twenty-seven he let a club bill go unpaid, although he received an allowance of twenty-five hundred dollars a month. When this came to Reid's attention he chided his son but was more displeased at the club manager's rude manner of sending second notices of unpaid dues.

Later, after Ogden became managing editor, his inattention affected the paper. On one occasion he ignored the pleas of the *Tribune*'s London correspondent so long that the man went to see Reid. Reid gave the correspondent the relief he had been unable to get from Ogden and criticized his son severely for carelessness that might have cost the paper a good reporter. More important, when Reid, seeking to improve the editorial and literary quality of the *Tribune*, asked that marked copies of the paper be sent to London, Ogden ignored the request, and Reid had to bring the matter to Lyman's attention.[31]

A little less than three years after Jean's wedding her brother decided to follow the example. Early in February 1911 Ogden astonished his father with the news that he was engaged and planned to marry at once. Ogden's bride-to-be was Helen Rogers, a native of Wisconsin who was Mrs. Reid's private secretary and an intimate friend of Jean. She had left the state of her birth to enter Barnard College in New York, where she did typing, tutoring, and other work to earn part of her expenses. After graduating she was recommended to Mrs. Reid, who wanted a private secretary, and was immediately accepted. Helen Rogers went to London in that capacity in 1905.[32] The warmth and personality of the diminutive (five-feet, one-inch) Miss Rogers endeared her to Jean, and her relationship with Ogden became more than casual in the summer of 1910 when the younger Reid accepted his father's invitation to spend a season in London as private secretary to the ambassador.[33]

Reid, in the United States on leave when Ogden made his announcement, had arranged to return to England at the end of February but hastily obtained Secretary of State Philander Knox's permission to extend his leave in order to attend the wedding. The marriage took place in Racine, Wisconsin, in mid-March 1911, and Reid was back at his post at the end of the month. He arrived just in time to attend the American and Foreign Bible Society's commemoration of the tercentenary of the King James English translation of the Bible.[34]

Attending such affairs and frequently making a few remarks, if not a speech, were a regular part of the American ambassador's duties, and Reid knew this when he went to London. English expectations were greater than he had anticipated, however, and he soon discovered that, as he put it, Thomas F. Bayard and Joseph H. Choate had thoroughly demoralized the British by their willingness, not to say eagerness, to speak publicly. It was assumed he would do so at any time and with little or no notice.

Reid had been accustomed to appear before audiences from the beginning of his membership in the Lotos Club and especially during his long presidency of that body. The campaign in 1892 gave him valuable speaking experience of quite another kind. Extemporaneous remarks were no problem for him, especially since so many talks could, as they were expected to, deal simply with Anglo-American friendship, a subject of intense and continuous interest to Reid since the Diamond Jubilee of 1897. Reid's anglophilism even caused him to adopt a slight British accent. Although he spoke well without preparation he preferred to make a set speech, which he frequently put in the form of an essay. Much research went into the best of these, frequently involving the use of statistics, exact dates, and detailed facts, for which he relied on his secretary or members of the *Tribune* staff. Even after thorough preparation and after nearly half a century of experience, he still offered his thoughts to an audience with some trepidation. "Next to the decisions of a petit jury, there is nothing in Heaven above, the earth below, or the waters under the earth, more absolutely uncertain than the reception any speech is likely to get," he told Roscoe Brown after more than six years as ambassador.[35]

Most of the speeches were well received, nearly all were reported in the *Tribune*, and Reid had many of them made into pamphlets, sometimes printing five hundred to a thousand copies, which he sent to his friends. He not only wanted the major addresses read, he wanted to see in print the routine remarks he made at presentations of medals, at unveilings, commemorations of Washington's birthday, Independence Day, Thanksgiving, and other occasions. Reid did not always tell Lyman to use his speeches in full but he sent copies to New York when there was time. He also frequently suggested the use of explanatory comments to precede the printed speech. One was newsworthy because it was made in response to the first request ever made to an American to talk about the Revolution to a great English university, he informed Lyman; another could be used in full because of "an unusual interest in Thanksgiving this year"; another had attracted wide interest in the English press. Reid liked to have the *Tribune* quote the text of a speech from London papers when possible. This will enable you, he told Lyman, to preface the report with "from the London _____," and to put in notes of "cheers" and other interruptions, which lend vivacity to the report.[36]

Reid sent copies of his major addresses and some minor ones to individuals ranging from the king and Roosevelt to William Conley, the farm manager in Xenia, and offered to send the latter extra copies if he knew anyone in Xenia or Cedarville who might be interested.[37] One of his more impressive addresses was on Abraham Lincoln and was delivered at the University of Birmingham near the end of 1910. This publicly expressed estimate of Lincoln was more generous than earlier judgments. Reid still saw the warts and pointed them out, but he now said that the patience, wisdom, final success in war, and statesmanlike leadership of the nation were far more important. Privately he still had many reservations about Lincoln's statesmanship, popular leadership, and executive capacity, but thought that despite these lacks the wartime president was one of the great leaders in the history of the English-speaking race. When Roosevelt read the Lincoln address he told Reid that it was the best thing of its kind any American ambassador to Great Britain had ever done, "even Lowell."[38]

Reid's speeches and entertaining during his years in London gained more attention and left stronger impressions than did his negotiations in Anglo-American political and economic relations. Sydney Brooks, writing in *Harpers Weekly* early in 1909, said that American ambassadors in London were expected to be agents of good will rather than professional diplomats. Reid's urbane handling of the exacting social requirements demanded of the ambassadors and his superior abilities as a speaker had made him an outstanding success in London,

Brooks believed. A decade after Reid's death Chauncey Depew wrote that his friend of forty years had been ideal as the American ambassador to Great Britain. He was a cordial and charming host who entertained lavishly and delightfully, and he was an excellent speaker, Depew recalled.[39]

16

Mission to Great Britain: II

"IN THE years from 1905 to 1912 there was not much in the handling of public affairs between the Government of the United States and ourselves that retains sufficient interest to be described here." Thus Lord Grey, British foreign minister during most of those years, writing his memoirs a decade later, recalled the period during which Reid served as the American ambassador to Great Britain.[1] After six and a half years in London Reid remarked to his predecessor there, speaking of his own incumbency, "Happy is the embassy whose annals are dull." He then added that with minor exceptions there was nothing to occupy him or his counterpart in Washington but the "monotony of constant good feeling between the two countries."[2]

Indeed, critical problems did not arise while Reid was in London, although a number of matters required his attention and occasionally some diplomatic maneuvering was necessary. Even here, however, Reid was not often called on for serious effort. His first secretary, John Ridgely Carter, was a capable officer in his own right, widely known and highly respected in diplomatic circles. When he left the embassy to become minister to Rumania in 1909 he was succeeded by the equally capable William Phillips, who served until the eve of Reid's death. These two relieved the ambassador of all routine matters and of much work at high levels of diplomacy.[3] In addition to the indispensable first secretaries, the chancery staff included second and third secretaries, military and naval attachés, a personal secretary for the ambassador, plus two messengers and a stenographer. These took pride in serving under an ambassador of Reid's background, distinction, and international reputation. At the same time some found him cold and withdrawn as a person, without "the easy friendliness of Mr. Choate."[4]

The only purely Anglo-American question of major proportions that was at issue in Reid's incumbency was that of the Newfoundland fisheries, and this was largely handled in Washington. Lesser negotiations involved an Anglo-American arbitration treaty, a commercial convention, and the Panama tolls controversy. Other matters

231

that involved the United States and England concerned other countries as well and were only Reid's responsibility in part. These included mediation of the Russo-Japanese War, the Moroccan dispute, arbitration agreements, Chinese loans, and minor matters. Reid's role in most of these was peripheral.

One reason for this was that Theodore Roosevelt watched closely over the nation's foreign affairs himself while he was in the White House. He was not only his own secretary of state, he frequently used his personal friends rather than his ambassadors as his diplomatic emissaries. He could do this because of his character and personality and because of some circumstances of his younger years. In the 1890s "in the gay social circle in which he moved in Washington, he dined, danced, rode horseback, discussed literature, argued about the affairs of the world and formed permanent friendships with young diplomats serving apprenticeships at their legations in Washington who were to occupy much more important posts while he was President."[5] Two of the most important were Cecil Spring-Rice and Hermann Speck von Sternburg. A third was Roosevelt's tentmate in the Spanish-American War, the British military attaché, Arthur Lee. Lee later was a member of Parliament and served in Arthur Balfour's government. Further intimate relationships were formed later during President Roosevelt's informal hikes and rides through Rock Creek Park and swims in the icy Potomac in springtime. Speck von Sternburg, then the German ambassador, and Jules Jusserand, the French ambassador, renewed Roosevelt's confidence and friendship while accompanying him in such activities. Others suffered in Roosevelt's eyes when they could not keep up. One such, to his mortification, was Britain's ambassador, Sir Mortimer Durand.[6]

Reid's work as ambassador was affected by these relationships from the beginnings of his mission, and the origins of the Algeciras Conference make this aspect of his tenure quite plain. At the beginning of the twentieth century France sought to extend her influence in Morocco, and early in 1905 Germany decided to oppose the effort. Wilhelm II precipitated a crisis when he visited Tangier and spoke on March 31 in support of Moroccan independence from foreign influences. This serious German challenge to French policy concerned the powers to such an extent that by June Roosevelt had decided to attempt to bring about an international conference. He discussed the matter at length privately, unofficially, and frankly with Jusserand and learned that

France was eager for a peaceful settlement. He learned through Speck von Sternburg that the German emperor was willing to compromise. When Roosevelt assured each power that the other was interested in a settlement, Germany and France agreed to meet at Algeciras. The president's "crony diplomacy" thus brought about a conference that might have been very difficult for others to arrange. Roosevelt told Lodge, Taft, and Root of his efforts. He did not tell Secretary of State Hay and he did not inform Reid.[7] In fact, in February 1906, a month after the conference opened and ten months after Roosevelt's first efforts in the matter, Reid was so much in the dark that he complained to Root, Hay's successor in the State Department, that he knew little more than what appeared in the papers and asked for a statement he could use if questioned.[8] Eventually, long after the conference was over, Roosevelt sent his ambassador in London a "quarto-volume," as the president called it, about the preliminary negotiations. Marked "Absolutely Private and Confidential," the long letter included copies of correspondence between the president, von Sternburg, the kaiser, Taft, Jusserand, and Root and gave Reid a complete account of Roosevelt's diplomacy.[9]

Some events that took place in the second year of Reid's mission provide another example of relationships in Rooseveltian diplomacy. In that year the president refused to permit his ambassador to Great Britain to show the king some of Roosevelt's correspondence with the kaiser, fearing a possible misinterpretation of some exchanges. In the fall of 1906, however, the president asked Arthur Lee to cross the Atlantic for a visit. Lee went to Washington, and Roosevelt gave his former tentmate information he would not give to his ambassador but that he wanted the British government to have. He told Lee about his roles in the Algeciras and Portsmouth negotiations, his actions in the Bering Sea seal controversy, the Newfoundland fisheries question, the Chinese customs problem, and his attitudes in other matters. Lee returned to London and gave the king and Sir Edward Grey, the new foreign secretary, their first direct information about Roosevelt's position and thoughts in those affairs.[10]

Reid's most intimate friend among the people near Roosevelt in Washington, Secretary of State John Hay, died less than a month after Reid's arrival in London. This, however, deprived Reid of very little private information about presidential policies or plans. Roosevelt thought of the two men in somewhat the same way. Both had been friends of his father and had known him as a boy. Neither was in the inner circle of Roosevelt's intimates that included Lodge, Taft, and Root. The president confided in Root in all matters, in Lodge and Taft in most, and in Arthur Lee, Cecil Spring-Rice, Jules Jusserand, and Speck von Sternburg in areas of international affairs. Root, athough a leading New York Republican, had never been close to the editor of the *Tribune*. Thus, in matters of big importance involving America and Britain, the president and the secretary of state frequently used other channels of communication than that of the embassy in London.

This is not to say that Roosevelt distrusted Reid, did not have confidence in him, or disliked him. Reid wrote long, chatty letters to Mrs. Roosevelt about things that he and his popular, well-acquainted first secretary picked up at dinners, balls, the races, formal teas, and informal talks. The sidelights on events of the day, London gossip, the royal household, the diplomatic set, and the streams of visitors who flowed through the embassy and the chancellery fascinated the president as well as his wife. "Don't stop writing Mrs. Roosevelt," he urged, while telling Reid that he'd better communicate directly with Secretary of State Root on official matters, rather than through the White House.[11]

In another vein the president entrusted Reid with a delicate task he had earlier given to Lodge while Choate was ambassador. Lodge had not succeeded. When Britain's ambassador to the United States, Sir Michael Herbert, died in 1903 Roosevelt wanted his old friend Spring-Rice to succeed Sir Michael. But the foreign office sent Sir Mortimer Durand to Washington. Durand admired Roosevelt and had actively sought the post but he failed to win the president's friendship and trust.[12] In 1905 Roosevelt sent Lodge to see the Foreign Secretary, the Marquess of Lansdowne and the king about an appointment for Spring-Rice as ambassador. Lodge had no success. Reid was told of the matter soon after his appointment but his first approaches to the Foreign Office were so timid that the British did not understand what he sought.[13]

A year later, after Grey replaced Lansdowne in the Foreign Office, Reid tried again. This time he was very frank and presented Roosevelt's position strongly. Grey was equally frank: Spring Rice was not even a minister; he could not be given an ambassadorship so soon; there was no other suitable place for Durand and if dropped from the foreign service, he would lose his pension. Roosevelt persisted and at the end of of 1906 succeeded in having Durand recalled, but it was James, First Viscount Bryce, who replaced Durand rather than Spring-Rice.[14]

Reid did not play a role in the Moroccan affair, and elsewhere in Africa, a continent in which the United States had almost no interests, there was little call for his efforts. He became slightly involved once in a matter regarding Liberia.

Early in the century Liberia's bankrupt condition drew the interest of the major powers, and in 1909 the little country asked the United States for help in analyzing its financial difficulties. A commission was sent that at the end of the year recommended an American loan to Liberia as a temporary expedient while international support was considered.[15] The loan was made and the larger arrangement was concluded in 1912. Reid had no part in the negotiations. His contribution to the result of the effort to bolster Liberia's financial structure was an indirect one. He kept the State Department well informed about Britain's interest in and attitude toward the problem. He conferred with the Liberian Minister to Great Britain and ascertained his views on France's participation in a loan. He said frankly that he only knew about the general situation from London's point of view, but within that limitation he relayed to Philander Knox the pros and cons of Germany's and Holland's interests in Liberian stability. Reid favored making "only three bites" of the "insignificant little cherry" and suggested that the United States, France, and England comprise the loan syndicate. Germany and Holland should be excluded, he recommended.[16] His views did not prevail, but his analyses were useful to Knox's assistant, Huntington Wilson, and others in the State Department who concluded the financial arrangement of June 1912.

Reid's attention was drawn to another area, Asia, early in his London mission. A few weeks after his arrival in London, Roosevelt sent him a general summary of the president's views about a reasonable settlement of the Russo-Japanese war. Reid relayed these informally to Prime Minister Arthur Balfour simply as a matter of information.[17] There was little further communication on the subject between the White House and the London embassy. Roosevelt had found that he could expect little help from the English in bringing about a peace because of the Anglo-Japanese alliance, and the British embassy in Washington served well enough for the transmission of routine reports on the progress of the negotiations. Jusserand and Sternburg were at hand and Roosevelt kept France and Germany informed through them.[18]

Another matter of Asian affairs took little more of Reid's time. This was the long and tedious negotiation that preceded the Opium Convention signed at The Hague in January 1912 by the United States, Great Britain, and ten other nations. The problem was an old one but not, in Britain's or America's view, a critical one. Reid communicated with the Foreign Office about a general conference on the subject at some time during each of his seven years in London. His principal contribution to the negotiations was made in June 1910. He successfully brought together Bishop Charles H. Brent, an old friend and the chief American delegate to the conference, and the British leaders who guided policy for their country. Brent acknowledged the importance of Reid's help. The associations were so productive that at the end of 1911, six weeks before the convention was signed, Brent turned down Reid's offer to arrange interviews with the Foreign Office on the ground that things were going so well that further bilateral discussions were not needed.[19]

The most important venture into Asian affairs that engaged Reid's energies during his mission to Great Britain concerned loans to China. In 1898 the American-China Development Company had made a contract with the Chinese government to build a railway from the port of Canton to the great inland city of Hankow. So little interest in the project developed in the United States that the company fell into the hands of Belgian financiers. In 1905 J. P. Morgan purchased it and quickly sold it to the government of China.

Meantime, European capitalists were becoming much interested in the construction of railroads in China. British, French, and German firms, after long and complex negotiations, succeeded in concluding an agreement with the Chinese in June 1909. At this juncture the newly installed Taft administration decided that it was now in the national interest for American capitalists to participate fully in the financing of Chinese railroad construction and development. Secretary of State Philander Knox instructed Reid to sound the Foreign Office on the possibilities of American entrance into the three-power group. Reid at once approached Grey, who sent him a memorandum about the history of the loan arrangements. Among other things, Grey pointed out that on three separate occasions in 1905, during the early stages of the negotiations the Foreign Office had communicated with the State Department or the American Embassy in London about American participation in the consortium and had received negative answers. The

Foreign Office, satisfied that the Americans were not interested, had then approved the continuance of negotiations, and after four years English, French, and German financial houses had completed agreements with China. Under these circumstances, Grey said, His Majesty's Government would scarcely feel justified in interfering with the bankers' arrangements.[20]

Undeterred, Taft and Knox tried to prevent China from signing the agreement while trying to persuade England to support American admission to the consortium and while attempting to find evidence of prior American expressions of interest. On this last point there was complete failure. William Phillips, then chief of the Far Eastern Division of the State Department, was unable to find evidence that any American financial house had showed a desire to participate in a railroad construction loan to China. Even so, Phillips, who had served in the Peking legation for two years, believed the United States should insist on its rights to join the consortium.[21] In Peking the Chinese brushed aside the American argument, and Henry P. Fletcher, then in the legation, admitted that the records did not show that America's position was "as strong as one could wish."[22] In the same weeks Willard Straight, perhaps partly because Reid had made no headway with Grey but more because of his own position as a liaison between the State Department and large financial interests who might be persuaded to enter the loan negotiations if permission could be gained, went to London in July 1909. There he presented the case for American participation. Grey was no more moved by Straight than he had been by Reid. American bankers who went to London to ask for admission to the consortium fared no better despite Reid's efforts. He had all the bankers, three English, three American, two French, and two German, along with John Ridgely Carter, to dinner at Dorchester House. He also invited Grey and the undersecretary who was in charge of Chinese affairs, Sir Francis J. Campbell, but these declined. Grey told Reid later that he was very regretful he did not know of American intentions six months earlier. When Reid reported this comment to the State Department the venerable Alvey Adee, then in his thirty-first year in the department and his twenty-third as second assistant secretary, remarked to Huntington Wilson, "Did we know our own intentions six months ago?"[23] Negotiations were in such a critical state in August that Knox asked Reid to postpone his vacation, something that had not happened to the ambassador before.[24]

Despite these efforts little was accomplished by the end of the year and early in 1910, while on a visit to the United States, Reid was orally instructed to tell Grey that the State Department was much dissatisfied with British failure to cooperate with American policies in the Orient. The ambassador discussed these and other matters in interviews with Grey in February. Meantime, Knox's scheme of a great consortium to "neutralize" railroads in Manchuria by buying them up and then selling them to China, had further complicated the loan negotiations. Grey again had to remind Reid that earlier developments, beginning with an Anglo-Russian agreement in 1899, gave Britain a perspective on the issue that differed from Washington's.[25]

By the spring of 1910 the neutralization scheme had collapsed and Reid had decided privately that the deterioration of the Manchu government, active hostility to the loans in China, and passive resistance to American entry on the part of the western powers gave little encouragement. The Americans finally overcame the resistance and made an agreement with the other three powers, only to have China refuse to sign. Reid had no further connections with the negotiations, which dragged on for another year before the reluctant Chinese officials were persuaded. They signed on May 20, 1911, but before the end of the year the Manchu Dynasty was toppled and American relations with China were virtually suspended.[26]

In the same months, the first half of 1911, the matter of an Anglo-American arbitration treaty came under discussion in Washington and London. The ambassador was in the United States on a visit when, early in 1911, Taft instructed Knox to negotiate treaties of general arbitration with England and France. The idea was a popular one and when Reid returned to London he found widespread public enthusiasm for the treaty as well as support within the government. In the meantime Grey had sent Bryce an outline of a treaty and the British ambassador worked on details with Secretary Knox.[27]

Reid's role was again that of a messenger between Knox and Grey. His first assignment was to clear up the question of the effect that certain articles in the Anglo-Japanese alliance might have on an Anglo-American arbitration arrangement. Grey assured the ambassador that the matter had been considered and discussed with the Japanese. When the arbitration treaty was completed the alliance treaty would be revised so as to make it of no effect regarding any country with which Britain had a general arbitration treaty, the foreign secretary assured the ambassador. Grey, worried about embarrassing the Tokyo government before all arrangements were completed, swore Reid to secrecy. He confided that Bryce knew the details of the agreement but had been instructed not to inform Taft or Knox. Reid told the president only that he was certain the British alliance with Japan would not be an obstacle when the Anglo-American treaty went to the Senate.[28] At the same time he informed Knox that the Foreign Office had made confidential arrangements with Japan to avoid the possibility of Anglo-American conflict because of England's alliance with Japan.[29]

Ultimately all of this was to no avail. The Anglo-Japanese alliance was revised and signed July 12. Bryce and Knox completed the Anglo-American arbitration treaty and sent it to the Senate in August, where it was drastically amended after much debate. Reid privately informed Hart Lyman that he feared for the treaty in the Senate, but confessed that he was no longer a frontline fighter.[30] On their side the British were annoyed and irritated. After their efforts to mollify Washington by amending the Japanese alliance, the American delay seemed uncalled for. Taft was also critical. He would not ask England to accept the emasculated treaty and it was never ratified.[31]

While the arbitration treaty was being discussed Reid had concluded an Anglo-American accord of lesser import. In November 1907 he and Grey had signed a commercial convention that provided for free admission into Great Britain of American commercial travelers' samples. In exchange the United States was to apply minimum tariff rates to British works of art. The arrangement was adopted but unfavorable congressional legislation killed the convention a year and a half later.[32]

None of these negotiations nor any other that involved Reid as a diplomat approached in significance the fisheries issue. Reid inherited from most of his predecessors at the Court of St. James a share of the problem of dealing with disputes about the use of fishing grounds off Newfoundland. The matter was first discussed near the end of the American Revolution. An agreement was made a part of the Treaty of Paris of 1783 and was modified in the Anglo-American Convention of 1818. Thereafter periods of comparative quiet alternated with years of friction. By the time Reid arrived in London the dispute was being handled on a year-to-year basis and hostility was building up on both sides.[33]

Three years earlier Secretary of State Hay and the prime minister of Newfoundland had signed a treaty giving Americans free fishing privileges in Newfoundland and permitting fish and some other products of Newfoundland to enter the United States without payment of duty. New Englanders had opposed the scheme, and in 1905 Lodge succeeded in defeating the treaty in the Senate. The Newfoundlanders then contrived to lay punitive and discriminatory restriction on American fishing vessels.

When Root became secretary of state after Hay's death, he decided to treat the fisheries question as a matter between Washington and London and to deal informally with the "Colonials." Accordingly he instructed Reid to inform the Foreign Office that the United States would stand on the Convention of 1818. The United States would respond to points brought up through diplomatic channels but did not wish to consider problems resulting from the independent action of Newfoundland authorities, Root said. Reid talked to the Marquess of Lansdowne, who temporized, and the ambassador reported the exchange to the State Department. Meanwhile, Root was discussing the problems with Durand in detail, laying the ground for later American proposals for a permanent arrangement.[34]

The temporary arrangements continued while relations between American fishermen and their northern neighbors deteriorated. Lansdowne left the Foreign Office and was succeeded by Edward Grey, but Reid's discussions with the new foreign secretary were no more productive than with the old one.[35]

By September 1906, however, Root's diplomacy was bearing some fruit. Sir Charles Hardinge, permanent undersecretary in the Foreign Office, told Reid that the two nations were basically agreed. It was, Sir Charles said, "our Colonials" who made things difficult. Still, the Foreign Office continued to back the colonials. By this time, a year after he had defeated Hay's treaty in the Senate, Lodge was extremely anxious to develop an atmosphere in which a permanent solution of the fisheries question could be effected. With an eye to the political implications of such an arrangement, Lodge suggested that it would not only be in the interest of the two countries but also that Root would gain credit for settling an issue that has "been a thorn in our side since the Revolution."[36]

In 1906 the fishing season was to open on Monday, October 1, and as September wore on London and Washington became more anxious. On the seventeenth the State Department was "anxiously awaiting" a reply from Reid about England's answer to State's last offer. On the nineteenth, Acting Secretary Adee was "in urgent telegraphic communication" with Reid but regretted that a *modus vivendi* had not been reached, and on the same day Reid responded, "I have been and am urgent."[37] It was not until the season was open and American vessels were on the sea en route to the fishing grounds that Washington and London reached agreement on the terms by which fish could be taken during the season.[38]

Reid's conferences with Grey contributed to the making of the agreement. Details and much of the technical work were completed by First Secretary Carter. The ambassador was not in London when Root approved Reid's recommendation that the most recent British memorandum be accepted. He wrote at once to Carter. "I don't see but that you have provided for a *Modus*—whichever line our State Department on the one side and the Newfoundland people on the other finally may decide to take. So all's well that ends well."[39]

Lodge thanked Root for all his efforts and pledged that he would try to get the New England fisherman to comply with the terms of the *modus vivendi*.[40]

The arrangement permitted Americans to fish in Newfoundland waters but left them unsatisfied, as it did the British colonials. Ten months later Washington and London could do no better than renew the agreement without change for another year. At the expiration of that period another renewal, this time with some slight changes, was agreed upon but the dissatisfaction continued.[41] In 1909 neither the State Department nor the Foreign Office was willing to concede enough to do more than renew the *modus vivendi* with minor modifications for another year.[42]

Meanwhile Root had continued his efforts to find a permanent solution. In 1907 he had visited Newfoundland and Canada as a gesture of sincerity while seeking a formula by which differences could be adjusted. With Reid's active cooperation and with Lodge's reluctant consent, Root signed a treaty with Great Britain in April 1908. Under its terms the two countries agreed to submit their differences to the Permanent Court of Arbitration at The Hague. The Court ruled on the seven specific questions put before it and announced its decision in September 1910. The result was a compromise generally satisfactory to both sides. Two years later, in July 1912, an Anglo-American Commission signed a convention that modified the tribunal's decision slightly but accepted its main feature, and the dispute was ended.[43] Reid's role in the fisheries negotiation and settlement was marginal. Secretary of State Root took upon himself not only the responsibility for making a general settlement, but also the tedious tasks of detailed discussions. Afterward, he considered the diplomacy with Britain on this matter his "greatest diplomatic triumph as Secretary of State."[44]

Reid's last discussions with the Foreign Office were on the subject of the Panama tolls. As construction of the canal neared completion, the United States prepared regulations about its use. In the summer of 1912 Congress considered legislation that included clauses exempting American coastwise vessels using the waterway from the payment of tolls.

When this legislation came to Grey's attention he called Reid to the Foreign Office and complained that the proposals were in violation of the Hay-Pauncefote Treaty of 1901. That agreement provided that the canal was to be open to vessels of all nations on terms of equality, Grey pointed out. Reid had no instructions on the matter but he defended the American application of tolls on foreign ships. He took the ground that the United States had gone to great expense to build the canal and was entitled to some return from it. He pointed out that his country had virtually no merchant marine, so the waterway would be more beneficial to other nations that did have such fleets. Finally, he contended that, contrary to Grey's view, the building of the canal could hardly be ascribed to military-naval motives since the existing American fleet could have been duplicated in size to establish equal fleets in the Atlantic and Pacific at a fifth of the cost of the canal.[45]

Privately, Reid agreed with Grey's view. He told Root, now in the Senate and opposing the administration's bill, that the United States should abide by the terms of the Hay-Pauncefote Treaty and informed him that the proposed legislation was viewed in London with amazement and incredulity. Moreover, Reid endorsed Lyman's stand in the *Tribune* against the tolls. He strongly urged his editor to oppose congressional passage of the bill and to recommend that the president refuse to sign it.[46] Despite opposition the bill was passed and signed in late August. Although Knox had never bothered to communicate with Reid about the matter, the ambassador felt he should let Taft know of the depth of British feeling. He sent the president clippings and cartoons from English papers and told his chief that the United States had not had "so bad a press" on any other matter during his mission.[47]

After the bill became law the Foreign Office prepared an official protest. In mid-November Reid and Grey discussed the issue again. The ambassador supported the American position as best he could and urged the Foreign Secretary to consider the legal bases of that position before making final decisions.[48]

It was Reid's last diplomatic effort. His final illness began a few days later. During his mission to Great Britain, Reid's health was as good as or better than it had been in any seven-year period of the two decades before he went to London. He had some difficulties in July 1912 but had recovered and was riding horseback regularly at Wrest Park by mid-August, although he did not go to London for several weeks.

His first major effort after recovering was to undertake a trip to Albany, New York. Andrew Draper, commissioner of education, had persuaded Reid, as chairman of the Board of Regents, to make a speech at the opening of a long-wanted educational building of the University of the State of New York.[49] Reid went to New York at the end of September, delivered the address, conferred with his architect about Ophir, saw a few friends, and was back in London late in October. He left almost immediately to make an important address at the University College of Wales at Aberystwyth.

The addresses in New York and Wales were his last important public acts. The trips had weakened him. Early in December bronchial troubles developed and he did not recover. He died at noon on the fifteenth with Lizzie and Jean at his bedside.

An impressive memorial service was held on December 20 in Westminster Abbey attended by representatives of the royal family, by Prime Minister Herbert Asquith and scores of British and foreign officials and friends. On the following day Reid's body was moved from Dorchester House in a flag-draped coffin on a gun carriage with a military escort to Victoria Station and then to Portsmouth by train. The

British government provided an armored cruiser, the *Natal*, for the trip to New York. There on January 4 the body, still in its flag-draped coffin, was taken on an artillery caisson to the Cathedral of St. John the Divine where a service was held. Taft and Roosevelt were among the hundreds who attended. Hart Lyman and Donald Nicholson acted with James Bryce, the British ambassador, Elihu Root, J. P. Morgan, Chauncey Depew, and other notables as pallbearers. Later on the same day Reid was buried in Sleep Hollow Cemetery at Tarrytown.[50]

17

Summary and Conclusion

WHITELAW REID died as a distinguished American journalist, business-man, political leader, and diplomat. He gained his successes largely through his own efforts. Nothing in his early life pointed to the achievements that lay ahead. Xenia, Ohio, provided no challenges or opportunities for him, and there is no evidence that he would have responded positively had there been any. At the same time he was an avid reader of almost anything that came to hand. Moreover, his uncle was head of the Xenia Academy and gave the boy special tutoring to supplement the regular instruction. Thus when he went to Miami University at the age of fifteen, Reid was prepared to take full advantage of the opportunities there. He was introduced to new ideas, read widely, and participated freely in the life of the university not only in the classrooms but in the social clubs and, perhaps most importantly, in the activities of the literary societies. Traits of character and personality that had not been apparent earlier but became prominent later first appeared in his college years.

He strove for perfection and was willing to work long and hard for it. He desired a position of leadership among his fellows and he wanted recognition. He was highly competitive. These traits and a native intelligence that was obvious in his boyhood but that had had little opportunity for expression before he went to Miami enabled him to become the outstanding member of his class, and he graduated as its brightest scholar.

As a young man, after some false starts, Reid began to build a place for himself in the field of journalism. In the war years by hard work, careful analyses of events, and some luck he gained a national reputation as a reporter and critic. Later he gained success in business and influence in politics. His positions'in the latter two areas were established between the time he joined the staff of the *New York Tribune* in 1868 and his marriage in 1881.

In this period of his life he was distant in manner and slow to accept advances. In 1872 when he was thirty-five, fellow journalists who worked closely with him at the Cincinnati convention, Horace White, Samuel Bowles, and Murat Halstead, respected him but did not really know him as a person. He was surrounded by a wall of reserve, a result of his childhood environment and his almost unaided rise to prominence and position. This barrier was probably never removed, and the inner Reid, the complete person, was something of a mystery to his contemporaries.

His formal and somewhat cool personal relationship with others did not indicate a lack of interest in the society of his fellows. He was a popular member of the Lotos Club and its president for many years. He also belonged to the Union League Club, the Century Club, and others. These provided diversion, good company, and easy access to men in the business and professional classes of New York, all of which were important for the highly ambitious bachelor. Soon after he gained control of the *Tribune* he bought a house at a good address where he could entertain friends and repay social obligations. After his marriage at the age of forty-four, Reid's social life became fuller, his home much more elaborate, and the entertainment of friends far more lavish, since his young wife had much money and enjoyed spending it. They purchased and refurbished, added to and partly rebuilt palatial homes on Madison Avenue and at Ophir Farm and expanded a summer place on Upper St. Regis Lake.

Reid, from the time he was a young man, was interested in the business opportunities of newspaper publishing as well as in the journalistic aspects. His decision to remain with the *Cincinnati Gazette* when other places became available, a crucial move as it turned out, was importantly influenced by a chance to acquire shares in that paper. When he went to the *Tribune*, he invested in it, and when a chance came to buy a controlling interest, he was even willing to put himself under heavy obligation to the unscrupulous Jay Gould to obtain funds needed for the purchase. Once he became proprietor of the paper, he strengthened his position by putting up a new building for revenue as well as for housing improved press facilities, by withholding dividends from stockholders until the cost of the structure was amortized, and by doubling the number of shares and retaining most of the new ones. In line with his belief in the principles of laissez faire, he considered that since he took the risks and did the work he was entitled to the rewards of his enterprise.

In one development in newspaper publishing Reid was an innovator and a leader in his period. He was an important figure in the move toward the application of machinery to the printing and distribution of the news. He was among the first, if not the first, to use Barr patented typesetting machines in getting out a daily paper. He was the first to recognize the revolutionary possibilities of the Mergenthaler linotype machine, the first to use it, and he had an important role in its development. In 1875 the first of Richard Hoe's new web presses to be seen in New York was installed in the *Tribune* basement. Reid watched Hoe's improvements on presses and made suggestions to him and to others regarding refinements that would both reduce the cost and speed the process of getting newspapers out of the pressroom onto the streets, and into homes. The intensity with which he pursued these aims testified partly to an interest in the financial advantages of cheaper and faster production of newspapers and partly to his inner drive to achieve and to perfect this part of the operation of the *Tribune*. The use of machines became an element in the long conflict between Reid and workers in the composing room that began in the seventies because of his wage cuts. The introduction of Mergenthaler's invention eliminated the need for compositors, the editor contended, since the *Tribune* need only employ linotype operators and these were not entitled to the wage scales the union demanded for compositors. In truth, the matter of the machines was a peripheral one. He believed that trade unions had no right to intervene in negotiations between employer and employee. He opposed any limitation on his or any other employer's right to hire workers at any wage they would accept. The editor strongly supported this view in the *Tribune*. Virtually all of its subscribers, as well as most businessmen of the time, approved that position.

Reid was also involved in the expansion and consolidation of news-gathering agencies. Here he worked with a few other leading papers to secure control of the major collecting organizations for the financial rewards as much as, perhaps more than, for access to the supply of news. This area of his activity put Reid in a position somewhat parallel to that of his contemporaries who were, in the same decades, the eighties and nineties, building trusts and monopolies in transportation, industry, and other fields. It is a significant commentary on the men of the time that while the *Sun* and the *Tribune* were bitterly opposed to each other in most of their editorial views and political positions, their editors,

Charles Dana and Reid, worked harmoniously with each other for fifteen years as dominant figures in the news-gathering agencies.

When Reid took over the *Tribune*, his chief competitors in New York were Dana's *Sun*, James Gordon Bennett's *Herald*, George Jones's *Times*, and Manton Marble's *World*. These differed among themselves on questions of the day and in politics, but on the whole they were conservative in outlook and appealed largely to the middle and upper classes. Of these editors only Dana had begun to emphasize cleverness of style and human interest stories as means of increasing circulation by appealing to a broader class of readers. Reid did not follow Dana's lead, but by the end of the seventies he saw what might result if the trend away from the old ways were continued. A fortune, he said, could be gained by the man who would make a paper so "disreputable and vile" that 150,000 people would be willing to buy it. When Joseph Pulitzer took over the *World* in 1883 it seemed to other editors that Reid's prediction had been accurate. Pulitzer, and later William Randolph Hearst, developed practices that Reid refused to adopt despite the fact that the new ways built circulation which in turn increased revenues from advertising. Reid held to his idea that the *Tribune* was a paper for conservative, middle, and upper class, mainly Republican, readers. He regarded Republicans as the party of culture and respectability, as the party of the gentry. Pulitzer and Hearst went after the far more numerous working classes. Reid could not appeal to readers who wanted heavier taxes on men of wealth and on large corporations and who bought papers that called for public ownership of utilities. To do this would be to attack his own interests, those of his friends, and of the people he regarded as his paper's constituency. The image of the *Tribune* in the minds of these readers was more important to its editor than the money to be made from greater circulation, if that were increased through methods of which Reid did not approve. He would not follow the new tactics of emphasizing purely dramatic, curious, and odd happenings as news. He was slow to adopt the bold, eye-catching headlines that Pulitzer, Hearst, and others used to enlarge sales. He refused, even in the months preceding the outbreak of war with Spain, to take advantage of the public's interest in sensationalism. Despite, however, their differences in political policies and journalistic practices, Reid and Pulitzer liked and respected each other personally.

In sum, Reid clung to the belief that a paper that printed the news in a dignified way could be successful. His outlook and his view of his responsibility to his class and to his paper's reputation remained largely constant from the time he gained control of the *Tribune* to the end of his life. In his late years he seemed to consider his paper as a sort of keeper of the Republican party's conscience.

Reid's friends and his critics saw his motivations and his character traits in different lights. The critics considered that he had no political principles and constantly sought power and position. He was regarded as being self-engrossed, a money-worshipper, and unconcerned about anything that did not involve his own interests. His friends considered that Reid, through the *Tribune*, was a strong force for political stability, an asset to the Republicans, and therefore to the country. They agreed that he did seek influence and that he was not unselfish, but they believed he used his influence for honorable ends. Few denied his interest in wealth. His friends saw this characteristic as a genuine appreciation of fine possessions and a sincere love of grandeur. Thus both critics and friends saw somewhat the same person. They differed in their interpretations of the reasons behind his actions.

In fact, Reid was an introvert. He was more concerned with his own difficulties and problems, as well as with his rights and privileges, than with those of others. That he had made his own way by his own efforts undergirded this element in his personality. He was interested in profits because he wanted a strong financial position for his paper and the material appurtenances of gracious living for himself. His own integrity and that of his paper were also basic. Sometimes the desire for profit and the concern for integrity conflicted. In the seventies the money interest governed, as in his relations with Gould and in his agreement to soften criticisms of Thomas C. Platt in exchange for the boss's aid in increasing the *Tribune*'s circulation. Later the paper was more important, as in his unwillingness to gain readers by following the practices of sensationalism introduced by Pulitzer in the eighties and nineties. He was frequently charged with being an office-seeker. In the last third of his life he did indeed want appointment to a high place. He believed, justifiably, that his qualifications were at least equal to those of others who received such appointments and that he deserved the distinction and the recognition from the Republicans because of his long and substantial support of the party.

As editor of the *Tribune* Reid reported the political affairs of his city, state, and nation and interpreted them for his readers. He had been interested in politics since his college years and his acquaintance with leading political figures was increased during the war years. After he gained control of the *Tribune* he felt more personally involved in state and national affairs and was more concerned about his own relation to them. In the area of national politics most of the period between Reid's acquisition of the *Tribune* and the end of the century was, in Henry Adams' phrase, poor in purpose and barren in results.

So far as political issues were concerned, in these decades Reid's interests were more in economic matters than in others. He supported some civil service legislation but his first concern was for sound money. He supported a protective tariff, and here he was among the first to base his position not on the need to protect "infant industries," but on the point that the tariff level should be set to cover the difference in production costs caused by differences in American and foreign wage levels. Except for the impact of the silver issue on the sound money principle, these were not highly divisive issues within or between the major parties, although leaders on both sides frequently tried to make them seem so.

The essential struggles in this period were intraparty factional feuds. It was not the innovator, but the partisan who sought to unite his party against the wicked and perfidious other side who was most valued by the national leaders. Those who could reconcile the factions were more important than those who spoke of and worked for specific issues. Reid's standing as a national party leader was in considerable part due to his position as a New York figure who worked toward keeping different elements in that key state, with its large electoral vote, united behind Republican candidates. While he engaged in struggles for position within the party, in contests with the Democrats he worked untiringly, skillfully, and effectively to unite Republican factions. Thus he fought for Republican dominance in state and national political contests and at the same time for supremacy within the party of the men who he considered were able to win elections, who did not offend his sense of dignity, whose public and private conduct he could approve, and who would accord him the recognition and position he believed he deserved. Few men met all of these requirements. The *Tribune* supported those having more of the qualifications than others, since most of them were in agreement on general policy.

Reid had both successes and failures in the party feuds of his time. His most satisfying political experiences and his brightest days as a leader in the party came in the brief period between James A. Garfield's nomination for the presidency in 1880 and Reid's departure for Europe the following spring. Reid helped make his friend of long standing president of the United States. As candidate, president-elect and president, Garfield was grateful, turned to the editor for counsel, and considered his judgment in making major appointments, important decisions, and policy speeches. The two worked closely together in destroying Roscoe Conkling, Reid's bitter enemy, as a political power in New York. Reid was never again as close to a chief executive as he was to Garfield. Later failures to establish a place of influence near the White House irked him, as he felt that his advice and counsel ought to have been valued, if not actively sought.

The editor's longest and most frustrating struggle in the party feuds of his time was his unsuccessful attempt to dethrone Thomas C. Platt, Conkling's successor as the head of the Republican machine in New York. Reid and Platt cooperated or moved in the same direction at times but neither liked or trusted the other and each would have been glad to see the other's influence destroyed. The boss could not destroy the editor but for many years stood athwart his path to the embassy in London or to a major cabinet post. In the end they simply agreed to stop fighting, largely because of age and weariness. The editor's appointment to the embassy in London was delayed for some fifteen years because, although he could cooperate with Platt in some matters, he would not submit to him.

Reid struggled for a longer time with a problem of a different sort, one that caused him much suffering and possibly contributed to his self-concern. Throughout his life, from early manhood to his last years, he was troubled by asthmatic and bronchial ailments that sapped his strength and depressed him. In his youth and middle years the difficulties were not incapacitating but in the last third of his life the illness became more severe. After he turned the day-to-day operation of the paper over to others, he usually stayed away from New York City for at least a part of the winter. When minister to France he went to the Mediterranean area during the cold months when he could. In 1894 and 1895 he spent more than six months in Egypt and went to Arizona for several months in each of the following two winters. During the years as ambassador to

Great Britain he retreated from the London weather when circumstances permitted.

Reid's interest in diplomacy came in his later years. At the age of forty he declined to consider a diplomatic mission that was available from President Hayes, despite strong urging from Hay that he accept an appointment. Four years later Garfield offered the Berlin legation to the editor but he was only slightly interested. However, by the time Harrison was elected, Reid, then fifty-one, was not only ready for a diplomatic appointment but was highly interested. He was convinced that because of his long support of, and financial contributions to, the Republican party he was entitled to one of the best places available. He wanted the mission to the Court of St. James, and his friends tried to get it for him. The effort failed and with some reluctance he accepted an appointment as minister to France.

The term in Paris seemed to whet his appetite and to increase his desire for further recognition. In the following years his public posture was that the office should seek the man, and he repeatedly denied that he was seeking or had ever sought public office. Even in his private correspondence he was usually oblique rather than direct in putting himself forward. Nevertheless, he actively worked to obtain the London mission or the secretaryship of state or even a lesser cabinet post. Appointments to special diplomatic assignments, especially to that on the Peace Commission following the war with Spain, pleased him but did not satisfy his craving for the recognition he believed he deserved.

Reid was, for most of his life, less interested in United States foreign relations than in national and state politics. His position on policy, however, was clearer in the area of foreign affairs than in domestic matters. Questions of American involvement in Europe's problems rarely arose before the end of the nineteenth century. When a question did come up, Reid usually warned against making any commitment. He opposed any entanglement in European affairs. His most positive stance was his support of the Monroe Doctrine, and his position was consistent and unvarying. In the early seventies he held that the United States must dominate the Caribbean and that Spain should leave Cuba. The Clayton-Bulwer Treaty should be ended, he thought, so that Britain could not threaten American control of the Isthmus. In the mid-nineties he supported the Cleveland-Olney position that a British threat against Venezuela could not be tolerated. In 1903 in an address at Yale he again stated his view of the doctrine: uncompromising American dominance in the Caribbean. President Roosevelt praised the speech.

While Reid believed in American superiority in the Caribbean he opposed the acquisition of territory there by the United States. He also was against territorial expansion in the Pacific. Through the 1870s and 1880s he opposed annexation of Hawaii, a reciprocity treaty with its government, or the lease of a naval base there. In the 1890s his views about expansion began to change but he moved away from his earlier positions slowly. In 1891 he looked favorably on a Portuguese offer of naval stations in Africa but did not urge acceptance when the administration frowned on the proposal. By the end of 1896 he had come to believe privately that the United States some day would not only have to take Cuba and Hawaii but should hold them as colonies and not incorporate them or admit them as states. He did not, however, openly advocate the acquisition of island territories by purchase, treaty, or conquest until the war with Spain began. He opposed the idea of an armed conflict with that country until a few days before the administration asked for a declaration of war, and four years later he thought that war could and should have been avoided.

When hostilities began, however, Reid's position became one of outright imperialism. Privately he viewed with misgivings the idea of taking over all the Philippines, but publicly he argued that there was no way of avoiding doing so. He advocated a course of colonialism in the Caribbean as well. As a member of the Paris Peace Commission he continued to work for the "large policy." After the treaty was signed and for months after it was approved by the Senate, Reid's voice was loud in support of colonialism. He frequently mentioned duty in discussing this subject but his arguments were more deterministic than moralistic, which put him, in this area, with the social Darwinists. His work in Paris and during the great debate on the legitimacy and constitutionality of an American empire were his most important positive contributions to his country's foreign policy.

Reid never lost interest in the London mission, and in 1905 he finally gained the post he had long believed he merited when Roosevelt made the appointment. The president, who had neither liked nor trusted Reid before entering the White House, had come to respect him as a staunch and loyal Republican and to consider that he deserved recognition and honor for his long and useful support of the party. That the two men's views about the proper course of United States foreign relations were very similar made Roosevelt's decision easier. In the ensuing years they became good friends.

Reid's service as ambassador to Great Britain, which began in his sixty-eighth year, might have been the peak of his career as a diplomat had there been major problems or policies that required solution or adjustment. As it was, Anglo-American relations from 1905 to 1912 were harmonious and uneventful. In his years in London Reid received many honors and enjoyed great prestige, things for which he had worked for half a century. He filled the role of ambassador of good will with distinction.

Notes

CHAPTER 1

1. W. R. to Dear Brother [Gavin Reid], 10 Oct. 1853, Reid Papers, box 72. The Whitelaw Reid Papers are in the Manuscript Division of the Library of Congress. Most of Reid's letters are in bound volumes. These are cited by date only. Unbound materials in the papers are identified and cited by box number.

2. William Warren Sweet, *Religion on the American Frontier: The Presbyterians* (New York, 1936), pp. 29–35; Francis P. Weisenburger, *The Passing of the Frontier, 1825–1850*, p. 28; Walter Havighurst, *The Miami Years, 1809–1969*, pp. 39, 49, 103.

3. Henry Howe, *Historical Collections of Ohio*, 1: 701, 702, 718, 721; see Royal Cortissoz, *The Life of Whitelaw Reid*, 1: 5–10, for material on Reid's ancestry and youth. Cortissoz, a *Tribune* staff member, wrote a highly laudatory *Life*. The account is mainly useful for the numerous letters he printed, but many of them are edited without indication of omissions or changes; Gavin [Reid] to Nettie [Reid], 5 July 1856, Reid Papers, box 213; *The Seventh Census of the United States, 1850*, pp. 810–79; Weisenburger, *Passing of the Frontier*, p. 73, describes the fair of 1848; *Cincinnati Commercial*, 18 Jan. 1860 cited in Eugene H. Roseboom, *The Civil War Era, 1850–1873*, p. 6, indicates that Xenia residents were petitioning the General Assembly to bar free Negroes from Ohio. In his chapter on the war years Roseboom draws heavily on Reid's *Ohio in the War*.

4. Cortissoz, *Reid*, 1: 10–12. This was mentioned in a speech Reid made at Xenia in 1881; see Whitelaw Reid, *American and English Studies*, 1: 213; Hugh McMillan was the younger brother of Gavin McMillan, one of Marian Whitelaw Ronalds Reid's four brothers-in-law.

5. W. R. to Dear Brother, 10 Oct. 1853, Reid Papers, box 72; Howe, *Historical Collections of Ohio*, 1: 354–57; Samuel H. Stille, *Ohio Builds a Nation*, p. 226; Walter L. Tobey and William O. Thompson, eds., *The Diamond Anniversary Volume of Miami University*, pp. 66–85.

6. *Twenty-Ninth Annual Circular of Miami University* (May 1854), p. 29, cited in James G. Smart, "Whitelaw Reid: A Biographical Study," p. 8. Smart's useful study is highly informative; his main emphasis is on the political aspects of the years 1872 to 1884.

7. Roscoe C. Buley, *The Old Northwest: Pioneer Period, 1815–1840*, 2: 386; W. R. to Dear Brother, 10 Oct. 1853, Reid Papers, box 72; *Diamond Anniversary Volume*, p. 171.

8. See notes in Reid's pocket diary for 1853, Reid Papers, box 1.

9. *Diamond Anniversary Volume*, pp. 175, 308–9. The complaint resulted in an early return of the remaining volumes to Erodelphian.

10. Ibid., pp. 242, 248, 249, 300.

11. In his pocket diaries for 1854 and for 1855–57 Reid lists articles he wrote while at Miami; see Reid Papers, box 1; see also William E. Connelly, *Life of Preston B. Plumb, 1837–1891*, p. 20.

12. Nettie Reid to Gavin Reid, 16 Sept. 1856, Reid Papers, box 213.

13. Pocket diary for 1856 and notebook containing some 50 pages of clippings, Reid Papers, box 1.

14. Pocket diary for 1858, Reid Papers, box 1.

15. Ibid.

16. Ibid.; Cortissoz, *Reid*, 1: 29–31.

17. Pocket diary for 1858, Reid Papers, box 1; Cortissoz, *Reid*, 1: 37–38.

18. Cortissoz, *Reid*, 1: 51–52, quotes Reid in the *Xenia News* without giving a date.

19. Cortissoz, *Reid*, 1: 56–62.

CHAPTER 2

1. "Financial statement," Reid Papers, box 191.

2. Royal Cortissoz, *The Life of Whitelaw Reid*, 1: 20.

3. Willian Dean Howells, *Years of My Youth*, p. 144; *Cincinnati Gazette*, 26 Mar. 1861.

4. Cortissoz, *Reid*, 1: 62; Smart, "Reid," p. 23. Smart found that Reid was paid five dollars a week by the *Cincinnati Times*, fifteen dollars by the *Cleveland Herald*, and twenty dollars by the *Cincinnati Gazette*.

5. Howells, *Years of My Youth*, pp. 172, 183, 213–15; Smart, "Reid," p. 23.

6. Cortissoz, *Reid*, 1: 66–67; Whitelaw Reid, *Ohio in the War*, 1: 21–22.

7. Richard Smith's notes to Reid about this position were addressed to J. Whitelow Reed, J. W. Reed, etc. The beginning offer was for fifteen dollars a week, nearly double the Cedarville teaching salary but lower than the Columbus pay. "Cincinnati Gazette Co.," Reid Papers, box 11.

8. *Cincinnati Daily Gazette*, 8, 15, 22 July 1861; W. R. to Gavin Reid, 27 June 1861, cited in J. Cutler Andrews, *The North Reports the Civil War*, pp. 104–105; Robert H. Jones, "Whitelaw Reid," pp. 125–26.

9. Douglas S. Freeman, *Lee's Lieutenants*, 1: 23–29; Jones, "Whitelaw Reid," pp. 127–30. Jones puts the fight at Carrick's Ford on July 14, while Cortissoz and Freeman have it on the thirteenth. Jones's account, taken largely from Reid's reports to the *Gazette*, is very good; Howe, *Historical Collections of Ohio*, 1: 718.

10. Andrews, *North Reports*, pp. 106–7.

11. Freeman, *Lee's Lieutenants*, 1: 34–35; Cortissoz, *Reid*, 1:76–77, prints a part of Reid's report on the fight at Carrick's Ford.

12. *Cincinnati Gazette*, 16, 23 Aug. 1861 and 31 Jan. 1862, cited in Andrews, *North Reports*, pp. 109, 117.

13. *Cincinnati Gazette*, 16 Sept. 1861; Andrews, *North Reports*, p. 110.

14. *Cincinnati Gazette*, 30 Sept. 1861, cited in Andrews, *North Reports*, p. 112; *Cincinnati Gazette*, 4 Nov. 1861.

15. Lewis Wallace, *Lew Wallace: An Autobiography*, 1: 459, 501.

16. *Cincinnati Gazette*, 14 Apr. 1862; Thomas W. Knox, *Camp-fire and Cotton-field*, p. 150; Frank B. Wilkie, *Pen and Powder*, pp. 154–55; Frank Moore, ed., *The Rebellion Record*, 4: 385–400; Kenneth P. Williams, *Lincoln Finds a General*, 3: 391, 530.

17. *New York Tribune*, 8, 9 Apr. 1881; Reid, *Ohio in the War*, 1: 65, 370–78; Emmet Crozier, *Yankee Reporters, 1861–65*, pp. 218–19; Andrews, *North Reports*, p. 181.

18. R. C. Reid to Gavin Reid, 31 July 1862, Reid Papers, box 213.

19. Andrews, *North Reports*, pp. 46–48; W. R. to Ellis P. Oberholtzer, 10 Nov. 1905, quoted in Ellis P. Oberholtzer, *Jay Cooke: Financier of the Civil War*, 1: 480–83; Jones, "Whitelaw Reid," pp. 132–39; Reid's income was unencumbered except for his own needs. He received a note from his father for $1,631.37 in November 1862 for acting as guardian of Gavin's daughters. In January 1864 he received $350 for the same service; "Miscellaneous notes," Reid Papers, box 191.

20. Oberholtzer, *Cooke*, 1: 483, 553–54; W. R. to Nicolay, 21 Mar. 1865, John Nicolay Correspondence, 1865–67, No. 3, Library of Congress.

21. Andrews, *North Reports*, pp. 46–48, 302; War Department, *The War of the Rebellion*, Series II, 6: 183.

22. Andrews, *North Reports*, pp. 547–48.

23. Ibid., pp. 416–34.

24. *Cincinnati Daily Gazette*, 27 May 1864; Agate's analysis filled a column and a half on page 1; Joseph J. Mathews, "Civil War News," *South Atlantic Quarterly*, 52 (July 1953), 363.

25. Andrews, *North Reports*, p. 595, cites a manuscript story dated 15 July 1864 and written for the *Gazette* but not used.

26. Carl Sandburg, *Abraham Lincoln*, 2: 502.

27. W. R. to William Henry Smith, 6 Aug. 1863, cited in Andrews, *North Reports*, p. 47.

28. Andrews, *North Reports*, p. 47, cites several sources for the story, but it is certainly inaccurate in suggesting that Reid could not pay his rent.

29. James G. Randall, *Lincoln the President*, 2: 222; Tyler Dennett, *Lincoln and the Civil War in the Diaries and Letters of John Hay*, p. 138; Louis M. Starr, *Bohemian Brigade*, p. 312, cites W. R. to Greeley, 19 Jan. 1864, Sidney Howard Gay Papers, Butler Library, Columbia University; see Agate's letter from Washington dated 8 Apr. 1864 in *Cincinnati Daily Gazette*, 12 Apr. 1864; James G. Randall and David Donald, *The Civil War and Reconstruction*, pp. 373–74.

30. W. R. to Anna Dickinson, 11 Sept. 1864, facsimile in James G. Randall, *Lincoln the Liberal Statesman*, pp. 64–65; see Agate's letter of 6 June 1864 in *Cincinnati Daily Gazette*, 10, 11 June 1864; Sandburg, *Lincoln*, 3: 204; Edward L. Pierce, *Memoir and Letters of Charles Sumner*, 4: 196–97.

31. Andrews, *North Reports*, pp. 47 n.39, and 472 n.40, cites Richard Smith to William Henry Smith, 15 Nov. 1863 and W. R. to William Henry Smith, 6 Aug. 1863, Smith Papers, Ohio State Historical and Archeological Society, Columbus; Andrews, *North Reports*, pp. 471–72, cites W. R. to Greeley, 2 Nov. 1863; William S. Rosecrans to Charles A. Dana, 17 Mar. 1882, in Charles A. Dana Papers, Library of Congress; Dennett, *Lincoln and the Civil War*, p. 114; Agate in *Cincinnati Daily Gazette*, 4 Jan. 1864.

32. "Miscellaneous financial statements," Reid Papers, box 191.

CHAPTER 3

1. Charles J. Rosebault, *When Dana Was the Sun*, p. 128; *New York Tribune*, 10 Apr. 1865; J. Cutler Andrews, *The North Reports the Civil War*, pp. 633–34.

2. This account of Reid's trip in the spring of 1865 is from his *After the War* and from his pocket diary for 1865 in Reid Papers, box 1, except as noted.

3. Reid, *After the War*, pp. 316ff., and pocket diary for 1865.

4. Reid, *After the War*, chap. 43.

5. Ibid., p. 380.

6. Ibid., pp. 457, 470, 503, 564, 580.

7. W. R. to his mother, 11 Sept. 1866, quoted in Cortissoz, *Reid*, 1: 124–25; the pocket diary for 1866 contains some notes on financial aspects of the plantation venture; see E. D. Ross on Francis Jay Herron in *Dictionary of American Biography*; additional data on the venture is in "Financial statements," Reid Papers, box 191.

8. Dr. James I. Robertson examined Reid's treatment of the twenty major-generals in *Ohio in the War* and made his findings available to me. The generalizations above were made on the basis of Dr. Robertson's study. His principal criticism of Reid's account was that the estimate of Garfield was overgenerous.

9. Pocket diary for 1866, Reid Papers, box 1.

10. Scrapbooks containing Agate letters for March–May 1868 are in Reid Papers, box 219.

CHAPTER 4

1. *New York Tribune*, 30 Sept. 1868; Harry Baehr, *The New York Tribune since the Civil War*, is an excellent account of the development of the paper; see p. 67 on Reid.

2. *New York Times*, 28 Jan. 1868, cited in Candace Stone, *Dana and the Sun*, p. 57.

3. Greeley's letters to Reid in 1868–70 are filled with suggestions and directions; Horace Greeley Papers, Manuscript Division, Library of Congress; John Russell Young to W. R., 20 Feb. 1869, Reid Papers, box 112.

4. W. R. to Garfield, 27 Dec. 1868; *New York Tribune* 14 Sept., 17, 18, 19 Dec. 1868.

5. John Russell Young to W. R., 2 Apr. 1869, Reid Papers, box 112.

6. Charles J. Rosebault, *When Dana was the Sun*, p. 182.

7. *New York Sun*, 27 Apr. 1869, cited in Baehr, *Tribune*, p. 73; Stone, *Dana*, pp. 42, 125; Rosebault, *Dana*, p. 167; William Dean Howells, *Years of My Youth*, p. 214; Frank M. O'Brien, *The Story of the Sun, 1833–1928*, p. 266.

8. W. R. to Samuel Sinclair, 24 May 1869; W. R. to Franklin J. Ottarson, 7 June 1870; Baehr, *Tribune*, p. 395.

9. *New York Tribune*, 8, 9, 10 Apr. 1871; W. R. to Bigelow, 30 Dec. 1871, in John Bigelow, *Retrospections of an Active Life*, 4: 570–72; William H. Hale, *Horace Greeley: Voice of the People*, pp. 322ff.; Glyndon G. Van Deusen, *Horace Greeley: Nineteenth Century Crusader*, chap. 25.

10. W. R. to Garfield, 17 July 1871.

11. Edward L. Pierce, *Memoirs and Letters of Charles Sumner*, 4: 515–16; Don C. Seitz, *Horace Greeley: Founder of the New York Tribune*, pp. 370–71; W. R. to [Senator] Allison, 11 Apr. 1872; Reid to Bowles, 26 May 1872, cited in Royal Cortissoz, *The Life of Whitelaw Reid*, 1: 218; James G. Smart, "Whitelaw Reid," pp. 9–11.

12. *New York Tribune*, 13, 15 Apr. 1872.

13. W. R. to Joseph Millikin, 24 Apr. 1872; W. R. to Smalley, 25 Apr. 1872.

14. Ellis P. Oberholtzer, *History of the United States since the Civil War*, 3: 19–20; Henry Watterson, *Marse Henry: An Autobiography*, 1: 243.

15. Smart, "Reid," pp. 67–82; see Earle Dudley Ross, *The Liberal Republican Movement*, p. 96; Edward Stanwood, *A History of the Presidency*, p. 341.

16. Horace White, *Life of Lyman Trumbull*, p. 385; Frederic Bancroft, ed., *Speeches, Correspondence and Political Papers of Carl Schurz*, 3: 345; Ross, *Liberal Republican Movement*, pp. 97–99; James G. Smart, "Whitelaw Reid and the Nomination of Horace Greeley," p. 239.

17. William B. Hesseltine, *Ulysses S. Grant: Politician*, p. 273; Ross, *Liberal Republican Movement*, pp. 89 n.13, and 99; Cortissoz, *Reid*, 1: 210.

18. *New York Tribune*, 15 May 1872; Baehr, *Tribune*, p. 109.

19. Stanwood, *History of the Presidency*, p. 345; W. R. to Jay Cooke, 18 June 1872, cited in Oberholtzer, *Jay Cooke: Financier of the Civil War*, 2: 353; Ross, *Liberal Republican Movement*.

20. W. R. to George W. Smalley, 24 June 1872, cited in Cortissoz, *Reid*, 1: 223–25; *New York Tribune*, 9 July 1872; Stanwood, *History of the Presidency*, p. 345.

21. Hesseltine, *Grant*, pp. 279–80; Matthew Josephson, *The Politicos, 1865–1896*, pp. 168–69.

22. *Harper's Weekly*, 8 June and 3, 10, 31 Aug. 1872, cited in Oberholtzer, *United States since the Civil War*, 3: 57; William Murrell, *A History of American Graphic Humor*, plate 45; Hesseltine, *Grant*, pp. 280–81.

23. Horace White to W. R. ca. 15 Sept. 1872, cited in Cortissoz, *Reid*, 1:226–27.

24. W. R. to William Larimer, 11 Mar. 1873, cited in Cortissoz, *Reid*, 1: 244–45; W. R. to George W. Smalley, 21 Nov. 1872; Ross, *Liberal Republican Movement*, p. 183; Greeley's physician said that the editor died of inflammation of the lining of the brain; Baehr, *Tribune*, p. 116.

25. Bigelow to Huntington, 24 Nov. 1872, in Bigelow, *Retrospections*, 5: 89–90.

26. This sum is arrived at simply by saying the hundred *Tribune* shares were worth ten thousand dollars each. Obviously the market value could only be determined by buying all the shares, and no one did this. Sinclair estimated the worth of the property at $713,000, and Reid thought it was $800,000; Sinclair to W. R., 14 Dec. 1872; W. R. to Chase, 17 Dec. 1872, in Smart, "Reid," p. 86.

27. W. R. to John Russell Young, 27 July 1869; W. R. to Ben Perley Poore, 6 Nov. 1869.

28. W. R. to Poore, 6 Nov. 1869; W. R. to Murat Halstead, 20 Apr. 1870.

29. W. R. to E. S. Sanford, 26 Apr., 1 Nov. 1870.

30. William Walter Phelps to W. R., 30 May 1872, cited in Smart, "Reid," p. 83; W. R. to Phelps, 2 June 1872.

31. Seitz, *Greeley*, p. 408.

32. Ovando J. Hollister, *Life of Schuyler Colfax*, pp. 388–91; *New York Times*, 24 Dec. 1872.

33. Baehr, *Tribune*, p. 120.

34. *New York Tribune*, 25 Nov. 1872; Stone, *Dana*, pp. 128, 146, cites the *New York Sun*, 29 Oct. 1875, 19 Jan. 1876, 27 Apr. 1876; Baehr, *Tribune*, pp. 122, 146, 237; no clear explanation of Reid's arrangement with Gould has been found. Cortissoz's biography of Reid does not mention Gould. Baehr's study of the *Tribune* gives no details of the transaction. If there is a document describing the agreement in the Reid Papers, I do not know of it; see W. R. to Phelps, 24 Feb. 1874; W. R. to Hay, 6, 7 Oct. 1875.

CHAPTER 5

1. W. R. to Sinclair, 25 Aug. 1869.

2. W. R. to E. T. Kidd, 3 Mar. 1873; W. R. to Murat Halstead, 29 Nov. 1873, in James G. Smart, "Whitelaw Reid," p. 89.

3. W. R. to George H. Stout, 18 Feb. 1870.

4. Victor Rosewater, *History of Cooperative Newsgathering in the United States*, pp. 142–43, 145; W. R. to Simonton, 25 July–3 Oct. 1870, a score of letters detailing violations of rules by other papers.

5. W. R. to Sinclair, n.d. [ca 30 Oct. 1870].

6. W. R. to Hoe and Co., 29 Oct. 1878; W. R. to Murat Halstead, 12 Jan. 1870; *New York Tribune*, 10 Apr. 1875.

7. Whitelaw Reid, *American and English Studies*, 2: 270.

8. Ibid., 254, 258.

9. W. R. to George W. Smalley, 21 Feb. 1870; W. R. to Hay, 3 Dec. 1870, in Royal Cortissoz, *The Life of Whitelaw Reid*, 1: 165.

10. John Russell Young to Mrs. J. M. Cazneau, 11 Jan. 1869, 22 Feb. 1869, [ca. 1 Apr.] 1869, Reid Papers, box 112; Allan Nevins, *Hamilton Fish, The Inner History of the Grant Administration*, 1: 260.

11. Henry George, Jr., *The Life of Henry George*, pp. 186–87; Charles A. Barker, *Henry George*, p. 124.

12. W. R. to Howells, 18 July, 13 Aug. 1869.

13. W. R. to Ripley, 16 July 1869; W. R. to Kate Field, 17 July 1873; G. A. Custer to W. R., 26 Feb. 1876, and Walt Whitman to W. R., 7 July 1876, in Cortissoz, *Reid*, 1: 312.

14. W. R. to Ripley, 14 Jan. 1870.

15. W. R. to Thomas Marshall, 27 Feb., 1 Mar. 1870.

16. W. R. to J. C. Bancroft Davis, 12 July 1870.

17. W. R. to Sinclair, 30 Oct. 1870.

18. W. R. to Bayard Taylor, 4 Apr. 1873.

19. W. R. to Smalley, 21 Feb. 1870; W. R. to Hay, 21 Sept. 1870.

20. Hay to W. R., 24 July 1875; James to W. R., 23 Apr., 30 Aug. 1876; W. R. to James [10 Aug. 1876], cited in Cortissoz, *Reid*, 1: 307–8.

21. *New York Tribune*, 5, 6 Sept. 1870.

22. Harry W. Baehr, *The New York Tribune since the Civil War*, pp. 31, 76, 82; Reid, *American and English Studies*, 2: 245; W. R. to George W. Smalley, 13, 20 July 1870, 7 Apr. 1873, and letters to Smalley in Feb.–May 1878.

23. *New York Tribune*, 12 Nov. 1868.

24. Sinclair to W. R., 14 Dec. 1872; see above chap. 4, n.26; W. R. to Phelps, 22 Feb. 1874.

25. W. R. to Bigelow, 27 Aug.1879, in John Bigelow, *Retrospections of an Active Life*, 5: 414–15.

26. Baehr, *New York Tribune*, pp. 141–43; Cortissoz, *Reid*, 1: 301.

27. W. R. to Bayard Taylor, 10 Jan. 1873, cited in Smart, "Reid," p. 108.

28. Several such notices, dated 5 Dec. 1877, 5 Feb. and 12 Aug. 1878, are in the Gordon Ford Papers, New York Public Library.

29. Smart, "Reid," pp. 204–6, gives some details of these arrangements.

30. W. R. to Blaine, 8 Apr. 1879.

31. Platt to W. R., 13 Feb. 1878, cited in Smart, "Reid," p. 207.

32. *New York Tribune*, 20 Aug. 1879; Conkling to W. R., 21 Aug. 1879, cited in Cortissoz, *Reid*, 1: 372; Baehr, *Tribune*, p. 143.

33. N. W. Ayer and Son, *American Newspaper Annual, 1880*, p. 57; W. R. to Bigelow, 27 Aug. 1879, in Bigelow, *Retrospections*, 5: 414–15.

34. Baehr, *New York Tribune*, p. 126; W. R. to Bigelow, 18 Feb. 1873, "Bigelow," Reid Papers, box 6.

35. The indenture to Mary Bodine and agreements between the *Tribune* Association and various renters are in the Gordon Ford Papers, New York Public Library.

36. W. R. to A. C. Fahnstock, 21 July 1873; Claude G. Bowers, *The Tragic Era*, chap. 19; Matthew Josephson, *Politicos, 1865–1896*, pp. 187, 252; copies of the notices Reid sent are in the Gordon Ford Papers, New York Public Library.

37. W. R. to Tuttle, 31 Dec. 1874, 14 Jan. 1879.

38. Baehr, *New York Tribune*, pp. 128, 184–86; W. P. Thompson to W. R., 6 June 1877 and [27/28] June 1877, cited in Smart, "Reid," pp. 249–52; Josephson, *Politicos*, p. 252.

39. W. R. to Ripley, 16 July 1869, 14 Jan. 1870; W. R. to Sanford, [1] Nov. 1870; W. R. to Bigelow, 18 Feb. 1873, "Bigelow," Reid Papers, box 6.

40. W. R. to Edward McPherson, 25 June 1879.

41. W. R. to Hay, 20 Mar. 1879, "J. Hay to Reid, 1878–79," Reid Papers, box 105.

CHAPTER 6

1. *New York Times*, 28 Jan. 1868, cited in Candace Stone, *Dana and the Sun*, p. 57.

2. *New York Tribune*, 2 Sept. 1868.

3. *New York Tribune*, 22 Sept. 1868.

4. Whitelaw Reid, *After the War*; see for examples pp. 45, 292, 296, 298, 357, 365, 394, 404, 407.

5. W. R. to Bigelow, 10 Apr. 1871, in John Bigelow, *Retrospections of an Active Life*, 4: 487–90.

6. W. R. to Bigelow, 10 Apr. 1871, in ibid.

7. W. R. to Greeley, 18 Sept. 1871.

8. W. R. to John A. Dix, 11 Sept. 1874; *New York Tribune*, 20 Oct. 1874.

9. Tyler Dennett, *John Hay, From Poetry to Politics*, p. 123; W. R. to Watterson, 7 Nov. 1874; W. R. to Tilden, 31 Dec. 1874, 22 Feb. 1876.

10. Claude M. Fuess, *Carl Schurz: Reformer*, p. 217; Matthew Josephson, *The Politicos, 1865–1896*, p. 241; W. R. to E. A. Merritt, 18, 20, 21 Aug. 1876; Evarts to W. R., 24 Aug. 1876, in Royal Cortissoz, *The Life of Whitelaw Reid*, 1: 350; *New York Tribune*, 23 Aug. 1876.

11. W. R. to Bigelow, 8 June 1875, in Bigelow, *Retrospections*, 5: 207–8.

12. W. R. to Blaine, 23 Jan. 1876; W. R. to Charles Nordhoff, 28 Feb. 1876; Hay to W. R. [Feb.] 1876 and W. R. to Hay, 14 Mar. 1876, cited in Cortissoz, *Reid*, 1: 335, 337.

13. Harry W. Baehr, *The New York Tribune since the Civil War*, pp. 158–59; *New York Tribune*, 30 June, 29 Aug. 1876.

14. W. R. to Hayes, 21 July 1876.

15. Howells to W. R., [n.d.], in Cortissoz, *Reid*, 1: 344–45.

16. *New York Tribune*, 8, 9 Nov. 1876.

17. Whitney to W. R., 9 Nov. 1876, in Cortissoz, *Reid*, 1: 356.

18. W. R. to Garfield, 9 Jan. 1877; the best account of the compromise is in C. Vann Woodward's *Reunion and Reaction: The Compromise of 1877 and the End of Reconstruction*. Woodward believes that the disputed election was one of the most severe political crises in the United States in the nineteenth century.

19. W. R. to Hayes, 21 Feb. 1877.

20. W. R. to Evarts, 1 Mar. 1877; Ellis P. Oberholtzer, *A History of the United States since the Civil War*, 2: 321.

21. *New York Tribune*, 2 Mar. 1877.

22. Josephson, *Politicos*, p. 248.

23. Carl Schurz, *Reminiscences of Carl Schurz*, 3: 391; Josephson, *Politicos*, 237–41; W. R. to Mary A. Dodge, 28 Aug. 1877, cited in Smart, "Reid," p. 198; see *New York Tribune*, 9, 16 June, 4 Aug.1877, for articles on civil service reform.

24. Full accounts of the strikes and the repercussions are in Robert V. Bruce, *1877: Year of Violence*.

25. Baehr, *New York Tribune*, p. 182; *New York Tribune*, 18–28 July 1877; see especially, "No Compromise with Rioters," "Wages of Railroad Men," and "The Duty of Good Citizens," in the paper for 27 July 1877.

26. Good summaries of the cipher dispatches expose are in Baehr, *New York Tribune*, pp. 168ff., and in Leon B. Richardson, *William E. Chandler: Republican*, pp. 226–33.

27. *New York Tribune*, 3, 5, 8, 9 Oct. 1878.

28. *New York Tribune*, 8 Oct. 1878.

29. W. R. to Chandler, 17 Oct. 1878, Chandler Collection, New Hampshire Historical Society, in Richardson, *Chandler*, p. 232.

30. W. R. to Hayes, 21 Feb. 1877; Hay to W. R. [4 Mar.] 1877, "J. Hay to W. Reid, 1876–7," Reid Papers, box 105.

31. Evarts to W. R., 10 Oct. 1878, "Evarts, William M. 1878–79," Reid Papers, box 19; Evarts to W. R., 23 Dec. 1878, in Cortissoz, *Reid*, 1: 365–66; there is no way to prove a direct connection between the exposés and the offer. Hay told Reid that Evarts thought the exposures did more for the Republicans than Conkling did in his whole life and that Reid was offered Berlin for his practical contributions to the party.

32. W. R. to Evarts, 30 Dec. 1878.

33. Hay to W. R., 30 Mar. 1879, in William R. Thayer, *The Life of John Hay*, 1: 456.

34. W. R. to Hay, 20 Mar. 1879; "J. Hay to W. Reid, 1878–9," Reid Papers, box 105.

35. W. R. to Hay, 13 Oct., 4 Nov. 1879; Dennett, *Hay*, p. 129; Cortissoz, *Reid*, 2: 8–9, prints the notes and telegrams exchanged.

36. H. Wilson, comp., *Trow's New York City Directory*, is on file in the New York Public Library. Volumes 82–100 cover the years 1868–69 through 1886–87. The first directory in which Reid's name appears, vol. 83, for the year ending May 1, 1870, lists "Reid, Whitelaw, editor, 154 Nassau, H 667 Second av."

37. W. R. to F. A. Wheeler, 23 Aug. 1873; W. R. to Henry Holt, 19 Sept. 1873; W. R. to P. W. Townsend, 12 Feb. 1876; pocket diary for 1866, but containing entries dated Apr. 1878, Reid Papers, box 1; W. R. to Hay, 1 Dec. 1884; W. R. to Lyman, 9 Dec. 1911.

38. W. R. to Blaine, 28 Feb. 1876.

39. Baehr, *New York Tribune*, p. 114; Cortissoz, *Reid*, 1: 250; pocket diary for 1876, Reid Papers, box 1.

40. If Reid was interested in any girl the matter was of too little moment to be mentioned in his outgoing correspondence. Occasionally his name was linked with that of Anna Dickinson. Interested readers may attempt to decipher Reid's note of 6 Feb. [1871?] in Private [letterbook] 3 A, Reid Papers, box 113.

41. Stone, *Dana*, p. 128; Henry Watterson, *Marse Henry*, 1: 244.

42. Hay to Bigelow, 12 Mar. 1871, in Bigelow, *Retrospections*, 4: 478–80.

43. Almost any sampling of Reid's correspondence with Phelps in the seventies will indicate the closeness of the personal relationship and the financial content of their communications with each other. See for example Phelps to W. R., 19 Mar., 1 Apr., 16 Oct., 11 Dec. 1873. Hugh M. Herrick's highly laudatory *William Walter Phelps* must be used with much care.

44. Pocket diary for 1876, Reid Papers, box 1.

45. W. R. to Stedman, 21, 27 May 1879.

46. W. R. to H. E. Riedel, 28 May 1879.

CHAPTER 7

1. Theodore C. Smith, *The Life and Letters of James Abram Garfield*, pp. 947–58; Sherman to W. R., 21 Dec. 1879, in Royal Cortissoz, *The Life of Whitelaw Reid*, 2: 14; Blaine to W. R., 10 Dec. 1879, in ibid., 2: 15–17; Phelps to W. R., 15 Mar. 1880, in ibid., 2: 21; W. R. to Hay, 24 Jan. 1880; W. R. to Platt, 17 Feb. 1880.

2. *New York Tribune*, 28 May 1880, 8 June 1880.

3. *New York Tribune*, 1 June 1880; only a few months earlier Reid had showed a marked lack of patience with bolters and considered the practice of bolting bad politics as a general rule; W. R. to Platt, 17 Feb. 1880.

4. *New York Tribune*, 8 June 1880.

5. See above, chap. 3, n.8, and Cortissoz, *Reid*, 2: 30.

6. *New York Tribune*, 9 June 1880.

7. W. R. to Garfield, 12 June 1880, 19 July 1880.

8. W. R. to Garfield, 19 July 1880.

9. W. R. to Garfield, 15 Aug. 1880.

10. W. R. to Garfield, 26 June 1880.

11. Smith, *Garfield*, 2: 652–54, 1002–4.

12. Smith, *Garfield*, 2: 996, 1002–4.

13. Smith, *Garfield*, 2: 1012; W. R. to Marshall Jewell, 2 Aug. 1880; W. R. to Blaine, 11 Sept. 1880.

14. Joseph Keppler in *Puck*, 25 Aug. 1880.

15. Garfield to W. R., 7 Dec. 1880 and Hay to W. R., [9?] Dec. 1880, in Cortissoz, *Reid*, 2: 41; Hay to Garfield, 25, 31 Dec. 1880, in William R. Thayer, *The Life and Letters of John Hay*, 1: 442–47.

16. Lizzie Mills to W. R., 23 Jan., 26 Feb., 4 Apr., 13 May 1880, Reid Papers, box 53.

17. Blaine to Mrs. Garfield, 20 Dec. 1880, Blaine to Garfield, 20 Dec. 1880, in Mary A. Dodge, *Biography of James G. Blaine*, pp. 494–95.

18. W. R. to Phelps, 24 Dec. 1880.

19. Lizzie Mills to W. R., 21 Nov., 7, 16, 23, 29 Dec. 1880, 2 Jan. 1881, Reid Papers, box 53; the correspondence suggests that Reid proposed sometime during Christmas week.

20. Benjamin Perley Poore, *Perley's Reminiscences of Sixty Years in the National Metropolis*, 1: 384.

21. W. R. to Phelps, 31 Dec. 1880.

22. *New York Tribune*, 3 Jan. 1881; W. R. to Garfield, 1 Jan. 1881; Smith, *Garfield*, 2: 1056–57.

23. W. R. to Garfield, 16 Jan. 1881; Cortissoz, *Reid*, 2: 51; Platt to W. R., 3 Jan. 1881, cited in Smart, "Reid," p. 233.

24. Lizzie Mills to W. R., 2 Jan. 1881, Reid Papers, box 53.

25. Lizzie Mills to W. R., 15 Jan. 1881, Reid Papers, box 53; W. R. to Garfield, 16 Jan. 1881; Hay to W. R., 15 Jan. 1881, Reid Papers, box 105.

26. W. R. to Hay, 18 Jan. 1881; W. R. to Blaine, 18 Jan. 1881, Reid Papers, box 34.

27. Smith, *Garfield*, 2: 1074.

28. Lizzie Mills to W. R., 5 Feb. 1881; W. R. to D. O. Mills, 6 Feb. 1881, Reid Papers, box 53; Hay to W. R., 11 Feb. 1881, in Thayer, *Hay*, 1: 405; Blaine to W. R., 13 Feb. 1881, in Cortissoz, *Reid*, 2: 70.

29. W. R. to Lizzie Mills, 1, 2, 3, 4, Mar. 1881, in Cortissoz, *Reid*, 2: 54–57; Robert G. Caldwell, *James A. Garfield: Party Chieftain*, p. 329.

30. W. R. to Garfield, 21 Apr. 1881, Reid Papers, box 30.

31. W. R. to Lizzie Mills, 1, 2, 3, 4, 5 Mar. 1881; Cortissoz, *Reid*, 2: 54–57.

32. Accounts of the Robertson affair are in Smith, *Garfield*, 2: 963, 1103; Caldwell, *Garfield*, pp. 319–21; Matthew Josephson, *The Politicos, 1865–1896*, pp. 306–9. See *New York Tribune*, 3 Jan. 1881, for Blaine's editorial.

33. W. R. to Garfield, 24 Jan. 1881, Reid Papers, box 30.

34. W. R. to Garfield, 16 Jan. 1881; W. R. to Garfield, 11 Apr. 1881, Reid Papers, box 30; W. R. to Hay, 27 Mar. 1881; Garfield to W. R., 30 Mar. 1881, in Cortissoz, *Reid*, 2: 60–63; see also Harriet Bailey (Stanwood) Blaine, ed., *Letters of Mrs. James G. Blaine*, 1: 283–87.

35. Hay to W. R., 31 Oct. 1881, Reid Papers, box 105; May D. Russell Young, ed., *Men and Memories: Personal Reminiscences by John Russell Young*, pp. 460–61.

36. Pocket diary 2 July [1881], Reid Papers, box 1; Hay to W. R., 4 July 1881, Reid Papers, box 105.

37. Blaine to W. R., 21 Dec. 1881, Reid Papers, box 104.

38. W. R. to Blaine, 28 Oct. 1881, in Cortissoz, *Reid*, 2: 76–77.

39. *New York Tribune*, 15, 26 May 1882.

40. Ward Thoron, ed., *The Letters of Mrs. Henry Adams, 1865–1883*,

p. 337; the Henry Adamses were no more Arthurites than Blaine and Reid.

41. Cortissoz, *Reid*, 1: 236; *New York Tribune*, 17 March 1889.

42. Reid Genealogy, 2, Reid Papers, box 191.

43. A pamphlet, *Administrative Office Building of the Archdiocese of New York*, printed by that body, has descriptions and photographs of the house as it was about 1950; W. R. to Hay, 9 June 1886, Reid Papers, box 34.

44. Cortissoz, *Reid*, 2: 104–5; see LeRoy R. Hafen's sketch of Ben Holladay in *Dictionary of American Biography*.

45. W. R. to Hay, 9 June 1886; D. O. Mills to W. R., 8 Nov. 1886, Reid Papers, box 52; W. R. to W. H. Robertson, 25 Jan. 1890.

46. W. R. to Olmstead, 25 Jan. 1890; W. R. to J. M. Logan, 22 Nov. 1889; W. R. to D. O. Mills, 20 July 1888, 21 Feb. 1890; W. R. to Tuttle, 12 Aug. 1890; *New York Tribune*, 15 July 1888.

47. "Financial statement" in Private [letterbook], No. 57, pp. 199, 354, 509, in Reid Papers, box 57; W. R. to Logan, 18, 20 Dec. 1888, 17 Jan., 16 Feb. 1889.

48. W. R. to Fred Barnes, 14 Aug. 1890, 4 Aug. 1891, 7 Dec. 1891, 9 Apr. 1892.

49. W. R. to Hay, 9 June 1886; W. R. to William H. Reid, 10 Apr. 1889.

50. *The Money Makers: A Social Parable* (New York, 1885) was written by Henry F. Keenan who worked in the *Tribune* office at the time Reid took the paper over in Greeley's last years. It was a bad novel but had a certain vogue because the authorship was widely known and the characters were easily recognized. Hay's father-in-law, Amasa Stone, was viciously portrayed under the name of Grimstone. Hay was furious when he learned about the book but could do nothing to prevent its circulation. Reid did not seem particularly disturbed; Hay to W. R., 2 Feb. 1885, Reid Papers, box 105; see Tyler Dennett, *John Hay, From Poetry to Politics*, p. 111.

CHAPTER 8

1. Oliver Gramling, *AP: The Story of News*, pp. 88–91; Melville Stone, *Fifty Years a Journalist*, pp. 209–210.

2. Gramling, *AP*, p. 91; Victor Rosewater, *History of Cooperative News-gathering in the United States*, pp. 166–67; W. R. to W. H. Smith, 26 Dec. 1883, 5 Feb. 1885; Edgar Laughlin Gray, "The Career of William Henry Smith, Politician-Journalist," pp. 68, 172; Gray cites a copy of the contract in William Henry Smith Papers, William Henry Smith Memorial Library, Indianapolis, Indiana.

3. Charles H. Dennis, *Victor Lawson*, pp. 186–87; Gramling, *AP*, p. 94; Stone, *Fifty Years*, pp. 209–10.

4. Gramling, *AP*, p. 113; Rosewater, *Cooperative Newsgathering*, pp. 183–84.

5. Rosewater, *Cooperative Newsgathering*, pp. 185–86.

6. W. R. to Richard Smith, 18 Aug. 1883; W. R. to Edward Mitchell, 15 Dec. 1883.

7. Stone, *Fifty Years*, pp. 165–66; Dennis, *Lawson*, pp. 175–76; W. R. to Phelps, 2 Mar. 1885, cited in James G. Smart, "Whitelaw Reid," p. 269; Thomas Dreier, *The Power of Print—and Men*, pp. 29ff.

8. Dennis, *Lawson*, pp. 176–77; Dreier, *Power of Print*, p. 32; W. R. to Stilson Hutchins, 7 [or 17] Mar. 1885; Reid's correspondence with Lawson is in Reid Papers, box 44. The comparative nearness of the *Tribune*'s presses to the Baltimore shop where the machines were built and to the mechanics there was of great benefit to Reid in the first years when breakdowns were frequent.

9. W. H. Smith to W. R., 11 Dec. 1886, Reid Papers, box 191; Reid held 7,045½ shares, Clephane 3,916⅓; the syndicate total was 16,302½.

10. Dreier, *Power of Print*, pp. 51–52; Henry W. Baehr, *The New York Tribune since the Civil War*, p. 201; Royal Cortissoz, *The Life of Whitelaw Reid*, 2: 105–6; W. R. to Tuttle, 20 Nov. 1889.

11. Baehr, *New York Tribune*, pp. 184–85; George A. Stevens, *New York Typographical Union No. 6*; in 1887 the *Tribune*, in its third reduction since 1873, set the wage scale at forty cents per thousand ems on night work and thirty-three cents on day work. This and other changes resulted in a loss, from prepanic levels, of almost half of the compositor's dollar income.

12. David M. Ellis et al., *A Short History of New York State*; W. R. to Richard Smith, 18 Aug. 1883, indicates Reid's attitude about the union. The numerous strikes in New York City in the eighties were naturally opposed by nearly everyone in positions similar to that of Reid, which made his attitude easier to assume.

13. Dennis, *Lawson*, p. 183.

14. Baehr, *New York Tribune*, pp. 185–86; Lawson to E. A. Grozier, 3 Aug. 1890, in Dennis, *Lawson*, p. 183.

15. Baehr, *New York Tribune*, pp. 125, 237; Frank L. Mott, *American Journalism*, pp. 418–492; George P. Rowell, comp., *Rowell's American Newspaper Directory*; the Directory for 1880 shows circulation of thirty thousand for the *Tribune* in that year; Henry Hall to W. R., 6 July 1885, Reid Papers, box 33.

16. Baehr, *New York Tribune*, p. 234.

17. Baehr, *New York Tribune*, p. 143; Hall to W. R., 6 July 1885, Reid Papers, box 33.

18. Candace Stone, *Dana and the Sun*, p. 385; W. R. to Richard Smith, 11 Oct. 1883; W. R. to Thomas B. Asten, 27 Mar. 1884.

19. Reid's correspondence with Mrs. Taylor on this point is in Reid Papers, vol. 45, box 136. At these figures Reid's seventy-five shares paid him $28,125.00 a year.

20. Baehr, *New York Tribune*, p. 237; W. R. to Hay, 22 May 1880; see also "Financial statement (F)," in Reid Papers, box 191.

21. *New York Tribune, A Sketch of Its History* (New York, 1883), pamphlet in Boston Public Library; W. R. to Nicholson, 24 Apr. 1891.

22. W. R. to Blaine, 28 Oct. 1881, cited in Cortissoz, *Reid*, 2: 76–77.

23. Matthew Josephson, *The Politicos, 1865–1896*, pp. 337–38; Blaine's letters to Reid during Arthur's administration are in Reid Papers, box 104.

24. W. R. to Chandler, 27 Dec. 1883.

25. W. R. to Phelps, 14 Feb. 1884; *New York Tribune*, 6 Feb. 1884.

26. George F. Howe, *Chester Arthur*, p. 265; W. R. to Phelps, 14 Feb. 1884.

27. Leon B. Richardson, *William E. Chandler, Republican*, p. 60; Stanley P. Hirshson, *Farewell to the Bloody Shirt: Northern Republicans and the Southern Negro*, pp. 108–114, cites *New York Tribune*, 17, 26, 31 Oct., 2 Nov. 1882, and Chandler to W. R., 17, 20 Dec. 1883.

28. David S. Muzzey, *James G. Blaine: A Political Idol of Other Days*, p. 293.

29. Muzzey, *Blaine*, p. 307; W. R. to Smalley, 19 June 1884.

30. Smart, "Reid," p. 292, cites Blaine to W. R., 14 June 1884, and W. R. to Blaine, 25 June 1884.

31. W. R. to S. B. Elkins, 8 Oct. 1884; W. R. to Blaine, 18 Oct. 1884. Elkins' letters to W. R. are in Reid Papers, box 19.

32. *New York World*, 30 Oct. 1884; Muzzey, *Blaine*, pp. 318, 322–23, describes the dinner and reproduces the cartoon.

33. W. R. to Blaine, 18 Oct. 1884.

34. Hugh M. Herrick, *William Walter Phelps*, p. 151; W. R. to W. R. Halloway (*Indianapolis Times*), 5 Nov. 1884; W. R. to W. W. Clapp (*Boston Journal*), 5 Nov. 1884.

35. Baehr, *New York Tribune*, p. 191; Hay to W. R., 28 Nov. 1884, Reid Papers, box 105.

36. Smart, "Reid," p. 310; *New York Tribune*, 3, 31 Dec. 1884, 12 Feb. 1887; Ellis P. Oberholtzer, *A History of the United States since the Civil War*, 4: 318, 465.

37. Charles C. Tansill, *The Foreign Policy of Thomas F. Bayard, 1885–1897*, pp. 300, 321.

38. W. R. to Hay, 10 June 1886.

39. *Puck*, 22, 29 Sept., 13 Oct., 3, 10, 17, 24 Nov., 15, 29 Dec. 1886.

40. Hirshson, *Bloody Shirt*, p. 155, cites *New York Tribune*, 2, 3, 4, 5, 9, 12 Jan. 1888; Lamar was confirmed, 32–28, when three Republicans voted with the Democrats; Chandler to W. R., 26, 30 Dec. 1887, Reid Papers, box 19.

41. Muzzey, *Blaine*, pp. 364, 367.

42. Muzzey, *Blaine*, pp. 367–68, 372; W. R. to Clapp (*Boston Journal*), 2 May 1888, in Cortissoz, *Reid*, 2: 116; *New York Tribune*, 30 May 1888.

43. Joseph B. Foraker, *Notes of a Busy Life*, 1: 341.

44. Muzzey, *Blaine*, pp. 373–76, 381 n.1.

45. Edward Stanwood, *A History of the Presidency*, pp. 482–85; *New York Tribune*, 25–31 Oct. 1888.

CHAPTER 9

1. Albert T. Volwiler, ed., *The Correspondence between Benjamin Harrison and James G. Blaine, 1882–1893*, pp. 5, 299.

2. W. R. to Albert G. Porter, 10 Dec. 1888; W. R. to Harrison, 10 Dec. 1888.

3. Volwiler, *Harrison and Blaine*, pp. 5, 299, 300; Elkins to Phelps, 9 Feb. 1889, Reid Papers, box 19.

4. In the usage of the day, in ordinary conversation about American legations abroad, London, Great Britain, and England were interchangable terms. This practice is followed here despite the technical inaccuracy of references to an American minister to London or to England.

5. Hay to W. R., 13 Nov., 2 Dec. 1888; 9, 26 Jan. 1889, Reid Papers, box 105; Elkins to Phelps, 9 Feb. 1889, and Phelps to W. R., 13 Feb. 1889, Reid Papers, box 19.

6. Edward Younger, *John A. Kasson*, p. 353; *New York Tribune*, 1 July 1888; Hay to W. R., 31 Aug. 1884, 14 Oct. 1889, Reid Papers, box 105.

7. Elkins to W. R., 13, 28 Mar. 1889, Reid Papers, box 19.

8. Memorandum: Hay to W. R., 14 Oct. 1889, Reid Papers, box 105; W. R. to Blaine, 16 Mar. 1889.

9. Memorandum: Hay to W. R., 14 Oct. 1889, Reid Papers, box 105; Reid's own summary of the "negotiations" about the appointment is in his letter to Smalley of 8 April 1889. He repeated the substance of the matter to A. K. McClure in a letter of 19 March 1889 and in one to Murat Halstead on 23 March 1889.

10. Hugh M. Herrick, *William Walter Phelps*, p. 209; Tyler Dennett, *John Hay, From Poetry to Politics*, p. 172.

11. *New York Tribune*, 24 Mar. 1889; W. R. to McClure, 19 Mar. 1889; W. R. to Halstead, 23 Mar. 1889; W. R. to Hiscock, 1 Apr. 1889.

12. *New York Tribune*, 17 Mar., 28 Apr. 1889.

13. Roosevelt to Lodge, 27 Mar. 1889, in Elting E. Morison, ed., *Letters of Theodore Roosevelt*, 1: 155.

14. *New York Tribune*, 20 Apr., 13 May 1889.

15. Beckles Willson, *America's Ambassadors to France, 1777–1927*, pp. 329–37.

16. Willson, *Ambassadors to France*, p. 335; *New York Tribune*, 16, 22 May 1889.

17. Willson, *Ambassadors to France*, p. 337; *New York Tribune*, 21 July 1889; Bailly Blanchard to H. C. Hall, 19 Oct. 1891, Reid Papers, box 145; Reid paid 27,500 francs rent per quarter; the franc exchanged at $0.193.

18. Willson, *Ambassadors to France*, p. 338; *New York Tribune*, 16 July 1889; W. R. to Smalley, 15 July 1880; Reid to Blaine, 16 July 1889; U.S., Department of State, *Foreign Relations of the United States, 1890* (Washington, D.C., 1891), pp. 276–80, hereafter cited *F. R.* [*date*]; U.S., Department of State manuscript, Instructions, France, 21, No. 9, 9 May 1889, National Archives, Washington, D.C. These manuscript records will be called Instructions or Dispatches as appropriate, followed by country designation; W. R. to Smalley, 15 July 1889.

19. W. R. to Nicholson, 19 July 1889.

20. Whitelaw Reid, *After the War*, p. 194; pocket diary [1865], Reid Papers, box 1.

21. Ernest R. May, *American Imperialism*, p. 61; in a short sketch May describes Reid as having mixed views, part antiexpansionist and part outward looking. This is correct to an extent but does not apply to Reid's views on territorial expansion before 1898. May has misread a speech Reid made in 1881 (see ibid., p. 61 n.26). There is nothing in the speech about the nation being destined to stretch into the Pacific; *New York Tribune*, 5 Feb. 1869; the evidence that Reid wrote the editorial on Cuba is in W. R. to Garfield, 7 Feb. 1869, cited in Royal Cortissoz, *The Life of Whitelaw Reid*, 1: 145–46; W. R. to Elihu Washburne, 11 Sept. 1869; J. R. Young to Mrs. J. M. Cazneau, 11 Jan., 22 Feb. 1869, Reid Papers, box 112.

22. W. R. to Schuyler Colfax, 13 Jan. 1870.

23. David M. Pletcher, *The Awkward Years*, pp. 22–24; *New York Tribune*, 28 Apr. 1880, 20 Dec. 1881; *New York Tribune*, 31 Jan. 1885; Blaine to W. R., 1 Feb. 1885, Reid Papers, box 104; see Philip M. Brown's essay on Frelinghuysen in Samuel F. Bemis, *The American Secretaries of State and Their Diplomacy*, 8: 3–43.

24. Pletcher, *Awkward Years*, pp. 59–63; Harry W. Baehr, *New York Tribune since the Civil War*, p. 32; *New York Tribune*, 12 Apr., 30 May, 19 Dec. 1873.

25. See Walter LaFeber, *The New Empire*, p. 60, for a comment about the lack of a consensus on the need for a strong navy at this time; *New York Tribune*, 22 Jan. 1887.

26. *New York Tribune*, 31 Jan., 5 Feb. 1885.

27. Hay to W. R. [4 March 1877], 3 Jan. 1879; Evarts to W. R., 23 Dec. 1878 and W. R. to Evarts, 30 Dec. 1878; all of these letters are in Reid Papers, box 105.

28. Instructions, France, No. 24 (5 July 1889).

29. Allan Nevins, *John D. Rockefeller: The Heroic Age of American Enterprise*, 2: 27–28, 34; Allan Nevins, *Study in Power*, 2: 96–128.

30. Bayard to McLane, 1 Sept. 1885, *F.R., 1885*, pp. 376–77.

31. *New York Tribune*, 30 Apr. 1887; *Journal de St. Petersburg*, 14–26 Sept. 1887, cited in Lothrop to Bayard, 6 Oct. 1887, *F.R., 1887*, pp. 968–69; W. R. to Blaine, 25 July 1890, enclosing W. R. to Ribot, 9 July 1890, and Thompson and Belford Co., Ltd., to W. R. [n.d.], Dispatches, France, 104.

32. W. R. to Blaine, 21 Aug. 1890, enclosing Ribot to W. R., 14 Aug. 1890, Wharton to W. R., 22 Sept. 1890, Dispatches, France, 104.

33. W. R. to Blaine, 31 Dec. 1891, enclosing W. R. to Ribot, 29 Dec. 1891, Dispatches, France, 106; W. R. to Blaine, 15 Jan. 1892, Dispatches, France, 107; Blaine to W. R., 3 Feb. 1892 (telegram), Instructions, France, 22.

34. W. R. to Blaine, 12 Feb. 1890, enclosing an unsigned letter dated 4 Feb. 1890 and addressed to the minister of foreign affairs of the United States of North America, Dispatches, France, 104; Blaine to W. R., 5 Mar. 1890, enclosing

Blaine to the French Society of Arbitration, 5 Mar. 1890, Instructions, France, 22.

35. W. R. to Blaine, 13 June 1891; a copy is in the Reid Papers and the original is in Dispatches, France, 105.

36. W. R. to Halford, 9 July 1891.

37. Harrison to Blaine, 3 Aug. 1891 and Blaine to Harrison, 10 Aug. 1891, in Volwiler, ed., *Harrison and Blaine*, pp. 169, 173.

38. W. R. to Harrison, 9 Oct. 1891; *New York Tribune*, 10 Mar. 1892.

CHAPTER 10

1. W. R. to Logan, 28 Dec. 1889; 31 July, 19 Oct., 7 Dec. 1891; W. R. to Olmstead, 6 Mar., 30 June 1890, 9 March 1891.

2. W. R. to Judge W. H. Robertson, 25 Jan. 1890; Ophir was assessed at eighty-five thousand dollars when the Reids acquired it; the figure was raised to a hundred thousand dollars when they began work on the house. Efforts to have the assessment lowered were not successful.

3. W. R. to White, 10 Oct., 18 Nov. 1890.

4. W. R. to Mills, 31 Jan., 21 Feb. 1890.

5. W. R. to White, 16 June, 2 Sept. 1890; Blanchard to Jules Allard, 23 Mar. 1891; a full description of the work to be done is on page 441 of vol. 61 B, Reid Papers, box 145.

6. W. R. to Mills, 19 Oct. 1891.

7. W. R. to Mills, 31 Jan. 1890; W. R. to White, 20 July 1891.

8. W. R. to Tuttle, 20 Nov. 1889; Reid sometimes wrote Wildair, sometimes Wild Air, usually the latter.

9. W. R. to Nicholson, 8 Nov. 1889; W. R. to Smalley, 22 Oct. 1890.

10. W. R. to Nicholson, 19, 26 July 1889.

11. Harry W. Baehr, *New York Tribune since the Civil War*, p. 276; W. R. to Nicholson, 2 Jan., 29 Aug., 30 Sept., 25 Oct. 1890, 4 Jan. 1891.

12. Ellis to Nicholson [ca. 8 Nov. 1889], Reid Papers, box 143; W. R. to Nicholson, 2, 14 Jan. 1890.

13. W. R. to Nicholson, 10 Nov. 1890.

14. Harold F. Gosnell, *Boss Platt and His New York Machine*, p. 131; James M. Lee, *History of American Journalism*; Baehr, *New York Tribune*, p. 237.

15. W. R. to Tuttle, 29 Jan. 1890.

16. Hall to W. R., 11 Apr. 1891, Reid Papers, box 45; W. R. to Hall, 24 Apr. 1891.

17. W. R. to Milholland, 3 Mar. 1891.

18. W. R. to Nicholson, 3 Mar. 1891, enclosing W. R. to Milholland, 28 Feb. 1891.

19. W. R. to Nicholson, 28 Sept. 1891.

20. W. R. to Nicholson, 6 Oct. 1891.

21. W. R. to Nicholson, 13 Oct. 1891; W. R. to Hall, 11 Nov. 1891.

22. W. R. to Brannan, 13 Oct. 1891; W. R. to Milholland, 13 Oct. 1891.

23. W. R. to Hiscock, 22 Oct. 1891; Reid told his friend that he knew Hiscock was not aware of this aspect of the matter.

24. W. R. to Milholland, 11 Nov. 1891.

25. George A. Stevens, *New York Typographical Union No. 6*, pp. 632–34.

26. W. R. to Bennett, 13 Jan. 1890; *New York Tribune*, 15 Jan. 1890; Reid believed that the union had exhausted its funds.

27. W. R. to Phelps, 15 Jan., 18 Feb. 1890.

28. W. R. to Ward, 17 Jan., 14 Feb. 1890.

29. W. R. to Phelps, 18 Feb.1890; W. R. to Nicholson, 9 May 1890.

30. W. R. to Halstead, 2 June 1890; W. R. to Ward, 4 June 1890.

31. W. R. to Nicholson, 19, 28 Aug. 1890; W. R. to Mills [ca. 12 Sept. 1890].

32. *New York Tribune*, 21 Sept. 1890; the Doyle bronze statue was unveiled on Memorial Day, 1894, at Broadway and Sixth Avenue; the site was named Greeley Square; Stevens *New York Typographical Union*, pp. 632–34; Doyle became convinced that he was entitled to the money raised in 1873 and later sued Reid. On 11 Nov. 1897 the Supreme Court of New York dismissed the suit; see *New York Tribune*, 11, 12, 13 Nov. 1897.

33. Charles H. Dennis, *Victor Lawson*, pp. 187–88; Victor Rosewater, *History of Cooperative Newsgathering in the United States*, p. 186; see Chap. 8 above.

34. Dennis, *Lawson*, pp. 187–88.

35. W. R. to Dana, 18 Feb., 15 Apr. 1891.

36. W. H. Smith to W. R., 6 Apr. 1891, Reid Papers, box 45.

37. Dana to W. R., 14 May 1891, telegram, Reid Papers, box 45. Reid thought the dividends he had received might amount to more than a third of a million dollars.

38. W. R. to Nicholson, 16 May 1891.

39. Dennis, *Lawson*, p. 189; Edgar Laughlin Gray, "The Career of William Henry Smith, Politician-Journalist," pp. 181–84.

40. W. R. to Dana, 6, 23 Oct. 1891; W. R. to Nicholson, 13 Nov. 1891 and enclosed memorandum, "Points understood."

41. W. R. to Dana, 3 Dec. 1891; W. R. to Nicholson, 4 Dec. 1891.

42. W. R. to Bennett, 14 Dec. 1891; W. R. to Nicholson, 10 Dec. 1891; W. R. to W. H. Smith [ca. 21 Dec. 1891], Private.

43. W. R. to Nicholson, 22 Jan. 1892.

44. Thomas Dreier, *The Power of Print—and Men*, pp. 51–52; W. R. to Mills, 10 Dec. 1891.

45. W. R. to Tuttle, 28 Dec. 1889, 20 Sept., 28 Oct. 1890; Reid sent the certificates, with a list, to Tuttle on 5 Dec. 1891.

46. Dennis, *Lawson*, p. 181; W. R. to Nicholson, 26 July 1889; W. R. to W. H. Smith, 19 Aug. 1889.

CHAPTER 11

1. This account is substantially the same as that in my "Protectionism and Pork," in *Agricultural History*, 33 (1959), 190–95. Beckles Willson, in his *America's Ambassadors to France, 1777–1927*, pp. 339, 340–41, mentions the problem but does not discuss it.

2. Blaine to W. R., 11 June 1889, U.S., Department of State, *Foreign Relations of the United States, 1889*, pp. 164–65.

3. W. R. to Blaine, 15 Aug. 1890, and enclosure, U.S., Department of State Dispatches, France, 104; see Louis L. Snyder, "The American–German Pork Dispute, 1879–1891," *Journal of Modern History*, 47 (1945), 16–28, for an account of the German phase of the matter.

4. W. R. to Blaine, 19 Oct. 1889, Dispatches, France, 103; also *F.R., 1889*, pp. 166–67; for example, resolutions from the Boston Chamber of Commerce and from the Kansas City Commercial Exchange were forwarded in Blaine to W. R., 8, 27 July 1889, U.S., Department of State Instructions, France, 21.

5. See Edward Stanwood, *American Tariff Controversies in the Nineteenth Century*, 2: 243–95, on "The McKinley Bill."

6. Vignaud to Blaine, 27 Mar., 7 Apr. 7 1890, Dispatches, France, 104; W. R. to Vignaud, 3 Apr. 1890, Instructions, France, 22; W. R. to Phelps, 3 May 1890; see France, *Journal Officiel*, 22 July 1890 (*Chambre des députés*), pp. 1561ff., for discussions of the administrative bill.

7. See France, *Journal Officiel*, 22 July 1890 (*Chambre des députés*), pp. 1561ff., for comments of Charles Dupuy on the administrative bill. W. R. to Blaine, 19 June 1890, Dispatches, France, 104.

8. W. R. to McKinley, 1 Sept. 1890.

9. W. R. to Blaine, 20 June 1890; W. R. to McKinley, 1 Sept. 1890; W. R. to Phelps, 3 May 1890; W. R. to M. G. Seckendorff, 8 July 1890; W. R. to William B. Allison, 1 Sept. 1890.

10. W. R. to Ribot, 3 July 1890, enclosed in W. R. to Blaine, 4 July 1890; W. R. to Blaine, 15 Aug. 1890, Dispatches, France, 104.

11. David S. Muzzey, *James G. Blaine: A Political Idol of Other Days*, pp. 442–50.

12. W. R. to Ribot, 3 July 1890, enclosed in W. R. to Blaine, 4 July 1890, Dispatches, France, 104; also *F.R., 1890*, pp. 283–86.

13. W. R. to Blaine, 4 July 1890, Dispatches, France, 104; the same letter, same date, is in the Reid Papers; W. R. to Seckendorff, 8 July 1890; Reid expected Seckendorff, in the normal course of his work, to exchange information with leading members of Congress and other officials in Washington.

14. W. R. to Nicholson, 8 July 1890.

15. This information appears in notations on the original dispatches, those cited in n.10 above.

16. *New York Tribune*, 16, 17 Aug. 1890.

17. *New York Tribune*, 31 Aug., 9 Sept. 1890.

18. W. R. to Blaine, 10 Sept. 1890, telegram, Dispatches, France, 104; *New*

York Tribune, 7 Dec. 1891; W. R. to Wharton, 3 Sept. 1890, telegram, Dispatches, France, 104; W. R. to Blaine, 16 Oct. 1890, Dispatches, France, 105.

19. Blaine to W. R., 11 Nov. 1890, telegram, 13 Nov. 1890, Instructions, France, 22; W. R. to Blaine, 20 Nov. 1890.

20. W. R. to Ogden Mills, 24 July 1890; W. R. to Nicholson, 15 Sept. 1890.

21. W. R. to Foster, 6 July 1891.

22. France, *Journal Officiel*, 28 May 1891 (*Chambre des députés*), pp. 1040–1046; W. R. to Blaine, 29 Oct. 1891, telegram, Dispatches, France, 106.

23. W. R. to Blaine, 20 Nov. 1890; U.S. Congress, *Congressional Record*, 51st Cong., 2d sess., 1891, 22, pts. 1–4: 3788, 3824, 3882.

24. Reid's reports to Blaine cover the French legislative action in detail; see W. R. to Blaine, 29, 30 Oct., 6, 16, 20 Nov., 11 Dec. 1891, Dispatches, France, 106; France, *Journal Officiel*, 29 Oct. 1891 (*Senat*), pp. 708–21, 723–30.

25. Reid also claimed much credit, with some justification, for having precipitated the removal of bans against American pork in three other countries through the pressure he exerted in France against the idea and practice of prohibition; see W. R. to Nicholson, 10 Nov. 1891. Certainly the dropping of the prohibitions against American pork in Germany and Denmark in September and in Italy in October 1891 were not entirely coincidental; see *F.R., 1891*, pp. 487, 517, 727.

26. See Muzzey, *Blaine*, pp. 448–58, for a discussion of Blaine's relation to the reciprocity problem.

27. W. R. to Blaine, 23, 24 Dec. 1891, telegram, 31 Dec. 1891, with enclosures, Dispatches, France, 106.

28. Blaine to W. R., 28, 31 Dec. 1891, telegram, Instructions, France, 22; James L. Laughlin and H. Parker Willis, *Reciprocity*, p. 21.

29. Blaine to W. R., 28 Jan. 1892 and through Feb., Instructions, France, 22; W. R. to Blaine, 24 Mar. 1893, Dispatches, France, 107. Subsequent complications in France prevented the reciprocity agreement from going before the Chambers, and it was not put into effect.

30. David Hunter Miller, ed., *Treaties and Other International Acts of the United States of America*, 1: 103–112.

31. Blaine to W. R., 9 May 1890, Instructions, France, 22.

32. W. R. to Blaine, 28 Jan. 1892, Dispatches, France, 107; W. R. to Mills, 10 Dec. 1891.

33. W. R. to Ribot, 23, 26, 28 Nov., 3 Dec. 1891 and Ribot to W. R., 1 Dec. 1891, enclosed in W. R. to Blaine, 3 Dec. 1891, Dispatches, France, 106.

34. Blaine to W. R., 1 Mar. 1892, with enclosures, Instructions, France, 22.

35. Discussions of the treaty are in nearly every communication from Reid in March to the time of his departure, Dispatches, France, 107.

36. *New York Tribune*, 27 Mar. 1892; Willson, *Ambassadors to France*, pp. 335–45.

37. *New York Tribune*, 19, 22, 25, 28, 30 Mar. and 2 Apr. 1892.

38. Bliss to Morton, 30 Mar. 1892, in Robert McElroy, *Levi Parsons Morton,*

Banker, Diplomat and Statesman, pp. 73, 79, 195; Philip C. Jessup, *Elihu Root*, 1: 167–73.

39. *New York Tribune*, 10, 17 Apr., 1 May 1892.

40. *New York Tribune*, 29 Apr., 12 May 1892; Reid was still minister to France during the convention. His letter of resignation to Harrison was written April 21. Harrison's reply, dated April 26, accepted the resignation effective when a successor was appointed or sixty days from the date of Reid's return to the United States. T. Jefferson Coolidge's appointment as minister to France was effective May 12.

41. Donald M. Dozer, "Benjamin Harrison and the Presidental Campaign of 1892," p. 54; W. R. to Elkins, 26 May 1892.

42. *New York Tribune*, 2, 29 Apr., 23, 26 May 1892.

43. Dozer, "Harrison and 1892," pp. 63–64, cites W. R. to Elkins, Feb. 1896, McKinley Papers.

44. Howard Wayne Morgan, *From Hayes to McKinley: National Party Politics, 1877–1896*, p. 403; *New York Tribune*, 6, 7, 8, 9 June 1892.

45. *New York Tribune*, 11 June 1892.

46. Spooner to Morton, 29 June 1892; Porter to Morton, 13 July 1892; Bliss to Morton, 30 Mar. 1892, in McElroy, *Morton*, pp. 195, 199, 201. *New York Tribune*, 11 June 1892.

47. Thomas C. Platt, *The Autobiography of Thomas Collier Platt*, pp. 246–47.

48. Dozer, "Harrison and 1892," p. 72.

49. Ibid., pp. 72–73; James G. Blaine, "The Presidential Election of 1892," pp. 513–525; Mrs. Harrison died at the White House on October 25.

50. Dozer, "Harrison and 1892," p. 73; Elkins to W. R., 15 July 1892, Reid Papers, box 19.

51. *New York Tribune*, 17 June, 26 Oct. 1892.

52. W. R. to Harrison, 4 Aug. 1892, with enclosure, Harrison Papers, cited in Dozer, "Harrison and 1892," p. 76; Hugh O'Donnel to W. R., 16 July 1892, Reid Papers, box 29, in folder "Foster, John W., 1891–92."

53. *New York Tribune*, 18, 19, 25, 29 Sept., 5, 9, 25 Oct. 1892.

54. *New York Tribune*, 5, 19 Oct. 1892.

55. Hay to W. R., 20 Oct. 1892, in William Thayer, *The Life of John Hay*, 2: 134–35; George H. Knoles, *The Presidential Campaign and Election of 1892*, pp. 213–14.

56. See sketch by H. Weidner in *The Diamond Anniversary Volume of Miami University*, pp. 277–91, which closely follows the sketch in the *New York Tribune*, 11 June 1892; if the latter was not written by Reid he certainly approved it; Charles R. Williams, ed., *Diary and Letters of Rutherford Burchard Hayes, Nineteenth President of the United States*, 2: 376.

57. Dozer, "Harrison and 1892," p. 76.

58. Knoles, *Campaign and Election of 1892*, p. 232; *New York Tribune*, 10 Nov. 1892.

59. New York *Tribune*, 16 Nov. 1892.

60. W. R. to Harrison, 28 Nov. 1892.

CHAPTER 12

1. Henry Adams, *The Education of Henry Adams*, p. 347.

2. Fahnstock to W. R., 7 June 1892, "Fahnstock, H.," Reid Papers, box 28.

3. Hay to Adams, 3 Sept. 1895, in Thayer, *Hay*, 2: 124–26.

4. *New York Tribune*, 21 Mar. 1894.

5. *New York Tribune*, 4 May 1894.

6. Royal Cortissoz, *The Life of Whitelaw Reid*, 2: 196; Charles H. Dennis, *Victor Lawson*, p. 416.

7. W. R. to Hay, [n.d., 1896?], cited in Cortissoz, *Reid*, 2: 198; W. R. to Hay, 6 Jan. 1897; W. R. to D. O. Mills, 15 Jan. 1897.

8. This was not, of course, done without Reid's knowledge and concurrence. The dispute was not reopened in his lifetime. The agreement is printed in full in George A. Stevens, *New York Typographical Union No. 6*, pp. 395–96.

9. Victor Rosewater, *History of Cooperative Newsgathering in the United States*; chaps. 16–19 contain a good account of the struggle; see also Oliver Gramling, *AP: The Story of News*, Dennis, Lawson, and Edgar Laughlin Gray, "The Career of William Henry Smith, Politician-Journalist," 181–84; there are a few pertinent items in "Assoc. Press," Reid Papers, box 107.

10. Rosewater, *Cooperative Newsgathering*, p. 246.

11. *New York Tribune*, 29 Mar., 12 Apr., 4 July 1896.

12. Theron G. Strong, *Joseph H. Choate: New Englander, New Yorker, Lawyer, Ambassador*, p. 87; Franklin Matthews in *Harper's Weekly*, 41 (25 Sept. 1897), 60; see Allan Nevins' sketch of Thomas C. Platt in *Dictionary of American Biography*.

13. See "Elkins, S. B., 1892;" Reid Papers, box 19; several of Elkins' letters of early 1896 indicate his recognition of McKinley's strength but his preference for Allison; McKinley to W. R., 21 Mar. 1896, in Cortissoz, *Reid*, 2: 204.

14. *New York Tribune*, 26 Apr. 1896.

15. *New York Tribune*, 26 Apr. and 2 May 1896.

16. *New York Tribune*, 1 June 1896; Reed was widely considered to be McKinley's strongest opponent for the nomination.

17. W. R. to McKinley, 11, 13 June 1896, in Howard Wayne Morgan, *William McKinley and His America*, p. 212.

18. Morgan, *McKinley*, pp. 207–20; Margaret Leech, *In the Days of McKinley*, p. 83.

19. The message is printed in the *New York Tribune*, 9 Sept. 1896.

20. *New York Tribune*, 4 Nov. 1896.

21. W. R. to McKinley, 6 Nov. 1896; *New York Tribune*, 11 Nov. 1897.

22. W. R. to Hay, 17 Nov. 1896.

23. Hay to W. R., 10 Dec. 1896, Reid Papers, box 105.

24. W. R. to Garfield, 19 July 1880.

25. W. R. to Depew, 26 Nov. 1896; W. R. to Hay, 26 Nov. 1896.

26. W. R. to McKinley, 5 Dec. 1896; the copy of this letter in the Reid Papers is typewritten on five double-spaced and three single-spaced pages.

27. W. R. to Hay, 6 Jan. 1897; W. R. to Depew, 12 Jan. 1897.

28. Loomis to W. R., 3 Dec. 1896, "Loomis, Francis G., 1896," Reid Papers, box 47; W. R. to Hay, 6 Jan. 1897.

29. Hay to W. R., 10 Dec. 1896, Reid Papers, box 105; W. R. to Vignaud, 31 Dec. 1896; W. R. to Hay, 6 Jan. 1897.

30. W. R. to Hay, 8 Feb. 1897; W. R. to Milholland, 13 Feb. 1897.

31. Leech, *McKinley*, p. 109; Hay to McKinley, 16 Feb. 1897, McKinley to W. R., 19 Feb. 1897, McKinley Papers, cited in Morgan, *McKinley*, p. 266.

32. *New York Tribune*, 27 Feb. 1897.

33. W. R. to McKinley, 3 Mar. 1897; W. R. to Nicholson, 16 Mar. 1897.

34. Hay to W. R., 24 Oct. 1902, (J. Hay to W. Reid, 1902–1905), Reid Papers, box 105; Hay to W. R., 14 Sept. 1898, (J. Hay to W. Reid, 1897–98), Reid Papers, box 105.

35. Arthur W. Dunn, *From Harrison to Harding . . . 1888–1921*, 2: 204.

36. Pauncefote to Sherman, 30 Mar. 1897, Sherman to Pauncefote, 2 Apr. 1897; *Foreign Relations of the United States, 1897*, p. 249.

37. Morgan, *McKinley*, p. 282; Pauncefote to Sherman, 14 Apr. 1897, *F.R., 1897*, p. 249.

38. Henry Pringle, *Theodore Roosevelt: A Biography*, p. 173; Sherman to Pauncefote, 29 Apr. 1897; Sherman to Hay, 29 Apr. 1897; *F.R., 1897*, p. 249.

39. Tyler Dennett, *John Hay: From Poetry to Politics*, p. 192.

40. Dennett, *Hay*, p. 193; Sherman to Hay, 21 May 1897, telegram, *F.R., 1897*, p. 250; Seckendorff to W. R., 21, 24 May 1897, enclosing undated memorandum, Reid Papers, box 107.

41. Dennett, *Hay*, p. 193; Sherman to Hay, 24 May, 1 June 1897, *F.R., 1897*, pp. 250, 251.

42. W. R. to Depew, 27 May 1897; [W. R.'s] Secretary to Thouvard, 27 May 1897.

43. McKinley to Hay, 29 May 1897, Hay Papers, cited in Dennett, *Hay*, p. 194.

44. Lizzie Reid to W. R., 27 May 1897, telegram, Reid Papers, box 107.

45. The request for a loan was an indication of the unexpectedness of the appointment and of Reid's haste to leave, rather than of his lack of funds; W. R. to Ogden Mills, 28 May, 4 Aug. 1897; [Ogden Mills to W. R.], 1 June 1897, "Corresp., etc., re Spl Embassy," Reid Papers, box 107.

46. Sherman to Hay, 28 May, 1 June 1897, *F.R., 1897*, pp. 251, 252.

47. [Ogden Mills to W. R.] 1 June 1897, Reid Papers, box 107; J. H. Godber to Ellis and Ellis, 10, 19 July 1897; Ellis and Ellis to Godber, 12, 19 July 1897, "Misc.," Reid Papers, box 19.

48. W. R. to Seckendorff, 17 June 1897; W. R. to Hall, 17 June 1897; see correspondence for 12–20 June in letters and telegrams, 12 June–24 July 1897, Reid Papers, box 153.

49. Hay to H. Adams, 25 July 1897, in William R. Thayer, *The Life of John Hay*, 2: 161.

50. See *New York Tribune* for June 1897, especially June 12, 13, 16, 19, 20, 22, 23; in 1853 Marcy ordered that the "simple dress of an American citizen" be worn by official representatives of the United States when abroad. The "dress circular" came to mean that a full dress suit was the most elaborate formal outfit that an American envoy should wear, regardless of the occasion.

51. *New York Tribune*, 6, 10, 19, 20 July 1897; W. R. to Seckendorff, 18 Oct. 1897.

52. *New York Tribune*, 25 July 1897; Nevins, *White*, p. 126.

CHAPTER 13

1. *New York Tribune*, 18, 22 Dec. 1872.

2. See chap. 9.

3. See chap. 11.

4. Edward Stanwood, *A History of the Presidency*, pp. 496–97.

5. *New York Tribune*, 30 Dec. 1895; W. R. to Francis B. Loomis, 15 Dec. 1896.

6. W. R. to McKinley, 5 Dec. 1896; W. R. to Nicholson, 22 Dec. 1896.

7. *New York Tribune*, 7 Dec. 1897; Ford to W. R., 7 Jan. 1898, Reid Papers, box 29.

8. W. R. to Seckendorff, 17 Jan. 1898.

9. *New York Tribune*, 1 Apr. 1898; W. R. to Nicholson, 30 Mar. 1898; W. R. to Nicholson and to Seckendorff, 6 Apr. 1898; Margaret Leech, *In the Days of McKinley*, p. 182.

10. *New York Tribune*, 6, 7, 13 Apr. 1898.

11. *New York Tribune*, 19 Apr. 1898.

12. *New York Tribune*, 21, 22, 23, 26 Apr. 1898; W. R. to Seckendorff, 17 Feb. 1902.

13. W. R. to McKinley, 19 Apr. 1898; see Paul Holbo, "Presidential Leadership in Foreign Affairs," pp. 1321–25, for an interpretive comment on one aspect of McKinley's policy.

14. W. R. to Seckendorff, 19 Apr. 1898.

15. Ford to W. R., 19 Apr. 1898, Reid Papers, box 29.

16. W. R. to Barnard, 30 June 1898, 22, 23, July 1898.

17. W. R. to McKinley, 5 Dec. 1896.

18. Leech, *McKinley*, p. 382; extracts from the *New York Sun*, printed in *New York Tribune*, 24 Sept., 29 Oct. 1897.

19. *New York Tribune*, 4 Aug. 1897; Ford to W. R., 7 Jan. 1898, Reid Papers, box 29; W. R. to Seckendorff, 17 Jan. 1898.

20. Elkins to W. R., 22 Apr. 1898, Reid Papers, box 19; W. R. to Seckendorff, 24 Apr. 1898.

21. Leech, *McKinley*, p. 382; Platt to McKinley, 14 Aug. 1898, in Thomas Collier Platt, *The Autobiography of Thomas Collier Platt*, pp. 256–64.

22. *New York Tribune*, 2–7 May 1898, especially 5 May.

23. *New York Tribune*, 7 May 1898.

24. W. R. to Barnard, 23 July 1898.

25. Richard Olney, "International Isolation of the United States," pp. 577–588.

26. *New York Tribune*, 7 May 1898.

27. W. R. to Nicholson, 20 July 1898; W. R. to Hay, 11 Aug. 1898, in Royal Cortissoz, *The Life of Whitelaw Reid*, 2: 224–25.

28. *Century Magazine*, 56 (Sept. 1898), 781–88 and 788–94.

29. Note dated 28 July 1898 sent over the *Tribune*'s private wire from New York to Washington, Reid Papers, box 154; W. R. to Hay, 11 Aug. 1898, in Cortissoz, *Reid*, 2: 224–25.

30. W. R. to Nicholson, 8 Aug. 1898.

31. Leech, *McKinley*, p. 329; Howard Wayne Morgan, *William McKinley and His America*, p. 401; *New York Tribune*, 18, 26, 27 Aug. 1898.

32. W. R. to McKinley, 25 Aug. 1898; Hay to W. R., 14 Sept. 1898, Reid Papers, box 105; Tyler Dennett, *John Hay, From Poetry to Politics*, p. 195.

33. W. R. to Nicholson, 26 Aug. 1898; *New York Tribune*, 3 Sept. 1898.

34. Letters and telegrams, Aug. 10–Dec. 31, 1898, Reid Papers, box 154; Leech, *McKinley*, p. 330; Morgan, *McKinley*, pp. 400–1.

35. H. Wayne Morgan, ed., *Making Peace with Spain: The Diary of Whitelaw Reid, September–December, 1898*, pp. 31–32; hereafter cited as *Diary*. Because of the excellent editorial work and the general availability of the printed version, Professor Morgan's rendition of the diary, rather than the original, is cited throughout this chapter.

36. *Diary*, pp. 26–31.

37. *New York Tribune*, 14–18, 24 Sept. 1898; *Diary*, p. 85.

38. W. R. to McKinley, 4 Oct. 1898.

39. W. R. to McKinley, 4 Oct. 1898; *Diary*, p. 34.

40. *Diary*, pp. 34, 44, 167; Reid's hotel bills amounted to more than thirty-two thousand francs, nearly as much as the combined charges against the other four commissioners. The franc exchanged at $0.193. At his suggestion Reid received from the United States an amount equal to the average paid to the others, and made up the difference out of his own pocket; see "State Dept. accounts," Clark to W. R., 13 Dec. 1898, in Reid Papers, box 191.

41. *Diary*, p. 49.

42. *Diary*, pp. 219–20.

43. Day to Hay, 22 Nov. 1898, Reid Papers, box 154.

44. "Barnard's daily reports" are in three volumes in Reid Papers, box 155.

45. *Diary*, pp. 97–98.

46. *Diary*, pp. 78, 168.

47. *Diary*, p. 53.

48. W. R. to Hay, 16 Oct. 1898.

49. *Diary*, p. 112.

50. Day to McKinley, 27 Oct. 1898, U.S., Department of State, *Foreign Relations of the United States, 1898*, pp. 936–37; Hay to W. R., 13 Nov. 1898, Reid Papers, box 105; Hay's comment was a reference to a Scottish saying regarding seating at any table, which is approximately, "Where McGregor sits, there is the head of the table."

51. *Diary*, pp. 44, 88–89.

52. *F.R., 1898*, pp. 932–35; *Diary*, Appendix III.

53. Hay to Day, 28 Oct. 1898, telegram, *F.R., 1898*, p. 937; Hay to Day, 28 Oct. 1898, private telegram, ibid.

54. Hay to W. R., 13 Nov. 1898, Reid Papers, box 105.

55. *Diary*, pp. 146, 150; Frye to McKinley, 30 Oct. 1898, Hay to [Frye?], 1 Nov. 1898, *F.R., 1898*, p. 939; Hay to Frye, 2 Nov. 1898, Reid Papers, box 34; Frye to the president, 30 Oct. 1898, through Adee, State Department, Reid Papers, box 30.

56. W. R. to McKinley, 29 Nov. 1898.

57. *Diary*, p. 71.

58. *Diary*, pp. 120–21, 141–42.

59. Day to Hay, 22, 26 Nov. 1898, Reid Papers, box 154.

60. Samuel F. Bemis, *Diplomatic History of the United States*, 5th ed., (New York, 1965), pp. 466–67; *Diary*, p. 223.

61. *Diary*, pp. 158, 160.

62. *New York Tribune*, 29 Nov. 1898.

63. Hay to Lodge, 5 Apr. 1898, William R. Thayer, *The Life of John Hay*, 2: 165.

64. *Diary*, pp. 178, 190, 193, 221.

65. *Diary*, pp. 222, 225–27.

66. *Diary*, pp. 221, 227; *New York Tribune*, 13 Dec. 1898.

67. W. R. to Hay, 16 Oct. 1898, 29 Nov. 1898; Hay to W. R., 13 Nov. 1898; [13 Dec. 1898] telegram, Reid Papers, box 105.

68. Parsons to Sackett, 4 Jan. 1899, Hewitt to the president, 4 Jan. 1899, Hall to W. R., 5 Jan. 1899, and Seckendorff to Hall, 5 Jan. 1899, in "Henry Hall, 1899," Reid Papers, box 33.

69. W. R. to Hay, 31 Dec. 1898.

CHAPTER 14

1. Theron G. Strong, *Joseph H. Choate: New Englander, New Yorker, Lawyer, Ambassador*, p. 81.

2. W. R. to Seckendorff, 31 Dec. 1900.

3. W. R. to Nicholson, 21 Mar. 1901; W. R. to Ford, 27 May 1901.

4. Roosevelt to Lodge, 12 Jan. 1899 in Elting E. Morison, *Letters of Theodore Roosevelt*, 1: 909; Roosevelt to Fox and McFarland, 1 Aug. 1899, ibid., 2: 1042–43; Roosevelt to Lodge, 10 Aug. 1899, ibid., 2: 1048; Roosevelt to

Lodge, 11 Sept. 99, ibid., 2: 1069; Roosevelt to White, 9 Oct. 1899, ibid., 2: 1080.

5. W. R. to Parsons, 23 Jan. 1900.

6. W. R. to Doane, 27 Feb. 1900; W. R. to Seckendorff, 15 May 1900.

7. W. R. to Nicholson, 23 Apr. 1900.

8. W. R. to Roosevelt, 15, 21, 27 Aug. 1900; Roosevelt to W. R., 25 Aug. 1900, in Morison, *Letters of Theodore Roosevelt*, 2: 1390; W. R. to Seckendorff, 30 Sept. 1900.

9. *New York Tribune*, 1 Jan. 1901.

10. *New York Tribune*, 15 Sept. 1901.

11. W. R. to Nicholson, 16 Sept. 1901.

12. *New York Tribune*, 12, 14, 24, 26 Feb. 1899.

13. *New York Tribune*, 15 June, 25 July 1899.

14. "Territorial Expansion," in Whitelaw Reid, *American and English Studies*, 1: 127–66.

15. Walter L. Tobey and William O. Thompson, eds., *The Diamond Anniversary Volume of Miami University*, p. 19.

16. W. R. to Ford, 5 Aug. 1899; Ford replaced Smalley in 1895 when the latter left the *Tribune* to join the *Times* (London) staff.

17. W. R. to Ford, 5 Aug. 1899; Davis to W. R., 7 Aug. 1899, Reid Papers, box 16.

18. *New York Tribune*, 16 June 1899, Reid, *American and English Studies*, 1: 127–66.

19. Davis to W. R., 7 Aug. 1899, Reid Papers, box 16.

20. Hay to W. R., 7 Feb. 1900, Reid Papers, box 105.

21. W. R. to Seckendorff, 6 Oct. 1899.

22. *New York Tribune*, 22 Oct. 1899.

23. *New York Tribune*, 13 Oct. 1899.

24. W. R. to A. J. Beveridge, 7 Feb. 1900; W. R. to Chandler, 22 Jan. 1900, cited in Royal Cortissoz, *The Life of Whitelaw Reid*, 2: 266–67; *New York Tribune*, 4 March 1900, 18 Feb. 1901, 26, 31 May 1902.

25. W. R. to Charles Francis Adams, 15 Aug. 1902; W. R. to Nicholson, 12 Jan. 1905; W. R. to Root, 9 Feb. 1903.

26. *New York Tribune*, 23 Dec. 1903; W. R. to Fearn, 13 Oct. 1903; Reid asked his Washington reporter to get information from the Census Bureau for this speech.

27. *New York Tribune*, 3 June 1899.

28. *New York Tribune*, 22 Nov. 1899, 27 Aug. 1901.

29. *New York Tribune*, 20 Nov. 1901.

30. W. R. to Seckendorff, 17 Feb. 1902.

31. Memo, W. R. to Nicholson, 18 Nov. 1899.

32. *New York Tribune*, 22 Nov. 1899, 1 Dec. 1900.

33. W. R. to Seckendorff, 2 Sept. 1899.

34. Hay to W. R., 7 Feb. 1900, Reid Papers, box 105.

35. W. R. to Hay, 9 Feb. 1900; *New York Tribune*, 20 May 1901.

36. *New York Times*, 2 Apr. 1903.

37. *New York Times*, 3 Apr. 1903; *New York Tribune*, 3 Apr. 1903.

38. An American Businessman, "Is the Monroe Doctrine a Bar to Civilization?," *North American Review*, 176 (Apr. 1903), 518–29; W. R. to Fearn, 9 May 1903; W. R. to Loomis, 5 June 1903.

39. New York *Tribune*, 23 June 1903.

40. Roosevelt to W. R., 24 July 1903, in Morison, *Letters of Theodore Roosevelt*, 3: 527; according to Morison, Roosevelt wrote Mediterranean but he must have meant Caribbean.

41. W. R. to Roosevelt, 27 July 1903.

42. Memo, W. R. to Nicholson, 6 Nov. 1903.

43. W. R. to Roosevelt, 9 Nov. 1903.

44. *New York Tribune*, 15 Jan. 1902.

45. White to [Hay], 12 Feb. 1902 and Hay to Reid, 26 Feb. 1902, Reid Papers, box 105.

46. Letters and telegrams, 1 Apr.–12 Aug. 1902, Reid Papers, box 160, and 14 Feb.–25 May 1905, Reid Papers, box 164.

47. *New York Tribune*, 5, 9 Aug. 1902.

48. *Encyclopaedia Britannica*, 9th ed., s.v. "Newspapers"; W. R. to Seckendorff, 9 Jan. 1900; W. R. to *Encyclopaedia Britannica*, 8 June 1900, 29 August 1900.

49. *New York Tribune*, 4 Oct. 1902.

50. See for example W. R. to Melville Dewey in October, November, 1896, in letters and telegrams, 20 Oct.–31 Dec. 1896, Reid Papers, box 152.

51. Harlan H. Horner, comp. and ed., *Education in New York State, 1784–1954*; W. R. to James Russell Parsons, 23 Jan. 1900.

52. Reid's speech at Union College, Schenectady, N. Y., 27 June 1900, as reported in the *New York Tribune*, 28 June 1900, and his speech at Stanford University on "University Tendencies in America," in *New York Tribune*, 26 Aug. 1901.

53. See Reid's speech at the convocation of the University of the State of New York, Albany, 27 June 1904, as reported in the *New York Tribune*, 28 June 1904.

54. W. R. to Roosevelt, 14 Jan. 1903; W. R. to B. B. Odell, 16 Jan. 1902, 26 Feb. 1903; W. R. to Draper, 3 Dec. 1912; *New York Tribune*, 5 Dec. 1902, 27 May 1905.

55. Horner, *Education in New York State*, p. 20; *New York Tribune*, 9 Mar. 1904; W. R. to Lizzie Reid, 14, 27 Apr. 1904.

56. Memo to Nicholson, Tuthill, Hall, n.d., [ca. 3–18 Nov. 1899], Reid Papers, box 157; Hall to W. R., 5 Jan. 1899, Reid Papers, box 33; W. R. to Kellogg, 8, 20 June 1901; W. R. to Hall, 10 June 1901.

57. W. R. to Kellogg, 7 Mar. 1905.

58. Harry W. Baehr, *The New York Tribune since the Civil War*, p. 224; W. R. to Fearn, 18 Oct. 1902.

59. W. R. to Seckendorff, 20 Sept. 1902; W. R. to Nicholson, 20 Sept. 1902.

60. W. R. to Hall, 28 Dec. 1899.

61. W. R. to Nicholson, 6 July 1900.

62. W. R. to Tuttle, 26 May 1905; W. R. to S. F. Strong, 8 Mar. 1905.

63. W. R. to Nicholson, 15, 28 June 1901; W. R. to D[onald] N[icholson], n.d. [ca. 30 Nov. 1902].

64. W. R. to Nicholson, 17 Apr. 1902; by the term "typewriter," Reid meant the operator rather than the machine itself.

65. See W. R. to J. A. Browning in letters and telegrams, 6 Apr.–22 Aug. 1899, box 157; W. R. to Tuttle, 15, 26 Sept. 1899; W. R. to Ogden Reid, 19 Mar. 1901.

66. W. R. to Ogden Reid, 1 Apr. 1902, 27 Apr. 1904; W. R. to Lizzie Reid, 14, 27 Apr. 1904; W. R. to Browning, letters and telegrams, 6 Apr.–22 Aug. 1899, box 157.

67. W. R. to Hay, 8 Oct. 1901; W. R. to Roosevelt, 20 Jan. 1905.

68. *New York Tribune*, 10 Mar. 1901, 2 May 1901.

69. W. R. to Mrs. Roosevelt, 31 Oct. 1905; Mona Gardner, "Queen Helen [Rogers Reid]," in John E. Drewry, ed., *More Post Biographies*.

70. W. R. to J. Q. A. Ward, 21 Jan. 1903.

71. W. R. to L [ouis] T [houvard], n.d. [ca. Feb. 1902].

72. Lida Rose McCabe, "Winter Life Outdoors at Ophir Farm," *Town and Country*, vol. 56, no. 52 (8 Mar. 1902), pp. 9–13.

73. W. R. to Hay, 29 Mar. 1902.

74. W. R. to Ford, 31 May 1899, 5 Dec. 1899.

75. Roosevelt to White, 9 Oct. 1899, in Morison, *Letters of Theodore Roosevelt*, 2: 1080; "Memorandum," n.d., in letters and telegrams, 24 Aug.–16 Dec. 1899, pp. 62–64, Reid Papers, box 157.

76. *New York Tribune*, 12 Nov. 1899; Reid said that he wrote this editorial, W. R. to Seckendorff, 12 Nov. 1899.

77. W. R. to Ford, 2 Mar. 1901.

78. Finley Peter Dunne, *Observations by Mr. Dooley*, pp. 183–84.

79. *New York Tribune*, 7, 8 Nov. 1902.

80. *New York Tribune*, 27, 29 June 1890, 15 Mar. 1904.

81. Baehr, *Tribune*, pp. 182, 269–72, 282.

82. W. R. to Nicholson, 25 Aug. 1904.

83. W. R. to Hay, 2 Aug. 1903.

84. W. R. to Seckendorff, 7 Oct. 1901; *New York Tribune*, 31 Dec. 1904; Roosevelt to Joseph B. Bishop, 23 Nov. 1904, in Morison, *Letters of Theodore Roosevelt*, 4: 1040.

85. Choate to W. R., 6 Feb. 1905, Reid Papers, box 11.

86. Lizzie Reid to Anna Cowles, 15 Feb. 1905.

87. W. R. to Hay, 16 Feb. 1905, 10 Mar. 1905.

88. W. R. to Choate, 15 May 1905.

89. W. R. to White, 31 Jan. 1905; W. R. to Carter, 27 Mar. 1905; Emily Bax, *Miss Bax of the Embassy* (Boston, 1939), pp. 97–99.

90. W. R. to Lyman, 26 May 1902; W. R. to Martin, 7 Sept. 1899; Baehr,

Tribune, p. 274; Albert Stevens Crockett, *When James Gordon Bennett Was Caliph of Baghdad*, pp. 121, 182.

CHAPTER 15

1. *New York Tribune*, 4 June 1905.

2. Emily Bax, *Miss Bax of the Embassy*, p. 98.

3. *New York Tribune*, 6 June 1905.

4. The judgment is that of Emily Bax, an Englishwoman who served as a clerk and secretary in the embassy from 1902 to 1914; see Bax, *Miss Bax*, p. 155. William Phillips, *Ventures in Diplomacy*, pp. 48–49; *New York Tribune*, 17 Aug. 1905; W. R. to D. O. Mills, 11 Oct. 1905; W. R. to Ogden Mills, 27 Oct. 1905; [W. R.] to C. Inman Barnard, 13 Dec. 1905.

5. W. R. to D. O. Mills, 28 Dec. 1908; W. R. to Cunliffe-Owen, 13 Jan. 1909; W. R. to Ogden Reid, 12 Aug. 1912; W. R. to Phillips, 12 Aug. 1912.

6. Auditor's reports on household accounts, 1907–12, Reid Papers, box 188; the pound sterling exchanged at $4.867; W. R. to Mrs. Roosevelt, 31 Oct. 1905; W. R. to Lyman, 19 June, 13 July 1906, 6 Aug. 1907.

7. F. M. Huntington-Wilson, *Memoirs of an Ex-Diplomat*, p. 230; Albert Stevens Crockett, *When James Gordon Bennett Was Caliph of Baghdad*, p. 112.

8. *New York Tribune*, 9 July 1905, 20 July, 11 Sept. 1906; letters and telegrams, 1 May–31 July 1911, Reid Papers, box 176.

9. Irving Blake [Reid's private secretary] to Lyman, 2 June 1909; W. R. to Van Duzer, 7 June 1909; W. R. to Lyman, 21 June 1909; W. R. to Mr. President [Taft], 3 Sept. 1909.

10. W. R. to Roosevelt, 3 Nov. 1908; W. R. to Roosevelt, 22 Jan. 1909.

11. Details of the events of these weeks are scattered through the letters and telegrams for 1 Jan.–31 Mar. 1910 and 1 Apr.–31 May 1910, Reid Papers, box 174; see also Allan Nevins, *Henry White*, pp. 302–304.

12. W. R. to Draper, 20 Jan. 1910; W. R. to Mrs. [William H.] Taft, 8 July 1910.

13. Ferdinand Lundberg, *America's 60 Families*, p. 99; receipt from the Republican National Committee for $10,000 dated 11 Sept. 1908, "Financial Statements," Reid Papers, box 191; W. R. to Hughes, 11 Nov. 1908; W. R. to Roosevelt, 22 Jan. 1909; Anderson was appointed Minister to Belgium in 1911.

14. Carter [for Reid] to AP and to UP, 5 Nov. 1908; W. R. to Taft, 20 Nov. 1908.

15. Elkins to W. R., 17 Jan. 1909, 13 Feb. 1909, Reid Papers, box 19; Lodge to W. R., 8 Feb. 1909, Lyman to W. R., 27 Mar. 1909, Reid Papers, box 47; W. R. to Roosevelt, 22 Jan. 1909; W. R. to Taft, 22 Jan. 1909; W. R. to Lizzie Reid, 25 Jan., 2, 3 Feb. 1909; W. R. to Mr. Senator [Lodge], 28 Jan. 1909.

16. W. R. to Lyman, 14 Apr. 1909.

17. W. R. to D. O. Mills, 5 May 1908; W. R. to Root, 30 June 1908.

18. W. R. to D. O. Mills, 25 Sept. 1908.

19. W. R. to Meade, 5 June 1908, 30 June 1909; W. R. to Lizzie Reid, 15 Dec. 1908; W. R. to McKim, Meade and White, 6 Dec. 1909.

20. Mona Gardner, "Queen Helen," p. 297; see also letters and telegrams, 1 June–31 Aug. 1910 and 1 Sept.–31 Dec. 1910, Reid Papers, box 175; W. R. to Van der Bent, 19 Apr. 1912.

21. W. R. to Fred Barnes, 9 Jan. 1906.

22. See Phillips, *Ventures*, p. 48, for comments on Lizzie Reid's expertise and interest in architecture; see letters to Fred Barnes in letters and telegrams, 1 Jan.–31 Mar. 1908, Reid Papers, box 170.

23. For example Conley sent Reid $335.19 for 1909 and $263.10 for 1911; W. R. to Conley, 6 Feb. 1908, 7 Feb. 1910, 7 Feb. 1912.

24. W. R. to James L. Lantz, 10 Apr. 1912.

25. [W. R.'s secretary] to White Star Line, N. Y., 17 Feb. 1912.

26. W. R. to Lyman, 26 May 1902, 24 Sept. 1906; W. R. to Tuttle, 1 June 1905.

27. Harry W. Baehr, *The New York Tribune since the Civil War*, p. 274 and chap. 13; W. R. to Martin, 7 Sept. 1899.

28. W. R. to Lyman, 21 Oct. 1908; A New York editor, "Is an Honest Newspaper Possible?" *Atlantic Monthly*, 102 (October 1908), pp. 441–47.

29. W. R. to Tuttle, 17 July 1905, 22 Apr. 1907, 26 Mar. 1908; W. R. to Ogden Reid, 27 Jan. 1909, 30 Aug. 1911.

30. W. R. to George Benton, treasurer, Bankers Trust Co., N. Y., 25 Nov. 1912.

31. W. R. to Ogden Reid, 30 Mar. 1910, 8 Dec. 1911, 10 July, 18 Sept. 1912; W. R. to Lyman, 20 Nov. 1912.

32. Gardner, "Queen Helen," pp. 289–314.

33. W. R. to Ogden Reid, 16 Apr. 1910; W. R. to Cunliffe-Owen, 18 June 1910.

34. W. R. to Knox, 11 Feb. 1911.

35. See Whitelaw Reid, *American and English Studies*, for most of his major addresses while in England; see also bibliographical note. The Library of Congress catalogue lists twenty-six titles in Reid's name; W. R. to R. C. E. Brown, 22 Dec. 1911.

36. W. R. to Lyman, 3 Aug. 1906, 7 Feb. 1907, 29 Nov. 1907, 3 July, 8 July 1908.

37. W. R. to Conley, 21 Nov. 1911.

38. Roosevelt to W. R., 3 Jan. 1911, Reid Papers, box 105; W. R. to Brooks Adams, 16 Jan. 1911.

39. Sidney Brooks, "How London Spoils Our Ambassadors," *Harper's Weekly*, 52 (27 Feb. 1909), 15; Chauncey Depew, *My Memories of Eighty Years*, pp. 198–200.

CHAPTER 16

1. Viscount Grey of Fallodon, *Twenty-Five Years, 1892–1916*, 2: 88.

2. W. R. to Choate, 18 Dec. 1911.

3. Phillips left the embassy in 1912 and Irwin Laughlin was first secretary at the time of Reid's death.

4. W. R. to H. M. Secretary of State for Foreign Affairs, 30 Jan. 1906; see also Emily Bax, *Miss Bax of the Embassy*, for lists of persons in the chancellery during Reid's mission.

5. Howard K. Beale, *Theodore Roosevelt and the Rise of America to World Power*, p. 20.

6. Beale, *Roosevelt*, p. 27.

7. Beale, *Roosevelt*, pp. 315–18; Roosevelt to Lodge, 11 July 1905, Henry Cabot Lodge, ed., *Selections from the Correspondence of Theodore Roosevelt and Henry Cabot Lodge, 1884–1918*, 2: 165–67.

8. W. R. to Root, 21 Feb. 1908.

9. Roosevelt to Reid, 28 Apr. 1906 in Elting E. Morison, ed., *Letters of Theodore Roosevelt*, 5: 230–51.

10. Beale, *Roosevelt*, pp. 129, 133–34.

11. Roosevelt to Reid, 29 Sept. 1905, Reid Papers, box 105.

12. Roosevelt to Reid, 30 June 1905, in Morison, *Letters of Roosevelt*, 4: 1257–58.

13. W. R. to Roosevelt, 17 June 1905.

14. Beale, *Roosevelt*, pp. 127–28; W. R. to Anna Roosevelt Cowles, 21 May 1906; W. R. to Roosevelt, 17 July 1906; 23 Oct. 1906.

15. Unsigned note [n.d.] from the Department of State, Office of the Solicitor, in Department of State Manuscripts, National Archives, State Decimal File, 1910–29, 882, 51/240–882.51/415½, box 10025.

16. W. R. to Huntington Wilson, 12 Aug. 1910; W. R. to secretary of state, 16 Apr. 1912, Wilson to Reid, 17 Apr. 1912, State Dec. File, 1910–29, 882, 51/240–882.51/415 ½, box 10025.

17. W. R. to Roosevelt, 15 Aug. 1905.

18. Roosevelt to Reid, 29 Sept. 1905, Reid Papers, box 105.

19. See Reid's memoranda on the Opium Conference, 11 Feb. 1907 and 28 Jan. 1909; W. R. to secretary of state, 4 Oct. 1908, 30 Nov. 1908; W. R. to Mrs. Taft, n.d. [ca. 30 June 1910], 12 Dec. 1911; Brent to Knox, 8 July 1910, letters and telegrams, 1 June–31 Aug. 1910, Reid Papers, box 175; Great Britain, *British and Foreign State Papers*, vol. 105 (1912), "Opium Convention," pp. 490–503.

20. W. R. to secretary of state, 8 June 1909.

21. Phillips to Knox, 10 June 1909, Knox Papers, Library of Congress, cited in Alfred Whitney Griswold, *The Far Eastern Policy of the United States*, p. 143; Phillips to Knox, 21 May 1909, Department of State Manuscripts, National Archives, State Numerical File, 1906–10, vol. 445, cases 5315/176 to 5315/413.

22. H. P. F. [Henry P. Fletcher] to Secretary of State [4 June 1909], State Num. File 1906–10, vol. 445.

23. "Memorandum from British Foreign Office," 7 June 1909, U.S., Department of State, *Foreign Relations of the United States, 1909*, p. 149–50; W. R. to secretary of state, 8, 23 July 1909; W. R. to Huntington Wilson, 12 July 1909; A. A. A. [Alvey A. Adee] to Huntington Wilson, 26 July 1909, State Num. File, 1906–10, vol. 446, cases 5315/414 to 5315/627.

24. Royal Cortissoz, *The Life of Whitelaw Reid*, 2: 399–400; W. R. to Knox, 31 Aug. 1909.

25. Griswold, *Far Eastern Policy*, p. 163; W. R. to secretary of state, 18 Feb. 1910; draft of letter to the Foreign Office, 12 Feb. 1910.

26. Griswold, *Far Eastern Policy*, p. 163; W. R. to Phillips, 20 Apr. 1910.

27. W. R. to Taft, 29 Mar. 1911; W. R. to Knox, 6 Apr. 1911, Bryce to Knox, 12 Apr. 1912, State Dec. File, 1910–29, 711.41/155–711.4112/79, box 6583.

28. Memo of Reid-Grey conversation, 13 Apr. 1911, W. R. to Taft, 13 Apr. 1911.

29. W. R. to Knox, 21 Apr. 1911.

30. W. R. to Lyman, 18 Aug. 1911; the Bryce-Knox and other correspondence on this is in State Dec. File, 1910–29, 711.4112/80–711.4112/193, box 6584.

31. W. R. to Huntington Wilson, 30 Sept. 1911.

32. Reid to secretary of state, 19 Nov. 1907, Great Britain, *British and Foreign State Papers*, vol. 100, 1906–07, p. 590; see also ibid., vol. 102, 1908–09, p. 154.

33. Charles C. Tansill, *Canadian-American Relations, 1875–1911*; Tansill treats the controversy fully.

34. Tansill, *Canadian-American Relations*, pp. 100, 106; Root to Reid, 13 Oct. 1905, and Root to Durand, 19 Oct. 1905, *F.R., 1905*, pp. 489, 490; Lansdowne to Reid, 16 Oct. 1905, Department of State Manuscripts, National Archives, Dispatches, Great Britain, vol. 213, Whitelaw Reid, 1 Oct. 1905–31 Jan. 1906.

35. W. R. to Root, 31 Aug. 1906; Reid-Grey correspondence in Great Britain, *British and Foreign State Papers*, vol. 100, 1906–07, pp. 578–83; Tansill, *Canadian-American Relations*, pp. 110–11.

36. H. C. Lodge to Robert Bacon, 13 Sept. 1906, State Num. File, 1906–10, vol. 86, cases 566–573/25.

37. Adee to Gardner, 19 Sept. 1906, Reid to secretary of state, 19 Sept. 1906, State Num. File, 1906–10, vol. 86.

38. Bacon to Adee, 17 Sept. 1906, State Num. File, 1906–10, vol. 86.

39. Reid to secretary of state, 26 Sept. 1906, 4 Oct. 1906, and Root to embassy, London, 30 Oct. 1906, State Num. File, 1906–10, vol. 86; W. R. to Carter, 3 Oct. 1906.

40. Lodge to Root, 6 Oct. 1906, State Num. File, 1906–10, vol. 86.

41. Tansill, *Canadian-American Relations*, p. 116; Reid to Grey, 4 Sept. 1907 and Grey to Reid, 6 Sept. 1907, Great Britain, *British and Foreign State Papers*, vol. 100 (1906–07), pp. 588–90; Grey to Reid, 15 July 1908 and Reid to

Grey, 23 July 1908, ibid., vol. 102 (1908–09), pp. 908–10; W. R. to secretary of state, 16 July 1908; Reid to secretary of state, 9 Aug., 7 Sept. 1907, State Num. File, 1906–10, vol. 87.

42. Reid to Grey, 22 July 1909 and Grey to Carter, 8 Sept. 1909, Great Britain, *British and Foreign State Papers*, vol. 102 (1908–09), pp. 908–10.

43. See Great Britain, *British and Foreign State Papers*, vol. 105 (1912), pp. 244–88.

44. Philip C. Jessup, *Elihu Root*, 2: 83, 86–90; Samuel F. Bemis, *The American Secretaries of State and Their Diplomacy*, 9: 231–37; Reid approved this arrangement. He probably did not recall that in 1888 Cleveland had made a very reasonable agreement that Reid had condemned as "the lowest point of degradation which American diplomacy has ever reached"; see chap. 8.

45. W. R. to secretary of state, 15 July 1912.

46. W. R. to Root, 7 Aug. 1912; W. R. to Lyman, 12 Aug. 1912.

47. W. R. to Taft, 6 Sept. 1912.

48. W. R. to Grey, 12 Nov. 1912.

49. W. R. to Draper, 21 Sept. 1912.

50. *New York Times*, 16 Dec. 1912 and 4, 5 Jan 1913; *Times* (London), 20, 21, 23 Dec. 1912.

Selected Bibliography

MANUSCRIPT AND NEWSPAPER SOURCES

THE basic sources for this study are the Whitelaw Reid Papers. They are in the Library of Congress in 343 containers. The first two boxes hold his diaries. Numbers 3 through 111 hold general correspondence, mostly incoming, and some other material. The most valuable part of the collection for this study is in containers 112–178, "outgoing correspondence," Reid's own letters from January 1869 through December 1912. The remaining boxes contain a wide variety of material, all of which is in some way related to Reid. The Horace Greeley Papers, Library of Congress, contain much material relating to Reid's first years with the *Tribune*. The Gordon Ford Papers, in the New York Public Library, have useful data about the *Tribune* Building.

Manuscript materials in Record Group 59, General Records of the Department of State in the National Archives are the basic sources for the study of Reid's work in diplomacy. The pertinent documents for this study are in the Diplomatic Instructions of the Department of State, France, Dispatches from U. S. ministers to France, Diplomatic Instructions of the Department of State, Great Britain, and Diplomatic Dispatches from U. S. ministers to Great Britain, for the years through 1905. For 1906–1910 the correspondence is in the numerical files of the Department of State and thereafter the documents are in the decimal files of the Department of State.

The *New York Tribune* was, after the Reid Papers, the most important source for this study. It accurately reflected the attitudes and opinions that Reid wished to express publicly during the forty years that he controlled the paper. It is widely available on microfilm. A fairly good file of the *Cincinnati Daily Gazette* for the years when Reid was with it is in the New York Public Library. Other newspapers that are consulted appear in the notes.

DOCUMENTS AND PERIODICALS

The Annual Register of World Events. London: Longmans, Green, 1758–.
N. W. Ayer and Son's *Directory of Newspapers and Periodicals*. Philadelphia: N. W. Ayer and Son, 1880–.
France, *Journal Officiel de la Republique Française*. Paris: 1789–.
Great Britain, *British and Foreign State Papers*. Foreign Office 1812/14–.
Miller, Hunter, ed. *Treaties and Other International Acts of the United States*

of America. Vol. I (Short Print). Washington, D.C.: Government Printing Office, 1931.

Moore, Frank, ed. *The Rebellion Record: A Diary of American Events*. 12 vols. New York: G. P. Putnam and Henry Holt [1863–69].

Rowell, George P. *Rowell's American Newspaper Directory*. New York: G. P. Rowell, 1869–1908.

U.S., Department of the Interior, Census Office. *The Seventh Census of the United States, 1850*. Washington, D.C.: Robert Armstrong, Public Printer, 1853.

U.S., Department of State. *Papers Relating to the Foreign Relations of the United States*. Washington, D.C.: Government Printing Office, 1862–.

U.S., War Department. *The War of the Rebellion . . . Official Records of the Union and Confederate Armies*. 70 vols. Washington, D.C.: Government Printing Office, 1880–1901.

Wilson, H., comp. *Trow's New York City Directory*. New York: John F. Trow, 1868–69—1886–87.

PARTIAL LIST OF WORKS BY REID
AND MISCELLANEOUS RELATED PAPERS

BOOKS

After the War: A Southern Tour. Cincinnati: Moore, Wilstach and Baldwin, 1866.

American and English Studies. 2 vols. New York: Charles Scribner's Sons, 1913.

Careers for the Coming Men. New York: Tribune Association, 1902; New York and Chicago: Saalfield Publishing, 1916.

Ohio in the War: Her Statesmen, Her Generals, and Soldiers. 2 vols. New York: Moore, Wilstach and Baldwin, 1868.

Problems of Expansion. New York: Century, 1900.

ARTICLES, SPEECHES, AND PAMPHLETS

Abraham Lincoln. London: University of Birmingham, Harrison and Sons, 1910.

Byron. London: University College of Nottingham, Harrison and Sons, 1910.

Colossal Philanthropy. Luton, England: Harrison and Sons, 1910.

Commencement Address before Phi Beta Kappa Society of Vassar College. New York: [DeVinne Press], 1903.

A Continental Union: Civil Service for the Islands. New York: Henry Hall, 1900.

Education in England. Albany, N.Y.: 1908.

Great Britain and the United States Need Each Other. London: Harrison and Sons, 1907.

The Greatest Fact in Modern History. New York: Thomas Y. Crowell, 1907.

Horace Greeley. New York: Charles Scribner's Sons, 1879.

How the United States Faced Its Educational Problem. London: Harrison and Sons, 1906.

Later Aspects of Our New Duties. New York: Henry Hall, 1899.

London Commemorations, 1908–1909. The Poe Centenary, The Bacon Tercentenary, The Milton Tercentenary, The Washington Anniversary. London: Harrison and Sons, 1909.

Making Peace with Spain: The Diary of Whitelaw Reid, Sept.–Dec. 1898. Edited by Howard Wayne Morgan. Austin: University of Texas Press, 1965.

The Monroe Doctrine, the Polk Doctrine and the Doctrine of Anarchism. New York: [DeVinne Press], 1903.

One Welshman: A Glance at a Great Career. London: Harrison and Sons, 1912.

Our Foremost Friend in Great Britain . . . Edmund Burke. London: Harrison and Sons, 1908.

The "Practical Side" of American Education. London: Harrison and Sons, 1907.

Scientific and Technological Education in the United States. London: Harrison and Sons, 1906.

The Scot in America and the Ulster Scot. London: Harrison and Sons, 1911.

Some Consequences of the Last Treaty of Paris. London: John Lane, 1899.

Some Newspaper Tendencies. New York: Henry Holt, 1879.

Two Speeches at the Queen's Jubilee, London, 1897. New York: DeVinne Press, 1897.

MISCELLANEOUS RELATED WORKS

Banquet to Whitelaw Reid, Delmonico's, 16 April 1892. New York: Press of the Chamber of Commerce, 1892.

Whitelaw Reid in France, 1889–1892: Formal Dinner to Whitelaw Reid, Paris, 24 March 1892. Oxford: Brentano's, 1892.

Smith, William Henry, *A Political History of Slavery*. With an introduction by Whitelaw Reid. New York: G. P. Putnam's Sons, 1903.

Memorial Service for H. E. the Hon. Whitelaw Reid, 20 Dec. 1912, 12 Noon. London: Vacher and Sons, 1912.

Reid, Elizabeth (Mills). *Art Treasures and Furnishings of Ophir Hall*. [New York?]: American Art Association, Anderson Galleries, 1935.

LETTERS, MEMOIRS, BIOGRAPHIES, AUTOBIOGRAPHIES, AND SPECIAL STUDIES

Adams, Henry. *The Education of Henry Adams*. Boston: Houghton Mifflin, [ca. 1918].

Armstrong, William M. *E. L. Godkin and American Foreign Policy, 1865–1900*. New York: Twayne, 1957.

Bancroft, Frederick, ed. *Speeches, Correspondence and Political Papers of Carl Schurz*. 6 vols. New York: G. P. Putnam's Sons, 1913.

Barker, Charles A. *Henry George*. New York: Oxford University Press, 1955.

Beale, Howard K. *Theodore Roosevelt and the Rise of America to World Power*. New York: Collier Books, 1962.

Beatty, Richmond C. *Bayard Taylor: Laureate of the Gilded Age*. Norman: University of Oklahoma Press, 1936.

Bigelow, John. *Retrospections of an Active Life*. 5 vols. New York: Baker and Taylor, 1909–13.

Blaine, Harriet Bailey (Stanwood). *The Letters of Mrs. James G. Blaine*. 2 vols. New York: Duffield, 1908.

Blaine, James G. "The Presidential Election of 1892." *North American Review*, 155 (1892), 513–525.

Brown, Harry James, and Frederick D. Williams, eds. *The Diary of James A. Garfield*. 2 vols. East Lansing, Mich.: Michigan State University Press, 1967.

Bruce, Robert V. *1877: Year of Violence*. Indianapolis: Bobbs-Merrill, 1959.

Caldwell, Robert G. *James A. Garfield: Party Chieftain*. New York: Dodd, Mead, 1931.

Campbell-Copeland, Thomas, comp. *Harrison and Reid: Their Lives and Record*. 3 vols. New York: C. L. Webster, 1892.

Chester, Giraud. *Embattled Maiden: The Life of Anna Dickinson*. New York: G. P. Putnam's Sons, 1951.

Connelly, William E. *Life of Preston B. Plumb, 1837–1891*. Chicago: Browne and Howell, 1913.

Cortissoz, Royal. *The Life of Whitelaw Reid*. 2 vols. New York: Charles Scribner's Sons, 1921.

Crockett, Albert Stevens. *When James Gordon Bennett Was Caliph of Baghdad*. New York: Funk and Wagnalls, 1926.

Dennett, Tyler. *John Hay: From Poetry to Politics*. New York: Dodd, Mead, 1933.

———. *Lincoln and the Civil War in the Diaries and Letters of John Hay*. New York: Dodd, Mead, 1939.

Dennis, Charles H. *Victor Lawson: His Time and His Work*. Chicago: University of Chicago Press, 1935.

Depew, Chauncey. *My Memories of Eighty Years*. New York: Charles Scribner's Sons, 1922.

Dodge, Mary A. [Gail Hamilton]. *Biography of James G. Blaine*. Norwich, Conn.: Henry Bill, 1895.

Dozer, Donald M. "Benjamin Harrison and the Presidential Campaign of 1892." *American Historical Review*, 54 (1948), 49–77.

Drewry, John E., ed. *More Post Biographies*. Athens: University of Georgia Press, 1947.

Durden, Robert F. *James Shepherd Pike: Republicanism and the American Negro, 1850–1882*. Durham, N.C.: Duke University Press, 1957.

Foraker, Joseph B. *Notes of a Busy Life*. 2 vols. 3rd ed. Cincinnati: Stewart and Kidd, 1917.

Ford, Worthington Chauncey, ed. *Letters of Henry Adams*. 2 vols. Boston: Houghton Mifflin, 1938.

Freeman, Douglas S. *Lee's Lieutenants: A Study in Command*. 3 vols. New York: Charles Scribner's Sons, 1944.

Fuess, Claude M. *Carl Schurz: Reformer, 1829–1906*. New York: Dodd, Mead, 1932.

George, Henry, Jr. *The Life of Henry George*. New York: Doubleday and McClure, 1900.

Gray, Edgar Laughlin. "The Career of William Henry Smith, Politician-Journalist." Ph.D. dissertation, Ohio State University, 1951.

Grey, Viscount of Fallodon. *Twenty-five Years, 1892–1916*. New York: Frederick A. Stokes, 1925.

Gosnell, Harold F. *Boss Platt and His New York Machine*. Chicago: University of Chicago Press, 1924.

Grodinsky, Julius. *Jay Gould: His Business Career, 1867–1892*. Philadelphia: University of Pennsylvania Press, 1957.

Hale, William H. *Horace Greeley: Voice of the People*. New York: Harper, 1950.

Havighurst, Walter. *The Miami Years, 1809–1969*. New York: G. P. Putnam's Sons, 1969.

Herrick, Hugh M. *William Walter Phelps*. New York: Knickerbocker Press, 1904.

Hesseltine, William B. *Ulysses S. Grant: Politician*. New York: Dodd, Mead, 1935.

Hirsch, Mark D. *William C. Whitney: Modern Warwick*. New York: Dodd, Mead, 1948.

Holbo, Paul. "Presidential Leadership in Foreign Affairs: William McKinley and the Turpie-Foraker Amendment." *American Historical Review*, 72 (1967), 1321–25.

Hollister, Ovando James. *Life of Schuyler Colfax*. New York: Funk and Wagnalls, 1886.

Howe, George F. *Chester A. Arthur: A Quarter Century of Machine Politics*. New York: Dodd, Mead, 1934.

Howells, Mildred, ed. *Life and Letters of William Dean Howells*. New York: Doubleday, Doran, 1928.

Howells, William Dean. *Years of My Youth*. New York: Harper and Brothers, 1917.

Huntington-Wilson, F. M. *Memoirs of an Ex-Diplomat*. Boston: Bruce Humphries, 1945.

Jessup, Philip C. *Elihu Root*. 2 vols. New York: Dodd, Mead, 1938.

Jones, Robert H. "Whitelaw Reid." In *For The Union: Ohio Leaders in the Civil War*. Edited by Kenneth W. Wheeler. Columbus: Ohio State University Press, 1968.

Jusserand, Jean A. T. Jules. *What Me Befell: The Reminiscences of J. J. Jusserand*. Boston: Houghton Mifflin, 1933.

Kerr, Winfield Scott. *John Sherman: His Life and Public Services*. 2 vols. Mansfield, Ohio: 1907.

Knoles, George. *The Presidential Campaign and Election of 1892*. Stanford, Calif.: Stanford University Press, 1942.

Knox, Thomas W. *The Republican Party and Its Leaders . . . Lives of Harrison and Reid*. New York: P. F. Collier, 1892.

Lodge, Henry Cabot, ed. *Selections from the Correspondence of Theodore Roosevelt and Henry Cabot Lodge, 1884–1918*. 2 vols. New York: Charles Scribner's Sons, 1925.

McElroy, Robert M. *Levi Parsons Morton: Banker, Diplomat and Statesman*. New York: G. P. Putnam's Sons, 1930.

Moore, Charles. *The Life and Times of Charles Follen McKim*. Boston: Houghton Mifflin, 1929.

Morgan, Howard Wayne. *William McKinley and His America*. Syracuse, N.Y.: Syracuse University Press, 1963.

Morison, Elting E., ed. *Letters of Theodore Roosevelt*. 8 vols. Cambridge: Harvard University Press, 1951–54.

Muzzey, David S. *James G. Blaine: A Political Idol of Other Days*. New York: Dodd, Mead, 1935.

Nevins, Allan. *Hamilton Fish, The Inner History of the Grant Administration*. 2 vols. rev. ed. New York: Frederick Ungar, 1957.

———. *Henry White*. New York and London: Harper and Brothers, 1930.

———. *John D. Rockefeller: The Heroic Age of American Enterprise*. 2 vols. New York: Charles Scribner's Sons, 1940.

———. *Study in Power: John D. Rockefeller, Industrialist and Philanthropist*. 2 vols. New York: Charles Scribner's Sons, 1953.

——— and Milton Halsey Thomas, eds. *The Diary of George Templeton Strong, 1865–1875*. 4 vols. New York: Macmillan, 1952.

Oberholtzer, Ellis. *Jay Cooke: Financier of the Civil War*. 2 vols. Philadelphia: G. W. Jacobs, 1907.

Olney, Richard. "International Isolation of the United States." *Atlantic Monthly*, (1898), 577–588.

Phillips, William. *Ventures in Diplomacy*. Boston: Beacon Press, 1952.

Pierce, Edward L. *Memoirs and Letters of Charles Sumner*. 4 vols. Boston: Roberts Brothers, 1877–94.

Platt, Thomas Collier. *The Autobiography of Thomas Collier Platt*. New York: B. W. Dodge, 1910.

Poore, Benjamin Perley. *Perley's Reminiscences of Sixty Years in the National Metropolis*. 2 vols. Philadelphia: Hubbard Brothers, 1886.

Pringle, Henry. *Theodore Roosevelt: A Biography*. New York: Harcourt, Brace, 1931.

Randall, James G. *Lincoln the Liberal Statesman*. New York: Dodd, Mead, 1947.

———. *Lincoln the President*. 4 vols. London: Eyre and Spottiswoode, 1947–55.

——— and David Donald. *The Civil War and Reconstruction*. 2nd ed. Boston: D. C. Heath and Co., 1961.

Richardson, Leon B. *William E. Chandler, Republican*. New York: Dodd, Mead, 1940.

Rosebault, Charles J. *When Dana Was the Sun*. New York: R. M. McBridge, 1931.

Sandburg, Carl. *Abraham Lincoln: The War Years*. 4 vols. New York: Harcourt, Brace, 1939.

Schurz, Carl. *Reminiscences of Carl Schurz*. 2 vols. New York: McClure, 1907–8.

Seitz, Don. *Horace Greeley: Founder of the New York Tribune*. Indianapolis: Bobbs-Merrill, 1926.

———. *Joseph Pulitzer: His Life and Letters*. New York: Garden City, [ca. 1924].

Smart, James G. "Whitelaw Reid: A Biographical Study." Ph.D. dissertation, University of Maryland, 1964.

———. "Whitelaw Reid and the Nomination of Horace Greeley." *Mid-America*, 49 (1967), 227–243.

Smith, Theodore C. *The Life and Letters of James Abram Garfield*. 2 vols. New Haven: Yale University Press, 1925.

Stoddard, Henry L. *Horace Greeley: Printer, Editor, Crusader*. New York: G. P. Putnam's Sons, 1946.

Stone, Candace. *Dana and the Sun*. New York: Dodd, Mead, 1938.

Stone, Melville E. *Fifty Years a Journalist*. Garden City, N.Y.: Doubleday Page, 1922.

Strong, Theron G. *Joseph H. Choate: New Englander, New Yorker, Lawyer, Ambassador*. New York: Dodd, Mead, 1917.

Tansill, Charles C. *The Foreign Policy of Thomas F. Bayard, 1885–1897*. New York: Fordham University Press, 1940.

Thayer, William R. *The Life of John Hay*. 2 vols. Boston: Houghton Mifflin, 1915.

Thoron, Ward, ed. *The Letters of Mrs. Henry Adams, 1865–1883*. Boston: Little, Brown, 1936.

Tobey, Walter L., and William O. Thompson, eds. *The Diamond Anniversary Volume of Miami University*. Oxford, Ohio: Miami University, 1899.

Van Deusen, Glyndon G. *Horace Greeley: Nineteenth-Century Crusader*. Philadelphia: University of Pennsylvania Press, 1953.

Volwiler, Albert T., ed. *The Correspondence between Benjamin Harrison and*

James G. Blaine, 1882–1893. Philadelphia: American Philosophical Society, 1940.

Wallace, Lewis. *Lew Wallace: An Autobiography*. 2 vols. New York: Harper and Brothers, 1906.

Watterson, Henry. *Marse Henry: An Autobiography*. New York: George H. Doran, 1919.

White, Horace, *The Life of Lyman Trumbull*. Boston: Houghton Mifflin, 1913.

Williams, Charles R., ed. *Diary and Letters of Rutherford Burchard Hayes, Nineteenth President of the United States*. 5 vols. Columbus, Ohio: Ohio State Archeological and Historical Society, 1922–26.

Young, May D. Russell, ed. *Men and Memories: Personal Reminiscences by John Russell Young*. 2 vols. New York: F. Tennyson Neely, 1901.

Younger, Edward. *John A. Kasson: Politics and Diplomacy from Lincoln to McKinley*. Iowa City: State Historical Society of Iowa, 1955.

GENERAL WORKS

Andrews, J. Cutler. *The North Reports the Civil War*. Pittsburgh: University of Pittsburgh Press, 1955.

Baehr, Harry W. *The New York Tribune since the Civil War*. New York: Dodd, Mead, 1936.

Bemis, Samuel F. *The American Secretaries of State and Their Diplomacy*. 10 vols. New York: Alfred A. Knopf, 1927–29.

Bowers, Claude G. *The Tragic Era*. New York: Blue Ribbon Books, 1929.

Buley, Roscoe C. *The Old Northwest: Pioneer Period, 1815–1840*. 2 vols. Indianapolis, Indiana: Indiana Historical Society, 1950.

Campbell, A. E. *Great Britain and the United States, 1895–1903*. London: Longmans, Green, 1961.

Campbell, Charles S., Jr. *Anglo-American Understanding, 1898–1903*. Baltimore: Johns Hopkins Press, 1957.

Carroll, Eber M. *French Public Opinion and Foreign Affairs, 1870–1914*. New York: Century, 1931.

Crozier, Emmett. *Yankee Reporters, 1861–65*. New York: Oxford University Press, 1956.

Dreier, Thomas. *The Power of Print—and Men*. Brooklyn, N.Y.: Mergenthaler Linotype, 1936.

Dunn, Arthur W. *From Harrison to Harding . . . 1888–1921*. 2 vols. New York: G. P. Putnam's Sons, 1922.

Dunne, Finley Peter. *Observations by Mr. Dooley*. New York: Harper and Brothers, 1906.

Ellis, David M. et al. *A Short History of New York State*. Ithaca, N.Y.: New York State Historical Association and Cornell University Press, 1957.

Gramling, Oliver. *AP: The Story of News*. New York: Farrar and Rinehart, 1940.

Griswold, Alfred Whitney. *The Far Eastern Policy of the United States*. New York: Harcourt, Brace, 1938.

Hirshson, Stanley P. *Farewell to the Bloody Shirt: Northern Republicans and the Southern Negro, 1877–1893*. Bloomington: Indiana University Press, 1962.

Horner, Harlan H., comp. and ed. *Education in New York State, 1784–1954*. Albany: University of the State of New York, 1954.

Howe, Henry. *Historical Collections of Ohio*. 2 vols. Cincinnati: State of Ohio, 1900.

James, Edward T., ed. *Notable American Women, 1607–1950*. 3 vols. Cambridge: Harvard University Press, Belknap Press, 1971.

Johnson, Allen, and Dumas Malone, eds. *Dictionary of American Biography*. Centenary Edition. 22 vols. New York: Charles Scribner's Sons, 1946.

Josephson, Matthew. *The Politicos, 1865–1896*. New York: Harcourt, Brace, 1938.

Knox, Thomas W. *Camp-fire and Cotton-field*. New York: Blelock, 1865.

———. *The Republican Party*. New York: P. F. Collier, 1892.

LaFeber, Walter. *The New Empire: An Interpretation of American Expansion*. Ithaca, N.Y.: Cornell University Press, 1963.

Laughlin, James L., and H. Parker Willis. *Reciprocity*. New York: Baker and Taylor, 1903.

Lee, James M. *History of American Journalism*. Boston: Houghton Mifflin, 1923.

Leech, Margaret. *In the Days of McKinley*. New York: Harper, 1959.

Lundberg, Ferdinand. *America's 60 Families*. New York: Citadel Press, 1937.

May, Ernest R. *American Imperialism: A Speculative Essay*. New York: Atheneum, 1968.

Morgan, Howard Wayne. *From Hayes to McKinley: National Party Politics, 1877–1896*. Syracuse, N.Y.: Syracuse University Press, 1969.

Mott, Frank L. *American Journalism: A History, 1690–1960*. 3rd ed. New York: Macmillan, 1962.

Murrell, William. *A History of American Graphic Humor*. 2 vols. New York: Whitney Museum of American Art, 1933–38.

Oberholtzer, Ellis P. *A History of the United States since the Civil War*. 5 vols. New York: Macmillan, 1917–1937.

O'Brien, Frank M. *The Story of the Sun, 1833–1928*. New ed. New York: D. Appleton, 1928.

Pletcher, David M. *The Awkward Years: American Foreign Relations under Garfield and Arthur*. Columbia, Mo.: University of Missouri Press, 1962.

Roseboom, Eugene H. *The Civil War Era, 1850–1876. The History of the State of Ohio*, edited by Carl F. Wittke, vol. 4. Columbus, Ohio: Ohio State Archeological and Historical Society, 1941–44.

Rosewater, Victor. *History of Cooperative Newsgathering in the United States*. New York: D. Appleton, 1930.

Ross, Earl D. *The Liberal Republican Movement*. New York: Henry Holt, 1919.

Stanwood, Edward. *American Tariff Controversies in the Nineteenth Century*. 2 vols. Boston: Houghton Mifflin, 1903.

———. *A History of the Presidency*. Boston: Houghton Mifflin, 1898.

Starr, Louis M. *Bohemian Brigade*. New York: Alfred A. Knopf, 1954.

Stevens, George A. *New York Typographical Union No. 6*. Albany, N.Y.: State Department of Labor, 1912.

Stille, Samuel H. *Ohio Builds a Nation: A Memorial to the Pioneers and Celebrated Sons of the "Buckeye" State*. Chicago: Arlendale Book House, 1939.

Sweet, William Warren. *Religion on the American Frontier . . . A Collection of Source Material, etc*. New York: Henry Holt, 1931.

Tansill, Charles C. *Canadian-American Relations, 1875–1911*. New Haven: Yale University Press, 1943.

Weisenburger, Francis P. *The Passing of the Frontier, 1825–1850. The History of the State of Ohio*, edited by Carl F. Wittke, vol. 3. Columbus, Ohio: Ohio State Archeological and Historical Society, 1941–44.

Wilkie, Franc B. *Pen and Powder*. Boston: Ticknor, 1888.

Williams, Kenneth P. *Lincoln Finds a General*. 5 vols. New York: Macmillan, 1949–59.

Willson, Beckles. *America's Ambassadors to England*. New York: Frederick A. Stokes, 1929.

———. *America's Ambassadors to France, 1777–1927*. New York: Frederick A. Stokes, 1928.

Woodward, C. Vann. *Reunion and Reaction: The Compromise of 1877 and the End of Reconstruction*. Boston: Little, Brown, 1951.

Index